Full Range Leadership Development

Pathways for People, Profit, and Planet

Full Range Leadership Development

Pathways for People, Profit, and Planet

John J. Sosik

Don I. Jung

Routledge
Taylor & Francis Group
New York   London

Psychology Press
Taylor & Francis Group
711 Third Avenue, 8th Floor
New York, NY 10017
www.routledge.com

Psychology Press
Taylor & Francis Group
27 Church Road
Hove, East Sussex BN3 2FA

International Standard Book Number: 978-1-84872-805-9 (Hardback) 978-1-84872-806-6 (Paperback)

Library of Congress Cataloging-in-Publication Data

Sosik, John J.
    Full range leadership development : pathways for people, profit, and planet /
John J. Sosik, Dongil I. Jung.
        p. cm.
    Includes bibliographical references and index.
    ISBN 978-1-84872-805-9 (hardcover : alk. paper) -- ISBN 978-1-84872-806-6
    (pbk. : alk. paper)
    1. Leadership. I. Jung, Dongil I. II. Title.

HD57.7.S6928 2010
658.4'092--dc22   2009026078

Visit the Taylor & Francis Web site at
http://www.taylorandfrancis.com

and the Psychology Press Web site at
http://www.psypress.com

Contents

About the Authors.. xv

Foreword...xvii

Preface xix

1   Introducing Full Range Leadership Development 1
Why Full Range Leadership Development Is Essential
for Exceptional Performance Today 3
    Leadership for Our Dynamic World and Lives 4
        Demographic Changes 4
        Technology Trends 4
        Geopolitical Alterations 4
        New Generations of Workers Bring New Ideas.................... 5
        Organizational Modifications.................................... 5
        Environmental Issues... 6
    And the Research Says … 7
The Components of Full Range Leadership Development Theory 9
    Laissez-Faire 9
    Passive Management-by-Exception 10
    Active Management-by-Exception 12
    Contingent Reward 13
    The 4Is of Transformational Leadership 13
        Idealized Influence 15
        Inspirational Motivation....................................... 15
        Intellectual Stimulation....................................... 16
        Individualized Consideration 17
Full Range Leadership Development and the History
of Leadership Thought 19
    Trait Theory... 19

Psychodynamic Theory..22
Skills Theory..23
    Emotional Intelligence..23
    Pragmatic or Problem-Solving Leadership Theory.............24
Style Theory...25
Situational Leadership Theory 26
Contingency Theory..27
Path–Goal Theory 28
Leader–Member Exchange Theory 29
Authentic Leadership Theory...30
Putting Transformational Leadership Into Practice as You
Read This Book 32
    Meta-Cognition and Critical Questioning....................32
Summary Questions and Reflective Exercises 34
Notes 40

2 The Full Range Leadership Development System 43
Sidney Poitier and *To Sir, With Love* 45
Leadership Is a System 47
    Leader..50
    Follower...51
    Situation..53
        GE and Its Passion for Leadership Development 54
    Confluence of Leader, Follower, and Situation.............56
Full Range Leadership Systems Thinking 60
    Process Model for Understanding Full Range
    Leadership Development 61
        Outcomes of Leadership at the Individual, Team, and
        Organizational/Macro Levels 64
Putting Full Range Leadership Development Systems Thinking
Into Practice 67
    First Step Is the Most Difficult 67
    View Your World Through a FRLD Process Model Lens.............68
    Take the Multifactor Leadership Questionnaire Now...............68
    Establish a Personal Leadership Mission Statement 71
    Find a Learning Partner..71
    Make FRLD Reflection a Part of Your Schedule.....................73
    Use Self-Rewards and Positive Affirmations.....................73
    Set Goals With a Personal Leadership Development Plan............74
Summary Questions and Reflective Exercises 74
Notes 77

3 **Idealized Influence Behaviors and Attributes:**
The Humane Side of Transformational Leadership.........................79
The Idealized Leadership of Mohandas Gandhi....................................82
Idealized Influence Behaviors: Definition and Examples........................83
   Talk About Your Most Important Values and Beliefs..................84
   Talk About the Importance of Trusting Each Other...................86
   Specify the Importance of Having a Strong Sense of Purpose......88
   Consider the Moral/Ethical Consequences of Your Decisions.....89
   Emphasize the Importance of Teamwork....................................91
   Champion Exciting New Possibilities That Can Be
   Achieved Through Teamwork..92
Idealized Influence Attributes: Definition and Examples......................93
   Instill Pride in Others for Being Associated With You.................93
   Go Beyond Self-Interests for the Good of Others 95
   Act in Ways That Build Others' Respect......................................98
   Display a Sense of Power and Confidence....................................98
   Reassure Others That Obstacles Will Be Overcome................... 100
Thinking About Idealized Influence 101
   Close and Distant Leadership 101
   Impression Management, Self-Construals,
   and Self-Presentation 102
      Desired Identity Images... 103
      Hoped-for Possible Selves Versus Actual Selves
      and Impression Management Tactics............................... 103
      Self-Monitoring 105
Putting Idealized Influence Into Practice 106
   Display the Behaviors Described in This Chapter 106
   Identify and Leverage Your Strengths and Those of Others 106
   Improve Your Perspective-Taking Capacity............................... 107
   Work on Your Self-Awareness 107
      Gauging Your Leadership Self-Awareness 108
   Learn About Becoming an Authentic Transformational
   Leader... 112
Summary Questions and Reflective Exercises 112
Notes 114

4 **Inspirational Motivation: The Emotional Side of**
Transformational Leadership 117
Inspirational Motivation: Definition and Examples............................ 120
   Talk Optimistically About the Future 120
   Talk Enthusiastically About What Needs to Be Accomplished 122

Articulate a Compelling Vision of the Future 124
Provide an Exciting Image of What Is Essential to Consider 128
Express Confidence That Goals Will Be Achieved 130
Thinking About Inspirational Motivation.............................. 132
   The Dark Side of Charisma....................................... 132
      Personalized Versus Socialized Charismatic Leaders 133
      The Inspiring Leadership of Winston Churchill
      and the Fatal Attraction of Adolph Hitler...................... 136
      Perspective-Taking Capacity and Moral Development...... 140
   The Rhetoric of Inspirational Leadership 141
Putting Inspirational Motivation Into Practice 144
   Display the Behaviors Described in This Chapter 144
   Boost Your Self-Confidence....................................... 145
   Write Mission and Vision Statements for Your Organization..... 145
   Work to Improve Your Public Speaking Ability........................ 146
   Use Storytelling Techniques to Articulate Your Vision 147
   Build Consensus Around Your Vision 148
Summary Questions and Reflective Exercises 149
Notes 152

5   **Intellectual Stimulation:**
    The Rational Side of Transformational Leadership.................... 155
    The Dynamic Leadership Duo of Anne Mulcahy
    and Ursula Burns at Xerox.. 158
    Intellectual Stimulation: Definition and Behavioral Examples........... 159
       Reexamine Critical Assumptions to Question Whether
       They Are Appropriate 159
       Seek Different Perspectives When Solving Problems................. 161
       Get Others to Look at Problems From Many Different Angles....163
       Suggest New Ways of Looking at How to
       Complete Assignments 165
       Encourage Nontraditional Thinking to Deal
       With Traditional Problems 168
       Encourage Rethinking Those Ideas That Have Never
       Been Questioned Before 170
    Thinking About Intellectual Stimulation............................ 171
       Roadblocks to Intellectual Stimulation............................ 171
          Your Organization 173
          Your Leader 173
          Your Followers.. 174

Your Problem Orientation 174

Yourself.. 175

Intellectual Stimulation and Pragmatic/

Problem-Solving Leadership.. 175

Putting Intellectual Stimulation Into Practice................................. 179

Display the Behaviors Described in This Chapter 179

Use Brainstorming.. 179

Promote the Use of Fantasy 180

Imagine Alternative States 181

Learn to Think Differently 182

Ask Challenging Questions 183

Reverse the Figure and Ground 184

Summary Questions and Reflective Exercises 185

Notes 188

6   **Individualized Consideration:**

The Nurturing Side of Transformational Leadership.....................191

The Developmental Power of Pat Summitt 193

Individualized Consideration: Definition and Behavioral Examples ... 195

Consider Individuals as Having Different Needs, Abilities,

and Aspirations From Others.. 196

Treat Others as Individuals Rather Than a Member of a Group... 199

Listen Attentively to Others' Concerns....................................202

Help Others Develop Their Strengths......................................204

Spend Time Teaching and Coaching.......................................205

Promote Self-Development 207

Thinking About Individualized Consideration 208

Individuation...209

Diversity Leadership Issues.. 210

Diversimilarity and Transformational Leadership 212

Mentoring... 214

Benefits of Mentoring... 214

Mentoring Functions.. 215

Mentoring and Transformational Leadership 215

Two Faces of Transformational Leadership: Empowerment

and Dependency...216

Developing Followers Through Delegation..............................217

Putting Individualized Consideration Into Practice...........................218

Display the Behaviors Described in This Chapter 218

Become Interested in the Well-Being of Others........................219

Celebrate Diversity 219
Establish Mentoring Programs in Your Organization 220
Create Strategies for Continuous Personal Improvement 220
Summary Questions and Reflective Exercises 221
Notes 224

**7 Contingent Reward and Management-by-Exception Active:
The Two Faces of Transactional Leadership 227**
The Transactional Leadership of Sam Palmisano at IBM 229
Contingent Reward—Definition and Behavioral Examples 230
Set Goals for and With Followers 233
Suggest Pathways to Meet Performance Expectations 234
Actively Monitor Followers' Progress and Provide
Supportive Feedback 235
Provide Rewards When Goals Are Attained 236
Management-by-Exception Active—Definition
and Behavioral Examples 237
Closely Monitor Work Performance for Errors 238
Focus Attention on Mistakes, Complaints, Failures,
Deviations, and Infractions 241
Arrange to Know If and When Things Go Wrong 243
Thinking About Transactional Leadership 244
When Is MBE-A Appropriate? 244
Goal Setting 245
Set SMARTER Goals 247
Extrinsic Rewards and Punishments 248
Timing of Rewards 250
Advantages and Disadvantages of Extrinsic Rewards 250
Putting Transactional Leadership Into Practice 252
Applying Contingent Reward Leadership 252
Display the Behaviors Described in This Chapter 252
Give Praise When It Is Deserved 253
Provide the Resources Needed by Followers
to Reach Their Goals 253
Use Rewards to Support Six Sigma and Total Quality
Management Initiatives 254
Applying MBE-A Leadership 255
Display the Behaviors Described in This Chapter 255
Set Standards 256
Preach Accountability and Responsibility 256
Assess Risk and Be Alert 256

Summary Questions and Reflective Exercises 258
Notes 260

**8   Management-by-Exception Passive and Laissez-Faire:
      Inactive Forms of Leadership 263**
      The Legacy of Lazy Leaders 265
      Management-by-Exception Passive—Definition
      and Behavioral Examples 266
          Intervene Only If Standards Are Not Met 267
          Wait for Things to Go Wrong Before Taking Action 269
          Believe That "If It Ain't Broke, Don't Fix It" 270
          React to Mistakes Reluctantly 271
      Laissez-Faire—Definition and Behavioral Examples 272
          Avoid Getting Involved, Making Decisions,
          or Solving Problems 273
          Be Absent When Needed 275
          Delay and Fail to Follow Up 276
          Avoid Emphasizing Results 277
      Thinking About Inactive Forms of Leadership 278
          Social Loafing and Free Riding Are Outcomes
          of Passive Leadership 278
          Should You Let Things Settle Naturally? 279
          Is It Empowerment or Just Laissez-Faire? 281
          Exception Reporting and Reactive Leadership 282
      Putting Passive Forms of Leadership Into Practice 283
          Applying MBEP Leadership 283
              Display the Behaviors Described in This Chapter 283
              Place Energy on Maintaining the Status Quo 284
              Enforce Corrective Action When Followers Make
              Mistakes 284
              Fix the Problem and Get Back to Coasting Along 285
          Applying Laissez-Faire Leadership 286
              Please Avoid the Behaviors Described in This Chapter 286
              Talk About Getting Things Done, But Let Others
              Take the Lead 287
              Show Lack of Interest When Things Go Wrong 288
              Let Things Settle Naturally 289
      Summary Questions and Reflective Exercises 289
      Notes 291

9   Sharing Full Range Leadership Within Teams 293
Team Leadership Lessons From the Beatles 295
    Carry That Weight.. 295
    Don't Let Me Down 296
    Come Together.. 296
    Tell Me What You See... 297
    Within You Without You... 298
Team Leadership Defined 298
Thinking About FRLD in Groups and Teams.................................... 300
    What's in a Name? Differences Between Groups and Teams 301
        Information and Workflow.. 301
        Synergy.. 302
        Individual Versus Mutual Accountability 304
        Overlapping Versus Complementary Skill Sets................. 305
    Shared Leadership and the Miracle on Ice 307
    Levels of Team Development... 310
Putting FRLD Into Practice in Teams 312
    Instill Pride in Team Members for Being Associated
    With the Team 312
    Go Beyond Self-Interest for the Good of the Team.................. 313
    Emphasize the Importance of Having a Collective Sense
    of Mission... 314
    Help Your Team Members to Develop Their Strengths 315
Summary Questions and Reflective Exercises 316
Notes 319

**10   Full Range Leadership Development for Strategic, Social,
    and Environmental Initiatives 321**
Steve Jobs and the Resurrection of Apple.. 323
Strategic Leadership Defined 324
    Strategic Leadership and the Balanced Scorecard 325
    How FRLD Enhances This Process 330
    Triple Bottom Line 333
Thinking About Full Range Leadership Development
as a Strategic and Social Intervention.. 334
    Social Entrepreneurship... 334
        Social Entrepreneurship in Action 336
    Environmental, Health, and Safety Issues in the Workplace...... 339
    Environmental Leadership Initiatives 342
Putting Full Range Leadership Development Into Practice at
the Strategic Level.. 344

Use Transformational Leadership Measures
for Promotion and Transfer 344
Recruit and Select the Best 345
Use Transformational Leadership as a Career
Development Tool 345
Reengineer Jobs and Processes 345
Build a Strong Brand and Corporate Image.............................346
Periodically Examine and Redesign Your
Organizational Structure 347
More Evidence That FRLD Promotes Prosperity and Well-Being.......348
Empowering Women With FRLD 349
Life-Changing Experience 349
Creating Sustainable Changes With FRLD...............................350
Raising Funds and Lifting Spirits With FRLD..........................351
Developing Righteous Minds Through FRLD 352
Negating the Naysayers With FRLD..353
A Most Noble Form of Transformational Leadership 354
Summary Questions and Reflective Exercises 355
Notes 357

Appendix: Master of Leadership Development Program **359**

Author Index **371**

Subject Index..**377**

About the Authors

John J. Sosik (PhD, State University of New York at Binghamton) is professor of management and organization and professor-in-charge of the Master of Leadership Development program at the Pennsylvania State University, School of Graduate Professional Studies at Great Valley, where he has received awards for excellence in research, faculty innovation, and teaching. Dr. Sosik also is the recipient of the 2007 Center for Creative Leadership/Leadership Quarterly Award for his research on personality, charismatic leadership, and vision. His research focuses on leadership and mentoring processes in face-to-face and virtual environments, groups/teams, and organizations. He is an expert on transformational leadership, having published over 70 articles, book chapters, and proceedings and delivered over 60 academic conference presentations since 1995, and has conducted training and organizational development programs for profit and nonprofit organizations. He serves on the editorial boards of *The Leadership Quarterly, Group & Organization Management,* and *Journal of Behavioral and Applied Management*. His reviewing the scholarly work of colleagues in his field has been applauded by both the Academy of Management and the Institute of Behavioral and Applied Management. He is the lead author of the book *The Dream Weavers: Strategy-Focused Leadership in Technology-Driven Organizations* (2004, Information Age Publishing). His book *Leading With Character: Stories of Valor and Virtue and the Principles They Teach* (2006, Information Age Publishing) was named one of the 30 best business books of 2007 by Soundview Executive Book Summaries. Dr. Sosik was awarded a grant from the National Science Foundation to study e-leadership of virtual teams at Unisys Corporation. He is also a certified public accountant in Pennsylvania and a certified management accountant.

Dongil (Don) Jung (PhD, State University of New York at Binghamton) is professor of management at Yonsei University, School of Business, in Seoul, South Korea. He formerly taught at San Diego State University. He teaches organizational behavior, international/comparative management, leadership and group processes, and international negotiation at undergraduate and graduate (MBA) levels. He has also been teaching the International/Comparative Management course in executive MBA programs since 1998. His areas of expertise include strategic leadership and innovation, multinational and world-class organization, team dynamics, and international negotiations. He has worked for profit and not-for-profit organizations as a consultant and trainer, including the U.S. Army, Navy Seals, and Budget Rental Car in the United States as well as SK, LG, Hyundai, Shinhan Bank, and Samsung in South Korea. He is a frequent guest speaker for several multinational companies. As an active researcher, Dr. Jung's publications have appeared in many top-tier scholarly journals, such as the *Academy of Management Journal, Journal of Applied Psychology, The Leadership Quarterly, Organizational Dynamics, Group & Organization Management, Group Dynamics, Journal of Applied Behavioral Science, Journal of Organizational Behavior,* and *Journal of Occupational and Organizational Psychology,* among others. He is listed in the *Marquis Who's Who in Business Higher Education* and received the Ascendant Scholar Award from the Western Academy of Management in 2004. He also received the Faculty Contribution Award from the College of Business Administration at San Diego State University.

Foreword

Approximately 20 years ago, Bernie Bass and I were working with the Fiat organization to design a leadership training intervention for its top 250 managers around the globe. One of the main strengths we brought to the table in our discussions with Fiat was a model of leadership that was evidenced based. Thus, we repeatedly emphasized that if we could develop managers to be more transformational and active transactional leaders, we were confident performance outcomes would improve. The Fiat leaders in ISVOR, the training company owned by Fiat, were well versed in theory, research, and application. They had training partnerships with many of the top-branded organizations around the globe, including at that time Motorola.

As we built the program, we had many discussions on how we could best frame the type of leadership we intended to develop in individuals, teams, and indeed, entire organizations within the Fiat family of corporations. From the very outset in planning these interventions, we were taking a multilevel view of leadership, examining transformational leaders, shared transformational leadership, and transformational cultures. After a number of brainstorming sessions, we settled on the idea of calling the model "a full range model of leadership," as opposed to "the full range model."

Our choice of this term was based on three criteria. First, we wanted to challenge participants to continually expand the breadth and depth of "their range" as they learned about leadership throughout their careers. Second, we knew that by choosing the term *full range* that some of our academic colleagues would immediately challenge whether *full* actually was *full*. It was our subtle way of intellectually stimulating the field of leadership to ask, what's missing and why? Finally, we were well aware of the theories and models of leadership that preceded ours, and we wanted to honor and include them in the range.

You will see in this book that much of what Bernie and I had hoped for, regarding this slice of our work together, has come to fruition. For example,

I can tell you of numerous conversations and citations where someone has tried to add to "the" (we really meant "a") full range model with this or that leadership style or concept we had left out. Over the last two decades, we have also seen not only a substantial amount of evidence supporting the full range model in individual and meta-analytic studies published in the literature, but also training interventions that have provided support for challenging participants to expand their implicit notions of what constituted their leadership. Regarding our third criterion, the model has now been incorporated into the leadership literature and, in many ways, has become even more integrated with prior models of leadership, and has served as one important organizing mechanism for pulling together the leadership literature.

With that as background to this book, you will see in the following pages an evidenced-based model of leadership unfold in unique and creative ways before your eyes. This model still covers a very broad range of leadership styles, with many applications of the model that will help any reader come to understand what it means to lead across the full range of leadership behaviors, actions, and potential. John and Don attempt to convey in as many ways as possible the breadth and depth of these constructs of leadership and do so in a way that is both practical and fun. What I find interesting is how far this work has come, particularly in terms of application and relevance, and this book is a testament to those achievements.

In closing, if you engage this book from front to back, you will no doubt positively expand your leadership potential and impact. I say no doubt because after 20 years of accumulated evidence, there is *no doubt.* The only doubt I have regards how this model can be used to develop each reader's unique potential, and to accomplish that, you, the reader, must lead. Since I don't know you, I have some doubts. Since I know John and Don, and the great work they have done, my doubts are minimal, but still consequential. Now, go enjoy all of your travels along a full range of leadership challenges and successes.

Bruce J. Avolio

Bruce J. Avolio (PhD, University of Akron) is Marion B. Ingersoll Professor of management and executive director of the Leadership Center at the University of Washington's Michael G. Foster School of Business. Dr. Avolio previously developed and led research and training initiatives at the University of Nebraska–Lincoln and the Center for Leadership Studies at the State University of New York at Binghamton. He is a world-renown leadership researcher and consultant, having published 9 books and over 100 articles, developed the Multifactor Leadership Questionnaire with the late Bernard M. Bass, served on the editorial boards of numerous prestigious academic journals, and conducted leadership training and development programs worldwide.

Preface

The most beautiful discovery true friends make is that they can grow separately without growing apart.

—Elisabeth Foley

Transformational and transactional leadership and its elegant expression in Bernard Bass and Bruce Avolio's Full Range Leadership Development (FRLD) model has become the premier leadership research paradigm. More importantly, countless educators, trainers, and practitioners in a wide range of industries and countries around the world have embraced the FRLD model. We wrote this book with the objective of demonstrating how ordinary people in all walks of life have used FRLD to achieve extraordinary results of developing people to their full potential, boosting company profits, and creating sustainable business practices. In essence, our purpose is to tell the story of how research on FRLD is being taught at our universities, trained in our clients' organizations, and applied by aspiring leaders to sustain performance excellence.

We feel well qualified to tell this story. We earned our doctoral degrees under the tutelage of Bernie Bass and Bruce Avolio at the Center for Leadership Studies at the State University of New York at Binghamton. As their students, we worked with our colleagues on many research projects on transformational leadership conducted at SUNY–Binghamton and elsewhere. During this time, we became close friends, honed our research skills, and vowed to carry on the work of researching and training transformational leadership over our careers. Looking back, our Binghamton experience was nothing short of wonderful. It led us to one of the most exciting and important research topics in our field. We're glad it happened to us.

After graduating, we became accomplished leadership scholars, trainers, and educators in our own right at Penn State University and San Diego State

University. Our training, teaching, and life experiences inspired us to develop courses on FRLD at our schools, and an Association to Advance Collegiate Schools of Business (AACSB)-accredited Master of Leadership Development (MLD) graduate degree program at Penn State. By sharing our knowledge of FRLD with our students and clients, we have personally witnessed FRLD's effectiveness in promoting positive change in individuals, teams, organizations, communities, and nations. FRLD is part of what has kept us united as both friends and advocates of transformational leadership over the years.

Our story began in the early 1990s when we were attracted to SUNY-Binghamton's doctoral program in management for one primary reason: Bernie Bass and his colleagues. Bernie entered academia in 1946 and had published over 400 books and articles on leadership by the time we joined him. His association with the classic Ohio State leadership studies, excellent pedigree provided by Ralph Stogdill and others, tireless work on the *Handbook of Leadership* (an encyclopedic anthology of leadership research findings and applications), and *Leadership and Performance Beyond Expectations* (the seminal work on transformational leadership) were huge draws for us.

During our days at Binghamton, we learned an important lesson: Not only was Bernie a giant in the field of leadership, but he was an extremely kind and nurturing man with an overflowing wellspring of knowledge as well. Both of us remember spending time with Bernie in countless mornings, asking him many silly questions. At that time, we were deadly serious about our questions. We even dared to challenge him. However, he never showed any sign of getting tired of naïve doctoral students. He always smiled like a Zen master! His willingness to spend time nurturing us clearly demonstrated that he was a transformational leader himself. Bernie also helped launch many vehicles that advanced the field of leadership, such as *The Leadership Quarterly* and the Center for Leadership Studies. We were privileged to be able to study and work with someone who had such a profound impact on our field, and a heart of gold that personified idealized leadership. For these reasons, we dedicate this book to the memory of Bernie Bass.

Intended Audience

In the spirit of Bass's notion of transformational leadership, we wrote this book as an in-depth overview of the FRLD model and how it has been applied in a wide range of real-life situations by people just like you. We wanted to show our readers that the FRLD model was not designed exclusively for world-class CEOs and high-ranking executives. It was designed for leadership development for everyone. Therefore, the intended audience is undergraduate and graduate classes in management, leadership, educational leadership, faith community leadership, industrial and organizational psychology, social services, health care and biotechnology management, social entrepreneurship, public administration, criminal justice, and training and development.

This book is a suitable complement to a growing number of university programs, such as the MBA and MLD programs at Penn State University, that are using the Multifactor Leadership Questionnaire (MLQ; www.MindGarden. com) to assess students' leadership development. Thus, this book may be used as a central text in leadership courses or as a supplement in an organizational behavior or human resource management course. Managers of organizations at all levels in all industries, trainers, business professionals, entrepreneurs, community leaders, or any readers interested in becoming better leaders should also find this book motivating and useful.

Features

Our book has several important and distinctive features. It is written in a clear, conversational, and thought-provoking style. It challenges you to think about what you are learning and how you can apply this knowledge to your personal leadership situation. It contains many profiles of famous leaders and colorful examples that bring FRLD concepts to life. In addition, several other features make this book useful and unique:

- Much of the application of FRLD has been tested and applied in Penn State's MLD program. Our book gathers this evidence together to provide a rich description of how transformational and transactional leadership can be successfully applied in real-life situations. We buttress this evidence with results of scientific research that makes this book both rigorous and relevant. We believe that there are many leadership books available, but many of them lack a fine balance of practical discussion and rigorous scientific validation.
- Each chapter describes in actionable ways what leaders need to do to be more successful in demonstrating transactional and transformational leadership and reaping the benefits of developing associates into leaders themselves. Thus, the book can serve as a how-to training guide that explains *how*, *when*, and *why* FRLD leadership behaviors work.
- Each chapter provides vivid examples, vignettes, and anecdotes about the nurturing of FRLD in organizations. We share many personal examples of how ordinary managers became extraordinary leaders through the FRLD model and training.

- Each chapter contains summary and reflective questions that reinforce the learning process and provide ideas for applying what is learned through experiential exercises. These exercises are designed to develop your full leadership potential and facilitate your learning. These include exercises linked to the measurement of FRLD behaviors summarized on Mind Garden, Inc.'s MLQ feedback report.
- Chapter 1 links FRLD to other leadership theories. A brief history of the development of leadership thought provides you with an understanding of how FRLD fits into and extends the leadership literature.
- Chapters include testimonials of key FRLD scholars and practicing managers who have used the FRLD model in their personal and professional lives. Their words can help you to understand the history and nuances of FRLD and how you too can benefit from the lessons in this book.

The book contains 10 chapters and an appendix. Chapters 1 and 2 provide foundation material. Chapters 3 through 6 cover transformational leadership behaviors. Chapter 7 describes transactional leadership behaviors. Chapter 8 examines passive forms of leadership behavior. Chapter 9 explains how FRLD can be shared within teams. Chapter 10 presents how FRLD can be used as a strategic intervention in organizations and communities through evidence from research and testimonials from managers and other practitioners. The appendix describes the philosophy and content of Penn State's MLD program, which is structured around the FRLD model.

Acknowledgments

Working on this book has been a labor of love, a nostalgic return to our roots, and a hopeful vision of a bright future for our students, clients, colleagues, and you, the reader. It is a privilege to acknowledge the great debt of gratitude to those individuals whose cooperation, assistance, and advice have made this book possible.

The first word of thanks goes to Bernie Bass and Bruce Avolio for their tireless mentoring and collegiality over the years. In August 2004 at the National Meetings of the Academy of Management in New Orleans, Bernie asked if we would be willing to integrate material from the transformational leadership training workshops into book form. Shortly before Bernie's passing in October 2007, we spoke with Bruce to get his opinion on our interest to write such a book. He expressed a need for such a book and supported our idea to write the book in a style that is both relevant and rigorous in terms of research support and integration. Bruce kindly provided generous and excellent feedback on our book proposal, and we greatly appreciate his support and encouragement for this project, and his outstanding mentoring over the years.

We thank our colleagues at the Center for Leadership Studies at the State University of New York at Binghamton. We owe a considerable debt of gratitude and friendship to Fran Yammarino, Don Spangler, Ruth Bass, Surinder Kahai, Shelley Dionne, Howard Powell, Al Pellicotti, Lisa Wolf, Diane Thomas, and Wendy Kramer, for their counsel, mentoring, and assistance during our days in Binghamton and throughout our careers.

Our thanks go as well to our friends and colleagues at Penn State Great Valley and San Diego State University (SDSU): the late Effy Oz, Jae Uk Chun, Denise Potosky, Simon Pak, Daniel Indro, Janice Dreachslin, Barry Litzky, Pastor Robert Scott, Alex DeNoble, Lynn Shore, and Moon Song for their help and support during this project. We thank and continue to be inspired by the numerous Penn State and SDSU students who have contributed testimonials on the effectiveness of FRLD in developing people, building profits, and saving our planet's natural resources and environment. Our students are transformational leaders in every sense of the word, and we are very proud of them.

Our editor, Anne C. Duffy at Psychology Press, has been a valuable resource throughout the project. We also thank Robert Most at Mind Garden, Inc., Darryl Walker, and Louise Whitelaw for their super job of editing and critiquing the manuscript. We must also thank JoAnn Kelly, Susan Haldeman, Sue Kershner, June Gorman, Pat Misselwitz, Michael Lomax, Silviu Rechieru, Andrea Laine, Lisa Baker, Karen Norheim, Nisha Desai, Neal Generose, Brian and Cristina Powell, and Sean Travers for various forms of assistance and support.

Finally, our profound thanks to John G. and Josephine A. Sosik, the late Ann Drost, Sinyoung Choi, and Austin and Celeste Jung for their love, patience, perseverance, and support during this project and over the years. Their lives give meaning to transformational leadership, to which we owe a special debt of gratitude.

John J. Sosik

School of Graduate and Professional Studies at Great Valley
Pennsylvania State University

Dongil (Don) Jung

School of Business
Yonsei University

Chapter 1

Introducing Full Range Leadership Development

The task of leadership is not to put greatness into people, but to elicit it, for the greatness is there already.

— John Buchan

Ever since he was a child, John Juzbasich possessed an entrepreneurial spirit and the desire to help others. From paper routes to lemonade stands to designing computer games, he had a knack for enterprising ideas. Later in life, after leaving a long and successful technology career at IBM, Juzbasich joined Jim Wynn to form Merit Systems LLC, a Wayne, Pennsylvania, training solutions company. As Merit Systems grew into a respected and profitable business, Juzbasich thirsted for leadership knowledge and experiences to supplement his success as an entrepreneur. So he assumed responsibilities as scoutmaster, church committee chairperson, township government official, and board director in his local community. He also enrolled in and graduated from Penn State University's Master of Leadership Development (MLD) graduate degree program. This Association to Advance Collegiate Schools of Business (AACSB)-accredited specialized master's business degree program is built upon a foundation of research and practice supporting the Full Range Leadership Development model.

The MLD program inspired Juzbasich to establish the West Africa American Trading Company (WAATCO). This for-profit business is dedicated to helping rebuild the war-torn country of Liberia. During this leadership endeavor, Juzbasich met with President Ellen Johnson-Sirleaf of Liberia and other officials on numerous occasions in the United States and Liberia to establish a business aimed at producing a triple bottom line benefiting people, profit, and planet.[1] This enterprise has given hope through the pathway of education to children of a famished country. So far, over 11,000 textbooks and used computers have been distributed to schools in Liberia through WAATCO.[2] Juzbasich's example of outstanding leadership illustrates that you can do good for people and the planet while making a profit.

Outstanding leaders, like John Juzbasich, are committed to bringing forth and developing the greatness in their followers. If you aspire to be an outstanding leader, you need to consider several key issues as you start reading this book. Take a few minutes now to reflect upon your responses to each of the following questions:

- Do you have a workable plan to cultivate the greatness of the people in your organization?
- How will you help them realize their potential to excel?
- Are you able to carefully scrutinize and evaluate their actions?
- Are you able to set goals for them and use rewards and punishments to move them closer to these goals?
- Can you role model in your own behavior what you expect from them?
- Is it possible for you to inspire them to cooperate with your organization's internal and external stakeholders?
- Are you capable of challenging them to rethink their basic assumptions and rework their ways of doing things?
- Are you patient enough to coach them in a way that develops their strengths to their full potential, while recognizing and addressing their weaknesses?

If you are willing to work to achieve these ends, you are in good company. Recognizing and developing the full leadership potential of people has become a strategic initiative in some of today's most successful global organizations. For example, Proctor and Gamble selects employees based on their emotional intelligence, a set of traits and skills such as self-awareness, self-regulation, empathy, and relationship management, linked to leadership effectiveness.[3] Both Capital One Financial and Nokia use coaching and mentoring programs to empower and advance the careers of their employees. General Mills and S. C. Johnson challenge their associates to be prepared for various environmental stewardship issues that may arise by training them to be creative problem solvers. IBM motivates its employees to learn through sharing of best practices from companies it has recently acquired, thereby promoting synergies that foster innovation. The United Way of New York City sponsors its annual Executive Fellows Program to train directors of member agencies on key strategic and tactical aspects of leadership. While these organizations differ in size, age, industry, and mission, they have one thing in common—they realize that leadership development gives them a competitive edge in adapting to the rapid changes and challenges of our global and technology-driven world.[4]

These organizations have realized that leadership is not just about moving people, teams, and organizations to get from point A to point B, and simply achieving goals. It's also about displaying behaviors and creating organizational structures and policies that develop their associates and business partners along the way. It involves moving leaders and followers from passive to more active styles of leadership, elevating followers' motivation and performance to levels of excellence, sustaining a positive and results-oriented organizational culture, and being committed to environmental stewardship as well.

The big question is: How do we develop more proactive leaders in our organization who motivate employees to perform beyond their expectations? We believe that the Full Range Leadership Development model,[5] a research-based and validated leadership paradigm, can help accomplish that goal. That's why we decided to write this book, to share our experience in researching, teaching, and practicing the Full Range Leadership Model with you. The Full Range Leadership Development model is a leadership training system that proposes that leaders vary in the extent to which they display a repertoire of leadership behaviors, ranging from active and more effective leadership to passive and less effective leadership. To fully develop the potential of leaders and followers who can achieve extraordinary levels of success requires an understanding of a full range of leadership behaviors suitable for today's complex world. The focus of this book is to ensure that leaders who read it come away with that understanding.

Why Full Range Leadership Development Is Essential for Exceptional Performance Today

The time is right for leaders at all levels in today's organizations to use Full Range Leadership Development (FRLD). That's due to the many dramatic changes that we have and will face in our lives. Shifting demographics, workforce diversity, geopolitical alterations, technology innovation, threats to the environment, shifts in the economic prowess of nations, and collaborative business practices are just some of the trends today's leaders must face. These changes are occurring at an accelerated pace due to advances in technology, globalization, and the information age in which we live. We believe that the following changes have created a new need to develop and practice a relevant leadership paradigm such as FRLD.

Leadership for Our Dynamic World and Lives

We live in a world that is constantly changing—and changing at a rapid rate. These changes require leadership that is ready to adapt to and leverage opportunities to excel from such trends.

Demographic Changes

Each new generation of workers brings changes in preferences in values, mindsets, and ways of living. Do you understand how to motivate different generational cohorts (e.g., Baby Boomers, Generation X, Generation Y) in your organization? Increased diversity and shifts in demographics of national populations also add complexity and a need to appreciate and recognize individual differences among people. For example, the Hispanic and Asian populations in the United States have grown significantly over the last 20 years. These trends pose interesting leadership challenges. How has the collective face of your workforce changed in recent years, and what are you doing to leverage the power of such diversity? By the year 2050, today's majority groups will become minorities, and vice versa. Leadership can help by leveraging diversity, developing its innate talents into strengths, and matching its varied skill set to the important challenges facing organizations.

Technology Trends

Advances in technology bring new opportunities and methods to socialize, share ideas and experiences, and conduct business. The Internet, social networking sites (e.g., Facebook, Twitter, Flickr), Webcasting, Apple's iPods and iPhones, videoconferences, and virtual worlds such as Second Life bring both challenges and opportunities to excel. Leadership is needed to identify ways to use technology systems to build social and collaborative networks and accelerate the development of your associates and the success of your organization. Are you leveraging leadership in a way that coordinates both the social and technology systems in your organization?

Geopolitical Alterations

The geopolitical alliances and boundaries that you grew up with have morphed into new configurations that require novel approaches for conducting business. Who would have predicted that former Soviet bloc countries would become members of NATO, and that after the Cold War ended, a new "global war on terror" would begin? An increasing amount of political, economic, and social attention is shifting to the Asian and African continents. Forces of internation-alization and globalization bring both opportunities for market growth and the responsibility to address some of the world's most menacing problems, such as poverty and disease. Is your leadership operating in such a socially responsible fashion? Leadership can help by finding ways to answer these questions through relationship building, problem solving, and conflict resolution. The FRLD model presented in this book is a leadership system that can help you to answer these questions.

New Generations of Workers Bring New Ideas

The associates in your organization also bring with them leadership challenges. Because today's employees are better educated and more experienced than ever before, they demand more of an active role in the leadership of their organization. For example, the Generation Y "millennials" (those born between 1976 and 2001) find serving their organizations and communities to add meaning to their lives. They enjoy connecting with their friends and colleagues almost 24/7. They tend to be more inclusive and tolerant of different social groups than previous generations.[6]

Leadership is needed to bring such associates' knowledge, skills, and abilities into the leadership equation to offer optimal solutions to the problems we face. The FRLD model engages and develops employees' knowledge, skills, and abilities as part of a leadership system. Based on a large volume of research evidence accumulated to date, we know that people who display such leadership are more capable of producing and sustaining the high levels of performance required for succeeding in today's global market and society.

Organizational Modifications

Indeed, adaptation has become a fact of life for most organizations. Organizational challenges such as economic recessions, housing market meltdowns, rapid changes in technology, fierce global competition, and employee retention prob-lems demand such leadership. Increasingly, organizations are turning to their leadership at all levels to promote employees' level of interest and motivation in their jobs, create novel products and services that meet customers' needs, improve product and process quality, adapt technology appropriately, and execute strategy effectively. Organizations that support and develop this form of leadership across organizational levels are more productive and profitable, attract and retain high-quality associates, promote creativity and innovation, garner trust and commitment from employees, and are strategically positioned to respond well to changes in the market. Leadership can help by fostering strategies and systems that promote adaptation instead of rigidity. FRLD strives to grow change-oriented leadership in organizations at all levels (including followers), thereby generating these positive outcomes at all levels as well.[7]

Environmental Issues

Worldwide environmental problems pose additional challenges for contemporary leaders. Many of the world's metals and fossil fuels, such as oil, coal, and natural gas, are nonrenewable. In 2008, we heard a radio news report about Russia approaching the limit of its oil supplies and calls for the U.S. government to tap into its strategic energy reserves. With the world's demand for fuel increasing beyond what we can presently supply, leaders must help identify alternative sources of energy to meet demand.

In addition, a variety of pollutants are wreaking havoc on the environment. Forests are being destroyed at an alarming rate as the world is being concreted over with new developments. Land that was once functional is being rendered useless through desertification. An unholy host of pollutants are making their way into our water, soil, and air. These include chemical pollutants (e.g., fertilizers, detergents, pesticides, plastics), solid waste pollutants thrown out by individuals and industry, and water pollution coming from a plethora of nasty sources. Industry, farmers, and cities are producing toxic waste. Hospitals, universities, and industrial plants are generating radioactive emissions. Air pollution and acid rain represent additional environmental threats.

Most of these problems stem from cultural and structural sources that can be addressed by FRLD concepts. Cultural sources of environmental problems include the idea that nature is a vast storehouse of resources to which we are all entitled. Leadership that challenges the assumptions underlying this idea can help change this cornucopia view of nature. The misperception that science and technology (without leadership) will save the environment is a dangerous proposition. The unchecked growth ethic that "more is better" needs to be challenged through rational analysis and problem solving. Rampant materialism, conspicuous consumption, and products designed for expedited obsolescence are societal values that need to challenged through idealized leadership. The belief in individualism in certain Western countries has preempted collective rights that protect the environment. Leadership that inspires teamwork and cooperation is needed to produce a more collectivistic and other-oriented perspective in these situations.

Structural sources of environmental problems include capitalism's unending quest for profits. Unfortunately, this goal requires unending supplies of resources to expend, rather than sustainable and reusable resources. Overconsumption and creating demand where it does not exist is another issue that needs to be examined from different perspectives. Many governments have cozy relationships with polluting corporations. These questionable alliances may necessitate grass-roots and social entrepreneurship initiatives to tackle environmental problems. In addition, demographic patterns such as rapid urbanization, suburban sprawl, and population growth need to be reexamined by hearing from multiple constituents. Environmental classism/racism, where members of lower socioeconomic strata encounter various pollutants (e.g., lead poisoning, foul air) more than others, is often overlooked by community leaders.[8]

Taken together, the above-mentioned list of social, economic, political, and environmental problems represents a new frontier for research and practice applying FRLD. Leadership is needed to assume the responsibility to address these problems *now* instead of deferring these problems to the next quarter, administration, or generation. We need leaders like *you* to solve these problems.

And the Research Says …

To begin solving these problems with the right leadership paradigm, you need to seriously consider your options, just as you would if you were facing a major health concern. Would you subject yourself or your loved ones to a medical treatment or procedure that has not been validated in systematic evaluation? Probably not. Then why would you subject yourself and your associates to any leadership paradigm that has not been rigorously validated? Rest assured, the FRLD model is supported by an extensive research base and applications in corporate, military, religious, educational, and nonprofit training settings worldwide. It is based on Bernard Bass's *Leadership and Performance Beyond Expectations*, the seminal work on the transformational-transactional leadership paradigm published in 1985 and acclaimed by many top leadership scholars such as Francis J. Yammarino (see Table 1.1). Building upon Bass's work, Bruce Avolio published in 1999 *Full Leadership Development: Building the Vital Forces in Organizations*, which presents an integrated overview of full range leadership development. The book you are reading builds upon and extends their work.

The work of Bass, Avolio, and their associates at the Center for Leadership Studies at the State University of New York in Binghamton and at other universities has provided the foundation for leadership training around the world in many areas, including stand-alone specialized graduate degree programs in leadership development being taught at a number of universities. For example, Penn State University's MLD program, where John is the program director, uses the transactional-transformational leadership paradigm as the foundation for its courses. We will present evidence of the development of leaders from this program throughout this book to support many of its key lessons.

Table 1.1   FRLD Scholar Profile: Francis J. Yammarino

Francis J. Yammarino is distinguished professor of management and director of the Center for Leadership Studies (CLS) at the State University of New York at Binghamton. Yammarino joined Bernard Bass at Binghamton in 1985 and over the years has worked with Bass and Bruce Avolio to create and administer the CLS. He has been a significant contributor to FRLD in terms of his extensive stream of research on transformational leadership and levels of analysis. He has served as editor of *The Leadership Quarterly,* the premier journal in the field of leadership. Beyond that, Yammarino has been an excellent mentor to many FRLD scholars earning their doctoral degrees at SUNY-Binghamton, including the authors.

Yammarino recalls receiving an autographed copy of Bass's (1985) *Leadership and Performance Beyond Expectations* in the fall of 1985 and considers this seminal book on FRLD to be a monumental work in the field of leadership. In a book review published in *The Leadership Quarterly* in 1993, Yammarino deems the Bass book to be a catalyst for research on transformational and charismatic leadership theories. Besides outlining solid theoretical underpinnings for FRLD behaviors, Bass's work presented the original work on the Multifactor Leadership Questionnaire (MLQ), which measures FRLD behaviors. According to Yammarino, this influential work laid the groundwork for attempts to develop a solid understanding of FRLD behaviors.

Yammarino is proud of the theoretical and empirical work extending Bass's original work that has come out of the CLS and its faculty and students. Their dissertations and journal articles have added much to our understanding of FRLD and its application to organizations. He also notes the numerous conferences and conference sessions on transformational leadership at SUNY–Binghamton and elsewhere as indicators of the topic's importance. Yammarino points out that many trainers and consultants around the world use FRLD concepts, which illustrate its relevance and practicality. In addition, he highlights the large number of research grants and publications on FRLD topics as indicators of its significance. Indeed, FRLD is backed with a solid foundation of science and usefulness.

The advent of Bass and Avolio's FRLD model has lead to a surge in research attention on the transformational-transactional leadership paradigm. Leadership scholars Tim Judge and R. F. Piccolo argue that this paradigm is *the* premier leadership paradigm, currently garnering more research attention than any other leadership theory or model. Their meta-analysis (i.e., a quantitative academic study summarizing the results of many studies) by and large validated the FRLD model, as have other independent analyses.[9]

In summary, today's internal and external conditions for organizations demand FRLD. We live in turbulent times with uncertain markets, political instability, terrorism, a depleted environment, and rapidly changing technology and social forces. We are faced with challenging problems every day at work, and within and between the nations on earth. Solving these problems requires us to be creative and innovative. We need to constantly challenge and develop our colleagues so that we can select and retain the best and brightest. When we utilize FRLD, we are able to attract new high-quality personnel, and challenge and develop them more fully. We can respond more quickly and effectively to changes in the market. We are able to generate more creative solutions to our problems. We are able to project an image of confidence, commitment, and mission focus to our employees, customers, and other organizational stakeholders. All of these processes result in higher satisfaction, productivity, and profits.[10] And they have the wonderful potential to enhance the welfare of our planet as well.

The Components of Full Range Leadership Development Theory

Now it's time to briefly introduce the components of the FRLD model. Together, we will expand your understanding of these leadership styles in subsequent chapters. At this point, consider the FRLD model shown in Figure 1.1. According to this model, leadership across the range is represented by five specific behaviors and one attribute. A *behavior* is something a person does or says that can be observed, described, and recorded. In contrast, an *attribute* is a characteristic that is ascribed to a person by others based on what the person is perceived to do or say.[11] These five behaviors and one attribute describe different forms of leadership. According to the FRLD model, leaders display a repertoire of both passive and active forms of leadership. The more active forms of leadership are associated with higher levels of effectiveness and satisfaction than the more passive forms of leadership.

The passive forms of leadership in the FRLD model include laissez-faire and passive management-by-exception leadership. More active forms of transactional leadership include active management-by-exception and contingent reward leadership. At the uppermost end of the range is transformational leadership, which research has linked to the highest levels of individual, group, and organizational performance. Let's establish transformational leadership as our goal and work up the FRLD starting at the bottom of the model.

Laissez-Faire

Have you ever worked for a leader who sees the development and performance of followers as someone else's responsibility and avoids taking a stand on issues at all costs? How did you and your associates respond to this individual's behavior? What was the end result of such a lazy attitude toward leadership?

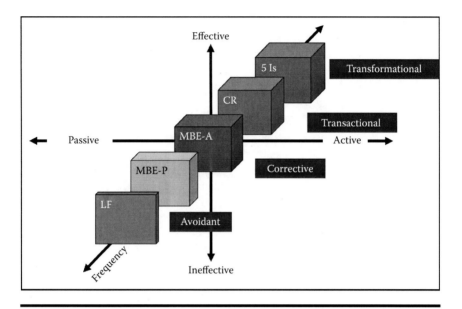

Figure 1.1 Full Range Leadership Development model. (Reproduced by special permission of the publisher, Mind Garden, Inc., Menlo Park, CA, www. mindgarden.com from the *Multifactor Leadership Questionnaire Feedback Report* by Bernard M. Bass and Bruce J. Avolio. Copyright © 1996, 2003 by Bernard M. Bass and Bruce J. Avolio. All rights reserved. Further reproduction is prohibited without the publisher's written consent.)

When leaders abdicate responsibility, delay in responding to urgent requests, or do not follow up on issues, they display laissez-faire leadership. When they are indifferent about important issues and avoid making decisions or dealing with chronic problems, they display laissez-faire leadership as well. Laissez-faire leadership is actually nonleadership because there is no exchange relationship between the leader and the follower. A leader who displays this form of nonleadership is perceived as not caring at all about others' issues. The laissez-faire leader shown in Figure 1.2 is on a personal phone call and is certainly absent from his professional responsibilities. Laissez-faire leadership is associated with the lowest levels of performance and satisfaction.

Passive Management-by-Exception

A slightly more effective style of leadership in the FRLD model is *passive management-by-exception*. When a leader waits for mistakes to happen before stepping in to attempt to fix the problem, the leader displays passive

Figure 1.2   Take it easy. Laissez-faire behavior is associated with the lowest levels of individual, team, and organizational outcomes.

management-by-exception. The leader's attitude is typically "if it's not broken, don't fix it." A leader who displays this form of leadership intervenes only when standards are not met. Figure 1.3 shows a leader pointing out to his follower that something has gone wrong after the fact. In this situation, the follower has not met a company standard and the leader is letting him know about it. Because the leader springs into action only when something went wrong, the leader is not perceived by followers as a worthy role model. As a result, followers show little trust in the leader. Their commitment level is low and their motivation is weak.

Passive management-by-exception leadership also can be illustrated with the "cop in the donut shop" stereotype often seen on television shows. Imagine a small-town policeman leisurely sitting in a Dunkin' Donuts® shop drinking coffee. Then his police radio goes off, beckoning him to a disturbance at the local

Figure 1.3   Here comes trouble. Passive management-by-exception leadership behavior points out what's gone wrong after the fact.

shopping mall. He takes no action unless a problem arises. After the problem is fixed, it's back to normal functioning—a warm and comfortable booth at the coffee shop.

Active Management-by-Exception

If passive management-by-exception behavior is like the cop in the donut shop, you can imagine *active management-by-exception* behavior as "Robocop," "Rambo-in-Pinstripes," or a heat-seeking missile. Instead of waiting for things to go wrong before taking action, a leader who displays active management-by-exception micromanages processes and takes corrective action, often before or soon after the problem arises. Such behavior involves closely monitoring work performance for errors and arranging to know if and when things go wrong. As shown in Figure 1.4, the leader pointing to the board is monitoring performance very closely. He is clearly focusing much attention on one down quarter instead of considering the entire year. Here the leader's attention is on mistakes, complaints, failures, deviations from standards, and infractions of rules and regulations.

While active management-by-exception may be effective in high-stakes or life-or-death situations (e.g., nuclear power plants, military operations) or in problem-solving contexts (e.g., auditing, information systems development and maintenance), leaders in other contexts who display this behavior are likely to promote fear and stifle innovation among associates. It is difficult for followers to identify with and place trust in a leader who constantly focuses on the negative and keeps systems in check all of the time. Consequently, followers' commitment and motivation levels are not typically optimized with active management-by-exception leadership.

Figure 1.4 Micromanager on steroids. Active management-by-exception leadership behavior seeks to avoid mistakes before they happen. But its focus on the negative can be de-motivating.

Contingent Reward

Moving up the FRLD model, we now come to *transactional contingent reward*, an active and generally effective leader behavior, often displayed by politicians and other dealmakers. Contingent reward leadership is a constructive transaction—a type of implied contract. It represents an exchange relationship between the leader and the follower. The leader sets goals, clarifies roles, and explains expectations for the follower regarding performance targets. In return, the follower promises to meet the performance expectations set by the leader. If the follower meets expectations by following through with his side of the deal, the leader rewards the follower in accordance with their implied contract. If the follower fails to meet the goal, he does not receive the reward, or is punished for failing to meet the goal.

In essence, contingent reward is a carrot-and-stick approach to leadership that relies on extrinsic motivation to drive followers toward the goal. In Figure 1.5, we see a leader praising his follower for a job well done. The follower was able to accomplish his task properly because of the fact that the leader was clear in setting and communicating his goals for the report. Research has shown that contingent reward leadership is generally effective in building base levels of trust and commitment in followers, and for meeting targeted performance levels.

The 4Is of Transformational Leadership

While contingent reward may be an effective way to motivate followers to reach targeted goals, such an approach might have limited success in today's knowledge-based economy, where people need to have both extrinsic and intrinsic motivation to succeed. We need someone who leads us with a vision

Figure 1.5 Keep up the good work. Transactional contingent rewards leadership behavior, sets goals for followers, and rewards them for a job well done.

Table 1.2   Leader Profile: Muhammad Yunus

Bringing vision into action is a hallmark of transformational leaders. One man's vision is the total eradication of poverty from the world. That man is Muhammad Yunus, recipient of the 2006 Nobel Peace Prize for his work in fighting world poverty. Yunus is the Bangladeshi economist, professor, politician, and founder of the Grameen Bank (Village Bank). This organization transformed the financial services industry by introducing the concept of providing small loans to poor people at reasonable interest rates. These microcredit loans have helped reduce poverty in Bangladesh and in hundreds of countries around the world. Grameen has diversified beyond banking into the agriculture, irrigation, software, telecommunications, and clothing industries—all with a focus on fighting poverty and helping to promote social entrepreneurship.

Yunus is using part of his Nobel Prize award money to create another company that will make low-cost, high-nutrition food for the poor. He also plans to establish an eye hospital for the poor in his country. He is a member of the Global Elders, a multinational group of political leaders, including Desmond Tutu, Nelson Mandela, and Jimmy Carter. This group shares their leadership wisdom in an effort to solve the world's most pressing problems of poverty, disease, and social and economic injustice.

Yunus displayed intellectual stimulation by venturing where traditional banks would not dare to go. He did this by extending high-risk microcredit loans to the poor. He displayed individualized consideration by expanding his business model beyond finance so that more poor people could benefit from the products and services of his Grameen enterprises. Yunus is the epitome of transformational leadership in the realm of social entrepreneurship.

Source: Yunus, M., & Jolis, A. (2001). *Banker to the poor: The autobiography of Mohammed Yunus, Founder of Grameen Bank.* Oxford: Oxford University Press; and http://www.muhammadyunus.org/. Retrieved December 18, 2007.

and confidence. Transformational leadership inspires followers to exceed these goals—to perform beyond expectations. Transformational leadership promotes positive and meaningful changes in people, teams, organizations, nations, and even societies, as illustrated in the leader profile of Muhammad Yunus in Table 1.2. There are four components of transformational leadership, which are called the 4Is of transformational leadership: idealized influence, inspirational motivation, intellectual stimulation, and individualized consideration. Let's briefly examine each of these components of transformational leadership.

Idealized Influence

You might have felt that Muhammad Yunus seems like a current-day version of Mohandas Gandhi, who advised his followers to always aim at complete harmony of thought, word, and deed. Transformational leaders, such as Yunus and Gandhi, often seek this authenticity by displaying high levels of moral behavior, virtues, and character strengths, as well as a strong work ethic.[12] Transformational leaders talk about the importance of universal or company values, beliefs, purposes, a collective mission, and the benefits of trusting each other. They set aside their self-interest for the good of the group. Their words and deeds represent *idealized influence behaviors*. When followers witness a leader's idealized influence behaviors, they attribute idealized influence to the leader, as shown in Figure 1.6. Here you can see that this leader is well respected and admired by his team member. This leader instills a sense of pride and respect in his team member because he speaks with confidence of a collective mission and the importance of living company values and beliefs.

The idealized leader's role modeling of high levels of performance and ethics is admired and respected by followers as well, thereby adding to the idealized influence followers attribute to a transformational leader. As a result, followers identify strongly with a leader, show high levels of trust in and commitment to the leader, and exert high levels of drive and motivation. Indeed, idealized influence (behavior and attributes) represents the very pinnacle of leadership within the FRLD model, as shown in Gandhi's call for authenticity, which increases followers' willingness to trust and emulate the leader.

Inspirational Motivation

Closely related to idealized influence is *inspirational motivation*, a leader behavior that involves developing and articulating a vision. Examples of positive visions

Figure 1.6   Hooray for our team! Idealized leaders talk about the importance of teamwork and the collective success that energizes followers to emulate the leader.

include U.S. President Barack Obama's inaugural address highlighting the price and promise of citizenship, Dr. Martin Luther King's "I Have a Dream Speech," Oprah Winfrey's encouraging young women with her Leadership Academy, and Professor Randy Pausch's "Last Lecture" on life lessons given at Carnegie Mellon University. (If you have not witnessed these visionary speeches, we encourage you to view them on http://www.YouTube.com.) Such visions paint an optimistic and enthusiastic picture of the future that "raises the bar" for followers. The status quo is unacceptable to the transformational leader; the alternate future presented in the vision is considered a must-achieve scenario. Often this vision elevates performance expectations and reframes the organization's purpose as meaningful. Raising the bar and highlighting significance is a way to inspire followers to put forth extra effort in their work.

By using inspiration, transformational leaders express confidence in followers and their shared vision. Through the content of this vision and behavior that is consistent with the vision, inspirational leaders energize followers to exert extra effort in challenging situations. In addition, they champion collective action and team synergy. These are essential ingredients needed to achieve the vision. As shown in Figure 1.7, the leader is giving a presentation in which he is articulating a clear vision of the future, and he is very confident in his message as he talks of team synergy.

Both inspirational motivation and idealized influence elicit very strong emotional bonds, deep trust, and commitment between leaders and followers. As a result, inspirational motivation increases followers' willingness to excel.

Intellectual Stimulation

While inspirational motivation triggers the emotions of followers, intellectual stimulation values followers' rationality and intellect. The great thinkers

Figure 1.7 I can see for miles and miles. Inspirational leaders motivate their followers by presenting them with an appealing and evocative vision of the future.

Figure 1.8 Let's try it this way. Intellectual stimulation gets followers to look at old problems in new ways.

of history, such as Thomas Aquinas, Albert Einstein, and Maria Skłodowska-Curie, were strong advocates of rational thinking, considering opposing points of view, and systematic analysis as means of creative problem solving and innovation. So too are contemporary leaders such as Howard Schultz of Starbucks, Meg Whitman of eBay, and Larry Page and Sergey Bren, the founders of Google, Inc. When leaders encourage the use of these methods of imagination and challenge old ways of doing things, they are displaying *intellectual stimulation*. Seeking different perspectives, reexamining assumptions that are no longer valid, getting others to look at problems in new ways, and encouraging nontraditional thinking as well as rethinking are all forms of intellectual stimulation. These behaviors get followers to become more creative and innovative, and more willing to change people, processes, products, and services for the better. In essence, intellectual stimulation increases followers' willingness to think.

As shown in Figure 1.8, the leader is challenging her team to reexamine assumptions and seek perspectives that are not the norm. She is encouraging her team to think in a different way and be creative. As a result, her intellectual stimulation creates an environment of rational thinking that supports the development and use of followers' natural talents and strengths.

Individualized Consideration

Transformational leaders' ultimate aim is to develop followers into leaders themselves.[13] Who in your life has been such a transformational leader to you? Who has helped you recognize the greatness that grows in you? Pause for a moment and think of some of those people who wanted the best for you in your life. Who has encouraged you to become who you are today? Who helped to transform you into your best possible self?

Figure 1.9   A helping hand. Individually considerate leaders coach and mentor followers by appreciating their uniqueness and helping them build their talents into strengths.

The developmental nature of transformational leadership is best illustrated through *individualized consideration*. When leaders spend time listening, coaching, and teaching for followers' development they are displaying individualized consideration. When leaders treat others as individuals with different needs, abilities, and aspirations (and not just part of a group of subordinates), they are displaying individualized consideration as well. As shown in Figure 1.9, the leader has taken the time to listen to his follower's concern. He understood the problem facing the follower and supported him in facing a challenge. Individualized consideration involves showing empathy, valuing individual needs, and encouraging continuous improvement. As a result of such attention, individually considerate leaders increase followers' willingness to develop.

To summarize, the FRLD model proposes the notion that leaders who achieve performance beyond expectations are those who build people up through transformational leadership. These leaders are exemplary role models, have an exciting vision, challenge the status quo and continually innovate (even at the peak of success), and coach and mentor their associates to achieve their full potential and performance. Effective transformational leadership is built upon a foundation of transactional contingent reward leadership, an exchange relationship between the leader and follower that sets well-defined roles and expectations and uses extrinsic rewards to achieve desired performance. Less effective leadership styles search for what's done wrong, not what's done right (active management-by-exception), patch problems and focus on mistakes only after they have occurred (passive management-by-exception), and avoid leadership and relinquish responsibility (laissez-faire).[14]

Full Range Leadership Development and the History of Leadership Thought

Theory and research on FRLD is connected to and built upon a long and interesting history. For centuries, man has considered the concept of leadership. But it was not until the 20th century that the disciplines of political science, psychology, sociology, history, anthropology, and management converged to make major contributions toward our understanding of leadership.[15] Guided by Table 1.3, let's briefly examine the history of leadership thought and how FRLD relates to a variety of other leadership theories. As we often tell our students, please consider a theory to be a useful tool that explains how and why things happen, rather than an abstract and useless idea. As psychologist Kurt Lewin once said, "There is nothing as practical as a good theory."

Trait Theory

Scholars first studied leadership in terms of the traits, or fixed personal characteristics and innate qualities, found in great leaders. These "Great Man" theories linked qualities such as intelligence, self-confidence, determination, integrity, and sociability to leadership effectiveness.[16] For example, think about the types of strong characters movie actors John Wayne, Denzel Washington, or Russell Crowe played across their careers and you will get a sense of what the Great Man theories espoused. These theories also described similar "great women," such as Margaret Thatcher, the strong-willed former prime minister of Great Britain, who was dubbed "Iron Lady" by the Soviets. Other examples include Sarah Palin, former governor of the U.S. state of Alaska, and Angela Merkel, the chancellor of Germany.

There are several problems with trait-based leadership theories. For example, leaders can share many of the same traits, yet behave in different ways and produce starkly different outcomes. Consider Mohandas Gandhi, Winston Churchill, Franklin Delano Roosevelt, Charles de Gaulle, Adolph Hitler, Joseph Stalin, Benito Mussolini, and Francisco Franco. Each of these charismatic leaders of the mid-20th century possessed self-confidence and determination, but some led followers in destructive ways, while others were constructive. This is also true for more contemporary leaders, such as Vladimir Putin, Osama bin Laden, Tony Blair, and George W. Bush. Trait theories ignore what these leaders do, namely, how they behave. Trait theories also ignore the characteristics of followers and the situation, which also determine leadership effectiveness. For these reasons, by the 1950s, leadership scholars shifted their attention to leader behaviors and characteristics of followers and the situation.

Table 1.3 How Full Range Leadership Development Relates to Other Leadership Theories

Theory	Source(s)	Key Concept(s)	Relationship to FRLD Theory
Trait theory	Bass (1990); Judge et al. (2002); Kirkpatrick & Locke (1991)	Innate qualities and personality characteristics are found in "great" leaders (e.g., intelligence, self-confidence, determination, integrity, sociability).	Traits and personality not considered in FRLD model. But research indicates that positive, adaptive, active, and developmental leader traits support social influence process for most effective leaders.
Psychodynamic theory	Freud (1938); Kets de Vries (1994); Shamir (1991); Zaleznik (1977)	Self-concept, ego states, and personality issues underlie a parent-child relationship for leaders and followers. Leaders and followers develop through self-awareness.	Ego, self-concept, and personality not considered in FRLD model. But research links positive life experiences, prior leadership experience, and other-oriented and positive self-concepts to most effective leadership.
Skills theory	Goleman (1995)	Emotional awareness and control are essential to leadership effectiveness.	Emotional connection and social comfort between leader and follower key to leadership effectiveness.
	Mumford et al. (2000)	Problem solving, social skills, and knowledge impact leadership effectiveness.	Rationality and intellectual curiosity required on part of leaders and followers.
Style theory	Cartwight & Zander (1961); Stodgill (1963)	Task and relationship leader behaviors influence followers' performance and satisfaction.	Most effective leaders pay attention to both task and relationship issues with followers.

Theory	Citation	Description	FRLD comparison
Situational leadership-oriented theory	Blanchard et al. (1985)	Followers' competence and confidence determines appropriate leader behavior (i.e., direct, coach, support, delegate).	Most effective FRLD behaviors universal across many situations and cultures. Most effective leaders can be either directive or participative.
Contingency theory	Fiedler (1967)	Match leaders to the appropriate situation depending upon task/relationship orientation, relations with followers, task structure, and position power.	Most effective FRLD behaviors universal across many situations and cultures. Some situations may require more task-focused and less developmental behaviors.
Path–goal theory	House & Mitchell (1974)	Leader considers task and follower characteristics and selects appropriate behavior (i.e., directive, supportive, participative, achievement).	Most effective leaders clarify expectations to clear a path for followers. Raising self- and collective efficacy is vital. Most effective leaders can be either directive or participative.
LMX theory	Graen & Uhl-Bien (1995)	Quality of leader–follower dyad determines in-group, out-group, and effectiveness.	Most effective leaders give individualized attention to followers through coaching, mentoring, and diversity.
Authentic leadership theory	Avolio & Gardner (2005)	Positive psychological states, organizational contexts, and self-development promote positive outcomes.	Most effective leaders are true to themselves and others, self-aware, positive, and development oriented.

FRLD primarily focuses on leader behaviors and does not consider leader traits and personality. However, a recent resurgence of interest in trait-based explanations of leadership has linked leader traits to aspects of the Big 5 personality model (i.e., emotional stability, openness, conscientiousness, extraversion, and agreeableness) and several other traits.[17] In general, this line of research indicates that leaders who are positive, adaptive, and developmental in nature are the most effective leaders.

Psychodynamic Theory

Some psychologists and sociologists have used psychodynamic theory to explain leadership processes as the making of meaning, protection of followers by the leader, and emphasis on development of the self and others. While psychodynamic approaches to leadership are varied, one common theme is that leaders play a key role in influencing how followers think, feel, and act. This theory assumes that the world can be a hostile, turbulent, and unpredictable environment. Followers look for a leader who can make sense of such crises for them. This way of describing leadership may explain why in the midst of major global economic, social, and political turmoil, Barack Obama received a large vote of confidence during the 2008 U.S. presidential election. Obama was able to make sense out of the turmoil for people and give them hope that they could meet these challenges.

Many of these leaders successfully overcome personal challenges or organizational crises in their own lives and share their life lessons with followers. Through introspection and learning, these leaders gain greater self-awareness of who they are, what their strengths and weaknesses are, and how they can best contribute in their leadership role. Some trainers schooled in the psychodynamic approach use the Myers–Briggs Type Indicator® (MBTI) to help leaders better understand their psychological type and preference for leadership or followership. While most MBTI consultants may not see themselves as psychodynamic counselors, they are coaching leadership as a personality style measured by the MBTI, as opposed to training leadership as a set of behaviors that can be learned independent of personality, as proposed by FRLD consultants. After experiencing personal growth through the psychodynamic approach, some leaders are able to present themselves as role models worthy of protecting and guiding followers, similar to parents with their children.[18]

For example, one of our colleagues uses psychodynamic theory with her executive clients to identify sources of their aloof leadership behavior. One such client is "Richard," a 50-year-old entrepreneur who identified several critical events in his early childhood that hindered his ability to interact effectively with his associates. Richard's father was very harsh, strict, and cold in his relations with his wife and children. To compensate for this liability, Richard's mother and sisters smothered him with love and affection because he was the baby and only boy in the family. Richard's upbringing has fed a strong need for attention, standoffishness, and huge ego. Doesn't he sound somewhat child-like? In addition, Richard has few male friends due to his hypercompetitive and manipulative manner. He also feels more comfortable around women at work, but only if he is in charge and gets his way. After counseling, Richard has identified these roadblocks to his leadership effectiveness, understands where they came from, and is working on a plan to address his issues.

Psychodynamic theory provides leaders such as Richard a better understanding of who they truly are so that they may grow in their self-awareness and improve their leadership. Concepts of self, ego states, and personality are not considered in FRLD theory. However, some evidence exists that transformational leaders have a preference for intuition, empathy, and extraversion, while transactional leaders have a preference for logical thinking and practicality. In addition, research indicates that positive life experiences (e.g., having challenging but supportive parents), prior leadership experiences, and other-oriented and positive self-construals are associated with the most effective leaders in the FRLD model.

Skills Theory

Some scholars take a more practical view by describing leadership as a way to solve problems. Here the emphasis is on solving social problems that arise in relationships, teams, organizations, communities, and nations. These perspectives are grounded in theory and research on emotional intelligence and problem solving.

Emotional Intelligence

Emotions and the information they contain can help leaders do their job. Emotions, such as happiness, amusement, sadness, and concern, influence our thinking and decisions on how to act. The emotional intelligence perspective proposes that emotional awareness and control is essential to leadership effectiveness. For example, the level of emotional intelligence that George W. Bush and Tony Blair used in their leadership pales by far when compared to that of Bill Clinton or John F. Kennedy.

While there is some debate on whether emotional intelligence is a constellation of traits or a collection of skills, most leadership trainers assume the latter to be true. Emotions contain valuable information such as hints at psychological states and underlying intentions. Many people think with emotion and also think about emotions. Therefore, there is skill and knowledge involved in dealing with emotion.

As such, emotional intelligence skills allow individuals to recognize their emotions and the emotions of others, and use this information to adapt their behavior and influence others' behavior to produce a more satisfactory and effective outcome.[19]

For example, Tanya received incorrect feedback from her manager, Clyde, who pointed out her "mistakes" in the presence of coworkers. By doing so, the boss sent an implied message to others that Tanya is incompetent and could not control situations. Such messages usually trigger emotions (e.g., fear and resentment) and physical reactions (e.g., tense body and wide-open eyes). These reactions typically produce a defensive mindset and a fight-or-flight behavioral reaction. Instead of allowing these effects to dismay her, Tanya recognized what she was feeling and was able to calm herself down by rationally challenging the underlying assumptions that triggered her fear. She calmly confronted Clyde and pointed out the error in his thinking. In this case, Tanya's emotional intelligence helped her exert upward influence on Clyde, her misinformed micromanaging boss.

According to FRLD theory, the level of emotional connection and social comfort between leader and followers is oftentimes associated with transformational leadership effectiveness. Emotionally intelligent leaders and followers are better able to create the positive and developmental relationships found at the pinnacle of the FRLD model.

Pragmatic or Problem-Solving Leadership Theory

Another skills-based leadership perspective proposes that leaders play a very practical role in helping followers solve organizational and career-related problems. According to this view, leadership is nothing more than a series of opportunities for problem solving. In these situations, leaders' cognitive and social skills, coupled with their life experiences and knowledge base, influence their leadership effectiveness. Problem-solving leadership theory also proposes that innate and learned intelligence and the abilities stemming from them, along with personality and motivation level, influence these problem-solving skills.[20]

For example, when Walt arrived at his new managerial post, he saw himself as the "organizational savior," who was appointed to fix all that was wrong in an organization that had run amok prior to his arrival. Based on his 20 years of experience in the Defense Ministry, Walt felt that he possessed the systems thinking skills, ability to judge under uncertain conditions, and judgment to determine whether or not a solution was a good fit for any organizational or personnel problem that came his way. He thought that these skills, along with his accumulated wisdom, allowed him to fix any problem, whether it was mentoring a colleague or designing a new metric to assess organizational performance. Walt's leadership strength could not be explained by personal charm, charisma, or inspiring words. Instead, his leadership prowess was based on his ability to use organizational resources to solve organizational problems.

The problem-solving perspective to leadership can also be illustrated by many politicians who claim that they have solutions for social, economic, or political problems. By framing themselves as a problem solver, they hope to appeal to the rationality and practicality of voters who are looking for someone who could address these problems. According to FRLD theory, such rationality and curiosity are required for the intellectual stimulation of both transformational leaders and their followers.

Style Theory

By the 1950s, scholars realized that the trait approach for explaining leadership was inadequate. It was not enough to know only what personal characteristics great leaders possessed; there also was a need to know what these leaders do (i.e., how they behave). So scholars from Ohio State University and the University of Michigan analyzed a wide variety of leader behaviors and distilled them into two main types of leadership: (1) *task- or production-oriented leadership*, which focuses on initiating structures and pathways for followers to perform effectively, and (2) *people- or relationship-oriented leadership*, which focuses on being considerate of followers' needs and building good leader–follower relations. Both task and relationship leadership behavior styles influence followers' performance and satisfaction. According to style theory, leaders who lack either of these leader behaviors can be problematic and less effective than those who display high levels of both styles of leadership.[21]

Consider the leadership style of a charming middle-aged professor named Norton. When Norton was appointed academic head of a department at a local college, faculty and staff were thrilled. Norton was famous for his brief interactions with colleagues that were laced with compliments, flattery, and humorous quips uttered in the style of a pompous, yet gregarious thespian. Norton would frequently utter comments such as "Erica couldn't get elected dog catcher," "The Papal decree is … ," "Now there's a dangerous duo … how are you, my young ladies?," or "I think I can work for the new boss—I can dance with her." Norton ingratiated everyone that he came into contact with, and as a result was well liked by a highly satisfied staff. He was very considerate and supportive with all colleagues and thus displayed very high levels of people-oriented leadership. Unfortunately, the faculty tired of Norton's excessive and almost exclusive display of people-oriented leadership, and he left the campus to work in a consulting practice for federal agencies.

As Norton's example shows, a leader's behavioral style matters. One thing in common between style theory and FRLD theory is that they both use leader behaviors to explain leadership processes and outcomes. These behavior-based theories make leadership development more promising because behaviors are a lot more changeable and thus trainable than personal attributes proposed in the trait theory discussed earlier.

Situational Leadership Theory

Situational leadership theory (SLT) seeks to match an appropriate leader behavior to various situations defined primarily by the follower's readiness to perform a task independently. These leader behaviors shift from task-oriented to relationship-oriented or supportive leadership, and from leader-dominated action to follower-dominated action. Followers' readiness is defined by their competence and commitment levels as perceived by the leader.

When the leader perceives the follower to possess low levels of competence and commitment, SLT prescribes the leader to be *directive* with the follower by making and announcing a decision. When the leader perceives the follower to possess a low level of competence but some commitment, the leader is advised to *coach* the follower by presenting ideas to the follower and asking for input regarding the decision. When the leader perceives the follower to possess a high level of competence and some commitment, the leader is advised to *support* the follower by presenting the problem, getting solutions from the follower, and making the decision based on that input. When the leader perceives the follower to possess high levels of competence and commitment, SLT prescribes the leader to use *delegation* with the follower by permitting the follower to make the decision within limits set by the leader. As followers' levels of competence and commitment increase, the use of authority by the leader diminishes and amount of empowerment of followers increases.[22]

To illustrate, Rhonda supervises a group of internal auditors at a large public accounting firm. Due to the high turnover rates in entry-level positions in public accounting, Rhonda's firm hires several college graduates every June. When the new hires join her group, Rhonda spends much time directing them regarding the firm's standard operating procedures and adherence to new statements published by the Financial Accounting Standards Board and the International Accounting Standards Board. Rhonda and her senior colleagues coach those that remain with the firm past the first year and whom they perceive to be increasing in their competence and commitment levels. As the junior staff gain more experience and knowledge, Rhonda spends less time with them and empowers them with the necessary resources and decision-making authority. Therefore, the leadership behaviors Rhonda displays with her staff members depend upon her perception of their competence and commitment to her group and the firm.

Many organizations use SLT in their training and development programs because SLT is intuitive and easy to understand. However, SLT also has been criticized by leadership experts on several fronts. For example, SLT has received little empirical support from rigorous scientific research. It also suffers from conceptual and measurement ambiguity, lacks a solid theoretical framework to explain the effects proposed by the theory, and fails to account for demographic differences in leaders and followers that may influence its predictions across situations.[23] In contrast, research on the FRLD model indicates that the most effective leader behaviors (i.e., transformational and transactional contingent reward leadership) are generally universal across many situations and cultures. Depending on the situation, leaders can blend directive or participative approaches with transformational and contingent reward leadership to maximize leadership effectiveness.[24] FRLD is conceptually sound, measurable with the Multifactor Leadership Questionnaire, and has been the subject of a vast amount of research in many different contexts. Both SLT and FRLD are developmental in nature as they seek to empower followers and develop them into leaders themselves, but FRLD is based upon a much stronger foundation of academic support.

Contingency Theory

Another popular situational approach to understanding leadership is contingency theory, developed by leadership researcher Fred Fiedler. Contingency theory seeks to match leaders to appropriate situations. Leaders are assumed to possess a preference for task- or relationship-oriented leadership. This preference is assumed to be measured with an instrument called the Least Preferred Coworker survey. Respondents who describe their least preferred coworker more critically are said to possess a task-oriented leadership style. Those who describe their least preferred coworker more leniently are said to possess a relationship-oriented leadership style. Since contingency theory assumes that leaders are fixed in either of these leadership styles, they must be fit into a situation that best suits their leadership effectiveness. This approach is much like a bullpen pitcher in baseball who is brought into the game based on whether he or she is right- or left-handed and whether the hitter bats from the right- or left-hand side of home plate.

The appropriate fit for task- or relationship-oriented leadership depends on the nature of the situation as assessed by three critical situational factors:

- The quality of the leader-follower relations
- The leader's position power (i.e., authority to reward or punish followers based on position in the organization)
- The task structure (i.e., whether the task is clearly defined and easily understood or ambiguous and complex)

Contingency theory predicts that task-oriented leaders are best suited for very favorable (e.g., good leader–follower relations, strong position power, structured tasks) or unfavorable (e.g., poor leader–follower relations, weak position power, unstructured tasks) conditions. In contrast, relationship-oriented leaders are said to be a good fit for moderate conditions (e.g., good leader–follower relations, weak position power, unstructured tasks). According to contingency theory, the relationship-oriented leadership style is a good fit for followers performing tasks that cannot be performed by simply adhering to standard operating procedures, but must rely on their collective experience and skill sets to make sense out of the difficult task. Based on these assumptions, top management should be familiar with their leaders' preferences for leadership and carefully assess the aforementioned situational characteristics so they can match the right leader to situations that arise.[25]

FRLD theory differs from contingency theory in at least two ways. First, FRLD theory does not assume that leaders are fixed in terms of their predisposition for a certain style of leadership. Rather, FRLD theory assumes that leaders possess the ability to display the repertoire of leadership behaviors shown in the model. Second, as noted above, the most effective FRLD behaviors are universal across many situations and cultures. Some of these situations may require more task-focused (e.g., active management-by-exception and contingent reward) and less developmental (i.e., transformational) behaviors, and vice versa. Therefore, FRLD argues that the leader must assess the situation to determine whether he or she is using the right mix of active or passive leadership behaviors.

Path–Goal Theory

Perhaps a more useful situational approach to understanding leadership is path–goal theory. According to path–goal theory, one of a leader's main functions is to pave the way for followers by clearing a path for them to achieve organizational goals. To do this, the leader must first assess (1) personal characteristics of the follower, such as perceived ability and locus of control (i.e., the degree to which you believe you control your own destiny), and (2) environmental characteristics, such as task structure, authority system, or work group characteristics. Once this assessment is made, the leader chooses one of four behaviors to display: *directive* (leader tells followers what to do), *supportive* (leader attends to needs of followers), *participative* (leader invites followers to share in the decision-making process), or *achievement-oriented* (leader sets high performance expectations and challenges followers to meet them). Path–goal theory proposes that selecting the right leader behavior for the personal and environmental characteristics results in followers' motivation to perform and reach high levels of productivity.[26]

While taking an MBA course on leadership that we taught, our students once produced a training film for path–goal leadership that we still use today in our teaching. This humorous video illustrates how Steven Peppers, an ex-Army sergeant, attempted to motivate a follower to perform a data analysis task. The video scenes depict Steven's successful and unsuccessful attempts at leadership. For example, Steven failed when he used participative leadership with an inexperienced follower working on an ambiguous task. Here Steven should have used directive leadership, which provides guidance and structure for followers working on complex tasks with unclear rules. Supportive leadership provides consideration to followers who desire affiliation with others working on mundane or repetitive tasks. Participative leadership works best when followers are experienced and professional, but need the leader to add some understanding to the complex tasks they perform. Achievement-oriented leadership is appropriate for leaders like Steven whose followers have high needs for achievement but are faced with challenging tasks. When Steven finally got it right, his followers called out for a group hug and exclaimed, "You're transformational beyond transformational!"

Path–goal theory teaches leaders how to structure the transaction they enter into with followers. This is what the most effective leaders using FRLD theory do when they display transactional contingent reward leadership and clarify expectations to clear paths for followers. Path–goal theory also describes how leaders can raise followers' self-efficacy and collective efficacy, as described in motivation-based theories of charismatic and transformational leadership. Transformational leaders in the FRLD model can use either directive or participative approaches to leadership, and these behaviors are listed among the choices for leaders in the path–goal theory.

Leader–Member Exchange (LMX) Theory

Ever wonder why some people get so worked up over leadership changes in their departments? One reason is provided by leader–member exchange (LMX) theory. According to LMX theory, leaders form a unique relationship with each of their followers. Instead of treating all followers the same, leaders form special individualized relationships with followers that create in-groups or out-groups. In-group members receive preferential treatment from the leader, such as receiving privileged information, highly sought-after resources, and mentoring. Out-group members receive support from the leader, but they are not treated as well as in-group members. Thus, in-group followers enjoy higher-quality relationships with the leader than do out-group followers. As followers demonstrate their competence and loyalty to the leader, their roles may change from being treated like a stranger, to being treated like an acquaintance, and finally like a partner in the high-quality exchange seen in in-groups.[27]

Consider the case of Eleanor, who was suddenly removed from a leadership post by senior management and replaced with Peter. All at once, it seemed that those who were close to Eleanor had lost their power derived from the perks of her position and their closeness with Eleanor. Because Eleanor was not friendly with Peter, those formerly in the in-group now found themselves part of the new out-group. Their influence on management was now second fiddle to that of Peter and his in-group. It would take time before the members of the new out-group could scheme to gain more influence over the senior managers. Indeed, LMX theory sheds light on the nature of the leadership dynamics for Eleanor, Peter, and their associates.

LMX theory is similar to FRLD theory in at least two ways. First, LMX theory describes the nature of the social exchange between the leader and the follower. FRLD's transactional contingent reward behavior is also based on an exchange relationship. Here, the leader clarifies goals and expectations, and in exchange for a follower's promise to meet the performance target, the leader rewards the follower for meeting the expectations. Second, transformational leaders give individualized attention to followers through coaching, mentoring, and appreciating the unique knowledge, skills, and abilities followers possess. This individualized approach to leadership is also described by LMX theory.

Authentic Leadership Theory

The recent affliction of lies, corruption, and other unethical behavior that plagued top management of organizations ranging from Enron to WorldCom to faith communities has spawned a call for more ethical approaches to leadership. But this new way of explaining leadership goes back to some very old ideas pondered by the Greek philosopher Socrates and English poet and playwright William Shakespeare. Socrates called for men to know themselves. His philosophy influenced Shakespeare in *Hamlet* to write: "This above all: To thine own self be true, and it must follow, as the night the day, Thou canst not then be false to any man." More recently, leadership practitioners and researchers have proposed that leaders and followers must also be true to themselves and others in order to produce exemplary, ethical, and sustainable results.

Such calls for authentic leadership have been made by Bill George, former CEO of Medtronic, Warren Buffet, CEO of Berkshire Hathaway, and Haruka Nishimatsu, Japan Airlines' CEO. Instead of limos and private jets, Nishimatsu takes the bus to work. Instead of spending a million dollars on an office, he works in an open-space office where associates can come and go. Instead of wearing Armani suits, Nishimatsu buys his suits from a discount warehouse. Instead of remaining aloof in his office, he walks around and helps associates perform their daily tasks. These authentic behaviors make him down-to-earth instead of distant and unapproachable. As a result, his associates feel close to him and encouraged.[28]

According to authentic leadership theory, a leader's positive psychological states, positive work contexts, and self-development processes create positive organizational outcomes. To be authentic, a leader must understand where he or she came from in terms of life experiences and strengths. This self-knowledge determines how he or she can invest in and contribute to the development of self and others through *positive psychological capital*, a psychological state consisting of confidence, hope, optimism, and resilience. At the same time, how a leader's situation is framed and shaped through his or her organization's vision, strategy, and culture can produce a positive organizational context that values human development and leverages followers' strengths. Together, the leader's positive psychological capital and positive organizational context allow the leader to respond favorably to events that can trigger positive self-development. This positive self-development comes from the leader understanding who he or she is and how he or she behaves toward others. Through increased self-awareness and self-regulated behavior one becomes an authentic leader.

Authentic leaders are transparent; they openly share appropriate information with their associates. They are moral and ethical in their personal and professional lives. They are future-oriented and lead followers with a compelling vision. They believe in associate building and developing the full leadership potential of their followers. And they aim to produce positive and sustainable impacts on individuals, team, organizations, and the environment. This set of qualities, developed through the processes described above, makes them authentic.[29]

To illustrate, consider Jim, a Canadian-born engineering executive. When Jim assumed a new leadership post, he promised himself that he would lead based on the same set of principles that he used in his personal life. He wrote out and posted these principles in his office so that he could read them any time he was challenged by a difficult boss or situation. Jim quickly became well liked by his staff because he stood up for them while he advanced the best interests of the organization. He is known as a man of his word as well. People know what Jim stands for and will not stand for. He openly communicates with his staff and doesn't hide things from them. He shares his positive vision of the future with them in a way that includes their opinions in the decision-making process. In many ways, Jim is considered to be an authentic leader by most of his associates.

Authentic leadership theory is proposed to subsume many forms of leadership, including FRLD theory. The most effective leaders in the FRLD model are true to themselves and others because they display and are attributed idealized influence. Research indicates that transformational leaders are self-aware, positive, and future-oriented in their vision and attitudes, ethical in their thinking and actions, and development-oriented in their quest to build followers into future leaders. These elements of authentic leadership share a common foundation with transformational leadership: promoting positive change in people, teams, organizations, communities, and the world.

Putting Transformational Leadership Into Practice as You Read This Book

Our experience in teaching and researching leadership has taught us that the best way to become skilled in FRLD, or any leadership topic for that matter, is *learning by deeply understanding and then doing*. To illustrate this point, think about what you are doing at this moment. You are currently reading. But are you actually comprehending and thinking critically about what you are reading?

With all the demands in our busy lives and the propensity to multitask these days, our inability to really focus on what we are reading may get in the way of our understanding. Sometimes our mind starts to drift as we read, and as a result, we lose out on important learning. That's because many of us are inefficient in acquiring and retaining information through our reading because we take a passive approach to reading. For example, we might skim over a sentence or paragraph when we come to a word or concept that is unfamiliar to us. Or we might not pay attention to what we are reading and think about everyday problems or things we still need to do today. Such passive forms of reading are less effective than more active forms of reading, just as passive forms of leadership are less effective than more active forms of leadership.

This metaphor gives us an opportunity to encourage you to apply the most active and effective form of leadership in the FRLD model (i.e., transformational leadership) to yourself as you read this book. Please use the following active reading techniques to improve your comprehension of the material in this book and your application of FRLD to your life. Transformational leadership is all about enhancing the process, so it's time to introduce some concepts to optimize your learning experience.

Meta-Cognition and Critical Questioning

Cognition describes mental processes regarding how humans come to understand things. Cognition involves how we select, process, and retain information and knowledge, and how we think about applying that knowledge to our lives. Cognitive processes are essential to how we accumulate, retain, and use knowledge. They are critical to reading comprehension and your ability to master the material in this book.

One way to improve your comprehension and learning involves *meta-cognition*, or the ability to "actively think about what you are thinking."[30]

For example, by periodically asking yourself if you understand what you are reading and how you might improve that understanding, you can become a more active reader through such meta-cognition techniques. As an active reader you can become aware that your mind is drifting and attempt to refocus your attention. If you are an active reader and you come across an unfamiliar word, you can use meta-cognitive techniques to recognize you do not know the meaning and look up the word. This process builds in self-reflection, which allows you to deepen your understanding of what you are learning about leadership, and most importantly how you may apply it to your personal life. Meta-cognition is a form of self-regulation that transformational leaders use to make sure their self-perception is in line with perceptions made by others. We will discuss this topic at length in Chapter 3, but for now, let's focus on applying transformational leadership to your learning.

Transformational leaders constantly question the status quo, including their understanding of facts and assumptions underlying concepts and situations. *Critical questioning* is a meta-cognitive technique developed by educational psychologist Alice King that can be used to improve your learning of the FRLD model. Critical questioning requires you to be an active reader. You can use critical questioning to develop your higher-level thinking skills by formulating questions that ask for more than a simple restatement of factual information. Critical questioning is similar to when transformational leaders use intellectual stimulation to get their followers to formulate questions in their mind to increase their understanding of problems or complex situations. Such techniques get followers to be more thoughtful by raising their level of thinking while reading and evaluating information.

Why don't you give this a try? Think about what and *how* you are currently reading at this moment. Are you engaging in lower or higher levels of thinking as you read this book? If you are seeking *knowledge* (i.e., reading to memorize) and *comprehension* (putting information in your own words), you are using lower-level thinking skills.[31] Knowledge-based learning skills help you to reiterate what others have said about a concept, whereas comprehension skills help you to understand the concept and explain it to others. However, a higher-level thinking and learning occurs when you get curious and think critically about a concept and how it relates to other concepts or to your life experiences. It allows you to make connections between new and old concepts, to see what is similar and what is different between concepts, and to create new ideas for your personal leadership development.

To reach this higher level of learning, you must use higher-level thinking skills. Four such skills include *application* (transferring knowledge and using it in a new way), *analysis* (taking a complex amount of information and breaking it into subcomponents), *synthesis* (taking discrete pieces of knowledge and producing a new whole), and finally, *evaluation* (thinking of different ways to synthesize information and making a judgment about which method is better than others).[32] Application helps you put into practice what you learn. Analysis helps you understand how a concept works. Synthesis helps you integrate concepts to create something new and useful. Evaluation brings together information to create the best possible solution to a problem. We encourage you to use all types of thinking skills listed above, but to focus your efforts on higher-level thinking skills to elevate your level of learning.

While reading this book, you can successfully learn to create higher-level thinking questions with the use of question stems. Examples of question stems include: "What is the difference between X and Y?" "How does X affect Y?" "Explain why …," "How is X related to Y that I read about earlier?" and "What would happen if …?"[33] Try this meta-cognitive technique as you read the chapters in this book. Compose questions in areas that you find interesting and challenging, and ponder them as you move through the chapters. Consider creating a FRLD book club of other readers and present your questions at your meetings. Your discussions are sure to enhance your learning.

Applying critical questioning as you read this book will serve three important purposes. First, the development of critical questions based on each chapter's readings will encourage you to actively read and apply learning from each chapter. Second, the presentation of your questions within discussion groups with others will allow you to reap maximum benefits from the knowledge and experience of your peers. Third, the development of critical questions allows you to engage in higher levels of thinking that increase understanding, promote self-reflection, and encourage application of the concepts to your personal leadership situation.

Let us now turn our attention to examining the dynamics of leadership situations, paying particular attention to how the leader, follower, and situation interact to produce outcomes.

Summary Questions and Reflective Exercises

1. As we go through life, we experience many opportunities to assume a leadership role. In which aspects of your life have you taken on a leadership role? How are these roles important to you? What is different about the leadership behavior you display in these roles? What is similar?

2. What is the greatest leadership challenge facing your organization today? What is your greatest personal leadership challenge? How can the behavioral components of the FRLD model help you to successfully face these challenges?

3. Think of an individual in your life who has had a profound effect on your personal development. For example, this person may be a parent, a boss, a pastor, a teacher, a coach, etc. With this person in mind, list three traits and three behaviors associated with him or her. (A trait is a stable personality characteristic, whereas a behavior is a specific action displayed by this person.) How do these traits and behaviors map onto the FRLD model introduced in this chapter? What situation gave rise to the effectiveness of this person's leadership effect on you?

4. Why is transformational leadership and not just transactional leadership needed in today's global and technologically advanced world?

5. Why should leadership be considered a developmental process?

6. You can measure your FRLD behaviors as perceived by yourself, your subordinates, peers, superior, and other associates with the Multifactor Leadership Questionnaire (MLQ). The MLQ is a reliable and valid online survey tool that provides feedback reports on how you and others perceive the frequency of different FRLD leadership behaviors that you exhibit, as illustrated in Figure 1.10. These customized reports can help you to develop plans for enhancing the full range of leadership potential for individuals, teams, and organizations. Visit www.mindgarden.com to learn more about the MLQ and to order this valuable tool prior to developing a plan for achieving your full leadership potential.

7. Distinguish between transformational and transactional forms of leadership. How are they similar and how do they differ? How are they related to each other?

8. Instructors in our FRLD university classes and corporate training workshops are often asked if leaders are born or made. The answer is both. We are yet to see a leader who was not born, although some are so bad that we wonder whether they need to be born again, or what Abraham Zaleznik called "twice born."[34] But seriously, leaders are shaped by both their genetics and life experiences.[35] Which of your personality traits are beneficial to your leadership development? Which are liabilities? What experiences in your life have shaped your current leadership abilities and potential?

9. Think of situations where you have used FRLD behaviors. How did your followers and associates react to your use of these behaviors? Which behaviors resulted in positive outcomes? Negative outcomes? Why?

10. After reading Chapter 1, compose critical questions using some of the question stems described above to elevate your level of active reading.

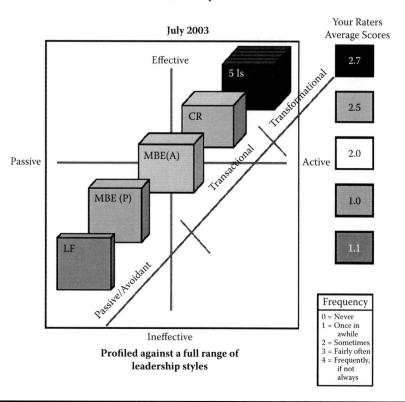

Figure 1.10   Selected pages from the *Multifactor Leadership Questionnaire Feedback Report.* (Reproduced by special permission of the publisher, Mind Garden, Inc., Menlo Park, CA, www.mindgarden.com from the *Multifactor Leadership Questionnaire Feedback Report* by Bernard M. Bass and Bruce J. Avolio. Copyright © 1996, 2003 by Bernard M. Bass and Bruce J. Avolio. All rights reserved. Further reproduction is prohibited without the publisher's written consent.)

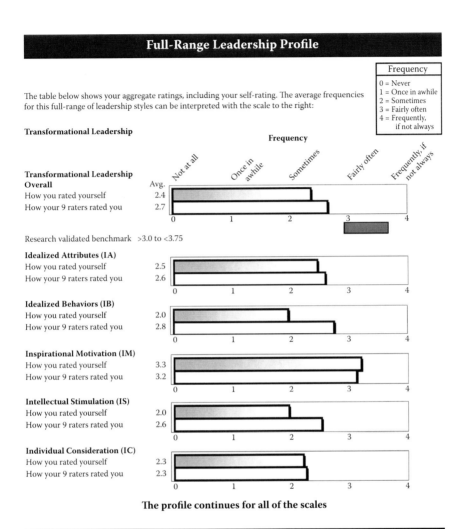

The profile continues for all of the scales

Figure 1.10 (Continued)

Self & Rater Group Feedback: Your Transformational Leadership

This section presents the average ratings given by each source for each leadership style.
Standard deviation refers to the amount of variation of your raters' responses for the leadership style. 0 indicates complete agreement; higher numbers indicate less agreement (higher variation) in your rater's evaluation of your leadership behaviors.

The average frequencies for this full-range of leadership styles can be interpreted with the scale below:

Your report was developed from the following number of raters providing you with feedback using the Multifactor Leadership Questionnaire (MLQ).

Frequency
0 = Never
1 = Once in awhile
2 = Sometimes
3 = Fairly often
4 = Frequently, if not always

Yourself
One Rater(s) at a Higher Organizational Level
Five Rater(s) at the Same Organizational Level
Three Rater(s) at a Lower Organizational Level

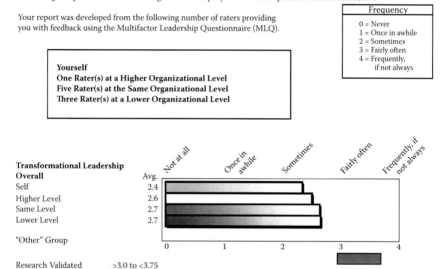

Transformational Leadership Overall	Avg.
Self	2.4
Higher Level	2.6
Same Level	2.7
Lower Level	2.7

"Other" Group

Research Validated Benchmark	>3.0 to <3.75
All raters average	2.7
All raters standard deviation	0.9

Figure 1.10   (Continued)

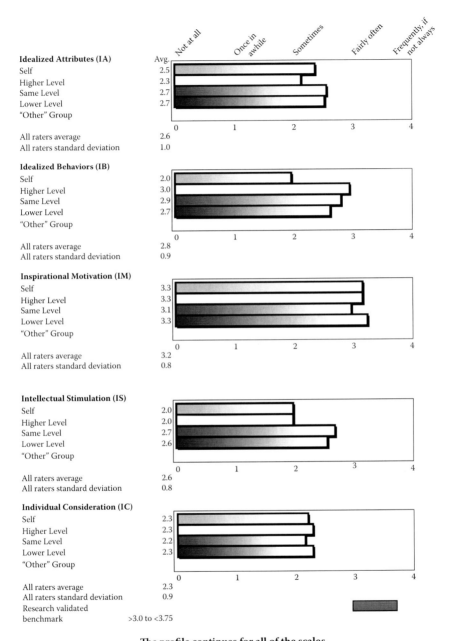

The profile continues for all of the scales

Figure 1.10   (Continued)

Record these questions in a journal for future reference. If you are reading this book as part of a leadership course, pose your questions to the other members of your class and listen to their reactions. In return, respond to the questions they pose to you.

Notes

1. Savitz, A. W., & Weber, K. (2006). *The triple bottom line: How today's best-run companies are achieving economic, social and environmental success—and how you can too.* San Francisco, CA: Jossey-Bass.
2. Retrieved April 15, 2008, from http://www.meritsystemsllc.net/team/j_juzbasich.html.
3. Goleman, D., Boyatzis, R., & McKee, A. (2002). *Primal leadership: Learning to lead with emotional intelligence.* Boston: Harvard Business School Press; and Sosik, J. J., & Megerian, L. E. (1999). Understanding leader emotional intelligence and performance: The role of self-other agreement on transformational leadership perceptions. *Group & Organization Management, 24,* 367–390.
4. Colvin, G. (2007, October 1). Leader machines. *Fortune, 156,* 98–106.
5. Bass, B. M., & Avolio, B. J. (1994). *Improving organizational effectiveness through transformational leadership.* Thousand Oaks, CA: Sage.
6. Alsop, R. (2008). *The trophy kids grow up: How the millennial generation is shaking up the workforce.* San Francisco: Jossey-Bass.
7. Bass, B. M., & Avolio, B. J. (1999). *Training full range leadership: A resource guide for training with the MLQ.* Palo Alto, CA: Mind Garden.
8. Adapted from a comprehensive analysis prepared by Russ Long. Retrieved April 17, 2008, from at http://www.delmar.edu/socsci/rlong/problems/chap-04.htm.
9. Several meta-analyses validate the Full Range Leadership Development model and its ability to predict individual, group, and organizational performance, including Judge, T. A., & Piccolo, R. F. (2004). Transformational and transactional leadership: A meta-analytic test of their relative validity. *Journal of Applied Psychology, 89,* 755–768; and Lowe, K. B., Kroeck, K. G., & Sivasubramaniam, N. (1996). Effectiveness correlates of transformational and transactional leadership: A meta-analytic review. *The Leadership Quarterly, 7,* 385–425.
10. Bass & Avolio (1999). As cited in Note 7.
11. Luthans, F. (2008). *Organizational behavior* (11th ed.). Boston: McGraw-Hill/Irwin.
12. Comprehensive overviews of authentic leadership are provided in Gardner, W. L., Avolio, B. J., Luthans, F., May, D. R., & Walumbwa, F. (2005). "Can you see the real me?" A self-based model of authentic leader and follower development. *The Leadership Quarterly, 16,* 343–372; George, B., & Sims, P. (2007). *True north: Discover your authentic leadership.* San Francisco: Jossey-Bass; Shamir, B., & Eilam, G. (2005). "What's your story?" A life-stories approach to authentic leadership development. *The Leadership Quarterly, 16,* 395–417; and Sosik, J. J. (2006). *Leading with character: Stories of valor and virtue and the principles they teach.* Greenwich, CT: Information Age Publishing.
13. Burns, J. M. (1978). *Leadership.* New York: Harper & Row.

14. Bass & Avolio (1999). As cited in Note 7.
15. Bass, B. M. (2008). *The Bass handbook of leadership: Theory, research and managerial applications* (4th ed.). New York: Free Press.
16. Bass (2008). As cited in Note 15.
17. Judge, T. A., Bono, J. E., Ilies, R., & Gerhardt, M. W. (2002). Personality and leadership: A qualitative and quantitative review. *Journal of Applied Psychology, 87,* 765–780; and Kirkpatrick, S. A., & Locke, E. A. (1991). Leadership: Do traits matter? *The Executive, 5,* 48–60.
18. Freud, S. (1938). *The basic writings of Sigmund Freud* (A. A. Brill, Ed.). New York: Modern Library; Kets de Vries, M. F. R. (1994). The leadership mystique. *Academy of Management Executive, 8,* 73–92; Shamir, B. (1991). The charismatic relationship: Alternative explanations and predictions. *The Leadership Quarterly, 2,* 81–104; and Zaleznik, A. (1977). Managers and leaders: Are they different? *Harvard Business Review, 55,* 67–80.
19. Goleman, D. (1995). *Emotional intelligence.* New York: Bantam.
20. Mumford, M. D., Zaccaro, S. J., Harding, F. D., Jacobs, T. O., & Fleishman, E. A. (2000). Leadership skills for a changing world: Solving complex social problems. *The Leadership Quarterly, 11,* 11–35.
21. Cartwright, D., & Zander, A. (1960). *Group dynamics research and theory.* Evanston, IL: Row Peterson; and Stogdill, R. M. (1963). *Manual for the Leader Behavior Description Questionnaire form XII.* Columbus: Ohio State University, Bureau of Business Research.
22. Blanchard, K. (2007). *Leading at a higher lever: Blanchard on leadership and creating high performance organizations.* Upper Saddle River, NJ: Pearson-Prentice Hall; and Blanchard, K., Zigarmi, P., & Zigarmi, D. (1992). *Leadership and the one minute manager.* Escondido, CA: Blanchard Training and Development.
23. Northouse, P. G. (2007). *Leadership: Theory and practice* (4th ed.). Thousand Oaks, CA: Sage; and Yukl, G. (2006). *Leadership in organizations* (6th ed.). Upper Saddle River, NJ: Pearson-Prentice Hall.
24. Bass, B. M., & Riggio, R. E. (2006). *Transformational leadership* (2nd ed.). Mahwah, NJ: Lawrence Erlbaum Associates.
25. Fiedler, F. E. (1967). *A theory of leadership effectiveness.* New York: McGraw-Hill.
26. House, R. J., & Mitchell, R. R. (1974). Path-goal theory of leadership. *Journal of Contemporary Business, 3,* 81–97.
27. Graen, G. B., & Uhl-Bien, M. (1995). Relationship-based approach to leadership: Development of leader-member (LMX) theory of leadership over 25 years: Applying a multi-level, multi-domain perspective. *The Leadership Quarterly, 6,* 219–247.
28. http://www.cbsnews.com/stories/2009/01/28/eveningnews/main4761136.shtml. Retrieved January 29, 2009.
29. Avolio, B. J., & Gardner, W. J. (2005). Authentic leadership development: Getting to the root of positive forms of leadership. *The Leadership Quarterly, 16,* 315–338.
30. King, A. (1991). Effects of training in strategic questioning on children's problem-solving performance. *Journal of Educational Psychology, 83,* 307–317.
31. Bloom, B. S. (1956). *Taxonomy of educational objectives. Handbook 1: The cognitive domain.* New York: David McKay Co.
32. Bloom (1956). As cited in Note 31.

33. King (1991, p. 669). As cited in Note 30.
34. Zaleznik (1977). As cited in Note 18.
35. Arvey, R. D., Zhang, Z., Avolio, B. J., & Krueger, R. F. (2007). Developmental and genetic determinants of leadership role occupancy among women. *Journal of Applied Psychology*, *92*, 693–706; and Sosik, J. J. (2006). Full range leadership: Model, research, extensions and training. In C. Cooper & R. Burke (Eds.), *Inspiring leadership* (pp. 33–6). New York: Routledge.

Chapter 2

The Full Range Leadership Development System

Our life is an apprenticeship to the truth that around every circle another can be drawn; that there is no end in nature, but every end is a beginning, and under every deep a lower deep opens.

—Ralph Waldo Emerson

The age of green is upon us. As the earth's natural resources are increasingly depleted, leaders like Andy Moses of Penske Trucking are promoting sustainable business initiatives. By focusing on Penske's impact on the environment, Moses is working to create jobs and lead projects that meet today's societal needs while not compromising the needs of future generations. Once solely focused on bottom-line results, he now considers how his company interacts with the natural environment. He believes that energy flows through the interactions organizations and their members, plants, and animals have. This energy is sustained by recycling resources that are the essence of life-support systems for "all of God's creatures, including people working in corporations." As a result of his Full Range Leadership Development (FRLD) training, Moses' thinking about what constitutes effective leadership outcomes has evolved into a global systems and environmental perspective.

The way we study and practice leadership has come a long way as well. We have broadened our perspective on leadership to focus not only on characteristics of leaders that make them great, but also on characteristics of followers and the situations that add to their greatness. Before taking action, outstanding leaders reflect upon the relationships between leader and follower, leader and situation, follower and situation, and the confluence of leader, follower, and situation. As this chapter's opening quote from Emerson suggests, even the immediate situation that embeds leader–follower interactions depends upon broader societal, cultural, historical, and technological trends and circumstances. Therefore, like Andy Moses, you also need to think of leadership as a system of which you are an integral part.

One way to gain this systems point of view about leadership is to develop your *perspective-taking capacity*. Higher levels of perspective allow you to look at a situation from many different viewpoints and to integrate these viewpoints in a way that is easily understood by others.[1] To better understand this, consider the concept of acting. Have you ever taken part in a theatrical production? If so, you may have been an actor, actress, or director and were responsible for specific tasks in preparing for and putting on the play. As an actor or actress, you are responsible for reciting your own lines and knowing when to come in on the script. As a director, you are responsible for much more. You have to understand set design, lighting, special effects, and how all the actors and actresses interact according to the script. You have to view the production from a systems perspective in the sense that you understand who, what, when, where, and how all the elements come together in the performance. Therefore, a director's perspective needs to be broader than an actor's perspective, but both must work together to satisfy the audience with a great production.

You can think of the leadership process as a type of drama production where the leader is the actor/director, and the followers are actors who play roles in the leadership performance for audience members made of followers, customers, and other key stakeholders.[2] Note that an outstanding leader must also possess a director's mindset, in addition to acting along with the followers. If, as a leader, you are always thinking about what's best for you, you have limited your perspective and range of potential, and you're likely to be a lousy actor (or a leader who displays laissez-faire behavior). Why? Because people put forth their best efforts for role models who make personal sacrifices for the good of everyone. If you want to limit your followers' potential, take care of your own needs with a laissez-faire approach to leadership. However, if you want to reach your full leadership potential and theirs, then act like a transformational leader by looking at things from their perspective, considering their needs, and making some sacrifices. The short-term sacrifices that you make will pay off in the long run with much more significant achievements and perhaps an "Academy Award" for your leadership performance.

This chapter shows you how to view FRLD as a system by broadening your perspective so that you can take away the skills required for that award-winning leadership performance. Let's begin by considering a case we use in class to teach graduate students how to view leadership as a system.

Sidney Poitier and *To Sir, With Love*

Films are a great way to illustrate various leadership behaviors and the dynamics of the leadership system as well. People often comment that once they watch the numerous film clips throughout their FRLD training, they can never view movies the same way. Hereafter, they view movies through a leadership systems lens.

One of our students' favorite films to illustrate leadership systems is *To Sir, With Love*,[3] starring Sir Sidney Poitier, the Academy Award-winning Bahamian American actor, film director, and social activist. In this classic movie, Poitier portrays Mark Thackeray, an unemployed communications engineer who takes a teaching job in a rough English high school in the late 1960s. The film shows how he is able to overcome many challenges to ultimately inspire his students to reach their full potential. The film deals with the timeless issues of social and racial prejudice, motivation, teenage angst, and inspirational leadership, among others.

Our students often comment that the film is as relevant today as it was when it was first released. They cite today's calls for social and economic change, workforce diversity issues, empowerment of youth, and troubled times as examples of its relevance. Many subsequent films, such as *Stand and Deliver, Dangerous Minds*, and *Friday Night Lights*, follow somewhat similar storylines. If you have never seen *To Sir, With Love*, we recommend that you view it on DVD or online. You are sure to thoroughly enjoy the film and Sidney Poitier's role.

Poitier's fine performance illustrates a teacher's evolution from a traditional transactional taskmaster. At first, he falls victim to the students' tormenting and unruly behavior. But over time he transforms into an inspiring and intellectually stimulating pragmatist who wins over his students and gains their respect and admiration. After watching this film for the first time in 1989, John was inspired to transition from a successful corporate career to an academic vocation where he too might encourage students to tap into their innate leadership greatness.

The movie's plot illustrates how characteristics of the leader, the follower, the situation, and their interaction come together to produce either positive or negative outcomes. According to the story plot, Mark Thackeray, the movie's aspiring leader, was born and raised in British Guyana. He goes on to earn his university degree in the United States. After graduating, he is frustrated by many unsuccessful applications to numerous engineering firms in England. The movie implies that he is turned down because he is a person of color. To make ends meet during his extended job search, he takes on a teaching post in a predominantly white high school in a lower-class East End London neighborhood.

Mark Thackeray stands in stark contrast to his jaded, bitter, and unmotivated fellow teachers who have been worn down over the years by their students. Instead, Thackeray presents himself as a sharply dressed, refined, calm and collected, intelligent, and idealistic teacher. As a victim of racial discrimination throughout life, he feels compelled to overachieve to fit in with his colleagues and gain the respect of his underachieving students. At first, he tries traditional teaching methods, strict discipline, and formality in his teaching. These methods do not work. Thackeray is baited, jeered, and easily manipulated by students who view the classroom as their domain and certainly not his.

Although Thackeray's humble background is similar to his students', he is at a big disadvantage because he is perceived as very different by them. His students have a problem identifying with him at first. He is a person of color, and the majority of them are Caucasian. They see him as having made a success of himself through his education and need for achievement. In contrast, they currently live among the working class, who do not see the value of education and lack any motivation to grow. They are rude in their demeanor, crass and obscene in their language, and selfish in their perspective. They show little concern for their appearance and less respect for their elders. They view their coursework as an impractical waste of time. They believe most of the boys will end up working in factories like their fathers, and most of the girls will end up as stay-at-home moms. These were typical career paths for students in economically disadvantaged areas in England during the 1960s.

The situation that surrounds Thackeray and his students makes matters even worse. The political and social climate of the 1960s promoted questioning of authority and nonconformity. These were ideas that students brought into the classroom and acted out on their teachers. The students' home lives were filled with parental disputes, alcoholism, and drug abuse, also depicted in contemporary films such as *Thirteen*. To make matters worse, they suffered from a lack of support and encouragement from their parents. Many were forced to take on part-time jobs to help make ends meet. At school, they were constrained by the rigid factory-like English educational system of the time that sought the mind control of students rather than developing their creativity and expressiveness. This approach to education viewed students as merely products who are churned out regardless of the amount of knowledge, skills, and abilities they possessed at graduation. The negative and cynical attitude of their prior teachers created an "us versus them" culture, so adeptly described by Roger Waters of Pink Floyd in his classic song entitled "Another Brick in the Wall (Part II)."[4] (Please view the video for this song on YouTube.com to see what we mean.) How can any teacher (or leader) make a difference in the lives of unmotivated and unruly students (or followers) given these circumstances?

Thackeray finds the answer to this question just in the nick of time. At the point Thackeray's "kids" are just about to drive him crazy, he realizes that treating them as kids is the problem that is derailing his leadership. He must stop treating them as kids by constantly focusing on correcting their mistakes. Instead, he must start treating them as adults by engaging them as partners rather than products of the learning process. Leadership scholar Bruce Avolio pointed out that treating followers as children who are at a lower stage of development is the way active management-by-exception leadership achieves its goals.[5]

Thackeray understood this concept and applied a new transformational approach to teach the class. He demonstrated intellectual stimulation by throwing out all of the textbooks and allowing his students to choose what topics they'll study. He showed inspirational motivation by taking his students on a field trip to a museum. He demonstrated individualized consideration by encouraging them to attend the funeral of a student's mother. Most importantly, he displayed idealized influence by insisting that they use proper forms of address toward him and among themselves, taking pride in their appearance, and fine-tuning their personal demeanor. By the end of the film, Thackeray is recognized as a gifted teacher by his colleagues. He also wins his students over as they present him with a pewter mug and serenade him with the movie theme song at the graduation dance.

Sidney Poitier's portrayal of Mark Thackeray in *To Sir, With Love* teaches us an important lesson: Coordinating all the roles your followers play and developing them along the way is essential to creating and sustaining a successful leadership system. What role will you play in optimizing your organization's leadership system?

Leadership Is a System

U.S. Secretary of State Hillary Clinton once said, "It takes a village to raise a child." Likewise, our examination of *To Sir, With Love* suggests that it takes a system to produce positive leadership effects. That is, it takes the right leader, followers, and situation, working in concert as a system, to produce outstanding leadership. To optimize your leadership, you must examine and understand the linkages and interactions between the leader, follower, situation, and the other miscellaneous elements that comprise the entirety of the system.[6]

To Sir, With Love illustrates several obvious components of the leadership system. Mark Thackeray represents the leader. His students represent the followers. The time and place (i.e., East End London high school circa 1967) represent the

Figure 2.1   Components of the leadership system.

situation. As shown in Figure 2.1, the leader, follower, and situation represent the core components of the leadership system, which we will elaborate upon below.

There are other system components that are not quite as obvious. Leadership systems also include evaluation, reward, and development subsystems. For example, the criteria that Thackeray used to assess his students' performance in class are part of the evaluation system. The way Thackeray's students and superiors perceived his teaching style and effectiveness served as an evaluation system for him. How are leaders and followers in your organization evaluated? Are they assessed based on their job performance or other tangible outcomes of their leadership? Are they also evaluated on the developmental processes they use to motivate and build up the people they lead?

In addition, the reward and development subsystems determine the behaviors and processes people use in the leadership system. People typically seek rewards and avoid punishments. Behaviors that are rewarded and developed through training and cultural practices are often reinforced, while those that are frowned upon or rebuked are often eliminated. These processes contribute toward the continuous process improvement of the leadership system. In *To Sir, With Love*, Thackeray discarded the traditional factory production and extrinsic reward approach to education. He learned that this approach resulted in being manipulated by students as well as students' feelings of manipulation and thought control by their teacher. It also generated students who were hopelessly disengaged in the classroom. To overcome these obstacles, Thackeray provided students with intrinsic rewards by letting them choose discussion topics and master practical skills that mattered most in their lives. In essence, he was putting a transformational twist on a transactional leadership system through the intrinsic motivation and continuous personal improvement of his students.

Figure 2.1 shows that the leadership system has resources, constraints, boundaries, opportunities, and challenges that change over time. Funding, technical support, and planning and implementation time are resources that are required for effective leadership system functioning, but they were not available for Thackeray. To work around these constraints, Thackeray drew upon the innate curiosity and creativity that his students possessed. He also highlighted the benefits that a practical education could bring to them.

Similar to what is depicted in *To Sir, With Love*, we've witnessed limitations that others can place on potential success in schools. For example, a top school administrator who micromanages and second-guesses decisions made by colleagues can constrain the effectiveness of the leadership system. Such an approach may have been appropriate in past decades, but is not consistent with expectations of today's workers for autonomy, inclusion, and ownership in leadership processes. In addition, environmental factors can pose important challenges to leadership systems in schools. These include sudden changes in student preferences and demographics, increased competition from neighboring schools, economic *downturn*, and nasty politics. The environment that surrounds the leadership system is constantly changing. That's why it's important to periodically assess the components of the leadership system to identify those that need to be retained and improved, as well as those that need to be retired and discarded over time.

To summarize, FRLD requires you to view leadership as a system. Like ecosystems, leadership is a dynamic and complex whole based on our relationships with others. It involves willing collaboration between leaders, followers, and other constituents. Energy (i.e., motivation and effort), materials and resources, and information flow between these elements of the system. These flows can be observed and described with effects traced back to specific activities or behaviors. Because of these actions, the leadership system is a community situated within a broader environment that can provide or take away the energy, resources, and information to and from the system. All components of the leadership system are interdependent. They can only exist as a whole; they cannot exist independently, especially the core systems components of the leader, follower, and situation.

Leader

A *leader* is someone who influences others to achieve a goal. Leaders are real people. They are not perfect. While they strive to display virtues and character strengths in their behavior, they also are challenged by their own personal vices and idiosyncrasies.[7] Their genetic makeup predisposes them to certain personality traits, such as confidence, extraversion, or narcissism. Such traits are generally stable over the life span. They have their own set of personal values, beliefs, and ideas about how things are and how they should be. Based on their life experiences, they think of themselves in a particular way, and this shapes their self-concept, the image some project to followers, and that some attempt to conceal.

Former U.S. president Richard Nixon attempted to present an image of strength and confidence despite possessing some self-esteem issues that stemmed from his physical stature and family background. Nixon suffered from an inferiority complex because he came from a family of modest means. He did not possess the resources and opportunities that others possessed. He was haunted and embittered by the image and background of John F. Kennedy, a child of a privileged family who seemed to have it all: looks, wealth, women, and power. Nixon's ambition and drive to overcome these challenges led to both his success and ultimate downfall.[8] You can witness many of Nixon's issues in movies such as *Nixon vs. Frost* and *Nixon*, or in various clips on YouTube.com.

Leaders' family background also shapes their attitude about themselves and about life in general. Upbringing by parents and relationships with siblings and other family members shape their willingness to influence others. Their motivation to lead often comes from other environmental influences, such as educational, religious, and leadership training experiences, support from peers, role models or mentors, unexpected opportunities, and overcoming personal and professional challenges.[9] These genetic and environmental influences shape the leader's character and style, which he or she brings into the leadership system. For example, former U.S. president Bill Clinton's father was absent during his childhood. This forced Clinton to assume a parental role of overseeing and nurturing his siblings. This role taught him the importance of building and maintaining personal relationships. Relationship building and maintenance is an essential principle of transformational leadership. These lessons were essential to Clinton's successful political career, but were ignored in the mistakes he made in his personal life.[10]

One mistake that aspiring leaders (even successful ones) often make is to assume that it is the job of leaders to get things done all by themselves. However, we do not believe that this process can be called leadership because it does not involve the whole leadership system. It is better called self-leadership.[11] That's because followers are not involved in the process. Leadership is about getting things done *with* followers, not *for* followers. This principle becomes even more important as the unit/organization you lead gets larger and the goal you are trying to accomplish gets more complicated. FRLD considers leadership to be a development process that views followers not only as a means to accomplish tasks, but also as an end in themselves. In the end, followers should be developed into self-actualized human beings who have reached their full leadership potential. In this way, they will have transformed into leaders themselves.

Self-centered leaders who ignore this developmental viewpoint are like Spanish playwright Miguel de Cervantes' character Don Quixote, the "Man of La Mancha." This elderly gentleman was so obsessed with notions of chivalry and righting injustice that he lost his mind and set forth as a knight on an ill-fated mission.[12] His only follower is his "squire," Sancho Panza. You might think of Don Quixote as somewhat like the clueless manager Michael Scott (Steve Carell) on the NBC TV hit series *The Office* (see Table 2.1). To "dream the impossible dream" with one or no followers is a nice notion for literature and Broadway or television. But it holds no value for leadership systems in the real world. Leaders need great followers to make organizational dreams come true.[13]

Follower

A *follower* is someone who chooses to follow a leader because of the leader's character, ability, or vision. Because of their respect and admiration for the leader, followers often imitate a leader in thoughts, words, and deeds. They become motivated to work in the service of the leader. Wouldn't it be nice if we could pick the best followers we could get, like schoolchildren who pick their own teams during recess? Nice thought, but highly unlikely.

Like it or not, most of us either inherit our followers or choose them through inadequate selection systems. Because followers are only human, they are imperfect, just like leaders. Followers bring into the leadership system the same baggage that leaders bring with them—all of the personal characteristics derived from one's genetic makeup and life experiences. If we have undeveloped followers in our leadership system (just as Mark Thackeray inherited), all we have is struggling leadership. Even if we have great followers in our system, we may still have struggling leadership. That's because the followers may lack direction that a good leader can provide. For example, if the students in *To Sir, With Love* were brilliant child prodigies instead of incorrigible hooligans and slackers, without a dedicated teacher with a clear vision and solid plan for developing their full potential, outstanding leadership would still not be possible.

We always encourage our students to be followers and great aspiring leaders at the same time. They possess a love of learning and a passion to put what they

Table 2.1   Leader Profile: Michael Scott

Michael Scott is a fictional character portrayed by Steve Carell on NBC's wildly successful television show *The Office*. Scott, the main character of the show, is the regional manager of a paper distribution company located in Scranton, Pennsylvania. He is also a bona fide male chauvinist, egotist, and bigot. Easily the most preposterous, and often most entertaining, character on the show, Scott holds inflated views of his leadership ability. At the same time, he seeks the type of adoration from his staff that is usually reserved for role models. In his role as branch leader, Scott will do or say anything for a laugh. He seemingly operates without any boundaries and is often cynical, politically incorrect, offensive, and downright mean in his commentary. Even when he attempts to be sincere, Scott always seems to find a way to put his foot in his mouth.

Scott is unapologetic about his stereotypical views of minorities and is quick to point out the faults of others. Then he tells them to follow his example so they can correct their faults, despite his utter lack of leadership talent. The only redeeming quality Scott has is that he is truly not a mean-spirited person. He really wants to help others, but he does it in such a way that he comes across to others as a jerk.

Despite his bravado, Scott is often weak and ineffective when dealing with his staff. His overestimation of his leadership abilities stems from his lack of maturity and self-awareness. He is a lonely individual who has few friends. He has trouble making friends because his attempts to do so usually end up with them being offended. Most of Scott's subordinates consider him to be an inept leader who lives in a dream world.

Source: Woglemuth, L. (2008, April 8). Seven career tips from NBC's *The Office*. *U.S. News and World Report* [Online]. Retrieved January 26, 2009, from http://www.usnews.com/articles/business/careers/2008/04/08/7-career-lessons-from-nbcs-the-office.html.

learn into practice. They are highly motivated and creative. They also possess a high level of commitment to each other and their academic program. They've taught us that the best followers not only practice what the leader preaches, but also believe in what they practice. They work together to move from what could be to what can be, from what is possible, through what is probable, to what is. And as a leader or a follower, that is your role.

Great followers sometimes follow and sometimes lead. They often possess detailed knowledge and personal connections that allow them to step up into leadership roles that the leader cannot assume. At other times, followers can struggle in areas of communication, teamwork, creativity, and ethics, and therefore require the guidance of a leader. Transformational leaders understand when followers must follow and when they are capable of leading. They provide followers with the resources, support, and confidence required to overcome these struggles.

Howard Schultz, CEO of Starbuck's Coffee, engages his people in a down-to-earth dialogue in town hall meetings. Founded under the principle of treating all people with respect and dignity at all times, Starbucks is consistently mentioned as one of the most caring and conscientious places to work. Schultz is referred to by many as a corporate caregiver and arbiter of the truth. He has developed a distinctive leadership style that is far-reaching and one that permeates his organization on all levels. Under his leadership, Starbucks has become one of the most respected global brands and a cultural icon. Throughout the company's growth, Starbucks has remained true to its coffee heritage by providing a connection and a sense of community for its employees and customers. Personal interactions between Schultz and his employees allow them to share their ideas and concerns and let him show that he cares.[14] If you keep this in mind and start viewing your followers as associates to develop rather than coworkers to tolerate, you are already moving up the FRLD model by imagining a better place for all of you.

Situation

A *situation* describes the relative circumstances, position, or context that surrounds the leader and followers. There are many ways to describe a situation. The historical context shapes the social culture, world events, and ways of thinking for a particular period of time. For example, the 1960s, with its antiestablishment and change-oriented values, were a perfect stage for Mark Thackeray's intellectually stimulating behaviors in *To Sir, With Love*, just as they are for today's business and national leaders. The economic, social, and political conditions that pervade a particular time period and geographic region place boundaries on what is possible for leaders and followers to achieve. For example, the civil unrest and bigotry in 1960's America severely limited Martin Luther King Jr.'s ability to enact many of his ideals outlined in his "I Have a Dream" speech. These limitations and his competition (i.e., enemies and racists) ultimately led to his death. Fortunately, Dr. King's followers and the majority of Americans have embraced many of his ideas, and we are making progress toward achieving his vision. In 2008, Americans elected Barack Obama as the first African American U.S. president. But we still have a way to go.

Situations have other elements as well. Competition can be nonexistent (as with monopolies) or it can be fierce. Business and political environments can be turbulent or relatively stable. Rising oil and food prices, depleted energy resources causing a competition between food and fuel, and home mortgage crises place many limitations on social and corporate growth. Such historical, political, and economic conditions are important aspects to consider when assessing the situation in the leadership system. These are issues facing today's world and business leaders.

Beyond timeframe and markets, the geographic context is important to consider. Geography specifies a particular national or regional culture with its own particular values, traditions, and practices. For example, collectivistic (group-oriented) national cultures that we find in China, North Korea, or Sweden and their clan modes of governance are appropriate contexts for transformational leadership. These contexts focus on cooperation and interpersonal harmony advocated by transformational leaders. In addition, the industrial context dictates specific laws, regulations, and technologies unique to a particular industry. Leadership styles that work in one industry (e.g., active management by exception in accounting and auditing) may be a big turn-off in others (e.g., marketing and biotech industries).

Organizational contexts define the situation as well. Whether an organization chooses an adaptive or rigid strategy to deal with the aforementioned external conditions also affects the situation. How the organization is structured also matters as well. Some organizations are structured as machine bureaucracies with tightly controlled top-down hierarchical communication and reporting structures, formalized policies and procedures, and specialized functions performed by particular personnel. Governmental agencies are notorious when it comes to such bureaucracy. So are companies like General Motors, with its history of red tape and mechanistic operations. No wonder GM and other major car manufacturers were on the verge of bankruptcy in 2009 and appealed to the U.S. government for a bailout. We do not believe that transformational leadership with its change-oriented nature will flourish under these environments.

Others are structured as organic organizations with flat communication and reporting structures, less hierarchy of authority and rules, and functions shared by crossed-trained employees and teams. Organic organizations, in contrast, facilitate transformational leadership. Some organizations deploy cutting-edge technologies as an integral part of their strategy, while others depend less on such technologies. All of these contextual characteristics determine whether or not a particular FRLD behavior is appropriate. We believe that General Electric (GE) is one of the best companies in which leadership development is not only encouraged but also required proactively.

GE and Its Passion for Leadership Development

GE is a world-class role model for building leaders. GE is a huge global organization formed in 1892 whose beginning can be traced back to Thomas Edison and the invention of the lightbulb. At that time, GE's leadership recognized the huge opportunity that tapping into electricity could provide for businesses and households alike. This imaginative quest parallels GE's current focus on innovation within and between the world's continents and industries and environmental initiatives for a more sustainable and greener world. GE's vast array of products and services include aircraft engines, power generation, water processing and security technology, medical imaging, business and consumer financing, media content, and industrial products. With customers in more than 100 countries, GE has more than 300,000 employees worldwide. Such a scope of operations presents both great opportunities and daunting challenges for its leadership, which has to a large extent successfully met these challenges.[15]

A recent survey of human resource managers worldwide ranked GE the top global and North American company for leadership development. This ranking was based on the company's long-time commitment to training and development at its famous Crotonville, New York, training facility, its off-site training programs in Europe and Asia, and its online leadership workshops offered to its global sites. At GE, leadership development is not just a program; it's a way of life.[16]

GE's large investment in leadership training is part of a culture of leadership development first embraced and supported by former CEO Jack Welch and continued by current CEO Jeffrey Immelt. Both of these top leaders realized that GE's priority is not only providing its wide variety of products and services globally, but also developing GE's associates into leaders through an emphasis on teamwork, ethics, innovation, and mentoring. In his letter to the shareholders in GE's 2005 annual report, Immelt stated, "At the top, we don't run GE like a big company. We run it like a big partnership, where every leader can make a contribution not just to their job, but to the entire company." Motivating individuals to share leadership through collaboration contributes to the collective success of GE. This is what FRLD strives to achieve.

The structure and demands of the task also dictate what FRLD leadership styles will work in a given situation and which ones will not. For tasks that are highly structured and easily understood, active management-by-exception leadership is likely to be perceived by followers as unnecessary and redundant. For tasks that are unstructured and complex, contingent reward and individualized consideration displayed by leaders are likely to be valued by followers. That's because such behaviors clarify how to perform the task. To master FRLD, you need to consider all of these aspects of the situation so that you will know the appropriate time and place for displaying each of the leadership behaviors in the FRLD model. In other words, the overall effectiveness of FRLD is determined not only by the transformational leadership qualities that a leader possesses, but also by the combination of other factors in the leadership system.

Confluence of Leader, Follower, and Situation

When we were in graduate school earning our doctorate degrees at the State University of New York at Binghamton, we experienced a blizzard of mammoth proportions. As the temperature plummeted below freezing, snow accumulated at record rates and the wind whipped up ferociously, reducing visibility to zero. Weather conditions were so bad that the administration closed the university. School closures were an extremely rare occurrence for a region that was used to a lot of precipitation throughout the year according to our good friend, colleague, and Binghamton native Shelley Dionne (see Table 2.2).

What made for Binghamton's weather woes during the "perfect storm of 1993"? A large amount of moisture heading up the U.S. East Coast fueled by relatively warm air, and very cold air in place contributed to the problem. Another key factor is Binghamton's geographic location. Binghamton sits at the confluence of the Susquehanna and Chenango rivers in the southern tier of New York State, just north of Pennsylvania's Endless Mountains region. This geographic setup has been described by meteorologists as a "magnet for precipitation." And in March 1993, everything came together to create one monster of a snowstorm.

Just as the right mix of ingredients is needed to fuel a blizzard, the right combination of leader, follower, and situational elements is needed to produce a potent leadership effect. To desire leadership, followers must feel challenged by their current situation or perceive themselves as victims of a crisis situation that is destroying their self-worth or well-being. When followers feel ready to embrace change, we have *follower–situation fit*. In this case, the leader must help followers make sense out of the crisis situation that threatens them. By rejecting the status quo and providing an evocative and compelling vision, leaders give new meaning to followers about the situation they face and build their hope for a better tomorrow. When the leader's vision is seen as a viable and inspiring alternate to the status quo, then the leader is the right person for the times and we have *leader–situation fit*. A leader must also provide the right message that followers are waiting to hear. Followers must view the leader as someone who is capable of giving them what they need to overcome their struggle and succeed. When these two conditions occur, the leader and followers are able to bond and we have *leader–follower fit*. Figure 2.1 suggests that when you possess good leader-follower, leader-situation, and follower–situation fits, your leadership system is primed to be the most powerful human force in the universe.

Over the course of history, we've witnessed many examples of this powerful force. General John Gronski's leadership in the dangerous Ramadi region of Iraq is one example (see Table 2.3). Another is Paul "Bono" Hewson, lead singer for the rock group U2. Bono has been a tireless champion of ridding the

Table 2.2   FRLD Scholar Profile: Shelley D. Dionne

Shelley D. Dionne is currently associate professor of management and a fellow at the Center for Leadership Studies (CLS), State University of New York at Binghamton. She is most proud to have been trained as a PhD student at the epicenter of the FRLD model at SUNY-Binghamton, and participated in research that advanced the FRLD model with Bernard Bass, Bruce Avolio, Fran Yammarino, Leanne Atwater, and Donald Spangler.

As a student, Dionne was an observer of the work ethic and scholarly dedication that Bass, Avolio, and their colleagues displayed in pursuit of the development and extension of transformational leadership into the FRLD model. Their commitment to research and teaching was outstanding. They worked tirelessly to promote and assist researchers around the world that were interested in testing or further developing the FRLD model, in part through the development of the CLS.

For over a decade, Dionne has been involved in a school leadership development program, initiated by Bruce Avolio and Fran Yammarino for the CLS. In response to a critical need for educational leaders throughout New York State, the Southern Tier Leadership Academy, a FRLD-based program, was designed to encourage high-potential public school teachers to consider pursuing educational leadership opportunities in the Binghamton, New York, regional area. Through a partnership with more than 16 local school districts, nearly 100 teachers have participated in the yearlong program, and more than half of those teachers have moved into educational leadership positions since participating.

As an accomplished researcher and teacher, Dionne believes that FRLD has the benefit of applying scholarly leadership theory and research to a practical framework for training and teaching leader behaviors. The FRLD model provides an easily understood progression of leader behavior to increase follower's positive response, namely, less of the ineffective and inactive leader behaviors, and more of the effective and active leader behaviors.

On the practical side, the extensive development of the FRLD model to make successful leader behavior more accessible to practicing and future leaders reinforces the notion that we can teach leadership based on a model grounded in theory and research. According to Dionne, there are an infinite number of self-help leadership development books, but many are based on a single person's opinion of how leaders succeed, without the benefit of literally hundreds of leadership studies. FRLD bridges that gap between research and practice better than any other leadership model.

Table 2.3   Leader Profile: Brigadier General John L. Gronski

Colonel John L. Gronski commanded a U.S. Army brigade combat team (2/28 BCT) in Ramadi, Al Anbar Province, Iraq, from July 2005 through June 2006. The 2/28 BCT's mission was to conduct counterinsurgency operations to neutralize the insurgency, develop the capability of the Iraqi Security Forces, and protect the population in order to improve stability in the area.

From the spring of 2004 and through the time the 2/28 BCT conducted operations in Iraq, Ramadi was characterized by great complexity and violence. Layers of insurgent groups, including Al-Qaeda in Iraq and "nationalists," conducted insurgent operations in Ramadi. Current U.S. military counterinsurgency doctrine was not yet fully developed. Gronski's challenge was to use transformational leadership as a means to achieve results in a very volatile, uncertain, complex, and ambiguous environment. This required comprehending all the elements in the leadership system.

Once gaining a feel for the area through FRLD systems thinking, Gronski displayed inspirational motivation. He developed and communicated a vision for what Ramadi should become at the end of 2/28 BCT's tour there. Under Gronski's direction, his staff put together a road map for what the area would look like at interim points of time and at the end state, in terms of areas controlled by coalition forces, Iraqi Army units, and Iraqi Police. Gronski and his staff also understood that the "key terrain" at stake was not physical ground, but rather the Iraqi civilians. He provided guidance to the soldiers and marines under his command regarding the need to conduct dismounted patrols in order to get closer to the populace and reinforced the tenet "first do no harm." This philosophy required restraint by American troops, even in the face of insurgent attacks.

Gronski realized he also had to exhibit idealized behaviors. He regularly participated in patrols and leader engagement activities to stay connected to the populace and share the danger junior leaders and soldiers had to undergo. Although force is still required when facing a fanatical enemy, Gronski also directed the use of certain techniques that demonstrated it was more important not to harm innocent Iraqi civilians than it was to detain or kill an insurgent.

Gronski exhibited intellectual stimulation by encouraging subordinate commanders from both American units and Iraqi Army units to try innovative approaches based on their specific areas of operation. This allowed the Iraqi Army to take ownership over specific areas and use techniques that worked effectively based on their deep understanding of the culture. It also leveraged the experience of commanders who had served in Iraq before or who were well versed in proven counterinsurgency techniques.

(continued)

Table 2.3   Leader Profile: Brigadier General John L. Gronski (Continued)

Gronski understood the importance of individualized consideration and his role as a coach and mentor. He continually circulated the area of operation to meet as often as possible with subordinate commanders and their troops. He participated in dismounted patrols and other operations with units throughout the area (both American and Iraqi) to get a firsthand impression of unit morale and how Iraqi civilians were treated by units. He spent time with company commanders, platoon leaders, and their noncommissioned officers to explain the importance of using restraint, in order to win over the innocent Iraqi civilians.
As a result of employing the 4Is of transformational leadership, commanders and their troops throughout the 2/28 BCT understood the behaviors necessary to win over the population and conduct successful counterinsurgency operations that set conditions to gain greater stability in a troubled area. A successful national election was held in Ramadi on December 15, 2005, in which 60% of the population voted (up from less than 10% only 10 months earlier). An effective police recruiting campaign was initiated where approximately 1,500 young men of Ramadi joined the Iraqi Police in the spring of 2006. Today the stability visible in Ramadi is a direct result of the effort of the 2/28 BCT and the other U.S. Army BCTs and U.S. Marine units that conducted operations there. For these and other acts of outstanding leadership, Colonel Gronski was promoted to the rank of brigadier general in December 2007.

Source: Gronski, J. L. (2008, January 7). Personal communication.

world of poverty, disease, and malnutrition by partnering with national leaders, as described in Table 2.4. Yet another is Anita Roddick, founder of The Body Shop, who was one of the world's first social entrepreneurs. She and her company exposed several large corporations that were wrecking havoc on the environment in poor Third World countries. At Southwest Airlines, we've seen how Herb Kelleher was able to create a fun-filled and positive organizational culture that selects and develops employees who are passionate about their jobs and company. The result is a company with a track record of financial success that is the envy of the airline industry. This reputation is one that current Southwest Airlines CEO Gary Kelly hopes to continue.

Other events, such as the war in Darfur and the Holocaust, provide somber reminders of the potential for disastrous effects of leadership. Such effects come from the confluence of an evil charismatic leader, visions of ethnic cleansing, followers thirsting for self-esteem, and untenable economic and social conditions that prompt followers to view the leader as a savior capable of extracting them

Table 2.4   Leader Profile: Bono

Paul "Bono" Hewson is the lead singer for the rock band U2, who has expanded his role to become a diplomat and philanthropist. The Irish musician has transcended his rock 'n' roll persona to champion the cause of global economic policy making and be a global leader in the war against AIDS in Africa. He has successfully leveraged his fame in the rock world for access to the world's most influential people. As a result, Bono has become a significant figure and leader in a world movement to end disease and poverty globally.

While many leaders would like to help solve global problems, such as curing an epidemic or eliminating poverty, the path to meaningful results is not always immediately apparent to them. Bono's leadership vision is to devise ways for everyday people to make a difference in the lives of others just by doing what they normally do. Bono has been the driving force behind a number of global initiatives that have married consumer purchasing power and philanthropy to help in the crusade against poverty. Bono also works tirelessly to get organizations to be more fiscally and socially responsible, thereby helping to pay for important causes such as inexpensive medicine to solve Africa's AIDS crisis.

Source: Assayas, M. (2005). *Bono on Bono: Conversations with Michka Assayas.* London: Hodder & Stoughton.

from their undesirable situation. We will elaborate on this important cautionary tale in Chapter 4.

Full Range Leadership Systems Thinking

Many aspiring leaders have focused on their own behavior, personality traits, self-awareness, and other types of personal attributes as their only means of leadership development. However, we have learned through our 25 years of research that several other components of leadership development are just as important. These include the characteristics of the follower, situation, and outcomes (discussed above), and the processes by which the leader, follower, and situation interact to produce leadership outcomes at multiple levels. It's not enough to display the right behavior and be aware of how we relate to others. We also need to understand *how* and *why* our leadership behavior influences followers to achieve leadership outcomes. When enhancing your own leadership development and that of your followers, it is only appropriate that you consider the FRLD model using a process model approach to improve your perspective and maximize your leadership outcomes. Let's examine one such process model that will guide your FRLD learning throughout this book.

Process Model for Understanding Full Range Leadership Development

To assist you in understanding and applying FRLD theory, we present a process model that allows you to predict what leadership styles will work with specific followers in particular situations to produce a variety of positive outcomes for individuals, teams, and organizations. This research-based model is shown in Figure 2.2.

Since we're using a systems-based approach, this model has a number of systems components. The inputs to the system appear on the left-hand side of Figure 2.2 and are labeled "Antecedents," because they come before behavioral actions and motivational processes in the model. These elements reflect the personal attributes of the leader and followers. Examples of these attributes include age, gender, race, religion, self-concept, self-esteem, life experiences, values, beliefs, attitudes, and

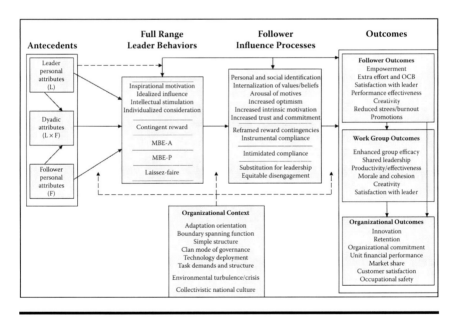

Figure 2.2 A process model for understanding Full Range Leadership Development. (Reprinted with permission from Sosik, J. J. [2006]. Full range leadership: Model, research, extensions and training. In C. Cooper & R. Burke (Eds.), *Inspiring leadership* [pp. 33–66]. New York: Routledge.)

personality traits. Take a few moments to reflect upon how each of these attributes shapes how you exercise leadership and how your followers react to your leadership. What new insights have you gained from your reflection?

Also included in the system are attributes that describe each unique leader-follower relationship or dyad. These elements include attributes of the dyad such as length of relationship, gender composition, attitudes toward learning, and mutual trust, loyalty, and commitment to each other. Dyadic attributes are important indicators of the amount of bonding between the leader and follower. They differ across each relationship a leader has with followers. These attributes determine the quality of each dyadic relationship; higher-quality relationships are closer and more productive than lower-quality relationships.[17]

Based on the quality of the relationship and the attributes of the leader, follower, and situation, leaders can choose which behaviors in the FRLD model to display. Each of the FRLD behaviors motivates followers in a unique way. We see from the two interior rectangles in Figure 2.2 that the 4Is of transformational leadership influence followers by making them identify with the leader and the organization's mission. Research has also shown that followers internalize and share values and beliefs of the transformational leader and work harder to fulfill their needs for achievement, power, and affiliation. Followers also become optimistic and work for the sake of the mission that they perceive as important or a job they perceive as meaningful. This is a powerful form of intrinsic motivation. Followers of transformational leaders are motivated by increased levels of trust and commitment as well.

These processes are illustrated by the way New Yorkers rallied around former mayor Rudolph Giuliani after the tragic events of September 11, 2001. Giuliani has been praised after 9/11 as a leader who was able to unite a diverse city during its darkest hours. Once viewed as a cold and power-hungry leader, Giuliani has become one of New York City's most beloved mayors and even made a brief run for U.S. president in the 2008 campaign. This case illustrates the power of transformational motivational mechanisms and their dramatic results.[18]

The motivational mechanisms for transactional contingent reward leadership differ from those for transformational leadership. Unlike transformational leadership, which relies on intrinsic motivation, extrinsic motivation is the primary driver that prompts followers of contingent reward leaders to work toward their goal. When leaders present clear goals to followers and offer them rewards upon successful attainment of the goal, followers become willing and able to meet performance expectations. These *reframed reward contingencies* help followers to see the path they must travel to reach their goal. They comply with the leader because it will result in receiving a reward that they value. Leadership researchers call this *instrumental compliance* because the follower complies since she perceives the leader's contingent reward behavior as being instrumental to her success. This is the kind of motivation we often see from politicians like former U.S. president Lyndon Baines Johnson, who cut deals with other players and constituents and mastered the political system to achieve specific goals.[19] A more misguided approach to deal making was seen in the case of Jeffrey Lauro, a smooth-talking southwest Florida entrepreneur. Lauro made millions during the recent real estate boom. But when the market went bust, he defaulted on the millions of dollars of loans to banks and investors, while stealing $200,000 through a crafty consulting loan scheme.[20]

Whereas contingent reward leadership uses reframed reward contingencies and instrumental compliance processes to motivate followers, management-by-exception (active and passive forms) relies upon *intimidation* to motivate followers and get them to comply with requests. When leaders wait for problems to arise or seek out problems before they occur, followers focus on avoiding mistakes or deviating from policies and standard operating procedures. They often fear the consequences of their failure to comply with standards, policies, regulations, and requests. For example, one school administrator used the guise of a social hour with students as a means for intelligence gathering of negative information to be used for reprimands. The days after these events were filled with phone calls to program administrators regarding "problems that needed to be solved." Research has shown that such a negative focus instills fear in followers because they become afraid of "being caught" and reprimanded by the leader for their miscues. Interacting in such police state conditions inhibits the innate creativity and proactive participation that are becoming more and more important in today's knowledge-based economy. So a primary reason that followers comply with leaders who display management-by-exception leadership is because they are afraid of the consequences of crossing the leader.

Fear of a different sort is involved in the motivational process associated with laissez-faire leadership. This type is a fear of failure. When asked how to deal with a superior who displays laissez-faire behavior, the majority of aspiring leaders we have taught over the years responded that they "do it themselves." In other words, they substitute for the superior's lack of leadership. They are able to do so because they possess the professionalism, knowledge, or character to make up for what their leader fails to add to the leadership system. However, those followers who lack these qualities engage in *equitable disengagement*. Since most people operate on principles of fairness or equity, these followers are likely to exert an amount of effort equal to the effort the leader exerts. If the leader is laissez-faire and thus exerts little or no interest or effort, such followers are likely to reciprocate and become disengaged from their work, thus displaying equitable disengagement. That's because they don't want to be perceived as suckers who are taken advantage of by others.[21]

Outcomes of Leadership at the Individual, Team, and Organizational/Macro Levels

As a result of the interaction of the leader, follower, and situation, numerous outcomes, shown in Figure 2.2, emerge from the leadership system. At the individual level, the active and effective leadership styles in the FRLD model result in more positive outcomes than the inactive and ineffective styles. For example, followers feel more empowered and engaged in their work and exert extra effort when they experience transformational leadership. Under such leadership, they engage in more organizational citizenship behaviors where they perform tasks that go beyond those described in their formal job description.[22] They are more satisfied with their leader and perform better and more creatively as well. They also report less stress and burnout and earn more job promotions when working with a transformational leader.

These types of outcomes are often reported by aspiring leaders in many leadership courses and workshops we taught in the past. For example, Aimee Firth was responsible for managing a large group of associates in the Revenue Analytics department at DaVita, the largest independent provider of dialysis services in the United States. The DaVita culture fosters teamwork and collaboration, continuous improvement, service excellence, accountability, fulfillment, and fun. These values are demonstrated from the top down, beginning with DaVita's CEO, Kent J. Thiry, who role models the 4Is of transformational leadership. One of his key phrases about DaVita is: "We said it, we did it." This motto illustrates idealized influence as demonstrated through the company's commitment to integrity and transparency by sharing not only the organization's strengths, but also its largest areas of opportunity for Aimee and other employees. Inspirational motivation is apparent through DaVita's acknowledgment of the contribution of all teammates in the fulfillment of its vision to become the greatest dialysis company the world has ever seen. This stretch goal challenged and invigorated Aimee and her associates. Additionally, intellectual stimulation is used to encourage employees to look at problems in new ways through DaVita's Continuous Quality Improvement program. And lastly, through individualized consideration, DaVita's culture and reward systems encourage Aimee and her teammates to develop not only professionally, but personally as well. DaVita reimburses its employees for university courses and degree programs in which they enroll.[23]

While at DaVita, Aimee encouraged several of her talented employees to develop their leadership potential. However, they had a difficult time maintaining a positive outlook and self-regulating their behavior during times of high pressure. That's when Aimee decided to intervene and teach her associates about leadership issues. One of the encouraging emails she sent to a colleague is shown in Table 2.5. As a result of this "leadership intervention," Aimee was able to bolster her associate's level of confidence and optimism, and his willingness to go the extra mile for both her and DaVita.

DaVita's collaborative culture underscores that followers typically do not work in isolation. They often work in groups or teams. Sometimes the positive individual-level effects cascade up to the team level to create a variety of group-level effects. For example, team members working under leaders who display transactional contingent reward and transformational leadership feel more confident about their team's ability to perform well. They possess high levels of morale and cohesiveness and are satisfied with leaders who display these active and effective styles of leadership. They tend to share leadership tasks more effectively. Their teams are very productive and effective. Their work products and processes are judged to be creative as well. These are the kinds of positive attitudes and habits that lead to the successful performance we see in championship sports teams or legendary rock groups like the Beatles or U2.

Since work groups and teams have become the basic building blocks for organizations, the aforementioned individual-level and group-level effects can cascade up to create organizational-level effects. This process is called *social contagion*, where organizational members come to share work attitudes, norms, values, and practices that they view in a positive light because they believe these practices lead to success.[24] This phenomenon may explain why several organizational-level outcomes have been shown to emerge from the more active and effective leadership styles in the FRLD model. These include innovation, employee retention, organizational commitment, increased unit financial performance, improved market share, customer satisfaction, and occupational safety.[25] Examples of organizations that have experienced these outcomes as a result of a transformational culture include Lockheed Martin, Vanguard, IBM, Intel, Qualcomm, and Barclay Global Investors, among many more.[26]

To summarize, FRLD is a process in which you must strategically assess your leadership situation to determine which FRLD behavior is appropriate for your circumstances. The choice of leadership behaviors to display depends on the nature of the followers and the situation. Followers who are developmentally ready for the 4Is of transformational leadership (i.e., good team players and principled individuals) are prime candidates for the 4Is, whereas self-centered followers who are not developmentally ready should be motivated with transactional forms of leadership. Using the 4Is is more effective for producing the follower, work group, and organizational outcomes of leadership (discussed above) when the organizational context includes one or more of the situational elements shown in Figure 2.2 that are conducive to transformational leadership.[27]

Table 2.5 An Online Leadership Intervention

From: Aimee Firth
Sent: Sunday, October 14, 2007 4:33 PM
To: Mark Cylinder
Subject: Aspiring to Great Leadership

Hello Mark,

I would like to provide you with some insights that I believe can provide you with focus and support toward developing your leadership talents. As we have discussed recently, I believe you demonstrate great leadership qualities. There are two idealized leadership principles that I think could be applied to help you develop in the areas of temperance and transcendence.

Temperance is related to the exercise of self-control in our interactions with others. This is critical, as our actions have great impact on our followers as well as the organization. Transcendence is a form of rising spiritually and psychologically above limitations placed on us by ourselves or others. More specifically, the leadership principles I have identified are related to self-regulation and optimism. I have found that by slowing down and paying attention to my own physiological cues during times of stress, as well as the nonverbal cues of others, I am better able to regulate my responses. I have also found that maintaining a sense of optimism while under pressure helps to maintain focus on things within my control.

As we have discussed, your role on the team is highly demanding, ranging from meeting customers' needs to providing mentoring and training to fellow teammates. In times of high stress it can be difficult to manage multiple conflicting priorities while maintaining a sense of optimism, and to not be overcome by negative thoughts and emotions. I have learned that by paying attention to verbal and nonverbal cues of followers, leaders can adjust their behavior to better control impulses, feelings, thoughts, and emotions. This self-control allows leaders to serve as positive role models, as well as to inspire others toward constructive behaviors. Our teammates look to you as a role model, not only for your technical skills, but in how you respond to conflicts and challenges. By maintaining a sense of optimism and practicing self-regulation during these times of extreme pressure, you will inspire and motivate your teammates to emulate your behaviors. This is referred to as inspirational motivation, and can be used to inspire others to achieve success.

I would like to explore these concepts with you in person and in more detail. It is my hope that I can help provide you with additional insights and guidance in your path to great leadership.

Respectfully,
Aimee

Putting Full Range Leadership Development Systems Thinking Into Practice

Books are great ways to learn the concepts of FRLD. If you use the critical questioning technique discussed in Chapter 1, books can be a learning laboratory for your mind. But the real learning laboratory is your personal and professional life. That's where you can put these ideas into action. Your world provides you with many opportunities to put the leadership concepts discussed in this book into practice. And that's the only real way to fully develop your leadership potential and that of your followers and associates. Developing leadership potential is a long and arduous journey that takes a lot of focus, dedication, and hard work. As they say, "Practice makes perfect."

You need to start by making a commitment to putting into practice what you've learned so far and will learn in subsequent chapters. Once you have made the commitment to start applying what you've learned from this book to your world, you're ready to move toward reaching your FRLD goal. Here are some steps to get started on your FRLD journey.

First Step Is the Most Difficult

You are trying to get in the habit of applying FRLD concepts to your world. Any new habit is difficult to establish, but it can be done. Realize that just as leadership is a complex process, so too is your leadership development. You will go through various stages of learning. First, you will learn the behaviors in the FRLD model. Then you will receive feedback from others on how they perceive your leadership. And you will reflect on what these results mean for you. You may become challenged by your results and even question the legitimacy of the scores you receive from your raters.

This was the case for Kurt Linneman, founder and president of Crocodile Catering, a quirky and successful food catering company and restaurant that is beloved by its fiercely loyal customers. Before he embraced FRLD, Kurt jokes that he was known by his employees as "Kurt-ler" (a sarcastic twist on Hitler). This nickname was the result of his single-minded focus on details and the bottom line, to the exclusion of his employees' needs, desires, strengths, and potential for development. With his newfound passion for FRLD principles, Kurt has evolved into a transformational leader who has created a strong culture that encourages leadership development, fun, employee engagement, and creativity at work. (Visit www.croccater.com for an in-depth look at this unique transformational culture.) As Kurt learned, once you begin to identify with the 4Is of transformational leadership, you can commit to developing an action plan to achieve your full leadership potential. Try to find a way to impose some reinforcement and accountability while practicing FRLD. Remember that if there are no serious consequences or rewards, people are not likely to change their behaviors and thoughts. Be patient, and plan to start slow and easy. The journey to leadership development is a marathon and not a sprint.

View Your World Through a FRLD Process Model Lens

System thinking requires a lot of reflection. It requires a lot of questioning, strategizing, and planning. Rethinking assumptions about leadership was the last thing that John Juzbasich had in mind when he joined Penn State's MLD program. John's goal was to learn skills and behaviors to better lead Merit Systems LLC, his management training company. Instead, he learned the need to expand his company's affiliations, partner with local universities and organizations, and pull all of these external elements into Merit's leadership system (see Table 2.6). After much hard work involving reflection and refining of his strategic plan, John became a FRLD systems thinker.

Fortunately, you have a tool that can help guide your systems thinking about FRLD—the FRLD process model shown in Figure 2.2. Consider the elements in this model. Think about what positive and negative personal attributes you bring to the table in interactions with your followers. Make a list of all of your key followers along with their strengths and weaknesses. Consider each of your followers one at a time. What is good about your relationship with each follower? What is bad? What is the level of developmental readiness that each possesses? What behaviors and motivational processes are likely to be useful to produce desired leadership outcomes for your associates, teams, and organization? Which of the organizational context elements in Figure 2.2 describe your leadership situation? Remember, if you don't think of leadership as a system that extends beyond your behavior, you won't be able to maximize the benefits of FRLD training and development.

Take the Multifactor Leadership Questionnaire Now

Since all leadership systems evolve over time, you will need to establish a baseline measure of your FRLD profile in order to track your progress over time. Your leadership behavior can be measured validly (what is supposed to be assessed is in fact assessed) and reliably (consistently over time) with the Multifactor Leadership Questionnaire (MLQ). It is easier to understand the concepts in this book when you see how they relate to you personally. Results from the MLQ make these concepts less abstract and easier to practice when they are quantified and measured within your personal situation. At this point, be sure to visit www.mindgarden.com to order the MLQ before you read the next chapter, especially if you have been inactive in your leadership or are just beginning FRLD training.

Table 2.6 Applying FRLD in Organizational and Social Development

The FRLD model has produced significant positive results in my professional and personal leadership endeavors. At our company, Merit Systems LLC (Merit), a professional training and development firm of which I am a partner, we not only teach FRLD to our clients, but we practice what we preach using FRLD in our strategic efforts. I also apply the model to my personal leadership activities and find that it has produced excellent results. Let's examine these three applications of transformational leadership.

Corporate cultural change is regularly sought, but is difficult to achieve because old habits die hard. One of Merit's clients, a large global corporation with a strong corporate social responsibility ethic, desires a cultural attitudinal change in its Environmental, Health and Safety (EHS) program. The executive team clearly envisions a future desired state, acknowledges the current state of affairs through metrics, and has established a multiyear timeframe to accomplish their goals. Working with their management team, I have devised a program using FRLD as the vehicle to transform their EHS culture and attitude from the current into the desired state of affairs. Working with their international management team, Merit produced a custom workshop in their EHS context that teaches the FRLD model and focuses on transformational leadership as the preferred style, their vehicle, to achieve the desired improvements and attitude changes. Thus far our work has been well received. We have developed a program to train a significant number of their senior-level managers worldwide.

Using transformational leadership, a small company such as Merit can practice corporate social responsibility in creative ways. During a lunch meeting with executives of a small nonprofit organization focused on prevention education services in the area of child sexual abuse, Family Support Line of Delaware County, Inc. (FSL), we discussed the shrinking pool of grant money and the difficulties this presents to growing nonprofit organizations. I wanted to do something to change the situation for FSL. Inspired and motivated by the intellectual challenge, the Merit team conducted an internal brainstorming session focusing on the nonprofit funding issue. We presented a mutually beneficial idea to their board and it was readily accepted.

Teaming with FSL staff and others knowledgeable in the subject of child sexual abuse, Merit produced and now distributes a DVD, *Recognizing and Reporting Child Abuse and Child Sexual Abuse*, for child care providers who are, by law, mandated reporters. The content was provided by subject matter experts; Merit created the script and directed the motion picture production process from filming to final editing and release. The marketing program designed by Merit has proven to be rather successful. The DVD is well

(*continued*)

Table 2.6 Applying FRLD in Organizational and Social Development (Continued)

received, and since its release in February 2008, the product has sold quite well. With each sale Merit provides a royalty fee to FSL for their contribution to the project, which helps them realize their mission of educational programs and aid to victims of child sexual abuse. Corporate social responsibility coupled with transformational leadership provides a powerful combination to shape and change the world.

Believing that leadership is a skill that can be learned and is developed through social interaction, I practice transformational leadership in my personal life to enhance my skill set. Three years ago I volunteered for the co-chair position of the Racial Justice Task Force (RJTF) at our church and later became the chair. The committee had been floundering with three members. At my first meeting a motion was made to disband the task force! The motion was defeated 3 to 1, and the proposer then resigned, leaving us with a total of three members.

Fortunately, the team was dedicated to the cause of racial justice and we resurrected the RJTF. Using the 4Is of transformational leadership, I inspired the RJTF to create our mission (inspirational motivation). I learned about and coached my two co-members and found out why they were interested in the committee. I then shared my personal interest in the task force, which developed from my work in Liberia (individualized consideration). We brainstormed, developed program ideas, explored those that they would like to lead, and discussed how we would bring them to fruition (intellectual stimulation). We implemented the new programs, and others came forth to join the RJTF. As the chair, I led efficient meetings and focused on our work with energy and enthusiasm, as best as I could (idealized influence). As a result of my transformational leadership behaviors, we all learned in context and via our interactions. Today the RJTF has 12 members and we have active adult education, advocacy, and social action programs touching hundreds of people.

Leadership opportunities abound; you need only to look about and they will become apparent. Reach out and take hold of one! Build your skill set, practice transformational leadership, and make a positive difference in the world.

—John Juzbasich, DEd (c), MLD

This is very important because the way you view your leadership behavior may be very different from the way your boss, peers, subordinates, and other raters perceive your style. This so-called "360-degree feedback" can provide you with a reality check on your leadership style and pinpoint any discrepancies that can limit your potential to become a transformational leader. We often find that people are shocked by these multisource views. Well, most of us tend to think of ourselves as an above-average leader. Right? After receiving this feedback, we should become more humble and more willing to change our leadership style.

Establish a Personal Leadership Mission Statement

Every exemplary leader has an overarching purpose that drives him to carry on in good times and bad. This notion has been explored by several psychologists, including Viktor Frankl, who calls this *purpose in life*, as well as Daniel Levinson, who discussed the importance of each person having a *dream* that directs one's life.[28] Sometimes these dreams also direct the lives of many others, as Dr. Martin Luther King showed us. Your purpose may be to create a new business, hire and develop the best staff possible, or reconcile a broken relationship with a follower. Your purpose may change over time, but the values that provide the foundation for your purpose are relatively stable. Examples of values include love of learning, truth, optimism, financial independence, and self-control, among many others. Values are abstract representations of what are deemed to be most important in life. They can be strong motivators of leadership behaviors that put these values into action.[29] For example, a leader who values love of learning may use intellectually stimulating behaviors to reflect this preference.

It is important for you to create a short personal leadership mission statement (PLMS) that links your purpose, values, and FRLD behaviors. This mission statement represents a constitution that can guide your leadership development and provide you with direction in the leadership roles you assume. It can also serve as a standard against which you can compare your MLQ results. When MLQ results are less desirable than what you espouse in your PLMS, you can create action steps in your leadership development plan to improve in these areas. An example PLMS of a former student who now manages a health care organization is shown in Table 2.7. A reflective exercise for creating your own PLMS is presented below.

Find a Learning Partner

Starting your FRLD training with a learning partner can increase your chances of benefiting from it and help you to stick with it as well. If you have a learning partner who is also interested in studying transformational leadership, you can encourage, motivate, and challenge each other. Learning partners make it easy to

Table 2.7   A Personal Leadership Mission Statement

My purpose in life is to ensure that every child is given the opportunity to receive the education he or she deserves, in order to lead a life full of respect and happiness. I will rely on my most important values of equality, creating a lasting impact, and family to help me succeed in this mission.

In my career, I will continually stress the importance of teamwork and that each staff member is an equally important part of our success. Since it is very rare that our available funds will cover our budget, by using the attributes of transformational leadership, most specifically, inspirational motivation, I will motivate my staff to work together to develop creative ways to get the most out of what we are given.

It is important to me that I have a lasting impact on others. By volunteering for organizations that take a sincere interest in other individuals, I have the opportunity to use another aspect of transformational leadership, individualized consideration. A lasting impact does not have to occur within a large group of people; if I am able to help just a few children realize their dreams, by the interest I have taken in their individual successes, I will have succeeded.

I value my family and the love and respect we have for one another. As the eldest of three children, my parents look to me to provide encouragement to my sisters in their own educational and personal journeys. Many times I am the "counselor" to whom my sisters look to offer a different perspective on a particular issue. By using intellectual stimulation, an attribute of transformational leadership, I will help them to see problems and successes from many different angles, so that they can make the decisions that will lead them to a successful outcome.

Finally, I know eventually I will have a relationship that leads to marriage and children, and when I have my own children, I will transfer my most important values into my personal life by being a good and active role model. By using the transformational leadership attribute of idealized influence, I want myself and my future husband to lead by example and by our own actions show our children that they can reach beyond any boundaries and strive to successes that now I cannot even imagine.

use the critical questioning approach discussed in Chapter 1. Learning partners can share their questions and comment on them. They can talk about the similarities and differences in their personal leadership situations and evaluate them from a different point of view. Besides, learning can be pretty lonely, so if you have a learning partner, it will make your journey to master FRLD far more enjoyable.

The benefits of learning with a partner are illustrated by Marty Moran and John McGroary, two managers from Lockheed Martin. Marty and John decided to start and complete Penn State's MLD degree program together. They took almost all of their courses together. They worked in the same teams. They challenged each other in all of their classes. They worked together to apply their FRLD knowledge at Lockheed Martin. Marty is now leading entrepreneurial programs within his company. John is leading engineering projects teams at work during the day, while pursuing a doctoral degree in organizational leadership.

Make FRLD Reflection a Part of Your Schedule

Include a 5–10 minute slot in your daily planner just as you would with any other appointment. At the end of each day, find a comfortable chair in which to sit and reflect upon what FRLD leadership behaviors you used during the day. What worked well? What didn't work so well? What lessons did you learn about leadership today? Use the FRLD process model in Figure 2.2 to explain how and why things went the way they did. This technique trains you to view leadership as a systematic process and to fine-tune your leadership skills over time as well. You can also plan ahead for the week so that you have an idea regarding what FRLD behaviors you can use with followers and associates. Even if you are pressed for time one day, a little self-reflection is better than none at all. Do what you can to fit it in, even if you have less time than you expected.

Gail Cooperman is no stranger to very hectic schedules. As a strategic marketing and growth consultant and busy working mom, Gail knows the challenges of time management. Despite her challenges, Gail stays focused on her daily FRLD reflection. This helps her to plan for unexpected leadership emergencies. As Gail says, "If you take the time to reflect and plan every day, you'd be amazed how that cuts out a lot of potential problems that spring up."

Use Self-Rewards and Positive Affirmations

When you receive MLQ feedback from your associates and get in the habit of thinking about your leadership on a daily basis, take some time to celebrate small successes. Giving yourself little rewards such as your favorite food or drink, socializing with friends and family, and taking some much needed rest and relaxation are great ways to help you stay on track. Affirmations can also help you train your mind to accept your new beliefs about leadership as a developmental process. You might say to yourself a few times a day: "I am evolving into a transformational leader by practicing what I am reading about." And, of course, be sure to be true to yourself and do what you're telling yourself. This can build your motivation and confidence levels as you develop your full leadership potential over time. It's the kind of confidence we see in leaders like Dan McKeon, who is developing www.LearnToBeALeader.com as an online portal for many of the FRLD resources and concepts described in this book.

Set Goals With a Personal Leadership Development Plan

Setting goals can be helpful in keeping you motivated and helping you to improve your leadership potential, but remember to keep them realistic. As part of the personal leadership development plans we create in our FRLD training and graduate courses, we specify action steps along with timetables and measurement requirements to help our participants stay on track. Short-term and long-term goals can make accomplishing these action steps easier. For example, what will you do to improve your idealized influence score? How much time will you give yourself to improve your score? How will you assess whether you have made any progress? Readministering the MLQ and reflecting upon its results is certainly a good means to answer these questions.

Congratulations! You are now ready to learn about each of the FRLD behaviors in detail. Let's start at the pinnacle of the model with idealized leadership. This form of influence exemplifies the essence of transformational leadership.

Summary Questions and Reflective Exercises

1. This exercise helps you to gain perspective on the role of leadership in your life. Develop your personal leadership mission statement (PLMS) by following these steps. Devote at least 30 minutes to this exercise. Go to a quiet room in your house or somewhere else that you can be alone. Set the tone by listening to some relaxing background music (perhaps classical or soft music—whatever soothes you) with earphones connected to your stereo or iPod. Then meditate on how you would answer the following questions:
   - Who is someone you deeply admire? Why?
   - Who are you without your job or your money? Describe in detail.
   - What activities could you add to your life that could be a source of joy for others?
   - What gives you the greatest joy, satisfaction, and renewal in your life? Can you do more of it?
   - If you were on your deathbed and you wanted to tell people close to you the three most important things that you learned in your life, what would they be?

   Once you have meditated on the questions above, your mind should be in tune to complete the actual PLMS. Be sure *not* to answer these questions in your PLMS. Instead, your PLMS should be written clearly and concisely and contain three paragraphs. In the first paragraph, describe your overall *purpose in life* at this point in your life. Be sure that your purpose is directed toward serving others. In the second paragraph, define your *personal values* that are reflected in your purpose in life. In the third paragraph, explain how you will put each of these values into action through *specific FRLD behaviors*.

2. This exercise helps you to view leadership as a system. Draft an outline for your personal leadership development plan by following these steps. Your complete leadership behavior profile will come from the MLQ report you will receive from www.mindgarden.com. The profile will contain a summary of leadership ratings generated by those who report to you directly, your superior, your peers, your self-ratings, and normative data for comparison purposes. Your MLQ report also will contain qualitative comments from your raters. You should use this array of data to examine your personal strengths and weaknesses with respect to the specific FRLD behaviors. Participants in our courses produce a 15-page doubled-spaced written report with the following sections:
   - Personal leadership mission statement.
   - Tabular or graphical summary of MLQ feedback. This section should describe how you saw yourself as a leader, how your followers saw you as a leader, the discrepancy between your self-ratings and your followers' ratings of you, how your results compare to those of others in your training program, and how your results compare to normative results.
   - Strengths.
   - Areas for development (weaknesses).
   - Organizational opportunities for leadership development.
   - Organizational stumbling blocks impeding leadership development.
   - Action steps to address weaknesses and accomplish personal leadership mission.

   Once you have received and analyzed your MLQ results, you can embellish your outline.

3. This exercise involves using systems thinking to analyze a real-world scenario. The names have been changed to protect the innocent. Imagine that you have been hired by Whitless Corporation, a privately owned 50-year-old medium-sized manufacturing firm, to develop an organizational change program to address its quality, employee, and customer satisfaction problems. Whitless's CEO, Bob Bossanova, utilizes top-down, authoritarian, and directive leadership to control the firm's specialized divisions. Whitless's organization structure is characterized by task specialization and rigidity, strict hierarchy of authority, centralized decision making (i.e., Bob calls the shots), and vertical/one-way communication.

   In recent years, Whitless's sales, profits, and employee morale have fallen off to uncomfortable levels. Puzzled as to why his management strategies are not as effective as they once were, Bob hollers, "I wonder if we have a *quality* problem! Who's @%*$ing up this time?" He has responded by tightening financial controls on each department, especially manufacturing, by requiring all department managers to prepare monthly budgets. Department managers receive monthly performance reports from Leona Ledger, CPA, Whitless's controller. These reports compare budgeted to actual costs and highlight variances between these costs. Managers are required to provide written explanations to Bob for unfavorable variances exceeding 5% of budgeted cost.

   a. Indicate reasons why Bob's management strategies may not be as successful as they once were. Be sure to consider factors both internal and external to the organization.

   b. How would you describe Bob's style of leadership in terms of the FRLD model? Why?

   c. Which styles of leadership do you feel would have positive effects on Whitless's total quality management (TQM) efforts? Negative effects?

   d. In developing a TQM strategy for Whitless, what specific behaviors would you prescribe for training managers and employees? How would you describe these behaviors in terms of the FRLD model? *Hint*: TQM is based on three concepts: customer satisfaction, continuous process improvement, and employee learning and empowerment.

4. This exercise develops your systems thinking and ability to apply FRLD concepts to real-world initiatives. Consider the Malcolm Baldrige National Quality Award, which is presented annually to U.S. organizations by the president to recognize quality and business accomplishments. Awards are given in manufacturing, service, small business, education, nonprofit, and health care sectors. Visit http://www.quality.nist.gov/Criteria.htm to review the criteria for winning the award. Then describe how elements of the FRLD leadership system can be applied to support the processes, goals, and measures of progress required to receive the award.

5. Choose a leadership-oriented film such as *Apollo 13, Hoosiers, Remember the Titans, Gettysburg, Norma Rae, Courage Under Fire, Twelve Angry Men, Dead Poets Society,* or *Wall Street* (for more ideas visit http://www. hartwickinstitute.org/) and view the movie with a friend or learning partner(s). Use a leadership systems model discussed in this chapter to identify the key elements in the systems and describe how these elements are dynamic and related to each other.

6. This creativity exercise is designed to enhance your perspective-taking capacity regarding viewing leadership as a system. Using a digital camera, illustrate several aspects of the leadership system described in this chapter by photographing people, processes, and outcomes at work or in your personal life. Present your photos to your learning partner(s), classmates,

or fellow aspiring leaders as illustrations of a leadership systems element. Explain to them why you feel they illustrate the concept. Discuss their reactions to your work.

7. Select popular songs that illustrate the essence of each of the FRLD behaviors described in Figure 2.2. Share the songs with your learning partner(s), classmates, or fellow aspiring leaders via .mp3 files, iTunes, or www.YouTube.com links. Explain why you feel they illustrate the concept. Discuss their reactions to your work.

8. Why is systems thinking required for effective FRLD? What happens to leaders who fail to use systems thinking? How can you train yourself and others to view leadership as a system?

9. Interview a top executive in your organization regarding how he or she evaluates the leadership potential of people in the organization. How much of a systems view does this leader possess? How can you help this leader to improve in this area?

10. Visit a few junior associates in your organization who may be struggling with a project or a business relationship. You don't have to know them personally. They just have to know that someone cares about them. Then follow up by offering to mentor them. By doing so, you'll expand your personal network and learn about another person's leadership system.

Notes

1. Sosik, J. J. (2006). *Leading with character: Stories of valor and virtue and the principles they teach* (p. 43). Greenwich, CT: Information Age.
2. Gardner, W. L., & Avolio, B. J. (1998). The charismatic relationship: A dramaturgical perspective. *Academy of Management Review, 23,* 32–58.
3. Clavell, J. (Producer/Director), & Braithwaite, E. R. (Writer). (1967). *To sir, with love* [Motion picture]. Culver City, CA: Columbia (British) Productions.
4. Waters, R. (1979). Another brick in the wall (part II) [Recorded by Pink Floyd]. On *The wall* [CD]. Hollywood, CA: Capitol Records.
5. Avolio, B. J. (1999). *Full leadership development: Building the vital forces in organizations.* Thousand Oaks, CA: Sage.
6. Ackoff, R. L. (1999). *Ackoff's best: His classic writings on management.* New York: Wiley; and Avolio (1999). As cited in Note 5.
7. Sosik (2006). As cited in Note 1.
8. Matthews, C. J. (1997). *Kennedy and Nixon: The rivalry that shaped postwar America.* New York: Free Press.
9. Arvey, R. D., Zhang, Z., Avolio, B. J., & Krueger, R. F. (2007). Developmental and genetic determinants of leadership role occupancy among women. *Journal of Applied Psychology, 92,* 693–706.

10. Clinton, W. J. (2004). *My life*. New York: Knopf.
11. Neck, C. P., & Manz, C. C. (2007). *Mastering self-leadership: Empowering yourself for personal excellence* (4th ed.). Upper Saddle River, NJ: Prentice-Hall.
12. Hiller, A. (Producer/Director). (1972). *Man of la mancha* [Motion picture]. Santa Monica, CA: Distributed by Metro Goldwyn Mayer.
13. Sosik, J. J., Jung, D. I., Berson, Y., Dionne, S. D., & Jaussi, K. S. (2004). *The dream weavers: Strategy-focused leadership in technology-driven organizations*. Greenwich, CT: Information Age.
14. Meyers, W. (2005, October 31). Conscience in a cup of coffee. *U.S. News & World Report*, *139*, 48–50.
15. http://www.ge.com/company/index.html. Retrieved July 18, 2008.
16. Hajim, C. (2007, October 1). The top companies for leaders. *Fortune*, *156*, 109–116.
17. Graen, G. B., & Uhl-Bien, M. (1995). Relationship-based approach to leadership: Development of leader-member exchange (LMX) theory of leadership over 25 years: Applying a multi-level multi-domain perspective. *The Leadership Quarterly*, *6*, 219–247; and Sosik, J. J., Godshalk, V. M., & Yammarino, F. J. (2004). Transformational leadership, learning goal orientation, and expectations for career success in mentor-protégé relationships: A multiple levels of analysis perspective. *The Leadership Quarterly*, *15*, 241–261.
18. Strober, D. H. (2007). *Giuliani: Flawed or flawless? The oral biography*. Hoboken, NJ: John Wiley & Sons.
19. Woods, R. B. (2006). *LBJ: Architect of American ambition*. New York: Free Press.
20. Braga, M. (2008, May 26). Deal maker facing criminal charges. *Sarasota Herald-Tribune* [Online]. Retrieved January 24, 2009, from http://www.heraldtribune.com/article/20080526/REALESTATE/805260573/1093/SPORTS.
21. Adams, J. S. (1965). Inequity in social exchange. *Advances in Experimental Social Psychology*, *62*, 335–343.
22. Organ, D. W. (1988). *Organizational citizenship behavior: The good soldier syndrome*. Lexington, MA: D. C. Heath and Company.
23. Firth, A. (2007). *Analysis of Leadership Potential Assessment Center (LPAC)*. Malvern, PA: Penn State Great Valley School of Graduate Professional Studies.
24. Jones, M. B., & Jones, D. R. (1995). Preferred pathways of behavioral contagion. *Journal of Psychiatric Research*, *29*, 193–209.
25. For a multilevel overview of outcomes of the FRLD system, see Sosik, J. J. (2006). Full range leadership: Model, research, extensions and training. In C. Cooper & R. Burke (Eds.), *Inspiring leadership* (pp. 33–66). New York: Routledge.
26. Sosik et al. (2004). As cited in Note 13.
27. Sosik (2006). As cited in Note 25.
28. Frankl, V. (2004). *Man's search for meaning: An introduction to logotherapy*. Boston: Beacon; and Levinson, D. J. (with Darrow, C. M., Klein, E. G., Levinson, M. H., & McKee, B.). (1978). *The seasons of a man's life*. New York: Knopf.
29. Sosik, J. J. (2005). The role of personal values in the charismatic leadership of corporate managers: A model and preliminary field study. *The Leadership Quarterly*, *16*, 221–244.

Chapter 3

Idealized Influence Behaviors and Attributes
The Humane Side of Transformational Leadership

It's important for people to know what you stand for.
It's equally important that they know what you won't stand for.

—Mary Waldrop

Some people seem to have it all. When it comes to charm, personality, intelligence, and friends, Bill Jordan can win a prize. As vice president of clinical research at pharmaceutical leader Sanofi-Aventis, Bill is well respected by many colleagues and is making his mark as a transformational leader. Bill's jet-set corporate lifestyle involves frequent travel to Europe, grueling 12-hour days, plus graduate school. His far-flung personal and professional network stems from his innate ability to connect with people at all organizational levels and in almost any walk of life.

Despite his corporate star power, Bill carries himself with an unusual air of modesty and quiet confidence. For an experiential exercise at school, Bill took his protégé Michael Agard back to Camden, New Jersey, where Bill grew up. Bill showed Michael his humble beginnings. Bill's parents operated an inner-city grocery store where he learned the importance of personal relationships and how to interact with all kinds of people. Bill worked three jobs to pay for college and help his parents and family. These experiences shaped the positive way Bill treats his associates today. Through hard work, insightfulness, and persistence, Bill now commands the loyalty, respect, and trust of his associates at Sanofi-Aventis and in his community.

Being recognized as a leader in your organization or community can bring many benefits. Like Bill Jordan, you may be viewed by others as an important authority on key issues, a spokesperson for your group, a provider of desirable resources, and a person of power and influence. You are likely to receive pref-erential treatment by others. You may command the attention and respect of your peers and subordinates as well. You may even become an idol to them. For example, consider the amount of idolization singer-actress Miley Cyrus has with young fans all over the world. As she outgrows her Hannah Montana image, it will be interesting to see whether she will adapt or entirely drop her role model image for her fans. Such great attention at a young age is sometimes difficult for role models to keep in perspective. That's why Malia and Sasha Obama are being carefully protected by their parents from the attention they receive from the media and opportunistic marketers.

Along with these perks comes the responsibility of being a role model for your associates. This can be a heavy cross to bear. As the leader, all eyes are fixed on what you do, all ears are tuned to what you say, and all minds are focused on evaluating how you think. People want to know if you exemplify your organiza-tion's values. They watch to see if you conduct yourself in a socially and morally acceptable manner. And they judge whether you can add social, economic, and market value for your organization through your leadership. In essence, every-thing you say, do, and think is scrutinized. People constantly test you to see what you stand for and what you will not stand for.

Yes, it's a tall order to embody societal virtues and character strengths, epitomize organizational values, and produce sustainable performance results through your leadership. And, that's precisely why we challenge our students to see if they are *ready* to lead. When people think about leadership, they often-times think about the many perks, not the added responsibilities that come with leadership. If they do, we don't believe that they are ready to meet their leader-ship challenges.

Many leadership challenges are easier to meet when you realize that the success of your leadership is achieved through the support from others. Your personality and behaviors have an effect on their motivation and influence the processes they use to achieve the outcomes of leadership. These outcomes of leadership are rarely directly related to a leader's personality or behaviors. A number of factors, such as economic conditions, strategy content and execution, and available resources, also determine organizational performance in today's complex environments. A single leader's personality and behaviors explain very little variation in organizational performance. This is why many leadership researchers have a hard time showing a direct and positive relationship between CEOs' leadership style and firm performance.[1] Nevertheless, how well your organizational unit performs can produce attributions of leadership effectiveness that can bolster your leadership prowess.

Consider Jack Welch, former CEO of General Electric (GE). If you browse Amazon.com or the business section of your favorite book store, you will likely find numerous books on leadership written either by or about Jack Welch.[2] With all this attention, it's as if he is the "patron saint of CEOs." Why? It's mainly because under Jack Welch's leadership tenure as CEO, GE was able to create a whopping $320 billion of stock market value for its shareholders. This represents phenomenal performance, especially compared to his two predecessor CEOs, who were only able to add about $1 billion in stock market value.[3]

How did Jack Welch do it? He used drastic cost cutting, including employee layoffs, in his early tenure. As a result, he was dubbed "Neutron Jack." He told his business units that their goal was to become number one or two in their markets, or they would exit that business sector. He championed continuous process improvement, total quality management, and Six Sigma initiatives aimed at promoting quality and efficiencies within and between GE's operating units. Later on at GE, Welch championed leadership development initiatives to enhance the knowledge, skills, and abilities of its employees. As a result, GE's achievements under Welch became the envy of corporations around the world. Today, many seek to follow his lead and replicate what Welch had done for GE in their own organizations. This is what it means to exert idealized influence in corporate settings.

Jack Welch's success story reiterates for us the main lesson of Chapter 2: Leadership and its outcomes are a function of the interaction of the leader, the followers, and the situation. The relationship that leaders have with their followers is created and maintained through social exchanges that go both ways. Leaders behave in certain ways that influence followers' motivation, values and beliefs, and organizational performance. Followers perceive these leader behaviors and performance outcomes and attribute either positive or negative characteristics to the leader. Because there is mutual influence in leadership systems, you should view leadership as a combination of actual leadership behavior displayed by the leader and socially constructed images of the leader created by followers.

This chapter shows you how to display idealized influence behaviors to gain attributions of idealized influence from your followers so that you can personify the very best of transformational leadership. Let's begin by considering the case of one of the greatest idealized leaders of the 20th century.

The Idealized Leadership of Mohandas Gandhi

Ever since we began teaching Full Range Leadership Development (FRLD), we've used the case of Mohandas Gandhi to illustrate idealized influence. His strong character and exemplary leadership led India to the successful quest for independence from Great Britain. He's been the subject of many books and movies. Indeed, Gandhi is perhaps the closest human example of idealized influence in history. His legacy is a collection of wise thoughts, ideas, words, and deeds that have changed the world. The changes he helped produce in India became the foundation for future social justice causes, such as the civil rights movement in the United States, the fight against Apartheid in South Africa, and the quest for increased human rights in China. His actions inspired leaders in other times and places to stand up for important principles such as human dignity, independence, and freedom of thought and expression. Gandhi's amazing story is relevant today because justice and human dignity are pro-social values that people will always be willing to live and die for.

The idealized leader reflects the most important pro-social values, beliefs, and aspirations of followers. Through consistency in thoughts, words, and deeds, the idealized leader becomes a symbol for the followers' cause. Recognizing his symbolic leadership role, Gandhi was very careful to portray himself as an imperfect "work in progress" instead of an infallible icon. He presented himself as being similar to his followers instead of being superior to them. He did this by shifting the focus of attention away from himself and toward important ideals and values he espoused. He did not want to create a "cult of personality" and receive the entire spotlight. Instead, he preached the importance of living a life of practical nonviolent moral action grounded in several spiritual and religious traditions. The only violence he condoned was "violence against the self" aimed at breaking down excessive ego. According to Gandhi, this helps one to be selfless by focusing on the needs of others and inspiring them to reach their full potential. These aspects of Gandhi's philosophy supported his ultimate quest and passion for truth in all situations.[4] Interestingly, Gandhi's words and deeds demonstrated the notion of "authentic leadership" long before former Medtronic CEO Bill George highlighted the term.[5] Most importantly, Gandhi practiced what he preached. His authenticity is why his followers and admirers even to this day respect him so.

One of Gandhi's quotes defines the essence of authentic leadership: "Always aim at complete harmony of thought and word and deed." The assumption in this statement and in theory on authentic leadership is that thought is indeed grounded in good or positive other-oriented values. However, it is also possible that a leader's thoughts are grounded in bad, self-centered, or egoistic values. What happens when a leader like Osama bin Laden, Saddam Hussein, or

Imelda Marcos is authentically self-centered or evil because he or she acts consistently with his or her egoistic beliefs at the expense of others? Being authentic does not always equate with good or moral leadership. Therefore, a high level of ethical standards and positive personal values are also important requirements of being authentic leaders.

Gandhi's ideas about service and stewardship (i.e., advocating the best interest of another person or entity) have influenced numerous leadership writers such as Robert Greenleaf, who identified Gandhi as an example of *servant leadership*. This notion of leadership spotlights the growth of those followers being served, as does transformational leadership. The literature on servant leadership identifies other-oriented, altruistic, helping, and moral/ethical behaviors as essential to followers' development. It emphasizes the development of skills and abilities required to serve followers, such as listening, self-awareness, foresight, and stewardship.[6] These behaviors and skills are key principles underlying the concept of idealized influence.

Greenleaf's research identifies two requirements for servant leadership: The servant leader must elicit trust and have a sustaining spirit. Gandhi elicited trust through his consistency between his thoughts, words, and authentically altruistic actions. Gandhi sustained his spirit through a deep Hindu faith and informed knowledge of other world religions, such as Christianity. Similarly, Greenleaf's conceptualization of servant leadership is not limited to one religious tradition or cultural context. In his writings, Greenleaf integrates ideas from Christian, Jewish, Hindu, and Buddhist traditions, and Western and Eastern cultural customs to explain his notion of servant leadership. And he illustrates this by pointing to Gandhi as the embodiment of servant leadership. To fully appreciate the example of Gandhi as an idealized leader, you should view Richard Attenborough's award winning film *Gandhi*.[7] To gain a rich understanding of how Gandhi's ideas are being applied in leadership situations, visit http://www.greenleaf.org/ and watch clips from the film *Gandhi* on DVD or YouTube.com.

Idealized Influence Behaviors: Definition and Examples

In order to gain the trust, respect, and admiration of your followers, like Gandhi, you need to display behaviors that demonstrate idealized influence. That's because *idealized influence* involves being a positive role model that exemplifies high levels of moral/ethical and performance standards. To be moral and ethical means that you hold and display character strengths and virtues valued by society. It also means that you put your group's best interests ahead of your own personal interests. To hold high performance standards means that you aim

Table 3.1 Leader Profile: Thurgood Marshall

As the first African American to serve as a justice on the U.S. Supreme Court, Thurgood Marshall represents an idealized leader. A turning point in his life occurred when, as a child, Marshall was punished for acting up in school. His penalty was to read the U.S. Constitution. That punishment fueled his curiosity and love of learning, thus motivating him to seek a career in the field of law. Despite many racial and social challenges in his life, Marshall persisted in his quest to graduate from college and law school. His law career was highlighted with arguing many successful cases upholding the rights of African Americans in their admissions to U.S. schools and universities. He went on to serve as chief counsel of the NAACP, successfully arguing many civil rights-related cases before the U.S. Supreme Court.

Through his idealized behavior and accomplishments, Marshall served as a positive role model for those advocating the civil rights movement he championed. As a result, Marshall was admired by Presidents John F. Kennedy and Lyndon B. Johnson, who recognized his high level of legal, moral, and performance standards. President Johnson appointed Marshall to the U.S. Supreme Court in 1967, where he served until 1991, when he was succeeded by Clarence Thomas. Marshall also served as a top aide to President Bill Clinton until his death in 1993.

Source: Bland, R. W. (2001). *Justice Thurgood Marshall: Crusader for liberalism: His judicial biography.* Bethesda, MD: Academica Press; and http://www.thurgoodmarshall.com/home.htm. Retrieved February 22, 2008.

high in all of your work processes, products, and outcomes, and you raise the bar for others. Unfortunately, this can sometimes detract from your popularity with some lazy or insecure followers in the short run, but it can build your reputation in the long run. Displaying idealized influence behaviors is a skill in which the first African American U.S. Supreme Court Justice, Thurgood Marshall, was quite adept (see Table 3.1).

Like Thurgood Marshall, you need to demonstrate idealized influence behaviors to be seen as a transformational leader by your followers. Let's now examine six key transformational leadership behaviors that embody idealized influence.

Talk About Your Most Important Values and Beliefs

Courtney was a supervisor of an accounts payable department at a large investment management company. Her department was responsible for processing cash disbursement checks for the company's purchases and expenditures. Her staff focused on technical details of their jobs and generally met their departmental goals within budget. However, they never really excelled or performed beyond expectations. Suddenly, the push from senior management was to exceed performance goals. Based on prior experience, Courtney felt that her use of extrinsic rewards and bonuses as motivators would not work. She felt disconnected from her staff, whom she felt didn't identify with her. One day after class, Courtney approached John and they started to talk.

Courtney said, "I don't feel that my staff connects with me. Today, you mentioned the importance of talking to staff about your important values and beliefs. But I'm not sure if my staff wants to hear about what I think. And besides, I'm not comfortable sharing my personal beliefs with my staff. I want more from my staff, but I don't know if I can show idealized influence that way."

John replied, "It's natural for some people to have trouble sharing their personal values and beliefs. In our society, we like to maintain our own personal space. We don't want to appear to be too pushy. However, one way to connect with your staff is to show them you are just as human as they are … that you have hopes, ideals, and aspirations, just like them. They want to see what is important to you as the leader … and to see what is most important for your company's success. So, you might start by picking one or two company values that you feel are important to your department's success. Talk them up with your staff. Show them that things like diversity, teamwork, innovation, and community service are essential for their success, and the success of the company. That way your staff will know what you stand for, and where your thinking is coming from."

Courtney's face lit up, and with a twinkle in her eyes, she told John, "OK, now I get it. If I want my staff to connect with me, they need to understand me. They need to see what I stand for, what I believe in, and what I value for our team. They'll never know this if I don't tell them." A few months later, Courtney emailed to say that she had been talking a lot lately to her staff about her love of learning (a personal value that is consistent with her company's emphasis on training and development), and what she was learning in graduate school. She explained to them that her company is actually investing in them by reimbursing their graduate and professional education expenses and how they should take advantage of this. Now she's "walking the talk" by role modeling the importance of graduate education and its application at work.

After that episode, Courtney gained confidence in her ability to talk about what's most important in her company. These values provide a strong foundation that motivates people to achieve collective confidence and success, not just personal confidence and success. And when followers see consistency among their leader's ideas, words, and actions, they are likely to attribute idealized influence to the leader. What important personal or company values can you highlight for your staff?

Talking about important values and beliefs is important in all areas of life. As shown in Figure 3.1, for people of faith, religious ceremonies often highlight

Figure 3.1 Values to live and lead by. The monsieur performing the baptism ceremony talks about the importance of Church values and beliefs associated with being a Catholic and the responsibilities of the parents and the godparents in leading and developing the child to be a person of faith.

what's most important to strive for and how to live one's life. Organizational leaders also must guide their followers and point them in the right direction. For example, Tony Dungy, the first African American NFL coach to win the Super Bowl, uses his faith to direct players and others in the game of life.[8]

Talk About the Importance of Trusting Each Other

A group of university business faculty members recently survived a marathon three-hour meeting. According to one observer, that particular meeting gave new meaning to the saying "Leading faculty is like herding cats." During the meeting, the group considered a motion to increase the required GMAT scores for MBA student applicants over a multiyear period. One faction of tenured faculty argued in favor of the motion, while another group of tenured faculty opposed it. When the call for a voice vote came, a large group of untenured faculty abstained from voting. They were afraid of being perceived by the group they disagreed with as not supporting their cause. Their fear came from the fact that tenured faculty sit on university committees that decide the promotion and tenure fate of untenured faculty, typically during the sixth year of service. What does this case tell you about the level of trust among the faculty in that meeting?

Yes, the level of trust among the colleagues in that meeting was quite low. On that day, the faculty failed to trust each other. However, trust is absolutely, positively essential in leader–follower relationships, as it is in any interpersonal relationship. While trust levels vary, most people believe that trust either exists or does not exist. Pretending that trust exists (when in fact it doesn't) runs counter to Gandhi's concepts of truthfulness and authenticity. If issues with trust exist in a group, they cannot be swept under the rug. Instead, they must be dealt with by discussing the sources of mistrust and working to eliminate them. Even when trust levels are sufficient, trust needs to be reinforced periodically so that the leader can continue to establish her image reflecting integrity, competence, openness, and consistency. When followers feel that they can count on their leader, they are more likely to go the extra mile for the leader and their team, as shown in Figure 3.2.

Leaders must also remember *not* to act in ways that make them appear to lack trustworthiness. In other words, if you talk about the importance of trust, you must act in ways that demonstrate your trustworthiness. This leadership

Figure 3.2 He's safe! The runner risked being thrown out at home plate because he trusts his idealized leader, who coached and watched over him.

principle should remind you of Gandhi's goal of complete harmony between thoughts, words, and deeds. When was the last time you talked to your followers about the importance of trusting one other?

Specify the Importance of Having a Strong Sense of Purpose

Have you ever felt like giving up when faced with a seemingly impossible task? Perhaps it was when you were working for a very difficult boss. Perhaps it was when you were completing your degree while you worked full-time. Perhaps it was when you were forced to take a statistics course you thought you'd never pass. Whatever the case, chances are you stuck it out because you had an important reason or motive for reaching your goal. Your reason might have been to make someone in your family proud of you. It might have been to establish or reestablish an important personal relationship. Or it simply might have been to complete an important work that no one else would be capable of doing.

This is the kind of motivation that sustained Lori in her leadership role as a middle manager in an international banking firm. Lori assumed her leadership post just as Willie joined her bank as the new director of operations and her superior. Willie had a notorious reputation for being an overbearing, number-crunching, command-and-control freak with an ego as tall as the Empire State Building. Willie had spent many years in the military's finance offices before he transitioned into industry a few years prior to a planned retirement at age 65. Imagine a cigar-smoking, crass, overweight, and opinionated middle-aged executive, and you'll get the picture. According to Lori, Willie is not a micromanager; he is a *nano-manager*! Sounds like active management-by-exception on steroids, doesn't it?

On account of Willie, Lori's days at work were replete with endless frustrations, nit-picky questions, illogical responses, and denials of resource requests. In short, Willie made Lori's and every other manager's life miserable. Escape from this situation was impossible because Willie's superior was his best buddy, and Willie had no intention of leaving. Like prisoners crossing off the days on a calendar as they passed, Lori and her colleagues counted down the days until Willie's planned retirement. What helped Lori and her colleagues sustain their wits and will power to carry on for the greater good of their firm?

It was their strong sense of purpose coming from a will to help their firm be successful despite Willie's mean-spirited motives and actions. This was their mission: to help each other and their associates get through the tough times, and to learn something from it. As mentioned in Chapter 2, their approach is what Viktor Frankl referred to as purpose in life and what Daniel Levinson referred to as the dream. When leaders talk about the importance of having a strong sense of purpose, followers are more likely to develop confidence, and it becomes

Figure 3.3 Catch a wave and you're sitting on top of the world. Idealized leaders inspire their followers to follow their dreams and live life to the fullest.

contagious to other people in their organization. Furthermore, leaders' strong sense of purpose gives followers a reason to persist, a cause to champion, and a reason to fight the good fight when times get tough. As shown in Figure 3.3, the surfing instructor is reiterating to his students their mission to experience life to its fullest, even in the face of monster waves. What purpose can be your sustaining force to help you weather the high seas or storms in your organization? How can you use purpose to help your organization survive difficult challenges that competitors inside and outside of your organization throw at you?

Consider the Moral/Ethical Consequences of Your Decisions

Joe Paterno, head coach of Penn State University's football team, is among the winningest coaches in college football. But Paterno stands for more than just the numbers in the win column. Paterno is famous for taking stands on issues based on honorable principles. He often talks about the importance of making decisions based on moral and ethical criteria. In a speech he gave to university honor students, Paterno highlighted honesty and integrity as the cornerstones of leadership. He talked about using virtues and role models of leadership as guideposts for making the many difficult decisions leaders must face. He illustrated the use of virtues by explaining how organizations such as the Boy Scouts can build character. He even recited the Boy Scout oath to point out its virtues and how they can be applied to everyday life. Paterno has used this decision-making framework in many situations, such as his support of using football to develop the whole person, a college football playoff system, modest stipends for players, philanthropy for education, and his opposition to gambling on college sports.[9]

Transformational leaders, such as Joe Paterno, are responsible for a broad range of followers with diverse interests and agendas. As role models for followers, transformational leaders must make decisions using a perspective that transcends their own narrow self-interests. This perspective-taking capacity, introduced in Chapter 2, is critical to the display of idealized influence behavior. That's because idealized leaders talk about important moral and ethical values and therefore must use these values in their own decision-making processes in order to gain credibility from followers. If your goal is to display idealized influence, it is not enough for you to talk about such values. You must use moral and ethical values to guide your decision-making processes and use them to justify your decisions if and when you come under fire from others. Like Gandhi and Paterno, you must strongly believe in a core set of moral and ethical values, use them in your decision making, talk about them to your followers and others, and bring them to life with behavior that is consistent with what you espouse. As shown in Figure 3.4, remember that your values and personal beliefs shape

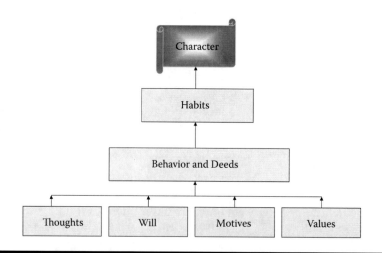

Figure 3.4 Building character. Idealized leaders build their character upon a solid foundation of ideals, behaviors, and practices. (Reprinted with permission from Sosik, J. J., Jung, D. I., Berson, Y., Dionne, S. D., & Jaussi, K. S. (2004). *The dream weavers: Strategy-focused leadership in technology-driven organizations* [p. 158]. Charlotte, NC: Information Age Publishing.)

your leadership behavior. As you continually display this behavior over time, your character is shaped.

However, our experience with many students and executives while teaching leadership has taught us about one common problem. People rarely spend time thinking about what values are important to them. To test this, we ask our students to write down the five most important values that they use to guide their behaviors and decision-making processes everyday. Surprisingly, more than half of them have a hard time writing down even two or three values. They are all managers, but they do not have a set of well-defined personal values. One common excuse for not having a set of personal values is that they are just too busy at work. Or, some people say that they will develop them when they become senior executives and when they really need them. We believe that it is very important to establish a clearly defined set of values early on and practice them every day. This will make you more of an authentic transformational leader. What are your top five important values? Can you pass this test by writing all five and living them?

Emphasize the Importance of Teamwork

If you have ever watched the Penn State Nittany Lions football team, you've probably noticed that the players do not have their last names printed on the back of their jerseys. While this is unusual, that's the way Joe Paterno likes it. Paterno feels that the absence of player names on jerseys places the focus of effort on the team instead of the individual player and therefore promotes team spirit and cooperation. What a great way to erase the big egos from these husky football players! This concept is what social psychologists call *de-individuation*, or the temporary loss of personal identity from being part of a group.[10] De-individuation shifts the attention of players from their individual needs and wants to those of their team because they are not easily identified at the individual level. They are, however, easily connected to their team because they share a common uniform and a common identity.

This shift of focus from individual to collective interests does more than promote teamwork. It also raises followers' level of moral development. Individuals whose perspective is on others rather than the self have high moral reasoning and perspective-taking capacities. Leaders like Gandhi or Paterno who focus the attention of followers on the cause rather than the leader are *idealized* rather than *idolized*. If the focus is mainly on the leader, a cult of personality is a real and dangerous possibility. But if the focus is on the team, vision, or mission, leaders are seen as servant leaders who display idealized influence. It's important for you to highlight the importance of teamwork to your followers so that they will identify with you as a worthy role model (see Figure 3.5). What can you talk about to foster teamwork in your organization?

Figure 3.5   All for one and one for all. Idealized leaders promote solidarity and teamwork with their followers, who look to them as role models.

Champion Exciting New Possibilities That Can Be Achieved Through Teamwork

Once you've established the importance of teamwork in conversations with followers, you need to get them excited about synergies that can emerge from teamwork. *Synergy* is defined as a process in which two or more entities acting together create an effect greater than any outcome resulting from the separate effects of the individual entities. For example, John can recall his first year after completing his doctoral degree. This was the year he came into his new job with strong training in leadership theory and research methods. Also new in her position at the time was Ronnie Godshalk, currently of the University of South Carolina at Beaufort. Ronnie brought with her a background in career management and mentoring. As they discussed their research interests, they found that Ronnie's knowledge of mentoring was a perfect complement to John's knowledge of transformational leadership, with its focus on development, role modeling (idealized influence), and coaching and mentoring (individualized consideration). Their unique knowledge bases and skills synergized into a productive relationship that has generated a solid stream of research exploring the intersection of leadership and mentoring.[11] Neither of them could have achieved alone what they achieved together.

Pointing out the potential for your followers to collaborate and attain such synergies builds your image as an idealized leader. Oftentimes, we have found that one of the most important reasons that a work group fails is that members don't recognize potential benefits of working together. Similarly, when your followers don't recognize you as someone who is instrumental in achieving success, you are not likely to win their support and willingness to collaborate. By explaining the needs and benefits of interdependence among followers, you will be perceived by your followers as a leader with high perspective-taking capacity associated with high levels of moral development. And that's the essence of idealized influence.

Idealized Influence Attributes: Definition and Examples

When your followers see you displaying these idealized influence behaviors, they are likely to attribute certain positive characteristics to you. Because of your idealized behaviors, your followers will reflect charisma back at you. That's because when you display idealized behaviors, you are a shining star in the eyes of your followers. They perceive you as a glowing role model, akin to a gem. The more they see your idealized leadership brilliance, the more they will polish your shine and admire your glimmer. Because followers naturally recognize and appreciate beauty and excellence, and leadership is a process of mutual influence, they ascribe attributes of idealized influence to you. *Idealized influence attributes* are positive personal characteristics of the leader that are socially constructed in leader–follower relationships. The range of these attributes is wide and varied. They occur across many leadership contexts, such as in the case of Katharine Graham (see Table 3.2).

Katharine Graham benefitted from the attributes of idealized leadership that her followers ascribed to her. So can you. Let's now examine five essential attributes of idealized leaders.

Instill Pride in Others for Being Associated With You

Why are so many sports fans extremely proud of their teams during winning seasons? The answer is that people like being associated with winners. It makes them feel good about themselves because they are seen by others in a positive light. Their team's success becomes their own success. Ask any fan of the Green Bay Packers during the Lombardi years or those of the Pittsburgh Steelers in more recent years, and they're sure to agree.

Table 3.2 Leader Profile: Katharine Graham

Idealized leaders set examples for others to follow. The example Katharine Graham set for publication owners, journalists, and all aspiring leaders is one of integrity, advancing the truth, and promoting workplace diversity.

Graham was born into a life of privilege, attending Vassar College and the University of Chicago, and going on to work for her father, who had purchased *The Washington Post*. Later she married Philip Graham, who went on to lead the newspaper company out of its financial troubles. From the late 1940s until 1963, Katherine left her job at the newspaper to raise a family until her husband's tragic suicide in 1963. It was at that time that Graham stepped into her husband's role and assumed the helm at the *Post*.

Graham is most famous for her decision to do the right thing by publishing the Pentagon Papers in 1971, as well as a series of articles by reporters Bob Woodward and Carl Bernstein. These publications exposed President Nixon's and his cabinet's involvement in the Watergate scandal, which eventually led to Nixon's resignation in the face of his likely impeachment. Graham also championed diversity within the *Post* by hiring more African American and female journalists.

Graham's high level of moral principles and authentic behaviors make her an excellent example of an idealized leader. In a 2001 article on the life and death of Katharine Graham, journalist Jessica Reaves of *Time* magazine wrote, "I never met Graham, was never, to my knowledge, anyway, in the same room with her. But like those who read her autobiography and followed the path of her career, I felt as if I knew her. Today, I feel profoundly sorry that I never will." Reaves's words illustrate what is meant by the attribution of idealized influence by followers to transformational leaders.

Source: Felsenthal, C. (1993). *Power, privilege, and the Post: The Katharine Graham story.* New York: Putnam; Graham, K. (1997). Personal history. New York: Knopf; and Retrieved February 22, 2008, from http://www.time.com/time/nation/article/0,8599, 167941,00.html.

If you are a top performer, chances are your associates will want to learn about your winning ways. They'll respect you for what you've accomplished and envy your success. They also may admire you for what you stand for as a person, as well as the tough stands you've taken during difficult times. They might like you for the values you demonstrate by your behavior. For example, we have always admired our mentor Bruce Avolio, currently of the University of Washington. Bruce demonstrated his love of learning through his strong work ethic and intellectually stimulating behaviors that challenged his PhD students'

Figure 3.6 Pride in the name of love. These team members are proud of the blueprints they created together and their team's excellence.

ways of thinking about leadership. Being associated with Bruce and all the other fine colleagues at the Center of Leadership Studies at the State University of New York at Binghamton has given us an immense amount of pride because of their positive values and achievements in cutting-edge research and training. As shown in Figure 3.6, pride is a powerful motivator for followers because it propels them to the same levels of excellence as their high-performing role models. If you want your followers to feel that same way about you, start thinking about what you can or should do to make your followers develop a sense of pride in being associated with you as a leader.

Go Beyond Self-Interests for the Good of Others

Peter accepted a challenging role as head of an academic department in a private university during a very difficult time. He put aside his research agenda for over two years to serve the faculty. He used a transparent and principle-centered approach to leading while dealing with the many challenges of a demanding faculty and administration and fierce competition from other schools. He led by following a set of virtues and principles outlined in Table 3.3. Peter often was the first to enter the office in the morning and the last to leave. Because of the grueling hours and nature of his leadership position, he was forced to forgo attending daily Mass, an experience he loved sharing with his wife for many years. These and other personal sacrifices did not go unnoticed by others as they attributed idealized influence to Peter. As a result, the vast majority of faculty and staff considered Peter to be the greatest department head in its history.

Table 3.3 Leadership Principles of Auxiliary Bishop Filipe J. Estevez

Bishop Filipe J. Estevez is truly a global transformational leader. Prior to assuming his current leadership role in the Archdiocese of Miami, Estevez came to the United States from Cuba, and is fluent in four languages. His impressive education includes a doctorate in sacred theology from Pontifical Gregorian University in Rome, Italy. He has served the Catholic Church in both Honduras and the United States in roles ranging from pastor to campus minister at Florida International University, and from seminary faculty member to the dean of spiritual formation at St. Vincent de Paul Regional Seminary, Boynton Beach, Florida.

Based on his extensive leadership experience, in 1984 he developed a set of 10 practical leadership principles that illustrate idealized influence and other aspects of transformational leadership:

1. People are more effective when they do what they can do best—discover *talents*, affirm talents, challenge talents.

2. Each one is part of a *team*, a body—a team is more effective than the individual—that seeks to promote a collaborative stand from each one of the team.

3. *Responsibility*. Be alert to respond well, as soon as possible and as far as possible to meet the need in its own terms.

4. *Clarity of direction*. Be sure to always have a vision and a plan of action—to know where the group is going. A sensitive plan is in touch with the history of the group and, above all, with the unique circumstances of the group.

5. Talk the language of *deeds*. Words fade away, but people esteem and respect you because of your deeds.

6. *Modesty*. The poor of the world are too many for seeking expensive, luxurious ways—modesty, sobriety, and simplicity at all times.

7. Seek the *involvement* of others. Delegate and share responsibilities as much as possible; then trust the persons involved. Praise their accomplishments publicly.

8. Seek *information*. It is indispensable for good decision making. Encourage people to make decisions, but hold them accountable to share information about what they are doing.

9. Value the *permanent education* of each person—the improvement of skills and acquisition of new methods and ways. Allow time for this!

10. Offer all your accomplishments to *the Lord*. Ask Him to purify your intentions so that His will may be done in all things at all times, and to make up for what our abilities may lack.

Source: Estevez, F. J. (2008). A vision of management and leadership (personal communication); and retrieved February 22, 2008, from http://www.miamiarchdiocese.org/ip.asp?op= A101010.

Idealized leaders such as Peter are seen as selfless servants to followers. Their followers perceive them as putting others' interests ahead of their own interests. Because of these idealized influence behaviors and perceptions, they are seen by others as possessing altruistic (i.e., other-oriented) goals as opposed to egoistic (i.e., self-centered) goals. Social psychologist C. D. Batson defined altruism and egoism in terms of goals. According to Batson, if the ultimate goal is to increase another's welfare, then the motivation is *altruistic* (even if the helper benefits in the process). If the ultimate goal is to increase one's own welfare (even if the one being helped benefits), the motivation is *egoistic*.[12] When followers see you as helping them achieve their goals, your behavior reflects the notion of altruism, as shown in Figure 3.7.

Altruism is a core behavior discussed in research on organizational citizenship behavior (OCB). This discretionary behavior is not part of one's formal job requirements, but promotes the effective functioning of organizations.[13]

Figure 3.7   Distant leader … only a click away. In the age of the Internet, it is important for leaders to take time out of their busy schedules to connect with their followers.

Research indicates a positive relationship between OCB and performance for leaders and their organizational units.[14] Whether you spend time being altruistic with your followers, promote interpersonal harmony between followers, or are conscientious about your role as leader, your followers will see you as a more positive role model. As a result, followers wish to develop an intimate association with you and will attribute idealized influence to you. Therefore, one important question you need to answer is: What sacrifices can you make for the betterment of your followers and organization?

Act in Ways That Build Others' Respect

Transformational leaders gain attributions of idealized influence from their followers the old-fashioned way: They earn it. They earn it by behaving in ways that reflect virtues and character strengths that are perceived as such by their followers.[15] Andee realized this when she accepted the role of development officer at a small nonprofit organization. Her first days on the job were quite challenging given a small group of needy and contentious direct reports. This demanding group introduced conflict into Andee's department and sought to undermine her authority in the eyes of the other staff members. Andee was initially upset by their escapades and quickly became disheartened by their motives. Andee knew she had to confront their dysfunctional behavior and "nip it the bud." How could she send a strong message without alienating all of her new staff?

Andee considered her conflict with this group as an opportunity to strengthen interpersonal relationships with them. She spent time in private meetings with each malcontent, listening to their opinions and ideas, and learning about how they best could serve her department. She framed the conflict as one of ideas or approaches, not of people. By keeping the conflict impersonal, Andee was able to present rational arguments that made sense to the large majority of her staff. She was not condescending and did not show contempt for those who threatened her by using sarcastic or abusive language. She did not shout or use emotional displays. Instead, she outwitted her challengers on a rational basis with calm and lucid reasoning supported by timeless virtues of wisdom, integrity, and justice. As a result, Andee was able to manage this initial challenge constructively and build her direct reports' respect for her.[16] A key challenge for many newly appointed leaders is how to go about building trust and gaining respect from their followers, as Andee did.

Display a Sense of Power and Confidence

One of the things that people most appreciated in Peter's leadership was his strong advocacy for the faculty. Rather than acting as a "leader on a leash" held by top administrators, Peter was a champion and spokesperson for his group. He championed the best interests of his faculty, while also seeking to cooperate to achieve broader university goals and policies. He was willing to stand up for them when they needed his support on important issues, such as faculty hiring, market equity in salaries, and funding for research. He didn't back down in the face of intimidating threats from individuals who possessed greater position power than he held. Peter made himself visible on important issues in a way that was consistent with leadership advice once given by civil rights activist and politician Jesse Jackson: "Leadership cannot just go along to get along.... Leadership must meet the moral challenge of the day." Peter's ability to meet his challenges was based on strong convictions in the moral justification of his actions and his strong faith. And that's a source of power and confidence that can move mountains.

Please do not confuse a sense of power and confidence with abuse of power, cockiness, or arrogant overconfidence. You must be careful to hold back on temptations to use your power in ways that are self-serving and dismissive of viewpoints of your followers and associates. Therefore, your ultimate leadership challenge is to be able to exercise influence over people around you even if you don't have any leverage, such as your title and authority. Here's a reality check for you: Do you believe that you can influence your subordinates when they no longer work for you?

As shown in Figure 3.8, displaying a quiet confidence can go a long way to avoid the pitfalls of an air of superiority. Remember that it takes many years

Figure 3.8 You can always count on me. This idealized leader is never too busy to offer guidance in a confident and friendly manner.

to gain the trust and respect of followers and associates. But it only takes a few minutes to destroy the idealized influence that you have built through your history of interactions with your followers. Next time you see a leader in your organization who displays a sense of power and confidence that benefits others, thank her for being a fine example of idealized influence, and ask her how she does this. Then reflect on how you too can gain such attributions of idealized influence.

Reassure Others That Obstacles Will Be Overcome

Our personal and professional lives present us with many challenges that can bring us down. It's nice to have friends and colleagues who can give us support and encouragement during these tough times. People like to surround themselves with people who are happy and positive. Their encouragement serves to lift our spirits and give us hope. French military and political leader Napoleon Bonaparte once said, "Leaders are dealers in hope." Jesse Jackson challenged his followers with the mantra "Keep hope alive!" And to many people, Barack Obama represents the great hope of a brighter future for the world. Followers look to their leader to make sense out of crises or challenges that they are struggling to overcome. It's the leader's job to explain why things are so, why the status quo is unacceptable, and what followers must do to overcome their struggle and prosper in the future. Transformational leaders are able to present an exciting and compelling vision of change that boosts followers' collective confidence that they can bring about positive change. Their positive words and "can do" attitude make them admired role models in their followers' eyes.

This form of reassurance worked well when Joseph, a local entrepreneur, was discouraged by numerous rejections on funding requests from venture capitalists. The stream of negative reactions on his idea for a new seafood restaurant made Joseph feel like throwing in the towel. As luck had it, Joseph decided to give it one more try. He retooled his idea after enrolling in a university course on creativity and new ventures. Motivated by inspiring and encouraging conversations with his professor, Joseph developed an idea for a family-oriented restaurant based on the *Forrest Gump* movie.[17] The idea for a theme-based restaurant tickled the fancy of a group of Baby Boomer venture capitalists. Joseph is now on his way to achieving his dream thanks to the positive encouragement of his optimistic professor. This example goes to show that hope and idealized influence "go together like peas and carrots." What challenges facing your followers provide you with opportunities to employ the power of positive thinking?

Thinking About Idealized Influence

Now that you've been introduced to the concept of idealized influence, we'd like you to start thinking deeply about what implications this concept has for two important leadership issues: close and distant leadership, and impression management. These are two issues that you are likely to confront in today's challenging leadership situations.

Close and Distant Leadership

As a member of an organization, you are part of an organizational hierarchy or chain of command. In any hierarchy, organizational members have both distant leaders and close leaders. For example, you report to your boss, and both you and your boss are subordinate to the CEO or top leader of your organization. In this case, your close leader would be your boss and your distant leader would be your CEO.

Take a few minutes to reflect upon your distant leader (e.g., CEO). What do you know about him or her? How do you get that knowledge? How much do you really know? How does what you know form your attitude toward him or her? Do you feel, behave, and perform positively in your current position based on your attitude toward him or her? Is there any difference between his or her public image and private life? Does he or she behave differently to his or her close and distant followers? Now answer these questions as they pertain to your close leader (e.g., boss). Did you notice any differences in your responses?

Once you have answered these questions, you can recognize the importance of idealized influence in both close and distant leader–follower relationships. The role of idealized influence is very important in your close leader–follower relationships because followers see their leader as a role model. Because they see the leader more frequently, they are more likely to witness the leader's quirks, weaknesses, and vices that are part of being human. As the saying goes, "No man is a hero to his valet." Therefore, as a close leader, you need to pay careful attention to what you say and what you do when interacting with your close followers. Demonstrating idealized influence can help you project an image of virtue and build a positive image with those who see you up close and personal.

When it comes to distant leader–follower relationships, you have more leeway because distant followers do not have the chance to see you as often as close followers. Distant leaders often communicate via media that can mask their inadequacies with carefully constructed self-presentations, such as email, texting, Web sites, or video conferences. Nevertheless, in distant leadership roles, it is important for you to build a positive image of favorable impressions with

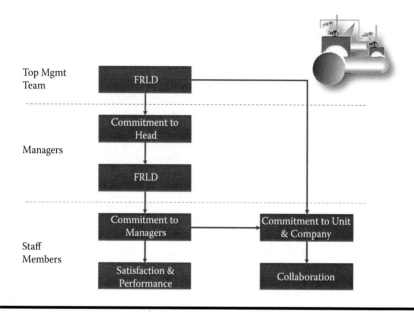

Figure 3.9   It starts at the top. To maximize the effects of FRLD, training must be championed by senior leaders because their behavior directly and indirectly affects followers through interactions and the organization's culture.

followers. That's because your words and actions are perceived by followers as part of the organizational values that you should aspire to portray in your leadership behavior. So in effect, your words and actions can bypass organizational hierarchies to directly influence what followers say and do through your idealized influence. It's also important to realize that your words and actions can cascade down the organizational hierarchy to create either a positive or negative organizational climate (see Figure 3.9). In other words, distant leaders who are top executives in an organization need to exert their influence through organizational culture, values, and norms. Therefore, your role modeling of idealized leader behavior is critical to the type of environment you create in your leadership role.[18]

Impression Management, Self-Construals, and Self-Presentation

Close and distant leadership situations highlight the importance of impression management in gaining attributions of idealized influence from followers. *Impression management* describes your ability to control the impressions others form of you. It involves your ability to help construct a certain image you want to project to your followers. This leadership tactic is commonly seen in political races such as the 2008 U.S. presidential campaign. Hillary Clinton presented herself as the experienced candidate who could provide solutions to the nation's domestic and foreign policy problems. Vietnam War veteran John McCain presented himself as the tough, no-nonsense experienced candidate who could bridge both conservative and liberal factions and stand up against threats to national security. In contrast, the charismatic Barack Obama presented himself as the "candidate of change," who could provide "change that we can believe in." Voters embraced Obama's presentation, and he was elected 44th president of the United States.

Desired Identity Images

Like these politicians, transformational leaders desire to project a certain image to their followers. These images range from being seen as trustworthy and credible to innovative and unique. Being seen as morally worthy of one's leadership position, attractive and held in esteem by others, and powerful are also desired identity images associated with transformational leaders.[19]

Projecting an image of trustworthiness and credibility is critical in building idealized influence because your ability to role model depends on your integrity as perceived by others. Being innovative and unique allows you to stand apart from others and be seen as an extraordinary leader, such as Andrea Jung of Avon and Indra Nooyi of PepsiCo. Because idealized influence involves displaying high standards of ethical performance and perspective taking, being seen as morally worthy can only add to the attributions of idealized influence reflected on you by your followers. If followers find you attractive and hold you in high esteem because of your accomplishments or character, they are likely to view you as a role model. Projecting an image of power and confidence makes followers feel more confident themselves and can serve to reinforce your attributions of idealized influence. Therefore, it is important for you to develop a very specific and concrete plan to create the type of personal image you'd like to project consistently. It will help you work to create these positive images in the eyes of your followers. What images do you desire to project to your followers?

Hoped-for Possible Selves Versus Actual Selves and Impression Management Tactics

These desired images come from your self-concept.[20] The image of who you are and what you stand for are part of your *self-concept*. Your self-concept is shaped through the social interactions you have with others throughout your life. There are aspects of your self-concept that you hope for, or wish that you should achieve. There are also aspects of your self-concept that you have actually achieved. When there is a gap between what you hope to become and what you really are, you are motivated to adjust your words and deeds so that there will be consistency between your thoughts, words, and deeds. Achieving this consistency involves demonstrating certain impression management tactics.

One such tactic is called *exemplification*, which involves role modeling positive organizational values and cultural virtues as a way to exercise influence over followers. Leaders who display this tactic are likely to gain attributions of idealized influence from their followers. Another positive impression management tactic is *ingratiation*, which involves making positive statements about another individual in order to "butter up" or "brown nose" him. This tactic may or may not be authentic, but research has consistently found that ingratiation is effective in influencing the target of your comments to like you, as shown in Figure 3.10.

Other impression management tactics are less positive in their goals. *Self-promotion* is a tactic that points out one's own accomplishments with the goal

Figure 3.10 Games people play. Ingratiation is an impression management tactic that may or may not be sincere. Be careful of leaders bearing gifts or offering flattery. What do they want in return?

of advancing one's career or self-interests. Former Hewlett-Packard CEO Carly Fiorina has been faulted for engaging in self-promotion at the expense of her leadership duties during her tenure at a large information technology company.[21] While self-promotion seeks to create an image of competence, *supplication* is a tactic that seeks to elicit sympathy from others because of a suggested weakness, misfortune, or inability to perform. Supplication is aimed at gaining the help of others. However, it is sometimes masked as a form of ingratiation, such as when Eleanor says to Erica, "You do such a great job with the budget analyses … much better than me. I'd really appreciate it if you would do them for me this quarter." These examples show that the ability to achieve your hoped-for possible selves by changing your actual self can be achieved by using impression management tactics that are appropriate for your particular leadership situation.

Self-Monitoring

Your ability to choose which impression management tactic is best suited to help create the desired positive image depends on your personality. One personality trait that is helpful in determining this is called *self-monitoring*. Some individuals are better than others at monitoring and controlling their expressive behaviors that are appropriate for a given situation. These individuals are called high self-monitors. They are good actors and actresses. You can think of them as human chameleons that are particularly sensitive to social situations. They size up situations and the people in them to correctly identify the most appropriate way to behave. As in acting, they possess a variety of mental scripts on how to behave in certain situations. These skills allow them to gain a most favorable impression from others. Former U.S. presidents Ronald Reagan and Bill Clinton are examples of high self-monitors. So too are actress and social activist Angelina Jolie and talk show host Ellen DeGeneres.

In contrast, low self-monitors wear their hearts on their sleeves. Regardless of the situation, they tend to behave in ways that are consistent with their personal values, ideals, and beliefs. They are not out to impress others. Rather, they are more interested in being true to themselves (i.e., authentic). They aim for consistency between their thoughts, words, and deeds. Former U.S. president George W. Bush is an example of a low self-monitor, as is Condoleezza Rice.

So, what's the challenge here? The challenge is how to maintain the appropriate blend of active self-monitoring and be true to yourself at the same time. In other words, your ability to gain attributions of idealized influence from your followers requires a delicate balance of self-monitoring and authenticity. A degree of self-monitoring can be helpful in portraying a leadership style that is flexible and your willingness to adjust your behavior when circumstances are changing. However, if you are seen by others as demonstrating excessive self-monitoring, you may be perceived as an inconsistent "flip-flopper," or a spineless "go along to get along" type. Such perceptions can cause big damage to your authenticity and your ability to be true to yourself. This can make it very difficult to be true to your actual self and hoped-for possible self. What degree of self-monitoring do you display in your leadership? How effective are you in adapting to the requirements of the situation? How true are you to yourself?

Putting Idealized Influence Into Practice

So far, you have learned what it means to display idealized influence. You have also thought about the implications of idealized influence for yourself, your followers, and your organization. You are now ready to identify action steps for putting idealized influence to work in your leadership system. Because every leadership system is different, it is up to you to determine how to best display idealized influence in your organization. This section presents a few suggestions that you may find useful in exemplifying idealized influence and building your full leadership potential.

Display the Behaviors Described in This Chapter

Put the idealized influence behaviors into practice at your job and in your home. When you demonstrate these behaviors at work, you will see the positive effects they can have on your followers' satisfaction and performance. When you display them at home with your family, you will come to understand that parenting may be the noblest form of leadership. That's the conclusion that Jay Wischum came to realize as he applied idealized leadership behaviors to encourage his daughter Erinn to study leadership as well. Jay served as a role model of love of learning, an important character strength to which Erinn aspired. Before long, both Jay and Erinn were enrolled in Penn State's MLD program. It was a unique and pleasant experience to have both father and daughter enrolled in John's research methods course. Because of Jay's exemplary role modeling, Erinn took on this challenging course and contributed to the intellectually stimulating environment that elevated students' thinking from the master's level to the PhD student level. Talk about performance beyond expectations! Their intelligence, enthusiasm, and drive never *cease* to amaze us.

Identify and Leverage Your Strengths and Those of Others

To be an idealized leader requires an understanding of your professional and character strengths. It requires that you appreciate your followers' strengths as well. You can achieve both of these goals by administering two reliable and valid surveys. Gallup's StrengthsFinder 2.0 survey identifies individuals' top talents that make them stand out from others. For more information, you are encouraged to visit their Web site (https://www.strengthsfinder.com/). Another valuable survey is based upon 24 character strengths that reflect the absolute best in humanity and transformational leadership. You can assess your character strengths using this framework at http://www.viastrengths.org/. Many of John's MLD students and their associates have taken these surveys. As a result of administering these surveys, they claim to possess a greater self-awareness of their strengths. They now have a more clear understanding of what they stand for, where they are strong, and where they need further development. This knowledge has helped them present themselves as idealized leaders in a more authentic manner. Remember, your leadership development journey should start from finding out what you don't know and what you need to know.

Improve Your Perspective-Taking Capacity

When you shift your perspective from a self-centered to an other-oriented focus, you make decisions that are in the best interest of your group. This selfless approach to leadership builds attributions of idealized influence. You can enhance your perspective-taking capacity by solving ethical dilemmas presented in corporate ethics training classes, courses on ethics in universities, or those embedded in tests of moral reasoning ability. One such test is James Rest's "Test of Defining Issues."[22] By taking this test, you can get a baseline measure on your perspective-taking capacity or level of moral reasoning. Do you reason at the preconventional level based on avoiding punishments or seeking rewards? Do you reason at the conventional level based on laws and conforming to group norms? Or do you reason at the postconventional level based on universal principles that sustain fairness, justice, and care in social systems? Once you gain an awareness of how you reason, you can work to broaden your perspective by immersing yourself in situations that take you out of your comfort zone. These experiences can make you question your basic assumptions about life and broaden your perspective.

Work on Your Self-Awareness

Understanding your self-concept and the image you desire to project to your followers requires a heightened degree of self-awareness. There are private and public aspects of self-awareness. Private self-awareness involves your understanding of your personal values, beliefs, and attitudes. Public self-awareness involves your understanding of how other people see you in your leadership role and requires a degree of self-monitoring, discussed above. You can enhance your private self-awareness by clarifying your purpose in life by writing a personal mission statement

(see Chapter 2), ranking your most important values, and ascertaining your character strengths. You can enhance your public self-awareness by participating in a
360-degree feedback assessment. (We assume that you have already or soon will
administer the Multifactor Leadership Questionnaire [MLQ]. Hint. Hint.)

This two-pronged approach to improving self-awareness is something that
Patricia Bonner, a high school administrator, found to be very effective. Prior
to undergoing this process, Patricia complained about never really understanding the real substance of her leadership. And her associates never understood
what she stood for. After examining her private and public self-awareness levels,
Patricia became better aware of her self-identity. As a result, she was better able
to present the leadership image she desired to share with others—an image of
care, concern, and quiet confidence.

Gauging Your Leadership Self-Awareness

An effective way of assessing your level of self-awareness as a leader involves
determining your level of self-other rating agreement. When you administer the
MLQ, you provide self-ratings of your FRLD behaviors. Your supervisors, peers,
subordinates, and others (e.g., customers, clients) also rate you on these leadership behaviors. These multiple sources of data allow you to determine the level
of agreement between your self-ratings and your superior's, peers', subordinates',
and others' ratings. In other words, this determines how you see yourself as a
leader versus how others see you. A comparison of self-ratings and the specific
other rating source of interest (e.g., subordinates) is made to classify you into one
of four categories:

- *Overestimators*, those who produce self-ratings that are significantly higher
  than others' ratings of leadership behavior
- *Underestimators*, those who produce self-ratings that are significantly lower
  than others' ratings of leadership behavior
- *In agreement/good*, those who produce self-ratings that are similar to others
  ratings of leadership behavior, when others' ratings are above the average
  of MLQ norms
- *In agreement/poor*, those who produce self-ratings that are similar to others
  ratings of leadership behavior, when others' ratings are below the average
  of MLQ norms[23]

Leaders categorized as overestimators and underestimators lack self-
awareness. Those who are in agreement/good or in agreement/poor are self-
aware, but the former is aware of her good performance while the latter
knows that she lacks the ability to display a specific leadership style. Table 3.4

Table 3.4   Attributes of Leaders Who Are Aware or Unaware of Their Transformational Behavior

	Self-Aware (In Agreement/ Good) Leaders	*Underestimator Leaders*	*Overestimator Leaders*
Personal characteristics	Emotionally intelligent	Lack self-confidence	Lack emotional intelligence
	Healthy self-concept	May be too hard on themselves; believe in continuous personal improvement	Hostile and belligerent toward others; easily angered by others
	Healthy level of public self-consciousness	Least publicly self-conscious	Publicly self-conscious
	Possess strong pro-social purpose in life	Lack strong purpose in life	Possess self-centered purpose in life
	Positive attitude	Pleasant to be around	Negative attitude
	Trusted	Most trusted	Least trusted
	Most trusting	Somewhat trusting	Untrusting/suspicious
	Committed to organization	Committed to organization	Least committed to organization
Behaviors	Adapt their behavior based on feedback	Raise self-evaluations when feedback is given	Ignore feedback from others

(continued)

Table 3.4   Attributes of Leaders Who Are Aware or Unaware of Their Transformational Behavior (Continued)

	Self-Aware (In Agreement/ Good) Leaders	Underestimator Leaders	Overestimator Leaders
Behaviors	Exemplify positive behaviors	Exemplify positive behaviors	Intimidate followers
	Effective rational persuaders	Very effective rational persuaders	Poor rational persuaders
	Very inspirational	Inspirational	Lack inspiration
	Adept at exchange relationships	Adequate at exchange relationships	Poor at exchange relationships
	Good mentors	Most effective mentors	Poor mentors
	Make good job-related decisions	Make ineffective job-related decisions	Make less effective job-related decisions
Performance outcomes	Very good; most innovative	Mixed, but generally positive	Poor, but can improve if they really want to

Source: Sosik, J. J., Jung, D. I., Berson, Y., Dionne, S. D., & Jaussi, K. S. (2004). *The dream weavers: Strategy-focused leadership in technology-driven organizations* (p. 230). Charlotte, NC: Information Age Publishing. Reprinted with permission.

Table 3.5   FRLD Scholar Profile: Yair Berson

Yair Berson is currently an associate professor of educational leadership at the University of Haifa in Israel. As a doctoral student of Bruce Avolio and Bernard Bass, he was involved in an extensive study of the U.S. Army leaders. This study validates the Multifactor Leadership Questionnaire (MLQ) using large samples and predicts the performance of military units with the leadership, in particular transformational leadership, of the platoon leaders and commanders.

As indicated by Bass in several places (e.g., in an interview to Robert Hooijberg published in *The Leadership Quarterly*), Berson's personal contribution has been in advancing alternative ways of measuring FRLD styles in order to triangulate the MLQ with other, mostly qualitative accounts of these leadership styles. Berson's other work has focused on applying FRLD to executive levels, where albeit strong theoretical support, there has been little empirical evidence for the importance of these styles.

According to Berson, the FRLD model and the MLQ have stimulated extensive research and theory development. He points out that in almost every second issue of the top leadership journals, one can find research and theoretical work associated with FRLD or transformational leadership. Although scholars had considered charismatic leadership prior to Bass and Avolio's seminal work on the topic, there was little measurement, and hence limited application, in both theory and practice in the field of management. For these reasons, Berson feels that the most significant achievement of FRLD is the valid measurement of leadership behavior and attributions and the extensive research associated with the MLQ.

Berson has used FRLD in teaching and with faculty members to provide examples of leadership styles and their effects on organizations. In addition to evidence that comes from research, FRLD is highly appealing to students and allows firsthand demonstration of the effects of leadership on multiple constituents. Berson feels that FRLD's efficacy comes from the fact that it is both research based and attractive to students. Students can easily apply it to different work settings and contexts. For example, using an interview protocol that he developed with Bass and Avolio, Berson asks students to videotape interviews with executives, which they later show and interpret in class. Students can easily see many examples of FRLD behaviors of senior executives and their impact on employees in organizations.

summarizes research findings that profile leaders classified as in agreement/ good, overestimators, and underestimators. As you examine Table 3.4, think about the personal characteristics, behaviors, and performance outcomes associated with these profiles and their potential implications for you. Then be sure to work on exercise 2 below.

Learn About Becoming an Authentic Transformational Leader

Greater self-awareness and self-regulation are required to be true to yourself and others. These concepts are at the core of authentic leadership, which builds upon ideas in the FRLD model, as mentioned to us by our good friend and colleague Yair Berson (see Table 3.5). While it is beyond the scope of this book, the concept of authentic transformational leadership is a subject worthy of additional study. Numerous books, articles, Web sites, and workshops on authentic leadership are available to assist you in developing your ability to display idealized influence.[24] The idealized influence that comes from being true to yourself and others is a powerful force that can help you inspire others to work together to achieve extraordinary outcomes. Let's turn our attention to such inspirational behaviors that motivate followers to perform beyond expectations in the next chapter.

Summary Questions and Reflective Exercises

1. This exercise uses results of your Multifactor Leadership Questionnaire (MLQ) report to assess your level of idealized influence behavior and attributes. Compare your idealized influence behavior and attributes ratings with the research-validated benchmarks. How did your self-ratings, ratings from subordinates, ratings from peers, ratings from superiors, and ratings from others compare against the benchmarks? On which specific MLQ items (i.e., questions) did you score highest? Lowest? What can you do to improve on the items where you scored lowest?

2. This exercise also uses results of your MLQ report to assess your level of idealized influence behavior and attributes. Compare your self-ratings on *idealized influence behavior* with ratings provided by subordinates, peers, superiors, and others. Compute the difference score (d) as the difference between your self-rating score and the specific other rating source score of interest. If d is less than .5 and the other rating source score is less than 2.73 (use 2.93 for idealized attributes), then you are considered to

be *in agreement/poor*. If d is less than .5 and the other rating source score is greater than 2.73 (use 2.93 for idealized attributes), then you are considered to be *in agreement/good*. If d is equal to or greater than .5 and the self-rating score is greater than the other rating score, then you are an *overestimator* on this dimension. If d is equal to or greater than .5 and the self-rating score is less than the other rating score, then you are an *underestimator* on this dimension. Consider the category under which you fall in terms of idealized influence behavior. What are the implications of this categorization for you? Are there any things you can do to improve in this area? Repeat this exercise for idealized influence attributes.

3. Visit http://www.viastrengths.org/ and take the Values in Action survey. What are your top five character strengths as described by the survey? How can you put these character strengths into practice through idealized influence behaviors? What specific idealized behaviors can reflect your character strengths in a way that allows you to be true to yourself and others?

4. Identify an individual in your organization or family whom you would consider a follower who needs attention. This may be a person who lacks self-confidence, self-efficacy, purpose in life, trust, or commitment. This person might be going through a personal or professional crisis. Alternatively, it might be someone who has great leadership potential but needs some direction and encouragement. Once you have identified this person, think about one or more of the behaviors of idealized influence to address the issue you identify. Then, compose and send an email to this person. The email should demonstrate your idealized leadership. Please be careful to compose your email in a way that makes the follower want to identify with you as an idealized leader.

5. Spend time coaching and mentoring the person you identified in exercise 4 once you have established a base level of trust. What expertise and knowledge can you share with this person? What can you learn from this person? Think about the outcome of your intervention and what you can do better in future interactions with him or her.

6. At your next department meeting, set some time aside to talk about your organization's core values. Highlight your personal values that are consistent with your organization's values. Ask your followers and associates what they can do to reflect those values in their behavior at work or in the organizational initiatives you are leading.

7. Come into work one hour early or stay late for one more hour one day this week. Spend this time helping one of your followers or associates who is

struggling with an assignment. This exercise demonstrates your willingness to make personal sacrifices for the good of the group.

8. During your next department meeting, spend some time reiterating your organizational mission. Explain to your staff how each of their jobs contributes to the mission. Be sure to highlight the interdependencies between staff members, the need for collaboration, and the way that you will reward teamwork. Take note of your staff's reaction to your emphasis on collective action and away from individual efforts.

9. Meet with four of your most trusted and sincere colleagues. Ask them to talk about what they find most appealing about your leadership. Probe deeper with questions about how they perceive your leadership behavior, the values that your behaviors reflect, and how they view your personality. Then ask them to identify one or two areas in which you can improve. Reflect upon their observations and work to accentuate the positive and eliminate the negative.

10. Before you turn in at night, spend five minutes reflecting on the leadership behavior that you displayed during the day. What did you do well? Where did you fall short of your expectations of being an idealized leader? What can you do to improve? Make a mental note of your intentions for the next day. Visualize opportunities to exert leadership over the next few days and think about how you can display idealized influence in these situations.

Notes

1. Meindl, J. R., Ehrlich, S. B., & Dukerich, J. M. (1985). The romance of leadership. *Administrative Science Quarterly, 30*, 78–102.
2. A variety of books have been written about or by Jack Welch. Some of our favorites include Baum, S. H., & Conti, D. (2007). *What made Jack Welch Jack Welch: How ordinary people become extraordinary leaders.* New York: Crown Business; Drexler, K. M. (2007). *Icons of business: An encyclopedia of mavericks, movers, and shakers.* Westport, CT: Greenwood Press; Lowe, J. C. (2008). *Jack Welch speaks: Wisdom from the world's greatest business leader.* New York: Wiley; and Welch, J. (2006). *Winning—the answers: Confronting 74 of the toughest questions in business today.* New York: Collins.
3. Bartlett, C. A., & Wozny, M. (2000). *GE's two-decade transformation: Jack Welch's leadership (multimedia case).* Boston: Harvard Business School Press.
4. Gandhi, M. (1957). *An autobiography: The story of my experiments with truth.* Boston: Beacon; and Weber, T. (1999). Gandhi, deep ecology, peace research and Buddhist economics. *Journal of Peace Research, 36*, 349–361.
5. George, B. (2003). *Authentic leadership: Rediscovering the secrets to creating lasting value.* San Francisco: Jossey-Bass; and George, B., & Sims, P. (2007). *True north: Discover your authentic leadership.* San Francisco: Jossey-Bass.

6. De Cremer, D. (2006). Affective and motivational consequences of leader self-sacrifice: The moderating effect of autocratic leadership. *The Leadership Quarterly, 17*, 79–93; Greenleaf, R. K. (1977). *Servant leadership: A journey into the nature of legitimate power and greatness.* New York: Paulist; and Greenleaf, R. K. (2003). *The servant-leader within: A transformative path.* New York: Paulist.

7. Attenborough, R. (Producer/Director), & Briley, J. (Writer). (1982). *Gandhi* [Motion picture]. Hollywood, CA: Columbia Pictures.

8. Dungy, T., & Whitaker, N. (2008). *Quiet strength: The principles, practices & priorities of a winning life.* Carol Stream, IL: Tyndale House.

9. Fitzpatrick, F. (2005). *The lion in autumn: A season with Joe Paterno and Penn State football.* New York: Gotham Books; and http://www.psu.edu/ur/2000/luchinsky3.html. Retrieved July 18, 2007.

10. Diener, E. (1977). Deindividuation: Causes and consequences. *Social Behavior and Personality, 5*, 143–155.

11. Godshalk, V. M., & Sosik, J. J. (2007). Leadership and mentoring: Standing at the cross roads of theory, research and practice. In B. R. Ragins & K. E. Kram (Eds.), *The handbook of mentoring at work: Research, theory and practice* (pp. 149–178). Thousand Oaks, CA: Sage.

12. Batson, C. D. (1991). *The altruism question: Toward a social-psychological answer.* Hillsdale, NJ: Lawrence Erlbaum Associates; and Sosik, J. J., Jung, D. I., & Dinger, S. L. (2009). Values in authentic action: Examining the roots and rewards of altruistic leadership. *Group & Organization Management, 34*(41), 395–431.

13. Podsakoff, P. M., & MacKenzie, S. B. (1997). The impact of organizational citizenship behavior on organizational performance: A review and suggestions for future research. *Human Performance, 10*, 133–151.

14. Cameron, K. S., Bright, D., & Caza, A. 2004. Exploring the relationships between organizational virtuousness and performance. *The American Behavioral Scientist, 47*, 766–790; Podsakoff et al. (1997). As cited in Note 13; and Sosik et al. (2009), as cited in Note 12.

15. Sosik, J. J. (2006). *Leading with character: Stories of valor and virtue and the principles they teach.* Greenwich, CT: Information Age Publishing.

16. Bass, B. M., & Avolio, B. J. (1995). *Multifactor leadership questionnaire: Leader's notebook.* Palo Alto, CA: Mind Garden.

17. Zemeckis, R. (Director), Finerman, W., Tisch, S., Starkey, S., & Newirth, S. (Producers), & Roth, E. (Writer). (1994). *Forrest Gump* [Motion picture]. Hollywood, CA: Paramount Pictures.

18. Chun, J. U., Yammarino, F. J., Dionne, S. D., Sosik, J. J., & Moon, H. K. (In press). Influence processes across hierarchical levels: Multiple levels-of-management and multiple levels-of-analysis perspectives. *The Leadership Quarterly*; and Shamir, B. (1995). Social distance and charisma: Theoretical notes and an exploratory study. *The Leadership Quarterly, 6*, 19–47.

19. Gardner, W. L., & Avolio, B. J. (1998). The charismatic relationship: A dramaturgical perspective. *Academy of Management Review, 23*, 32–58.

20. Sosik, J. J., Avolio, B. J., & Jung, D. I. (2002). Beneath the mask: Examining the relationship of self-presentation attributes and impression management to charismatic leadership. *The Leadership Quarterly, 13*, 217–242.

21. Karlgaard, R. (2005, February 11). Carly Fiorina's seven deadly sins. *Wall Street Journal*, A10.
22. Rest, J., Narvaez, D., Bebeau, M., & Thoma, S. (1999). DIT-2: Devising and testing a new instrument of moral judgment. *Journal of Educational Psychology, 91*, 644–659.
23. Yammarino, F. J., & Atwater, L. E. (1997). Do managers see themselves as others see them? Implications for self-other agreement for human resource management. *Organizational Dynamics, 25*, 35–44.
24. Gardner, W. L., Avolio, B. J., Luthans, F., May, D. R., & Walumbwa, F. (2005). "Can you see the real me?" A self-based model of authentic leader and follower development. *The Leadership Quarterly, 16*, 343–372; George, B. (2003). *Authentic leadership: Rediscovering the secrets to creating lasting value.* San Francisco: Jossey-Bass; Retrieved February 19, 2008, from http://www.authenticleadership.com/. Retrieved February 19, 2008, from http://www.authenticleadershipinc.com/; and Retrieved February 19, 2008, from http://www.shambhalainstitute.org/institute/home.html.

Chapter 4

Inspirational Motivation
The Emotional Side of Transformational Leadership

To accomplish great things we must first dream, then visualize, then plan ... believe ... and act!

—Alfred A. Montapert

A few years ago during the first day of the Full Range Leadership Development (FRLD) course, a confident executive MBA student stood up and made a bold statement. He said, "John, I'm expecting nothing less from this class than a Saul of Tarsus transformation!"And John wouldn't have expected anything less challenging from Phillip O'Reilly, who, at the time, was a swashbuckling CEO of an entrepreneurial firm specializing in mergers and acquisitions. Phil's positive attitude, intelligence, and enthusiasm inspired many business associates and friends. His gregarious and charming personality added to his love for adventure in all aspects of his life. Phil would often take colleagues and friends scuba diving or on rides in his small-craft airplanes. His zest for life and risk-taking behavior were apparent whether he was talking to his employees about his Multifactor Leadership Questionnaire (MLQ) results or charting the course for his next business venture or airplane glider trip.

Today, Phillip O'Reilly is senior vice president of U.S. sales at Juniper Networks, a Sunnyvale, California, developer of networking technology. Prior to his current role, Phil spent five years as president of Solunet, a Melbourne, Florida, value-added reseller of hardware and support services for data communications firms. In his present role, Phil is inspiring international growth for Juniper and partnering with other organizations to provide more "green solutions" for the computer industry.[1] For example, Juniper is partnering with Solunet to introduce eco-friendly infrastructure change into corporate data centers. The network servers and transport media that provide Internet services can consume huge amounts of space and power for operations and cooling. The Solunet–Juniper partnership has designed a new hardware appliance that reduces power consumption by 67% and takes 85% less space. This efficient solution provides outstanding HVAC operations and shows a genuine concern for the environment. Like Phil O'Reilly's passion for airplanes, his visionary leadership for providing eco-friendly data infrastructures is boosting sales and profits to ever higher levels.

Airplane pilots, like O'Reilly, are responsible for leading their craft from point A to point B. But airplanes do not fly in a vacuum. Rather, they fly in turbulent environments that include unpredictable weather conditions, strong airstreams, and wind shears. So if a pilot simply aimed his plane for point B (see Figure 4.1) without accounting for drift from downwinds, his plane would veer off course to point B' and he would miss his target destination. That's why pilots often compensate for such downwinds by aiming for Point B", as shown in Figure 4.1.

Just as pilots need to make adjustments to reach their targeted destination, so too must leaders in order for their associates to achieve their vision. As Viktor

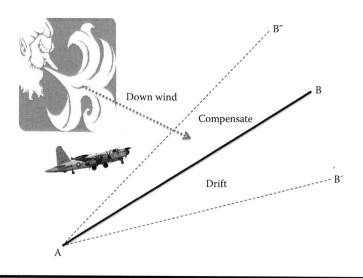

Figure 4.1 Charting the right course. Like airplane pilots, leaders must set their sights on the right path for their followers to take.

Frankl once said, "If we take man as he is, realistically, we make him worse due to drifts or detriments in him or his environment. However, if we take him as he should be, optimistically, we help him to become what he can be." If we apply these words of wisdom to leadership development, then leaders need to elevate their followers' expectations by inspiring them to work together toward a challenging and evocative vision. This requires leaders to aim for the ideal, seek virtue, and promote the greatness that lies dormant in followers who are capable of collaboration and professional development. In essence, this requires leaders to display inspirational motivation.

To better understand the notion of inspirational motivation, think of a time in your life that you were truly inspired by someone or something. Maybe you were inspired by how he overcame a significant challenge in his life. Maybe it was because of the courage he showed under tremendous pressure. Or perhaps it was his idea that resonated with you. Whatever it was, think about what it felt like to be truly inspired. Chances are that when you were inspired, you felt invigorated and energized. You felt enthusiastic and optimistic. You probably were filled with a sense of righteousness in your convictions that gave you a high level of confidence. That's because the word *inspire* comes from the Latin meaning "to breathe into." And when our bodies are refreshed with life-sustaining oxygen, we become energized in our thoughts, words, and deeds.

Transformational leaders trigger inspiration in followers. Inspiration involves three key concepts:

■ *Motivation*—Inspiration provides energy and direction that fuels the action of followers.
■ *Evocation*—You cannot force inspiration on someone through an act of will; instead, inspiration is evoked from within or through significant others (e.g., leaders) and their environment.
■ *Transcendence*—Inspiration moves followers through an appreciation of beauty and excellence that allows them to rise above ordinary preoccupations or limitations.[2]

These feelings and positive attitudes are commonly associated with visionary leaders such as Mark Zuckerberg of Facebook, Steve Jobs of Apple, and Richard Branson of Virgin. Each of these transformational leaders is visionary and confident. Since they see a brighter future that no one else sees, they openly challenge their followers by expressing their dissatisfaction with the status quo. But being discontented with the status quo is not enough for these leaders. They are also able to present a viable alternative to the status quo in a way that inspires others to work to achieve their vision. They reinforce their message of change through their language, which is filled with dynamic metaphors and colorful rhetoric (described below).

They also create unique ceremonies and rituals that symbolize their organization's purpose in working to achieve the vision. Such rituals include regularly scheduled "town meetings" that reiterate the company mission, vision, and values. Others include monthly birthday celebrations for staff, company picnics, sporting events, or award ceremonies that recognize employees for their key contributions for working toward the vision. These practices create magnetic imagery that inspires their followers and constituents to make the vision a reality.

This chapter shows you how to inspire your associates, teams, and organization to soar to new heights of success. By elevating expectations and boosting collective confidence through the power of teamwork, you can become an inspirational leader. Let's begin to learn about this process by considering the behaviors of inspirational motivation.

Inspirational Motivation: Definition and Examples

To inspire collective effort, hard work, and performance excellence like Mark Zuckerberg, Steve Jobs, and Richard Branson, you need to articulate your personal vision in a compelling way that energizes people around you. That's because *inspirational motivation* involves the energy, initiative, persistence, and vision that moves followers to achieve performance outcomes that exceed expectations and develops their leadership potential along the way. This high level of motivation comes from a message that gives meaning to what they aim to accomplish. It makes followers' work important to them because they see how their work contributes toward achieving the vision. Displaying inspirational motivation behaviors is a skill in which Richard Branson excels (see Table 4.1).

Like Branson, you need to demonstrate inspirational motivation behaviors to be seen as a transformational leader by your followers. Let's now examine five key transformational leadership behaviors that embody inspirational motivation.

Talk Optimistically About the Future

Barack Obama captured the imagination of voters during the 2008 U.S. presidential election campaign. Obama's messages highlighted hope for a better future and "change we can believe in." In the face of war, Obama advocated peace. In the face of despair, he believed there can be hope. In the face of politics that shut people out, tell them to settle, and divide them, Obama championed the belief that people can be one, reaching for what is possible.[3] These optimistic messages added substance to Obama's style, although some detractors claim that he lacks substance. According to his supporters, Obama's highly effective speaking skills are in part due to his sincere message of hope, positive change, and a brighter future for the country. In fact,

Table 4.1   Leader Profile: Richard Branson

How could a shy, academically underachieving child with dyslexia ever grow up to become a world-famous billionaire, entrepreneur, and adventurer? Ask Richard Branson, CEO of the Virgin Group, a holding company of over 360 organizations.

Branson is well known for his daring vision of creating complementary global businesses that cross over several industries and continents. For Branson, business opportunities are like buses: Another one is always coming. Starting in the mail-order record business, Branson dared to go where others did not and constantly adapted to the changing times and trends within the music business. His Virgin Records signed risky and unconventional musical acts, such as the Sex Pistols and Culture Club, which reaped large returns on investment. Branson then expanded his music empire by opening numerous mega-music stores in the United States and Europe. Building upon these successes, Branson entered the airline and aerospace, banking, and mobile phone industries, just to name a few of his enterprises.

Besides his many business ventures, Branson has also dabbled in humanitarian causes, world record sailing and ballooning attempts, television, film, and print ventures, and British politics as well. His vitality, optimism, and enthusiasm for life have inspired his associates and countless admirers to follow their own personal and professional dreams.

According to Branson, the secret to his success is perseverance, focus, determination, and pursuing only those things in life that are fun and challenging. The ability to dream and imagine possibilities that others dare not to has helped Branson to create and articulate several visions for successful businesses.

Branson's life teaches us to live our own life as one huge adventure, with an uplifting attitude that no challenge or risk is too big to take on. Branson's positive thoughts, stirring words, and unconventional behaviors give hope to aspiring entrepreneurs and leaders. Have the courage to overcome personal and professional challenges, dream big, talk confidently, and act boldly. That's the essence of inspirational motivation.

Source: Branson, R. (2007). *Losing my virginity: How I've survived, had fun, and made a fortune doing business my way.* New York: Three Rivers Press.

several political pundits and scholars have remarked that Obama's personal presence and oratory eloquence conjure up images of charisma not seen since Gandhi, Winston Churchill, Dr. Martin Luther King Jr., and John and Robert Kennedy. Voters embraced Obama's vision and persona, and they elected him president. The core messages of all of these leaders were infused with optimism.[4]

Figure 4.2 The power of positive speaking. Inspirational leaders talk optimistically and enthusiastically about what needs to be accomplished. They inspire followers to transcend difficulties through working hard and collective action.

By keeping the message positive and optimistic, transformational leaders motivate their followers through positive psychological states that are intrinsically motivating and satisfying. A message that satisfies intrinsically does not necessary depend upon any tangible outcome or success that followers will get to enjoy. Rather, the knowledge of working toward a noble goal is satisfaction in and of itself. In other words, the gift is in the giving. When people are in pursuit of any goal and what's driving them is internally focused, outcomes are likely to be more successful and effective. This is what academics call intrinsic motivation.

Positive psychological states, such as "being in the zone" or in "flow," generate several beneficial outcomes, such as increased persistence, creativity, and productivity. In addition, research has linked *positive psychological capital*, a related concept that includes hope, optimism, self-confidence, and resilience, to high levels of performance and satisfaction in several business contexts. These motivational forces encourage followers to work hard to overcome difficulties and crises. As depicted in Figure 4.2, such significant effort is often required to change the status quo and perform beyond expectations.[5]

Talk Enthusiastically About What Needs to Be Accomplished

Elaina held the position of chief coordinator of conference services at a large center city hotel. Her position required her to be a liaison with current and potential corporate customers. This was a very demanding, time-consuming, and emotionally laborious role to play. Despite her hectic and challenging schedule, Elaina always found time to get involved in important hotel initiatives such as diversity awareness and promotion of events. Those who knew and enjoyed working with Elaina were amazed by her seemingly eternal enthusiasm. She was always very excited about the work her group was performing. Her exuberance for the challenges her group faced energized the members of her group and created a positive attitude that they shared.

Elaina told us that her enthusiasm came from her difficult childhood. She was the product of a dysfunctional family and suffered as a victim of various types of abuse within her family. Instead of becoming bitter, she worked out any issues that stemmed from her upbringing. She was determined to hold a positive attitude no matter how bad her circumstances were. As if she were living on borrowed time, she resolved to live each day as if it were her last with a *vigorous love of life*, as depicted in Figure 4.3. She explained that when you love someone, you are willing to give everything. When you are willing to give everything, you give your all in an enthusiastic and energetic way.

However, there always seem to be people who attempt to extinguish the fire that fuels the enthusiasm of transformational leaders. How can transformational leaders maintain their enthusiasm in the face of difficult people and situations? Elaina answered this question for us by saying that she tries hard to let go of trying to control other people. She only has control over herself—her thoughts,

Figure 4.3   A zest for life. Inspirational leaders embrace all aspects of life and work with an enthusiastic level of vim and vigor that motivates followers to go the extra mile.

attitudes, and behaviors. She controls her attitude by continuously infusing it with enthusiasm. When Elaina's associates see her enthusiasm, they are inspired to also become enthusiastic about the things that need to be accomplished. Elaina's can-do attitude inspires rather than controls her followers. They rally around challenging work she presents as important and meaningful, rather than a task on a to-do list that needs to be checked off.

Articulate a Compelling Vision of the Future

As you read in Chapter 2, leadership is a dynamic system that evolves over time. As such, leaders who wish to inspire others must link the past with the present and future.[6] Barack Obama did this in his 2008 inaugural address, and when he modeled his cabinet after Abraham Lincoln's "team of rivals." Vladimir Putin fashioned his vision for Russia in an old-fashioned European sense infused with strong nationalism. When running for president, Hillary Clinton drew upon her earlier work as former First Lady to fight for the health care and well-being of children. Why do such leaders link the past, present, and future?

Fulton J. Sheen, philosopher, theologian, and seminal televangelist, once gave a fascinating talk with implications highlighting the importance of presenting a compelling vision of the future so that followers can understand their place in the larger picture. He began by talking about the notion of time being understood as the relationship between the past, present, and future.[7] Let's examine each element of time in Sheen's lecture to understand its relevance to inspirational leadership shown by many of today's top leaders.

What is the significance of *the past* for leadership? The past is important and should not be ignored. That's because the past is the source of traditions, history, customs, culture, or what organizational scholars call institutional memory. These aspects of the past give leaders and followers a sense of who they are and where they came from. Transformational leaders often remind followers of the great achievements in the past so that they can feel good about themselves and the rich tradition of which they are a part. We often see this in artifacts in collegiate and professional sporting arenas (e.g., the Los Angeles Coliseum), and U.S. military leadership training materials, such as those shown in Figure 4.4.

What is the significance of *the present* for leadership? The present is important because it reflects where leaders and followers are at this point in time. "The now" has its challenges and opportunities and particular circumstances. To make the most of the now, psychologists often advise people to live in the moment and seize the day. By making the most of the present, we are able to derive intrinsic satisfaction from where we are currently since our future is uncertain and the past is already gone. A challenging present is often needed for inspirational leaders to create and articulate their vision of a better future.

55th Brigade Combat Team

Command Philosophy

We will train, fight, and win as a team.

"Iron Soldiers"

During WWII 35 Pennsylvanians were awarded the Medal of Honor—that is more than any other state. One soldier from the 28th Division received our nation's highest military award during WWII. He was Technical Sergeant Francis J. Clark, a member of the 109th Infantry. From 12-17 Sep 1944 Sergeant Clark was a steady rock to the men he led in fighting along the Siegfried Line on Hill 515 known as "Purple Heart Hill". Along this battle ground of death, desolation, and hellfire Sergeant Clark moved with calmness and courage to reassure his men and provide them with ammo, water, medical aid, and direction. Even after he was wounded he refused to be evacuated. Although a squad leader, Sergeant Clark became the leader of two platoons and was the driving force in repelling an enemy counterattack on 17 September 1944.

Benjamin Franklin formed a militia in Philadelphia in 1747 in order to protect the colony of Pennsylvania from the threat of the Spanish and French military forces along the Delaware River. These citizen soldiers were the genesis of the Pennsylvania Army National Guard. In order to motivate and inspire these volunteers Franklin created the symbol of the rampant lion. The 55th Brigade crest portrays this rampant lion with a scimitar held in its upraised right paw and a shield held in its left paw symbolizing our determination to defend our nation against aggression as well as our willingness to live in peace.

On 14 July 1918 soldiers of the 55th Brigade's 109th Infantry fought heroically as part of the 28th Division's defense south of the Marne River in France. The soldiers fiercely repelled their German foe. So staunch was the Brigade's effort that General Pershing himself exclaimed, "They are Iron Men". With that said, the 28th Division became known and honored as the "Iron Division" due to the courageous fighting of the 55th Brigade's Iron Soldiers.

Figure 4.4 Brigadier General John Gronski's command philosophy. Notice the linking of values, vision, mission, and expected leadership behaviors.

55th Brigade Combat Team

In order to continue the 55th Brigade's outstanding tradition of service to our nation I provide these thoughts on mission, values, vision, and leadership. These ideas provide a point of departure so all soldiers of the 55th Brigade will have a hand in creating a vision we will all share.

John L. Gronski
COL, IN, PAARNG
Commanding

Mission

The 55th Brigade Combat Team will prepare for combat and provide military support to civilian authorities to achieve our country's national security and military objectives and provide for civil order.

"Leadership is the art of accomplishing more than the science of management says is possible"

Colin Powell

Vision

The 55th Brigade Combat Team will deploy in its entirety to conduct an operation or major exercise.

Core Values

- Loyalty – Be a soldier your buddies can count on. Stand behind your leaders and subordinates.

- Duty – Fulfill your obligations and do your job.

- Respect – Treat people as they should be treated.

- Selfless Service – Put the welfare of your unit and your subordinates before your own. Display a "mission first" attitude.

- Honor - Have pride. Do things to standard.

- Integrity – Be true to your values. Do the right thing even when no one is watching. Keep your word.

- Personal Courage – Stick up for what you believe in.

Brigade Commander's Leadership Philosophy

Lead by Example - Show uncompromising integrity and set the standard. Be where the action is. Share the load and hardships. Develop a spirit of teamwork & trust.

Create and Communicate a Shared Vision— Provide direction and inspire everyone to achieve the goal.

Competence—Work hard at being the best at your job and profession.

Coach—Be a trainer and mentor. Challenge & develop others by giving them responsibility & authority to act. The first duty of any leader is to develop more leaders.

Care — Care about your soldiers and their families. Provide challenging training and attend to administrative and personal issues. Ensure safety standards are met.

The fighting that occurred on 16-20 Dec. 1944 in the Ardennes displayed the courageous and tenacious spirit of the soldiers of the 109th Infantry and 28th Division. During these first days of the Battle of the Bulge the 28th Division held off 8 crack German Divisions and inflicted over 11,700 casualties. War correspondent Morley Cassidy called this action "one of the greatest feats ever performed in the history of the American Army".

Figure 4.4 (Continued)

What is the significance of *the future* for leadership? The past and present cannot be comprehended without an understanding of the future. Suppose you are traveling via train from Philadelphia to New York. At any point in time on your journey, the way you describe your travels is in terms of your final destination (e.g., "I'm in Trenton now en route to New York"). The same is true for leadership. The way you describe your leadership goal or destination is with a vision of the future. One reason that makes transformational leadership special and more effective than other leadership styles is that the vision transformational leaders develop is radically different from the status quo (i.e., the present).

For example, Hu Jintao, present-day leader of China, has created a vision for his nation that is unique, yet based on some fundamental Communist principles espoused by Chairman Mao. Jintao seeks a more harmonious society both within and the walls of China. He had adapted visions from earlier in China's history to meet his country's tremendous potential for growth and prosperity.[8] Another example is Pope John Paul II, who presented a vision of Poland transcending the ills of Communism. His vision included restoring traditional Polish values that had been taken away by the Communists. It also contained social, spiritual, and economic elements that improved upon the past.[9] In both cases, these leaders wanted their followers to embrace the future, while respecting the past.

However, some people reject the past and future and focus on getting the most out of the present. According to Sheen, they want to maximize their pleasure by intensifying the present through short-term rewards or "getting kicks." Their mentality is that the past is useless and the future is too uncertain. Only the present matters. We believe that this present-obsessed attitude is sadly too common today in many companies. This was best exemplified by the way Enron executives lived their corporate and personal lives, which was illustrated well in the documentary entitled *Enron: The Smartest Guys in the Room*.[10] The constant competition among Enron employees in the workplace to outperform each other was due to a survival of the fittest culture (a form of Social Darwinism) where the least effective employees are fired. The Enron philosophy was that there is no need to focus on the future since the present is so ecstatic, and the present is the only thing that matters. This phenomenon is intensified by corporate myopia on maximizing short-term profits and satisfying the analysts on Wall Street. This creates what Sheen likened to a rat race.

Unfortunately, the rat race notion of time distorts the real image of time. Time is not a meaningless race of vicious circles in which employees relentlessly chase dollars and compete with each other. Instead of being circular, time is a linear progression of days that add value to an individual's life through noble accomplishments and meaningful relationships. Some days add more value than others. However, there comes a point when the line is drawn and time ends for each of us. It's at that point that the daily values of our accomplishments and relationships are summed up and our contribution is assessed. So, time is more like our progression up a large hill with the ultimate goal of reaching the summit. And that summit is a compelling vision of the future for the leader and followers, a vision comprised of developing the self and others, building long-term relationships of loyalty and trust, and seeking truth and knowledge.

This metaphor begs the question: What makes for a compelling vision? The answer to this question is as complex as the many personalities that make up your organization and the circumstances that surround them. But one thing is certain: Visions are powerful motivational mechanisms that inspire followers to grow out of and improve upon the present. And compelling visions, such as that illustrated in Figure 4.4, have a few things in common. First, visions must be inspirational and contain shared values that are important to followers. For example, the values of innovation and collaboration have always been ideals that Steve Jobs has promoted at Apple. Second, visions need to be realizable. They can stretch followers out of their comfort zones, but they must be realistic and achievable. Third, the language describing visions must use superior imagery that touches followers' emotions. For example, Dr. Martin Luther King, Jr. did not say, "I have an idea." Rather, he said, "I have a dream." The word *dream* is more emotional and dramatic than the word *idea*. Fourth, the vision must be well articulated. It is one thing to draft a brilliant speech. It is another to have the ability to deliver it in a passionate and sincere way that moves people. We will discuss this topic in more detail below.

Provide an Exciting Image of What Is Essential to Consider

Inspiring your followers to work together toward a common vision is quite challenging. That's because they possess different personal agendas and strong egos. One way to find common ground among such followers is to focus on the content of the vision and make it evocative and appealing to followers. Richard Branson has effectively used this behavior over his career. Recently, Branson assembled a group of scientists and engineers to help achieve the vision of Virgin Galactic: to provide affordable suborbital space tourism for the first time in history.[11]

What an exciting and bold vision! Branson's vision for Virgin Galactic is thrilling because it demonstrates a revolutionary change in our perception of space travel. Traditionally, we have thought of space travel as being limited to NASA or government agencies. Branson has extended the boundaries of our perception of space travel to include ordinary citizens. According to Branson, this will represent "a new era in the history of mankind, one day making the affordable exploration of space by human beings a real possibility."

Figure 4.5 **Let's focus on this. Inspirational leaders show followers what is essential to achieve by clearly communicating the organizational vision.**

Who wouldn't want to be part of the team working to attain this exhilarating vision? Nevertheless, leading a team of brilliant professionals working on this project will be a challenge given human nature's competitive drive and innate self-interest. Fortunately, human nature also has the capacity for altruism, collaboration, and self-sacrifice. Therefore, all you need is to find a way to energize followers so that you can tap into the positive aspects of human nature. Transformational leaders inspire followers by pointing out what is most important and essential for achieving the vision, as shown in Figure 4.5.

There are many competing goals and objectives in organizations today. Needless to say, there are many projects that you and your followers may find on your plate. This can cause stress, lack of direction, and conflicts over limited resources within work groups. To be effective, leaders must prioritize what tasks are most important for followers to work on and explain to them why their completion is essential to achieving the overall vision. An evocative vision that is described in a colorful and appealing way will convince followers what they should focus on at the present. Such focus is essential for completing important tasks.

The task at hand at Amazon.com is marketing a digital book reader called Kindle that can store and download hundreds of titles. The vision of Amazon's founder, Jeff Bezos, is to allow readers to enter a video-game-like psychological state that draws them into the author's world. So far, Bezos's vision has Amazon's employees focused and their customers wondering what exciting experiences will come next.[12] So, the important questions you need to ask are: What is most important for your followers to focus on now in your organization? How can you convince them of its importance? What can you do to sharpen their focus?

Express Confidence That Goals Will Be Achieved

People working alone or in groups have different levels of confidence in their ability to perform tasks. The confidence a person possesses in the ability to perform a specific task is called *self-efficacy*. Two related concepts are collective efficacy and group potency. *Collective efficacy* describes the level of confidence an individual has in the ability of her group to perform a task. *Group potency* describes the group's collective perception of the group's general effectiveness.[13] Transformational leaders build these important motivational forces for their followers, as shown in Figure 4.6.

Figure 4.6   We can do it. MBA students Eric Santostefano, Melissa Shiu, and David Nguyen formed a potent team that possessed a can-do attitude in all of their FRLD projects.

One important reason that you should increase collective confidence among your followers before or while you work on achieving a challenging vision is uncertainty. No matter how well you articulate your vision for the future, it will entail lots of uncertainty and resistance because it is radically different from the status quo. In essence, achieving vision is all about motivating people to step out of their comfort zone and work toward a better future. When a leader displays such personal confidence, it helps followers get rid of their fear of navigating the unknown and unchartered path.

Thus, many successful transformational leaders try to elevate the confidence levels of their followers and work groups in mainly three different ways. First, they provide followers with experiences that demonstrate their effectiveness. Such experiences may be small tasks or projects that get progressively more complicated. Achieving small victories can boost confidence and performance on more difficult tasks. For example, Brian is a sales manager at Cisco Systems. Brian shared with us a series of emails he sent to Matt, an associate he was coaching for a big presentation to senior management. In his emails, Brian reminded Matt of the important tasks he would have to successfully complete in preparation for his presentation. Brian would send follow-up emails congratulating Matt as he completed each task. The practice and words of encouragement and congratulations boosted Matt's confidence as he prepared for presentation.

Second, leaders try to build confidence through vicarious experiences where they point out examples of similar people who were successful. If you use this process, make sure that you highlight the similarities between the exemplar and the person you are trying to persuade. Brian also used this approach in his emails. Brian described for Matt several similar situations he experienced and the presentation and reasoning approaches Brian had successfully used in the past. This sharing of experience and knowledge boosted Matt's confidence and ability.

Third, leaders build confidence by using rational arguments to persuade your followers and groups that they can be successful. Brian carefully described for Matt the reasons why he would be prepared for the presentation. Brian backed up his statements with evidence of Matt's prior successes on the small tasks and prior presentations. He pointed out that Matt's strengths were exactly those required for the upcoming presentation. Brian then told Matt that he was learning the best strategies for success. In the end, Matt wowed the audience with an exceptional presentation that generated a profitable contract with the customer. Most importantly, Brian was there for Matt during and after the presentation to see the results of his inspirational motivation. By continually expressing the confidence that goals can be achieved, you too can inspire your followers to focus on the task and direct their energies toward achieving your organization's vision.

Thinking About Inspirational Motivation

Now that we've introduced the concept of inspirational motivation to you, we'd like you to think deeply about what implications this concept has for two important leadership issues: the dark side of charisma and the rhetoric of charismatic leadership. A deep understanding of these topics will help you navigate the turbulent waters of leading in contemporary organizations.

The Dark Side of Charisma

Followers who are inspired and motivated by leaders often become mesmerized by their words, images, and actions. These followers see their leader as possessing a great amount of charisma. When most people hear the word *charisma*, they conjure up images of the leader possessing personal charm and having a way with words that makes people feel special. In fact, some people think that charisma is a gift from God that resides in the leader. In fact, one of the first places we find the word *charisma* is in the New Testament (1 Corinthians 12:8–10). Here, St. Paul talks about the spiritual gifts of wisdom, knowledge, faith, healing, miracles, prophecy, discerning of spirits, speaking in tongues, and interpretation of tongues. These represented extraordinary abilities bestowed unto the disciples of Jesus Christ. As a result of these gifts, the disciples gained new courage and confidence in their mission during the early days of the Church.

However, this notion of charismatic gifts residing in the leader is not consistent with current thinking on the topic. Sociologist Max Weber pointed out that charisma does not reside solely in the leader. Instead, charisma depends on the followers as well as the leader and can be intensified in times of crisis. The locus of charisma is in the leader and his emotional relationship with the follower during times that demand change. What matters most is how the followers feel about the leader and what special qualities they attribute to the leader. Charisma does not reside in traditional or formal authority or in ordinary exchange relationships with followers, but in followers' perceptions of the leader as being special. Thus, charisma is in "the eye of the beholder" when followers endow an extraordinary or magical quality, popularity, or celebrity status to the leader. Think about the amount of charisma associated with Miley Cyrus, Mariah Carey, Bruce Springsteen, or George Clooney in the arts and entertainment field. These charismatic leaders shape their image and emotional bond with the followers through their own energy, self-confidence, assertiveness, ambition, and seizing of opportunities.

Charismatic leadership often comes about in times of great distress. Followers look for a leader who can make sense out of stressful situations and crises. Charismatic leaders emerge with a radical vision offering a solution to these dilemmas. Their solutions attract followers who believe in the vision, especially if they experience some early successes in overcoming the crisis and make progress toward attaining the vision. As a result, followers come to perceive the leader as extraordinary. The bigger the crisis, the more the disturbance becomes emotional, and the more such emotionality can be invested in the charismatic leader who is perceived as "the savior."[14] Remember, a leader's self-confidence will play a big role in eliminating fear among followers while they are pursuing the leader's challenging vision. Charisma will surely add more confidence in this process.

For example, consider how much charisma the Dalai Lama is attributed by millions of people who turn to him for spiritual guidance. He's also admired for standing up to China's suppression of Tibet's freedom. Recall how much charisma Gandhi demonstrated as he led India's independence movement from Great Britain. And ponder the amount of personal power and charisma yielded by Osama bin Laden and Muqtada al Sadr as they mobilized their followers in their battles against American interests. Indeed, charismatic leaders yield immense influence and get strong emotional reactions from people. People either love them or hate them. That's why so many assassination attempts have been carried out on charismatic leaders over the years (e.g., John F. Kennedy, Robert Kennedy, Martin Luther King Jr., Malcolm X, John Lennon, Yitzhak Rabin, Pope John Paul II, and Benazir Bhutto).

Therefore, you can think of charisma as a form of influence exerted on a follower's emotional involvement and commitment. Charismatic leaders are known to inspire their followers because they present themselves as being dominant, self-confident, having a high need for power, and possessing strong convictions in the moral rightness of their beliefs. The presentation of this image in turn arouses followers' motives for achievement, affiliation, and power. It also increases followers' intrinsic motivation by linking the followers' self-concept with the mission advocated by the leader. This strong influence causes followers to go the extra mile for charismatic leaders, albeit sometimes down a path that should not be taken.

Personalized Versus Socialized Charismatic Leaders

Unfortunately, the immense personal influence and power over followers that charisma gives leaders can be dangerous and lead to destructive outcomes. Charisma is ethically neutral and can be used for either positive or negative ends. *Socialized charismatic leaders* use their charisma for the good of others and focus on advancing their cause. Examples of such leaders include Winston Churchill, Anita Roddick, Anwar Ibrahim, Pope John Paul II, Michelle Bachelet, and Benazir Bhutto. These leaders use their power to serve others. They align people around the vision and get them to commit to and share in the creation and attaining of the vision. They stimulate thinking and encourage open dialogue

Table 4.2   Leader Profile: Ken Lay

Former Enron chairman and CEO Ken Lay is best known for his role in the infamous corruption scandal that brought his company to ruins. Due to their arrogance and perceived invincibility, Lay and other Enron executives became prime examples of unethical leadership. Enron's bankruptcy in 2001 cost over 20,000 employees their jobs and many of them their life savings, since their Enron stock made up their entire pension portfolio. The demise of Enron wiped out more than $60 billion in market value and more than $2 billion in pension plans.

Lay reportedly dumped large amounts of his Enron stock as its price fell, while encouraging employees to buy more. Lay liquidated more than $300 million in Enron stock over an 11-year period, mostly in the form of stock options. He was one of the United States' most highly compensated CEOs as well. Lay's selfish approach to leadership was punished by U.S. courts, which found him guilty on 10 counts of securities fraud and other charges. Lay died of a heart attack four months before his scheduled sentencing in 2006. Academics and businesspeople alike often cite the Enron debacle as the epitome of accounting fraud and earnings management greed in the corporate world.

Source: Swartz, M., & Watkins, S. (2003). *Power failure: The inside story of the collapse of Enron.* New York: Doubleday; and retrieved January 30, 2009, from http://www.msnbc.msn.com/id/13715925/.

and debate. They learn from the criticism they receive from others. And they are influenced by their character strengths and virtues, which ground their decision-making processes.

In contrast, *personalized charismatic leaders* use their charisma for their own self-aggrandizement at the expense of others. Examples of such leaders include Adolph Hitler, Kim Jong-il, Jacob Zuma, Hugo Chavez, Saddam Hussein, Ken Lay (see Table 4.2), and Bernie Ebbers. In 2005, WorldCom co-founder and former CEO Bernie Ebbers was sentenced to 25 years in prison for his role in leading the largest corporate fraud in U.S. history. He was convicted of masterminding and guiding the $11 billion WorldCom fraud. Company stock that was once worth more than $60 per share was reduced to only pennies. Thousands of investors and WorldCom employees lost billions of dollars when WorldCom filed for bankruptcy and the company's stock price tanked. In one interesting account, Ebbers eliminated free coffee to company employees as a measure to save $4 million a year, while at the same time he watched his personal fortune grow to $1.4 billion.[15]

As Ebbers' example shows, such leaders use their power for personal gain because they are extremely narcissistic and self-centered. They use a heavy-handed approach to decision making and demand that their decisions be followed. They use fear and intimidation tactics that bully their followers into submission. Rather than promoting open discussion and debate, personalized charismatic leaders censure criticism. They are insensitive to others and do not tolerate dissent. Sometimes they get sidetracked by external factors instead of remaining true to themselves and others.[16]

These characteristics of personalized leadership illustrate several aspects of the dark side of charisma and its destructive outcomes. First, being in awe of the leader reduces the number of good suggestions offered by followers. This makes followers dependent on the leader and can promote an unhealthy group-think mentality within the organization. As psychologist Irving Janis pointed out, group-think occurs when emphasis is placed on maintaining solidarity within the group at the expense of quality of the discussion.[17] You have probably seen this emerge during meetings at work where subordinates use ingratiation tactics to "butter up" the boss, speak only when spoken to, and never disagree with the boss in meetings. What long-term effects do you think this has on followers and the leader?

Second, the desire for being accepted by the leader inhibits any criticism that followers may have for the leader. A lack of appropriate criticism can fuel the narcissistic flames of personalized charismatic leaders with hubris and a sense of invulnerability. Such excessive confidence and optimism on the part of the leader and followers can blind the leader to real dangers that lurk in the environment. Narcissistic leaders who carry on unchecked can quickly turn into monsters as well. How many times have we witnessed a situation where followers who inhibited their criticism of a narcissistic leader in public spend many hours privately venting about the leader, only to waste time and help fan the flames of the dysfunctional culture that they were trying to extinguish? What is the price followers pay for a desire at all costs to be accepted by a personalized charismatic leader?

Third, many personalized charismatic leaders take complete credit for their organization's successes. This can alienate some key followers who are essential for creating the real success. Followers like to be recognized for their contributions to the collective achievements. When they are denied such recognition, they grow resentful of the leader and dissent starts to emerge within the ranks. For example, Carly Fiorina, the charismatic former CEO of Hewlett-Packard, was faulted for her self-promotional style of leadership and excessive careerism. Followers viewed her message as "all about Carly and not about HP." What can you do to ensure that you share the credit with your followers so that you do not fall victim to the perils of personalized charismatic leadership?

Fourth, the impulsive nontraditional behaviors associated with being a charismatic leader can create enemies as well as supporters. Consistency of words and actions with organizational traditions and culture can inspire followers to work to achieve the mission. However, when charismatic leaders stray too far asunder from traditions and customs, they can fall out of favor with some less accepting colleagues. It is human nature to like those who are similar to us and be suspicious of those who are different. This is what happened in the case of minister and human rights activist Malcolm X, whom some claim was assassinated by his former associates within the Nation of Islam. According to this view, the top leadership of the Nation of Islam became jealous of Malcolm X's immense popularity and his unique way of communicating messages about current events (e.g., likening the assassination of John F. Kennedy to "chickens coming home to roost"). Members of Malcolm X's own fold became his enemies and had him gunned down as he spoke at a gathering in Manhattan in February 1965.[18] You can learn more about Malcolm X and his tremendous charisma by viewing various video clips on YouTube.com.

Finally, dependence on the leader holds back the development of competent successors and eventually creates a leadership crisis. When followers become so dependent upon the leader to make all decisions, their ability to learn on the job and expand their own leadership knowledge base is stifled. When the time comes that the organization needs a suitable replacement for the leader, the talent pool may be empty. That's because the followers will lack the independence and good judgment that can only come through proactive coaching and mentoring from the leader. Instead of perpetuating the dependence of your followers, why not work to promote their independence from you and interdependence among their colleagues in the organization and professions?

All of the above examples of destructive outcomes teach us to both *be aware* of and *beware* of charismatic leadership. At one point or another in your professional and personal life, you may have come in contact with a "little Hitler" running amok, bullying you and others in your organization. It's important not to get caught up in their deceptive images and words that at first may inspire, but later only intimidate. By knowing the circumstances that give rise to these villains and their characteristics, you can identify, isolate, and eliminate them before they inflict fatal damage to your organization. To learn what to look out for, consider the contrast between two famous charismatic leaders of World War II.

The Inspiring Leadership of Winston Churchill and the Fatal Attraction of Adolph Hitler

Former U.S. president George W. Bush imagined that he led the battle between good and evil in his military actions against Osama bin Laden and Saddam Hussein. He may have based his imagery on famous foes of years past. Two of the biggest adversaries of the Second World War were also two of the most charismatic leaders of their day. But Winston Churchill, the socialized charismatic leader, had the edge on Adolph Hitler, the personalized charismatic leader, when it came to inspirational motivation. That's because Churchill's leadership had substance in addition to his style, while Hitler's leadership was limited to style that only created a false and temporary impression of extraordinary leadership.

When Winston Churchill assumed his leadership of Great Britain in 1940, Hitler's armies were rolling across Europe. Nation after nation was overtaken by the Nazis. After France fell, the survival of Great Britain was in great jeopardy. Churchill's "Blood, Sweat, and Tears" speech, given on May 13, 1940, helped inspire his country to instill confidence in his new government and to carry on in the struggle against the Nazis despite formidable odds. In this speech, Churchill presented his vision:

> I say to the House as I said to ministers who have joined this government, I have nothing to offer but blood, toil, tears, and sweat. We have before us an ordeal of the most grievous kind. We have before us many, many months of struggle and suffering.
>
> You ask, what is our policy? I say it is to wage war by land, sea, and air. War with all our might and with all the strength God has given us, and to wage war against a monstrous tyranny never surpassed in the dark and lamentable catalogue of human crime. That is our policy.
>
> You ask, what is our aim? I can answer in one word. It is victory. Victory at all costs—Victory in spite of all terrors—Victory, however long and hard the road may be, for without victory there is no survival.[19]

What an inspiring and clear message! Churchill's words were grounded in the virtues of justice and national sovereignty as a just cause for Great Britain's fight for survival. The moral foundation for Churchill's vision was built upon just war theory, a notion originated by philosopher and theologian Thomas Aquinas in *Summa Theologicae*. This idea has been discussed by philosophers of the Scholastic and Jurist schools, and more recently in writings by Michael Walzer, Thomas Nagel, and others in the advent of the Al-Qaeda terrorist attacks on the United States on September 11, 2001.[20]

While Churchill was somewhat abrasive and insensitive in one-on-one interactions with his followers, his charm came from the content of his message and his personification of Victorian values and established English traditions. Churchill was inspiring because he was perceived by his followers as a tough bulldog fighting to save civilization from the evils of Nazi Germany. Churchill's tenacity of purpose was reassuring during the merciless German bombing of London and other cities during the Battle of Britain. Churchill reiterated this purpose time and time again as he challenged his nation to "never, never, never give up." As a result of his inspiration of the British people, Churchill gained the respect and admiration of people all over the world. Churchill's legacy is one of relevance and timelessness, especially in these dangerous days of threats against free nations posed by fundamental and extremist terrorist organizations such as Al-Qaeda or Hamas that challenge our way of life. His inspirational leadership and words remind us that "courage is rightly esteemed the first of human qualities ... because it is the quality which guarantees all others."[21]

In contrast, Adolph Hitler's legacy is a cautionary tale that warns us of the potential for charismatic leadership to run amok and produce disastrous results. It teaches us what we need to look out for, so we can catch it before charismatic leadership becomes destructive. What we need to look out for is the same thing that the German people failed to see through, that is, dramatic presentations high on style and emotion, and low on substance and reason. Hitler's drama amplified the effects of fear, intimidation, and excessive aspirations that strangled the reasoning ability of his countrymen.

Hitler was an evil master showman who excelled at creating an impression of power, righteousness in his beliefs, and superiority of his nation over all others. This message was quite appealing to the German people after their humiliation from losing World War I, their unfair treatment in the Treaty of Versailles, and the poor economic conditions of Germany during the Great Depression. All of these circumstances undermined collective self-esteem significantly among Germans. As Hitler entered the scene, he presented the German people with a vision to restore Germany's greatness by addressing their problems, righting their perceived wrongs, and in the process, elevating their collective self-esteem.[22]

What is fascinating about Hitler's leadership is that he was able to connect emotionally with the German people—a traditionally rational people known for their engineering and philosophical prowess. However, the majority of Germans failed to use their logic to question Hitler's leadership. They became mesmerized by his emotionally charged rhetoric that was high on passion and relatively low on reason. He spoke at rallies that were staged with the precision of a Hollywood movie production. In fact, Joseph Goebbels, Hitler's minister of culture and propaganda, was a huge fan of Hollywood movies. Goebbels worked with the top film producers of the day, such as Leni Riefenstahl, to create propaganda films such as *Triumph of the Will*.[23] He employed many of the film production techniques of the time to stage these events, which created a sense of awe in the audience members. Those who attended these rallies saw searchlights pointed to the sky marking the event, warm-up speeches given by key Nazi propagandists, immaculately dressed SS guards, torches, and neatly arranged seats filled with captivated audience members. Much detailed planning went into these events, which magnified Hitler's charismatic delivery and the emotional content of his speeches.[24] If you have never seen Hitler's staging of these events, you can view them on YouTube.com and see why the German people fell victim to his mesmerizing rhetoric.

Consider an excerpt from a speech Hitler delivered in the German Reichstag on January 30, 1937:

> The main plank in the National Socialist program is to abolish the liberalistic concept of the individual and the Marxist concept of humanity and to substitute therefore the folk community, rooted in the soil and bound together by the bond of its common blood. A very simple statement; but it involves a principle that has tremendous consequences. This is probably the first time and this is the first country in which people are being taught to realize that, of all the tasks which we have to face, the noblest and most sacred for mankind is that each racial species must preserve the purity of the blood which God has given it.[25]

Think carefully about what Hitler is saying here. While his rhetoric is highly charismatic in its content (note the emphasis on building collective self-esteem among Germans with words like *community* and *common blood*), it contains several flaws in reasoning. First, there is a difference between the concepts of "the individual" and "the person." The concept of the individual is considered to be an interchangeable element subsumed within a collective. For example, suppose you go to the supermarket and pick up an orange that you later realize is starting to spoil. You would then substitute another individual orange in its place. However, a truly humanistic view considers the person to be unique and of special value. That's because every person has a unique personality, spirit, soul, and dignity; it cannot be substituted for another as one would with individual components subsumed within a collective.

This kind of thinking was not part of the philosophy of the Nazis or the Soviets. Like Charles Darwin, they both emphasized the survival of the species or collective over the survival of the individual. This thinking is similar to that of a biologist who shows no concern over the death of a few thousand ants because what matters to him is the survival of the species. In his mind, who cares about a few thousand ants? Similarly, Hitler's obsession was the survival of the Aryan race (and elimination of other races), with no concern for the German individual. Similarly, Joseph Stalin's and other Communists' goal was the survival of the social class, with no concern for the individual worker. In their minds, workers are mere individuals, not persons.

Second, Marxism and its Communist application in the Soviet Union and other countries did not emphasize humanity as Hitler stated in his speech. Rather, it emphasized the importance and superiority of a common social (i.e., working) class or collective over the individual. Third, Hitler's obsession with maintaining the purity of racial species is inconsistent with contemporary trends of interracial marriage, globalization, and diversity—current realities that Hitler failed to foresee.

Despite his charisma, Hitler lacked a vision rooted in reality and ethics. His vision was full of biases, hatred, and manipulation. In the end, Hitler committed suicide in a Berlin bunker in April 1945 while his German nation was devastated by Allied bombing and overrun by Soviet forces entering from the East. For a German nation that fell victim to the fatal attraction of Hitler, his legacy is one of dangerous demagogue and personification of evil, only admired by neo-Nazis, radicals, thugs, and criminals. Even today, when we attempt to conduct leadership training in Germany, we are advised to substitute the word *management* for *leadership* in our training manuals because the German translation for the word *leader* is "Fuehrer." And that's an episode out of history that the German people would like to forget. Being able to identify "little Hitlers" you come across, based on your perception of their level of moral development, is another consideration.

Perspective-Taking Capacity and Moral Development

Recall from Chapters 2 and 3 the importance of perspective taking and moral development for leaders and followers. Developmental psychologist Lawrence Kohlberg identified three stages of *moral development*—preconventional, conventional, and postconventional. These stages are based on the progression of moral judgment over one's lifetime as one becomes educated and gains experience. *Preconventional moral reasoning* is based on a self-interested focus on avoiding punishment and seeking rewards. This is the kind of self-centered reasoning that a personalized charismatic leader would possess. *Conventional moral reasoning* is based on laws and rules that represent good interpersonal relationships and maintain social order. This is the most common level of moral reasoning found in the general population, and would be associated with transactional leadership.

Postconventional moral reasoning is based on universal principles and virtues such as justice and care, and establishing and upholding social contracts and individual rights.[26] Leaders at this stage of moral development typically maintain high levels of ethical and performance standards reflecting idealized influence. Similarly, postconventional moral reasoning is based on a holistic and broad perspective by focusing on social contracts and a shifting of interest from "me" to "we." This type of reasoning is required for leaders to display inspirational motivation aimed at building collective confidence and esprit de corps. Research has found consistently that leaders with higher moral standards have been shown to display higher levels of transformational leadership behaviors.[27]

Take a few minutes to reflect upon the level of moral development you possess. Are your decisions primarily driven by seeking rewards and avoiding punishments through obedience or naïve hedonism? Alternatively, do you make decisions by seeking to conform to group norms, laws, and conventional morality because doing so defines you as good in the eyes of society and maintains social order? Or, do you take a principled or conscience-based approach to decision making by maintaining social contracts that uphold the consensus of how people have agreed to live together? By broadening your perspective-taking capacity and shifting your focus from yourself to others, you can begin to use the type of post-conventional moral reasoning associated with transformational leaders.

The Rhetoric of Inspirational Leadership

Transformational leaders inspire their followers through their words and their deeds. In Chapter 3, you learned how to inspire your followers with idealized influence. Let's now spend some time exploring how to inspire followers with your words. To illustrate the content of inspirational messages, consider a passage from Barack Obama's 2008 presidential inauguration address:

> On this day, we gather because we have chosen hope over fear, unity of purpose over conflict and discord.
>
> On this day, we come to proclaim an end to the petty grievances and false promises, the recriminations and worn-out dogmas that for far too long have strangled our politics.
>
> We remain a young nation, but in the words of Scripture, the time has come to set aside childish things. The time has come to reaffirm our enduring spirit; to choose our better history; to carry forward that precious gift, that noble idea, passed on from generation to generation: the God-given promise that all are equal, all are free, and all deserve a chance to pursue their full measure of happiness.[28]

Do you remember how you felt when you heard this speech? Imagine how inspired those in the audience who marched with Dr. Martin Luther King Jr. must have felt when Obama delivered this speech. Now consider the following passage from Dr. King's "I Have a Dream" speech, one of the most influential orations of the 20th century.

> Let us not wallow in the valley of despair, I say to you today, my friends. And so even though we face the difficulties of today and tomorrow, I still have a dream. It is a dream deeply rooted in the American dream. I have a dream that one day this nation will rise

up and live out the true meaning of its creed: "We hold these truths to be self-evident, that all men are created equal."

I have a dream that one day on the red hills of Georgia, the sons of former slaves and the sons of former slave owners will be able to sit down together at the table of brotherhood. I have a dream that one day even the state of Mississippi, a state sweltering with the heat of injustice, sweltering with the heat of oppression, will be transformed into an oasis of freedom and justice. I have a dream that my four little children will one day live in a nation where they will not be judged by the color of their skin but by the content of their character. I have a dream today! ...

... And when this happens, when we allow freedom ring, when we let it ring from every village and every hamlet, from every state and every city, we will be able to speed up that day when all of God's children, black men and white men, Jews and Gentiles, Protestants and Catholics, will be able to join hands and sing in the words of the old Negro spiritual: "Free at last! Free at last! Thank God Almighty, we are free at last!"[29]

Can you feel the power of Dr. King's words? Do you get the usual feeling of electricity coming through you and get excited? Take a few minutes to reflect upon what makes this speech inspiring. What do you admire about this speech? What can you learn from the content of this speech?

Both Obama's and Dr. King's speeches provide several tips on creating an inspirational message. First, transformational leaders use inspirational messages to frame or reframe the big picture for followers. Their vision presents an appealing overarching end goal. The vision clarifies what the future state of affairs should look like by contrasting the future with the status quo. This typically involves demonstrating some revolutionary change that alters the present landscape. For example, Dr. King's speech contrasted the practices of segregation, discrimination, and injustice with an appealing vision of unity and equality. His compelling vision and well-articulated speech aimed at uniting the American people regardless of their gender, ethnicity, social status, and political parties. One important condition for a vision to be effective is that it has to be relevant and important to people you try to inspire. In Dr. King's speech we find the values of freedom, fairness, kindness, and love. These qualities inspire the best in humanity. And Obama's speech points his audience to the essential values of hope, unity, tolerance, perspective, freedom, and the pursuit of happiness.

Second, transformational leaders use words with content that stirs up the emotions of followers. Individuals are moved by their deep desires to be affiliated with noble causes, to strive toward significant achievements, and to exert influence over others. Obama's reference to words from the New Testament of the Bible (1 Corinthians 13:11), to set aside childish things, is an inspirational way to challenge citizens to "grow up" in their pursuits by focusing on priorities. Although Dr. King's vision was a great idea for humanity, he chose the word *dream* instead of *idea*. To say "I have an idea" has too much of an ordinary overly rational sound to it. In contrast, "I have a dream" conjures up positive images that can tap into followers' needs for affiliation with the worthy civil rights cause. This language has the same effect as when one listens to Beatle and peace activist John Lennon's classic song entitled "Imagine." That song just wouldn't have the same impact if it were entitled "Think."

Third, transformational leaders inspire their followers not only by what they say, but also by how they say it. They use special presentational techniques that can dramatically evoke deeply held values. *Metaphors*, or language that compares seemingly unrelated topics, can provide a visual depiction of the message. Dr. King contrasted Mississippi's "heat of injustice" with "an oasis of freedom and justice." Obama contrasted "hope" with "fear," and "unity of purpose" with "conflict and discord." *Analogies*, or the contrast of two pairs that have the same relationship, provide a standard of comparison to clarify a complex message. For example, Dr. King proclaimed that "we will not be satisfied until justice rolls down like waters, and righteousness like a mighty stream." By using these rhetorical devices, transformational leaders, like Dr. King, display confidence, poise, and a commanding professional presence. They also use simple visuals to support the message they want to get across to others. These visuals can be quite effective because a picture is worth a thousand words.

Transformational leaders who inspire followers speak with a captivating tone, appropriate inflection, and proper emphasis of key words. They may start off calm and somewhat monotone, but as they continue, they vary their intensity and build up to an emotional and dramatic climax. Their words come across as crisp and refreshing and seem to dance within their followers' hearts and minds. It's almost as if their words are beautiful music to the ears of their followers.

Jesse Jackson's speech to the National Convention of the Democratic Party in 1988 is another good example of delivery of an inspirational speech. Using all of these delivery techniques, Jackson's speech included references to hope and faith by linking the past (e.g., Dr. King) with the present by including 14 references to dreams and dreaming, and encouraged followers to "keep hope alive." Jackson's speech also included verbal persuasion to raise his followers' level of self-efficacy ("never surrender" and "you can make it") and to reinforce the collective efficacy and unity among members of his Rainbow Coalition (e.g., farmers, workers, women, students, African Americans, Hispanics, gays and lesbians, conservatives and progressives, right-wingers and left-wingers). To make an emotional connection with this disparate group of supporters, Jackson shared emotional stories of his disadvantaged past and upbringing. By presenting himself as a "working person's person," he was able to transcend the differences within his support base and get this diverse voter group to identify with him ("As I make it, so you can make it. You must never surrender to make America get better").[30] Later on, Obama used many of the same techniques in his campaign speeches in order to connect with a very diverse American voter population.

In summary, the rhetoric of inspirational leadership is not a special magical ability possessed only by a select few world-class charismatic leaders. Rather, it can be studied and learned by putting the above-mentioned tips into practice. By studying and practicing the techniques used by great orators, you will learn how inspiration can come from words and see its powerful effects on followers. By carefully crafting inspiring content for your own speech and delivering it in a dynamic and heartfelt way, you can inspire your followers in the style of the great inspirational leaders of history.

Putting Inspirational Motivation Into Practice

So far, you have learned what it means to display inspirational motivation. You have also reflected upon the implications of inspirational motivation for you and your organization. You are now ready to identify action steps for putting inspirational motivation to work in your leadership system. Because every leadership system is different, it is up to you to determine how to best display inspirational motivation in your organization. This section presents a few suggestions that you may find useful in displaying inspirational motivation and developing your full leadership potential.

Display the Behaviors Described in This Chapter

This chapter presented five behaviors associated with inspirational motivation. These behaviors focused on the importance of being optimistic and enthusiastic about the future, and presenting an exciting vision of the future to your followers with a great deal of self-confidence. By displaying these behaviors in your personal and professional lives, you can gain invaluable insight for your leadership journey.

That's what Michael Agaard, an executive at Sanofi Aventis, a French pharmaceutical company, found out after he completed his FRLD course at Penn State University. Always a thoughtful, intelligent, and caring person, Michael was inspired by the messages of hope and optimism associated with the transformational leaders he studied in class. The energy he derived as a by-product of his studies motivated him to share his enthusiasm for his work with his entire business unit. He scheduled meetings with key individuals in the company to present what he learned about FRLD. Michael made a strong business case for integrating FRLD behaviors into the culture of his company. Through his reasoned logic, passionate speeches, and examples of success stories, Michael was able to convince his associates to use FRLD to support their business initiatives.

Boost Your Self-Confidence

As a leader, the image you present to others is essential to the conclusions they draw about you. Therefore, you must project an image of confidence to your followers in order for them to become committed to you and the vision you share with them. When it comes to self-confidence, there is a plethora of advice available. Here are a few tips that can boost your self-confidence.

First, make sure that you have fully committed yourself to a vision or an idea you are about to communicate with your followers. If you have not, you won't appear to be confident and they will see it. Second, walk briskly and with a purpose. Instead of dillydallying, be sure to put some pep in your step. That can increase your energy level and give the impression that you are full of vitality. Third, be sure to maintain good posture when you walk or are seated. "Stomach in, chest out, shoulders back"—typical military counsel—is good advice to heed. Fourth, make eye contact with those with whom you speak. This builds trust and projects an image of poise. Fifth, speak up. Make it a point to interject at least one positive comment or probing question during meetings or gatherings. Those who speak first or frequently are often perceived as leaders who emerge within groups.[31]

We've seen all of these tips illustrated every time John Chambers presents Cisco's new products and technologies. With his highest level of self-confidence and carefully orchestrated speeches and presentations, his employees and customers believe that there is an exciting future for virtual meeting systems technologies today and in the future.

Write Mission and Vision Statements for Your Organization

One of the best ways to put inspirational motivation into practice is to lead a group effort to create the mission and vision statements for your organization. Most organizations hold annual strategic planning sessions. During these sessions, groups of organizational stakeholders (e.g., managers, employees, customers, suppliers, shareholders, business partners) meet to determine the purpose, values, objectives, and performance metrics of the organization. These exercises can put you in tune with what your organization stands for, and its purpose and greater role in society. This increased understanding provides information that can be used in the content of your speeches and to identify the organizational values to shape your organizational culture.

If you are not involved in such strategic organizational activities, be sure to position yourself so that you have the opportunity to get involved. No matter what role you play, whether it is key participant or member of a small focus group, the information you gain can provide a deep understanding of the opportunities, threats, strengths, and weaknesses facing your organization. This knowledge can help you imagine an inspiring future to describe in your vision, one that is realistic and links the present to both the past and the future. That's the kind of vision that can energize your associates and induce commitment and greater meaning to your mission.[32]

Work to Improve Your Public Speaking Ability

Numerous executive coaching firms and consultants provide training and development services designed to improve your public speaking ability. Such programs include the Dale Carnegie course (http://www.dalecarnegie.com/) or Toastmasters International (http://www.toastmasters.org/). These programs teach skills that make you feel more comfortable and confident in your speaking. Because command of language and its effective use are extremely important to the leadership influence process, your followers' perceptions of you as an inspiring leader depend very much on your public speaking ability.

The Toastmasters International Web site, noted above, presents 10 helpful tips for public speaking that can enhance your ability to inspire your followers. This organization encourages you to

1. *Know your material.* The content of your speech should contain material that is inspiring to your followers. Be familiar with it. When you use humor and speak from the heart by sharing personal stories, you can get people to identify with you as a leader they will follow anywhere.
2. *Practice over and over again.* Practicing out loud allows you to fine-tune your speech in terms of content, delivery, and timing. The more you practice, the easier it will be to deliver an inspiring speech. If possible, practice in front of a group of your colleagues. This will allow you to receive objective feedback and is an opportunity to observe others.
3. *Know the audience.* Make a personal connection with audience members by greeting them before you begin. They will look upon you as a familiar face rather than a stranger. Be sure to gather general information about them so that you can tailor aspects of your speech to their beliefs, desires, motives, and values. That's one way charismatic leaders connect with their followers.

4. *Know the room.* By arriving early and testing your equipment, you will be better prepared for any unexpected events. You will also feel more comfortable and engaged in your speaking role. This advice is similar to the need for leaders to understand the situation in which they are embedded, as discussed in Chapter 2.

5. *Relax.* A slow and relaxed start to a speech can convert nervous energy into enthusiasm that can build up to a positive emotional climax. A funny joke or friendly greeting can go a long way in connecting with the audience, who will be ready to receive an emotional story or two as your speech progresses.

6. *Visualize yourself giving the speech.* Visualization is a tactic frequently used by professional sports figures to boost their confidence. Prior to giving your speech, conduct a mental walk-through with positive imagery of clapping audience members. This is a good way to create optimistic and enthusiastic thoughts that can translate into an inspiring speech.

7. *Focus on the message, not the medium.* Any nervousness you may experience is likely to stem from public self-consciousness. So try not to think about yourself and your appearance once on stage. Instead, focus on the content of your speech and the way you will deliver it with appropriate volume, inflection, tone, and emphasis.

8. *Realize that people want you to succeed.* This is another tip that can boost your self-confidence. The audience is there because they want to learn from you and be inspired. That can only happen if you are successful. And that's an outcome you're both hoping for.

9. *Don't apologize for being nervous or any mistake you may make.* Audience members do not know what you were planning to say or do while you speak. Move forward in your speech with confidence and enthusiasm.

10. *Gain experience.* The more speeches you give, the more experience you gain. The more experience you gain, the more inspirational your speeches will become.

Use Storytelling Techniques to Articulate Your Vision

One of the best techniques for giving an inspiring speech is to tell personal stories that illustrate the values underlying the vision. Everyone has a story. When you speak from the heart, your ability to inspire others improves for several reasons. First, your talking points will come naturally to you because they are based on your personal experience. You are very familiar with your experiences. So talking about them should be easy and comfortable. Second, relating personal stories that are important to you is likely to evoke a wide range of emotions in you as you speak. When your followers witness these emotions in you, they too will feel your emotions and be inspired by the effect they have on you. Social psychologists call this phenomenon *emotional contagion.*[33] Third, people are generally interested in stories and the lessons they illustrate. Over the centuries, the great philosophers and teachers have taught their students with parables. As Bruce Avolio once pointed out, many of the early writings on leadership told its story through stories.

Steve Jobs used storytelling techniques in a commencement address he gave at Stanford University on June 12, 2005. In his speech, Jobs told three stories. His first story was about connecting the dots. This story was about trusting that the events in one's life are related to one another and will make sense in the long run. His second story was about love and loss. He talked about the importance of finding what you truly love in life and at work and not settling for second best. His third story was about death. This story was about the idea that your time is limited, so don't waste it living someone else's life—follow your heart and intuition. Each of his stories dealt with common life issues. As a result, many of the Stanford graduates and their proud parents in the audience could identify with the topics and with Steve Jobs as a human being rather than just another corporate leader.[34]

There are numerous resources available to aid in your storytelling competence. These resources range from books to articles to Internet Web sites. Spend some time reviewing these resources before you present the vision to your followers. You'll be amazed how inspired your followers will become by what you are teaching them through your personal stories.[35]

Build Consensus Around Your Vision

Once you present the vision to your followers, it is important to obtain their support and get them to share in the ownership of the vision. Nothing is more detrimental to your organization's success than a vision not being shared by its members. One way to do this is to hold formal and informal celebrations of the vision. During these ceremonies, you can recognize the key contributors who are working toward attaining the vision. It's also important to show associates how their work contributes to the progress and success of your organization. For example, every spring, Penn State Great Valley holds a Leadership in Action event that demonstrates to the public what our Master of Leadership Development program's vision and mission is, what the program means to our students, and how they have applied the knowledge they gained in the program to their professional and personal lives. These events are very popular and successful because they build cohesiveness and solidarity around the vision, and show the business community how the program benefits individuals, teams, organizations, and local and global communities through student initiatives.

While it is beneficial to promote the vision and celebrate success, visions need to be modified to adapt to the changing environment. Sharing information relevant to your organization's vision with followers is important to reinforce their feeling connected to the vision. You need to make sure that every new associate understands the vision and mission of the organization and clarify their role in accomplishing these goals. You should also seek opportunities to communicate and share ideas with people both inside and outside the organization. This communication flow can help in updating the vision by bringing new opportunities and threats to light, as well as strengths and weaknesses of your organization and its competitors. Remember that sharing the vision with followers increases their perception of you as an inspiring leader. It also enhances their emotional commitment to the organization because they see their role in helping attain the vision, which becomes a part of who they are. In the next chapter, we'll turn our attention to building followers' commitment to the organization by using rational means that spur creativity and innovation.

Summary Questions and Reflective Exercises

1. This exercise uses results of your Multifactor Leadership Questionnaire (MLQ) report to assess your level of inspirational motivation behavior. Compare your inspirational motivation ratings with the research-validated benchmarks. How did your self-ratings, ratings from subordinates, ratings from peers, ratings from superiors, and ratings from others compare against the benchmarks? On which specific MLQ items (i.e., questions) did you score highest? Lowest? What can you do to improve on the items where you scored lowest?

2. This exercise also uses results of your MLQ report to assess your level of inspirational motivation behavior. Compare your self-ratings on *inspirational motivation behavior* with ratings provided by subordinates, peers, superiors, and others. Compute the difference score (d) as the difference between your self-rating score and the specific other rating source score of interest. If d is less than .5 and the other rating source score is less than 2.83, then you are considered to be *in agreement/poor*. If d is less than .5 and the other rating source score is greater than 2.83, then you are considered to be *in agreement/good*. If d is equal to or greater than .5 and the self-rating score is greater than the other rating score, then you are an *overestimator* on this dimension. If d is equal to or greater than .5 and the self-rating score is less than the other rating score, then you are an *underestimator* on this dimension. Consider the category under which you fall in terms of inspirational motivation behavior. What are the implications of this categorization for you? Are there any things you can do to improve in this area?

3. The purpose of this exercise is to develop your inspirational speaking skills. Assemble a team of four members who will assist you in delivering and videotaping a speech. Assign the following roles to your team members:

Speaker: You will assume the speaker role.

Camera person: A technically competent individual who will videotape the speech.

Paralanguage specialist: An emotionally intelligent individual who will coach the speaker regarding nonverbal behaviors to be displayed during the speech.

Visionary writer: A thoughtful individual with foresight who will draft (i.e., outline) the content of the speech using tips presented in this chapter.

Literary writer: A literary ace and master of metaphors and analogies who will work closely with the visionary writer to embellish the speech with dramatic literary devices to evoke a potent emotional response from the audience.

   Once you have assigned roles to your team members, imagine that your team has been invited by the Public Broadcasting Service (PBS) to draft and deliver a three-minute speech using the rhetoric of inspirational leadership and the power of teamwork. Your message should focus on inspiring positive change in individuals, groups, organizations, and the community. Select one of the following audiences for your speech: Saints Phillips and James sixth grade class (http://www.sspj.net), Church Farm School (http://www.gocfs.net/docs/cfs.html), the Institute of Management Accountants (http://www.imanet.org), Big Brothers and Big Sisters (http://www.bbbs.org), or Willow Valley Retirement Home (http://www.willowvalleyretirement.com). Please tailor your speech to one of these audiences (i.e., where they are in their lives) and spend no more than 30 minutes drafting your speech. Then deliver and videotape your speech.

4. Review and critique the videotape that you created in exercise 3 with your team and other associates. Focus on what was said and how it was said. Discuss the language and behavior that made the speech inspirational. What verbal and nonverbal behaviors and actions worked well? What could have been improved?

5. Throughout history the future has been created in the minds of leaders and their followers. This exercise is designed to train your mind to create a positive future for your organization. Take a few minutes to think about the future and pay special attention to what you would be feeling or thinking as you entered work five years from today.

   a. What was going on at home before you left work?

   b. What were you thinking about on your way to work?

    c. What are you planning to do at work on that day?

    d. What new technologies will you be using?

    e. What is your staff like?

    f. What kind of relationships do you have with your boss, peers, and subordinates?

    g. What are the goals set for your unit?

    h. How do you communicate your enthusiasm for getting the work accomplished?

    i. What is the best thing that happened that day?[36]

6. Based upon your responses to exercise 5, create a vision statement for your organization. Use the tips on creating inspiring visions with the rhetoric of charismatic leadership presented in this chapter. Once you have drafted your vision statement, practice presenting it to an audience. Videotape your presentation and then assemble a group of colleagues to critique the presentation for its effectiveness in terms of content and delivery.

7. Conduct a literature review or Internet search on the topic of "improving self-confidence." Summarize five key findings of your research and present them to a group of coworkers or fellow students who may benefit from them. Explain to your colleagues how self-confidence is associated with transformational leadership.

8. Visit a local chapter of Toastmasters International and attend one of their meetings. For meeting locations and times, visit www.toastmasters.org. Talk with members to learn how to improve your poise when delivering leadership speeches. Share what you learned with your colleagues or leadership learning partners.

9. At your next company meeting, make a presentation on a FRLD topic and use one or two personal stories to make your point. Use personal or organizational values to link your stories to your topic. Your stories should be based on personal experiences that are interesting and relevant to the message you intend to communicate. Follow up with a few audience members regarding the impact of the stories on them and whether they were helpful in influencing them.

10. Work with a committee to plan and hold an event that celebrates the vision of your organization and the people who work together to attain it. This event should include individual and group presentations of success stories as well as stories that highlight great collective achievements linked to the vision. Integrate company values, history, and traditions that make your

organization special. During the event, be sure to reward and recognize associates who exemplify the organizational values reflected in your organization's vision.

Notes

1. Retrieved May 6, 2008, from http://www.btjonline.com/stories/0310exec.shtml. and retrieved January 25, 2009, from http://www.juniper.net/company/pr/2008/pr_2008_07_29-5_40.html.
2. Thrash, T. M., & Elliot, A. J. (2003). Inspiration as a psychological construct. *Journal of Personality and Social Psychology, 84*, 871–889.
3. Obama, B. (2008). *The audacity of hope: Thoughts on reclaiming the American dream.* New York: Vintage.
4. Bennis, W., & Zelleke, A. (2008, February 28). Barack Obama and the case for charisma. *The Christian Science Monitor.* csmonintor.com. Retrieved March 10, 2008.
5. Csikszentmihalyi, M. (2003). *Good business: Leadership, flow, and the making of meaning.* New York: Viking; and Luthans, F., Avolio, B. J., Avey, J. B., & Norman, S. M. (2007). Positive psychological capital: Measurement and relationship with performance and satisfaction. *Personnel Psychology, 60*, 541–572.
6. Shamir, B., House, R. J., & Arthur, M. (1993). The motivational effects of charismatic leadership: A self-concept based theory. *Organization Science, 4*, 1–17.
7. Sheen, F. J. (1988). *The psychology of the rat race; psychology of temptation* [Videocassette]. Victor, NY: Sheen Productions.
8. Cheng, T. J. (2005). *China under Hu Jintao: Opportunities, dangers and dilemmas.* New York: World Scientific Publishing.
9. Weigel, G. (1999). *Witness to hope: The biography of Pope John Paul II.* New York: HarperCollins.
10. Gibney, A. (Producer/Director), & McLean, B., Elkind, P., & Gibney, A. (Writers). (2005). *Enron: The smartest guys in the room* [Documentary film]. New York: Magnolia Pictures.
11. Retrieved March 28, 2008, from http://www.virgingalactic.com/.
12. Burrows, P. (2008, August 25). Here comes Kindle 2.0. Business Week.com. Retrieved January 25, 2009, from http://www.businessweek.com/the_thread/techbeat/archives/2008/08/herecomes_kind.html.
13. Bandura, A. (1997). *Self-efficacy: The exercise of control.* New York: Freeman; and Guzzo, R., Yost, P., Campbell, R., & Shea, G. (1993). Potency in groups: Articulating a construct. *British Journal of Social Psychology, 32*, 87–106.
14. Conger, J. A., & Kanungo, R. N. (1998). *Charismatic leadership in organizations.* Thousand Oaks, CA: Sage; and Weber, M. (1947). *The theory of social and economic organizations* (T. Parsons, Trans.). New York: Free Press.
15. Jeter, L. W. (2003). *Disconnected: Deceit and betrayal at WorldCom.* New York: Wiley.
16. Howell, J. M. (1988). Two faces of charisma: Socialized and personalized leadership in organizations. In J. A. Conger & R. N. Kanungo (Eds.), *Charismatic leadership: The elusive factor in organizational effectiveness* (pp. 213–236). San Francisco: Jossey-Bass.

17. Janis, I. (1972). *Victims of groupthink.* Boston: Houghton-Mifflin Co.
18. Bassey, M. O. (2005). *Malcolm X and African American self-consciousness.* Lewiston, NY: Edwin Mellen Press; and Helfer, A. (2006). *Malcolm X: A graphic biography.* New York: Hill and Wang.
19. Retrieved March 3, 2008, from http://www.historyplace.com/speeches/churchill. htm.
20. Fascinating reading on just war theory can be found in Brough, M. B., Lango, J. W., & van der Linden, H. (2007). *Rethinking the just war tradition.* Albany, NY: SUNY Press; Nagel, T. (1995). *Moral questions.* Cambridge, UK: Cambridge University Press; and Walzer, M. (1977). *Just and unjust wars: A moral argument with historical illustrations* (4th ed.). New York: Basic Books.
21. Best, G. F. (2001). *Churchill: A study in greatness.* London: Hambledon & London; and Roberts, A. (2002). *Hitler and Churchill: Secrets of leadership.* London: Weidenfeld & Nicholson.
22. Bullock, A. (1964). *Hitler: A study in tyranny.* New York: Harper & Row.
23. Riefenstahl, L. (1934). *Triumph of the will* [Videocassette]. Novi, MI: Synapse Films.
24. Roberts, A. (2002). As cited in Note 21.
25. Retrieved March 5, 2008, from http://www.calvin.edu/academic/cas/gpa/hitler1. htm.
26. Kohlberg, L. (1976). Moral stages and moralization: The cognitive-developmental approach. In T. Lickona (Ed.), *Moral development and behavior* (pp. 31–53). New York: Holt, Rinehart & Winston.
27. Kuhnert, K. W., & Lewis, P. (1987). Transactional and transformational leadership: A constructive/developmental analysis. *The Academy of Management Review, 12,* 648–657; and Turner, N., Barling, J., Epitropaki, O., Butcher, V., & Milner, C. (2002). Transformational leadership and moral reasoning. *Journal of Applied Psychology, 87,* 304–311.
28. Retrieved January 29, 2008, from http://www.nytimes.com/2009/01/20/us/ politics/20text-obama.html.
29. Retrieved March 20, 2008, from http://www.americanrhetoric.com/speeches/ mlkihaveadream.htm.
30. Shamir, B., Arthur, M. B., & House, R. J. (1994). The rhetoric of charismatic leadership: A theoretical extension, a case study, and implications for research. *The Leadership Quarterly, 5,* 25–42.
31. Retrieved March 20, 2008, from http://www.pickthebrain.com/blog/10-ways-to- instantly-build-self-confidence/.
32. Sosik, J. J., Jung, D. I., Berson, Y., Dionne, S. D., & Jaussi, K. S. (2004). *The dream weavers: Strategy-focused leadership in technology-driven organizations.* Greenwich, CT: Information Age Publishing.
33. Hatfield, E., Cacioppo, J. T., & Rapson, R. L. (1993). *Emotional contagion: Studies in emotion & social interaction.* Cambridge, UK: Cambridge University Press.
34. Retrieved March 25, 2008, from http://news-service.stanford.edu/news/2005/ june15/jobs-061505.html.
35. The following references provide excellent overviews of how storytelling is used to benefit leaders and their followers: Adamson, G., Pine, J., Van Steenhoven,

T., & Kroups, J. (2006). How storytelling can drive strategic change. *Strategy & Leadership, 34*, 36–41; Bai, M. (2005, July 17). The framing wars. *New York Times Magazine*, pp. 38–45, 68–71; Denning, S. (2005). Transmit your values: Using narrative to instill organizational values. In *The leader's guide to storytelling: Mastering the art of discipline of business narrative* (Chap. 6, pp. 121–148). Edison, NJ: Wiley; and Harris, J., & Barnes, B. K. (2005). Leadership storytelling: Learn how to get people to connect with you. *Leadership Excellence, 22*, 7–8.

36. Adapted from Bass, B. M., & Avolio, B. J. (1990). *Full range leadership development: Advanced workshop manual.* Binghamton, NY: Center for Leadership Studies, SUNY-Binghamton.

Chapter 5

Intellectual Stimulation
The Rational Side of Transformational Leadership

The world is but a canvas to the imagination.

—Henry David Thoreau

Imagine that you were tasked with helping children who have been affected by or infected with HIV/AIDS. You'd soon realize that these children suffer not only from physical symptoms that vary daily, but also from many emotional and social wounds inflicted by being labeled by their peer group and shunned by society. Imagine what it would be like if your children or children you loved either were infected with HIV/AIDS or were in a position where they had to care for someone living with this cruel disease. How would they feel? Could you empathize with them? What would you do to give them back their human dignity and precious childhood moments that this devastating disease takes away? How could you reach out in a way to help address this social problem?

Patty Hillkirk and a team of compassionate and imaginative transformational leaders committed their hearts and minds to the task of answering these questions. In August 1996, they established Camp Dreamcatcher (http://www.campdreamcatcher.org/) in Kennett Square, Pennsylvania, to address this issue. The camp's mission is to challenge society's views on HIV/AIDS and its effect on the lives of their campers. Camp Dreamcatcher is a unique organization because it is the only weeklong free therapeutic camp on the U.S. East Coast that offers a camping experience for HIV/AIDS-infected or -affected children between the ages of 5 and 17. Contrary to conventional wisdom, Camp Dreamcatcher assumes that these children can participate in and enjoy a full week of summer camp, just like healthy kids. That's because a talented team of experienced medical and counseling professional volunteers create a safe environment for the campers. Under proper supervision and leadership, the campers enjoy a wide variety of support group, recreational, training, and educational activities.[1]

Camp Dreamcatcher's success under Patty Hillkirk's leadership is well known. Media reporters and politicians have recognized that she gives children coping with HIV/AIDS both hope and an environment where they can develop socially, mentally, and spiritually within the physical limitations imposed upon them by their disease. Patty's efforts have been documented in *Tiny Tears*, a film produced by Robert Corna that examines the lives of AIDS orphans across the globe.[2]

Students in Penn State's Master of Leadership Development (MLD) program have worked with Patty and Professor Barrie E. Litzky to write a business plan for Camp Dreamcatcher because they want to purchase property and get accredited. Together, they have developed a strategy for accreditation in the American Camping Association. They have identified lists of potential collaborating organizations, HIV/AIDS organizations, and groups that may use the camp. They have also calculated Camp Dreamcatcher's social return on investment using metrics such as pre- and posttest surveys to campers and their parents/guardians measuring what they have learned in the camp, repeat attendance at the camp, and donations and fund-raisings to support the camp. These measures are factored into an innovative calculation of the camp's value to society based on inputs and activities that determine the camp's ultimate social outcomes (see Figure 5.1).[3]

Patty Hillkirk's intellectually stimulating leadership is a noble response to political scientist James MacGregor Burn's call to use transformational leadership to address the world's social problems and help people pursue happiness.[4] She is shifting society's views on HIV/AIDS from focusing on helping patients who are "dying from" to "living with" the disease. The traditional view of HIV/AIDS is that it represents a worldwide health crisis. By recognizing that the Chinese word for crisis includes both "opportunity" and "danger" at the same time, Hillkirk has seen the opportunity for Camp Dreamcatcher to "foster an atmosphere of tolerance, compassion, respect and understanding through volunteer opportunities, services and expanded community outreach," as stated in its mission statement.

Inputs	Activities	Outputs	Outcomes
• Volunteer's time • Fundraising/ donations • Year-round camp facility • Medical equipment • HIV/AIDS literature • Recreational equipment • Therapeutic equipment	• Recreational • Health/Wellness • Educational programs • Therapeutic programs • Social/ entertainment • Retreats • Reunions • Support groups • Teen speaker bureau • Documentary film "Tiny Tears"	• Medicine tolerance • Return enrollment • Parental satisfaction • Increased fundraising/ donations • Family support and advocacy • community outreach • Knowledge of life skills • Trained junior counselors	• Improved emotional health of campers • Increase awareness & tolerance of HIV/AIDS to local, national, and global community • Improved awareness of medical regimes by campers • Increase in # of infected/affected children having a real camp experience • Increase HIV/AIDS awareness programs in middle- and high-schools

Figure 5.1   Return on social investment. Camp Dreamcatcher uses these metrics to assess how resources and activities impact their organizational stakeholders and contribute to society.

Hillkirk's reframing of crisis as an opportunity is an example of intellectual stimulation. This behavior is often used by transformational leaders in for-profit organizations as well. For example, Dee Hock, former CEO of VISA International and Business Hall of Fame member, often talks about the need for organizations to get involved in solving societal problems by viewing them as incredible opportunities for positive change. In his writings, Hock embraces the seemingly incompatible notions of order and chaos in organizations. Through his Chaordic Alliance think-tank, Hock and his colleagues disseminate and implement his concept of the chaordic organization.[5] This notion espouses that organizations should evolve from traditional hierarchical command-and-control models to those that blend democracy, consensus decision making, cooperation, and competition. This nontraditional organizational structure reflects Hock's intellectually stimulating leadership and thinking.

This chapter shows you how to get your followers to think in unconventional ways about solving important leadership problems that face your organization. By showing your followers how to think for themselves, instead of relying solely on "tried and true" policies and procedures, you too can become an intellectually stimulating leader. Let's begin to learn about this rational approach to leadership by considering the case of a protégé learning from her mentor and vice versa.

The Dynamic Leadership Duo of Anne Mulcahy and Ursula Burns at Xerox

Xerox has always been known for innovation. The xerography technology for making copies has been revolutionary and has served as an invaluable business and commerce function for many years. In addition to advancing photocopying technology, Xerox engineers in the 1970s were experimenting with the graphical user interface and networks for computers when Steve Jobs of Apple and others visited their site in Palo Alto, California. Unfortunately, Xerox's top management lacked the vision to appreciate these technologies, which were quickly adopted by companies like Apple, IBM, and Microsoft. For this and other reasons, Xerox's performance floundered for some time, and by the year 2000, the company was in dire straits.

Enter Anne Mulcahy, a charismatic field representative who joined Xerox in 1975 and rose through the ranks to become its first female CEO in 2002. Through a series of aggressive strategic moves, Mulcahy and her top management team turned around Xerox's stock price, which had dropped from $64 to $4 per share in 2001. At that time, Xerox was burdened with $17 billion of debt and held only $154 million in cash. Besides the threat of bankruptcy, Xerox was plagued with a growing number of competitors and a government investigation of its books. Despite these challenges, Mulcahy returned Xerox to full-year profitability by the end of 2002, reduced its debt, and increased cash and working capital, while continuing to invest in research and development.

But Mulcahy did not achieve these phenomenal results alone. She was assisted by Ursula Burns, math wizard turned engineer turned executive extraordinaire. Burn's unconventional ways of thinking about traditional corporate problems at Xerox were the perfect complement for Mulcahy's ability to sell vision and ideas to organizational stakeholders. Burns was willing to embrace new ideas when other executives lacked the courage to stir the pot at Xerox. Burns, who is currently Xerox's president and heir apparent to Mulcahy, has a reputation for being a rational thinker and fearless in trying innovative initiatives.

So that Burns can copy Mulcahy's success, Mulcahy is currently grooming Burns to assume the CEO position. This high-profile mentoring relationship has been the subject of several articles in the popular press.[6] Mulcahy is teaching Burns how to be less of a micromanager and more of a listener and communicator. Burns is teaching Mulcahy how to be less of an intuitive thinker and more of a rational problem solver. As they learn to share power in their important leadership transition, Mulcahy is respecting Burns for her ability to challenge her colleagues, while having a reverence for the facts and the truth. But Mulcahy is harder on Burns because of their mentor-protégé relationship. She finds herself constantly challenging Burns to figure things out and work out of her comfort zone. Holding such high expectations for leadership and personal growth is helping these two corporate superstars find the right answers for Xerox.

Intellectual Stimulation: Definition and Behavioral Examples

To develop breakthrough strategies and champion innovation like Anne Mulcahy and Ursula Burns, you need to display intellectual stimulation behaviors. That's because *intellectual stimulation* involves rational thinking, creativity, and the freedom to fail. These concepts allow followers to think for themselves in ways that challenge conventional wisdom and seek continuous process and people improvement. It makes them feel fascinated with and curious about their work and challenged by their tasks. Like inspirational motivation, intellectual stimulation develops followers' leadership potential along the way because it forces them to exert cognitive (i.e., thinking and perceptual) energy to solve organizational problems. It challenges them to think in unconventional ways that moves them out of their comfort zone. This deep level of thinking comes from your willingness to question basic assumptions, policies, and procedures that may no longer be valid due to changes in your business contexts. It makes followers feel comfortable experimenting with new ideas, technologies, or management tools because they can try out new things without being viewed as undermining authority or being foolish. Displaying intellectually stimulating behaviors is a skill at which Craig Venter excels (see Table 5.1).

Like Venter, you can demonstrate intellectual stimulation by practicing behaviors that challenge the status quo. Let's now examine six key transformational leadership behaviors that allow you to display intellectual stimulation.

Reexamine Critical Assumptions to Question Whether They Are Appropriate

Think about the last time you or a member of your family was in need of health care. Whether you visited your doctor or the hospital, you probably experienced some agitation over the way you were treated during your wait and perhaps during your treatment. And don't forget about the hassles associated with your health care insurance and its reimbursement rules. Our life experiences seem to teach us that we must accept our flawed health care system as it is and simply go with the flow. Some of us may also assume that we should take a passive approach to our health and react only when something goes wrong. Some doctors

Table 5.1   Leader Profile: Craig Venter

Imagine working on a project to decode all of the approximately 20,000 to 25,000 genes in human DNA and its sequencing, store this information in a massive database, and begin to transfer this technology to industry within ethical, social, and legal constraints. Craig Venter not only imagined it, he did it.

Venter is the SUNY-Buffalo professor who challenged Celera (his former company) and U.S. government scientists to speed up the race to produce the first complete transcription of the human genome. As a result, he became well known as an adventurous and impetuous maverick entrepreneur. He is famous for adopting new technologies and processes in his 20+-year mission to sequence a human genome. His team's work has provided us with an opportunity to find the genetic components of diseases, help doctors provide personalized medical care, and create synthetic bacteria as a source of fuel and energy.

Ventor's early life events defy his present fame as the brilliant and spontaneous scientist. As a child, he was an underachiever, earning mostly Cs and Ds in school. As a teen, he was a California surfer and "beach bum" before serving as a Navy medic in Vietnam. While in Vietnam, he swam off China Beach intending to commit suicide, but fortunately he changed his mind. After surviving Vietnam, Venter returned to the United States with a newfound purpose and love of life. And it was *life* with which he became most fascinated as he completed college and earned a PhD in biochemistry.

Later on, during his quest to sequence the human genome, Venter constantly questioned government policies and procedures during the project. He championed new and improved methods to achieve success in faster and more effective ways. Venter has criticized the National Institutes of Health and corporate administrators for their traditional approaches to research as a business, and not about advancing health and ecological issues. Venter's unconventional style and maverick personality have been compared to those of Larry Ellison of Sun Micro Systems and Richard Branson of the Virgin Group.

Venter's story teaches us to live life to the fullest with a sense of curiosity and imagination that knows no bounds. We must always question the status quo even at the peak of success. His story reminds us of the words of Lieutenant General Willard W. Scott Jr.: "Any fool can keep a rule. God gave him a brain to know when to break the rule."

Source: Venter, J. C. (2007). *A life decoded: My genome: My life.* New York: Viking Adult; and retrieved May 18, 2008, from http://www.ornl.gov/sci/techresources/Human_Genome/project/about.shtml.

may presume that they are independent sources of knowledge and information on healing, and that their contact with us is "episodic, high intensity, and low touch."[7]

The U.S. health care system has been based upon these assumptions for many years, but not all doctors have accepted them. Consider Hunter "Patch" Adams, the maverick medical doctor and social activist portrayed by Robin Williams in the film *Patch Adams*. While attending medical school, Adams began to question the basic assumptions underlying the way health care is provided to patients. He asked himself and others why things could not be different.

Over his 35-year career, Adams has championed developing compassionate connections with patients. His philosophy is to use humor and the natural environment to forge a bond between the patient's physical, emotional, and spiritual well-being. Adams has always felt that a patient's wellness can be enhanced by the natural environment. Pending sufficient funding, Adams and his colleagues are planning the Geshundheit! Institute. This promises to be much more than a nontraditional hospital. The vision for this facility is to create a sustainable system including a free full-scale hospital, healthcare eco-community, center for the arts, nature, agriculture, and recreation with a focus on holistic medicine and overall personal well-being. Indeed, the Geshundheit! Institute seems to be a kind of Walt Disney World of holistic medicine and healing.[8] For a virtual tour of the Geshundheit! Institute, visit http://www.patchadams.org.

In many leadership courses and workshops we've conducted in the past, we've used Patch Adams to illustrate the power of questioning critical assumptions underlying strategic initiatives, work processes, company policies and practices, and cultural norms. As shown in Figure 5.2, you can achieve major breakthroughs in innovation and continuous improvement by questioning such basic assumptions. When elements in the leadership context change (see Chapter 2), the basic assumptions underlying policies and practices may no longer be valid and may require a change. When changes are made to basic assumptions, new models for organizing and operating can be developed. These new models can lead to innovative solutions to pressing problems.

Seek Different Perspectives When Solving Problems

Strategic planning is a perennial activity in most organizations, especially when they face challenging times. For example, a teaching-oriented university's revenue stream depends highly upon student enrollments. When student enrollments decline, the amount of available funds to finance operations comes into jeopardy and layoffs of untenured faculty and staff become a distinct possibility. Under these circumstances, a creative and effective strategic plan is typically required to address problems with enrollment. However, finding a

Figure 5.2 Imagine it this way. Penn State and Drexel University professors and students collaborate by sharing ideas on leadership development.

solution to a decline in student enrollments is complex. Enrollments are a function of many factors, including competition, economic conditions, perceived quality of programs, school reputation, marketing, and administrative leadership, among others.

A comprehensive analysis of these factors and the development of initiatives to address the complexity of this problem require the knowledge, skills, and abilities of many individuals. For this reason, universities often form strategic planning task forces consisting of administrators, faculty, staff, students, alumni, employers of students, advisory board members, and community members. That's because no one person has the knowledge to fully comprehend ambiguous and complex problems associated with creating a strategic plan. A team of diverse individuals from different functional backgrounds and areas of expertise can shed much more light on the problem than a single individual. Each individual possesses a distinctive collection of life experiences, intelligence, and skill sets that he or she can use to perceive and interpret problems in unique ways. A deep and wide range of perspectives provides for a more comprehensive understanding of the problem, which can allow for better solutions.

So when complex problems face your group or organization, it's a good idea to involve a diverse group of members in the decision-making process, as shown in Figure 5.3. Not just members of your organization, but customers, suppliers,

Figure 5.3 What do you think? Intellectual stimulation includes the sharing of perspectives on new ways to translate leadership research into action in corporations.

and even competitors can add value to the issue being considered. The varied perspectives that each member brings to the group can add the intellectual stimulation needed to produce a creative and effective solution.

Get Others to Look at Problems From Many Different Angles

Katrina leads a group of instructional designers in a large manufacturing company. She is well known for being a creative and insightful problem solver. Her reputation comes from a positive outlook on life that appreciates unique and quirky natural and man-made objects. Given her talent for appreciating beauty and excellence, Katrina has always been interested in artwork and photography and has taken up these activities as hobbies in her spare time. Over the years, she has taken several university-sponsored photography classes that have allowed her to use her talents to produce a most impressive gallery of photos. Katrina is always ready with her camera in hand to snap an interesting shot of nature, family gatherings, or events at work.

Photography has taught Katrina several important lessons about intellectually stimulating leadership. Katrina's photos often capture her subjects from an

Figure 5.4 Picture this. Several FRLD scholars are both subjects of a photo and the background for the photo they are examining.

unusual angle that reveals interesting details that would have gone unnoticed if not for her insightful positioning of the camera. This has taught her to consider leadership problems from different angles as well. These slants on perceiving leadership problems include considering short- and long-term implications of problems, most and least likely scenarios, best and worst case situations, and nuances in the behavior patterns of groups and their members. Katrina also considers issues of lightening, timing, and framing of the subjects of her photography using unorthodox approaches or unexpected situations, such as a photo of subjects looking at a photo, as shown in Figure 5.4. These unconventional tactics often produce behavioral snapshots rich in meaning from which personality characteristics of her human subjects can be gleaned. Applying this skill to her leadership at work, Katrina has learned the importance of hearing from individuals whom most people would likely pass up when gathering information. These people can provide information that adds value to the decision-making process.

The previous vignette teaches us that sometimes you can get this information from the least likely people. For example, Robert Scott works during the day as a maintenance man at Penn State. Robert grew up in Melbourne, Florida, as 1 of 16 children, the son of a Baptist minister. After finishing high school, Robert worked as a semipro boxer and then as a singer in several soul groups, including Philly Crème, an opening act for Harold Melvin and the Blue Notes. He always thirsted for the overflowing cup of love and attention that he thought only fame and fortune could bring. But the drink, drugs, women, and material possessions associated with the music business got the better of Robert. Physically, emotionally, and spiritually downtrodden, he realized that he was on the road to nowhere. And then one day before performing in Las Vegas, he heard the voice of the Lord telling him to clean up his act and pursue his real purpose in life. He was to follow his true calling of being a minister, but to do so unassumingly. Robert told us, "Just like the Apostle Paul was knocked down from his high horse on the road to Damascus, I had to start my life all over. Then I started to look at the world differently, with more humility."

To look at Robert in his unassuming maintenance uniform as he goes about his daily tasks, you would never know that he possesses a wealth of spiritual and philosophical knowledge from which many can benefit. But once you take the time to talk with Robert, you'll soon find out that his day job only pays the bills that allow him to pursue his real calling in life. That's because his true self is Pastor Robert Scott of the Holy Matrimony ministry serving Pennsylvania, New Jersey, and Delaware. As shown in Figure 5.5, Robert and his wife, Michelle, use their musical ministry to attend to the emotional and spiritual needs of individuals across the tri-state area. Robert possesses a "PhD in life," a source of wisdom and character that is truly hard to find in this day and age. His knowledge and way with words are so convincing that he's frequently spoken as a guest lecturer on issues of character strength and development in John's "Leadership across the Lifespan" class.

Robert Scott's story teaches us that you never know where you will find your next source of intellectual stimulation. Try looking at someone or something from a different angle; perhaps outside of the role that organizations or society stereotypically place upon them. And, be open-minded and listen to others' views on your issues. Allow them to share their perspective on your issues. No matter how many good ideas you have and no matter how many leadership workshops you've attended, unless you are open to embracing drastic and fundamental changes in the way you and your followers work, nothing will be useful as practicing your own intellectual stimulation.

Suggest New Ways of Looking at How to Complete Assignments

Corporations are notorious for benchmarking and prescribing the methods for their employees to use to complete tasks. Managers will frequently say, "But we always do it this way." Procedure manuals often spell out in excruciating detail how work should be performed, and supervisors often monitor its compliance. This approach stifles creativity and force fits people into procedural boxes that may not be natural for them. It assumes that all people are the same and possess the identical skill sets and preferences for completing assignments.

Figure 5.5   Pastor Robert Scott and his wife, Michelle, provide intellectual stimulation and inspirational motivation to their congregation and the many people they meet throughout the day.

However, research on diversity has shown us that this is not always true, and that people prefer choice and variety in the way they perform tasks.[9]

One way to use this preference to spur creativity and innovation is to suggest new ways to complete assignments and tasks, as shown in Figure 5.6. This can identify steps in the process that do not add value and can be eliminated to streamline the method to add efficiency. Or it can simply make the process more fun and encouraging of creativity. We know that freedom of choice regarding how to complete tasks is associated with creative outcomes in business, education, and entertainment.[10] Freedom of choice may also increase employee engagement, which is known to be an important foundation of innovation.

Figure 5.6   Let's try it this way. MLD professors and students learn about leadership on an enjoyable and intellectually stimulating field trip.

One of the most creative popular musical albums ever produced was the *Smile* LP, finally released in 2004. This musical masterpiece was the brainchild of the Beach Boy's leader and musical genius Brian Wilson and his lyrical collaborator, Van Dyke Parks. Instead of writing songs in the traditional way (e.g., in the office or studio, or at home), Wilson had a large sandbox installed in his living room with a baby grand piano placed in it. Wilson invited his collaborators to sit in the sandbox to compose songs with him for the *Smile* LP. The idea was to create a feeling of being at the beach and to inspire melodies typical of the Beach Boys' California sound. According to Wilson, several of the essential songs on *Smile* were written in the sandbox to the delight of the lyricists.[11]

This new approach to completing the assignment of songwriting for an album illustrates how intellectual stimulation can be used to create an environment that facilitates creative thinking and behavior. The next time your associates are planning the completion of a project, suggest that they consider alternative approaches to completing their work. A novel, amusing, or refreshing method may spur the creativity required to produce a project that is a hit with senior managers and customers alike.

Encourage Nontraditional Thinking to Deal With Traditional Problems

In 2008, the British rock band Radiohead released its album *In Rainbows* only online and asked customers to pay whatever price they felt was fair. Wow! Radiohead's nontraditional thinking signaled to record companies that the old business models of controlled access and distribution are passé. The band's innovativeness is helping to reshape the music industry.[12]

Dee Hock once said, "The problem is never how to get new, innovative thoughts into your mind, but how to get old ones out." And getting the old ones out requires developing new mindsets and behaviors, especially in organizations that are slow to change, such as academic institutions. For example, one of the mantras that some academic administrators chant to their faculty is "enrollment." Whether in strategic planning sessions or faculty senate meetings, their message is a constant call to raise student enrollment numbers: "the more enrollments, the better." This mantra is consistent with traditional enrollment-driven budget models that have influenced the thinking of academic leaders for many years. However, this mantra can irritate faculty members who value a more balanced approach of teaching, research, and service as a strategy to raise revenues.

One such irritated faculty member was Eloise, who pointed out an element that is glaringly missing in her school's strategic plan. The plan does not specify the ideal number of students the school would like in each academic program. She would not like to have "as many as students as we can" because, in her opinion, this is the greatest incentive for mediocrity. She would not like to grow without limits just for the sake of being large and perhaps rich. Instead, she would like a number of students in each program that can be supported by faculty, facilities, and other resources. She wants to see a combination of student body size and resources that can support a high quality of students, faculty, and the "holy trinity of research, teaching, and service." She has raised this issue over and over again during her decade-long service to the school—unfortunately to no avail. But the only mantra she and her colleagues hear from school leaders is "enrollment," and she strongly disrespects it as a strategic goal. In her opinion, enrollment is only a means to an end, not *the* end.

Eloise is intellectually stimulating her colleagues to use unconventional thinking when dealing with the traditional problem of enrollment. The administrators got into the habit of framing strategy solely in terms of enrollment, and Eloise is trying to break it. Psychologist William James once quipped: "Genius, in truth, means little more than the faculty of perceiving in an unhabitual way."

James's quote and Eloise's story suggest that you need to examine the habits you rely on in your thinking and work practices, as shown in Figure 5.7. This is called a *mental frame*. Most people rely on their existing knowledge base,

Figure 5.7 Think for yourself. Intellectually stimulating leaders challenge their followers to be independent thinkers who rethink the ways things are done at work and at home.

personal values, beliefs, life experiences, tried-and-true ways, and frames of reference to guide their thinking and actions. Your mental frame makes your thinking and work painless and efficient, but not necessarily innovative or intellectually stimulating. To break these habits requires an element of nontraditional, contrarian, and lateral thinking.[13]

Nontraditional thinking involves thinking outside of the traditional frames of reference. In the example above, the administrators failed to see beyond their enrollment-driven budget model. In contrast, Eloise was able to transcend the old budgetary rules and systems to encourage her colleagues to find a better answer and suggest that the old rules no longer apply. She also used *contrarian thinking* by playing the devil's advocate and taking a position that is totally opposite to the generally accepted beliefs of the administration. While contrarian thinking may make you come across as difficult or annoying to some, it certainly can help stem group-think problems and lead to higher-quality decisions that may have been overlooked under the tried-and-true problem-solving approaches. Contrarian thinking also helped Eloise use *lateral thinking* to look at the strategic planning process from a point of view that differs from the norm. Rather than framing success as money derived from student tuition, Eloise challenged her colleagues to consider additional revenue sources, such as research grants, consulting and outreach, executive education courses, and partnerships with corporations. Remember that what you often consider to be normal may be incorrect or may no longer apply because your leadership context is constantly changing.

Encourage Rethinking Those Ideas That Have Never Been Questioned Before

When it comes to creativity at work, John had an amusing experience in the early stage of his career as an accountant. Prior to entering academia, he worked as an internal auditor and financial analyst in industry. He can clearly remember his first day of work. As a newly minted CPA-MBA in a brand new job, he was very excited and looked forward to applying what he had learned in school to improve his company's operational systems and work processes. However, his enthusiasm was quickly diminished by Ted, his first supervisor. Ted's idea of employee orientation was to have John sit in a cubicle and read policy and procedure manuals all day "until new job assignments are assigned to us by the boss." By the end of the day, this lack of interpersonal interaction and intellectual stimulation prompted John to meet with Ted. John asked him questions about the department's auditing and systems policies and procedures. John's questions (Q) and Ted's responses (A) went something like this:

Q: Why do we limit our functions to only internal auditing?

A: Because that's what corporate headquarters defines as the mission for its internal auditing units and it's our job to go by the book. After all, we're accountants!

Q: But as internal auditors, we're often seen by the people we audit as cops looking for mistakes or ways to eliminate their jobs. Why can't we provide other services that help them when we aren't assigned our audits?

A: Because we speak only when spoken to and we don't want to "stir the pot." Besides, that's the way internal auditors have always and will always be seen. You've got to learn how to play the game and go along to get along. John, your idea is not all that bad.... Let me think about presenting it to the boss at the right time.

Q: These policies seem to apply to large units like our bakeries or corporate headquarters in New Jersey. Why not try something different here?

A: If it's not broken, don't fix it. It's not our job to worry about these things. We follow and enforce rules and do as we're expected and told. By the way, you ask too many questions.

Q: So, how have I been doing so far today? How about some feedback?

A: I'll let you know if you screw up. I got to get back to reviewing Joe, Rose, and Grace's working papers. See you tomorrow morning.

Talk about passive management-by-exception leadership! What a wasted opportunity! Ted could have used this opportunity to give his best intellectual simulation to this newly minted and highly engaging employee. But instead, he did the opposite thing, and it turned out as a big turnoff for John. As your author Don quipped, "No wonder John eventually changed careers and became an intellectually stimulating leadership professor!"

According to leadership scholars Bruce Avolio and Fred Luthans, moments matter when it comes to leadership.[14] Every interaction you have with your followers provides an occasion to teach, inspire, role model, or challenge them. It offers the chance to move them out of their comfort zones. It provides them with the opportunity to grow. For example, the interaction between Ted and John could have formed the foundation for new directions for the department and more positive attitudes toward internal auditing from our internal customers. Despite this missed opportunity, Ted and the department manager eventually did question and reevaluate the role of the department. As a result, they expanded its role beyond audits to creating PC and mainframe systems that made the jobs of employees more enjoyable and efficient. And when the internal audit team visited colleagues in the other departments, they greeted them with a friendly smile instead of the look of suspicion. Intellectual stimulation made even an audit team likable!

By encouraging your followers to rethink ideas that have never been questioned before, you too can steer your group in the right direction. This intellectually stimulating behavior gets followers to rationally evaluate old ideas and strategies that may need to be revised or totally eliminated. As shown in Figure 5.8, intellectual stimulation trains your followers to think critically and systematically. That allows them to use their reason and logic to address important issues and concerns. It also provides you with a wellspring of ideas that you can use to deal with problems that have been plaguing your organization.

Thinking About Intellectual Stimulation

You are now familiar with the concept of intellectual stimulation. Now it's time to start thinking deeply about what implications this has for implementing your own intellectual stimulation practices: setting the stage for intellectual stimulation and problem solving. A good understanding of these topics will help you to promote the innovation required for business survival, better returns on investment, and competitive advantage.

Roadblocks to Intellectual Stimulation

Former U.S. vice president Al Gore was awarded the 2007 Nobel Peace Prize winner for educating others around the world about man-made climate change.

Figure 5.8 All points considered. Aspiring leaders concentrate intently as they apply creative problem-solving methods to perform a group task.

Today, Gore spends much of his time addressing leadership and environmental issues of global warming and climate change and discussing these issues with political and business leaders. He also chairs the Alliance for Climate Protection, a nonprofit organization designed to help solve the climate crisis. They work to remove the roadblocks that stand in the way of solving the climate change problem.[15]

Al Gore's example teaches us that before we attempt to display intellectually stimulating behaviors, it's a good idea to identify (and then work to remove) any potential stumbling blocks that may get in your way. Displaying intellectual stimulation without considering potential stumbling blocks, or without building trust, can actually have negative effects on group creativity.[16] So you need to be more strategic about the content and timing of your intellectually stimulating initiatives because they may trigger resistance from several sources. These sources of resistance include your organization, leader, followers, problem orientation, and yourself. For each of these sources shown below, think about the following items that describe them and the degree to which they describe your organization. Keep track of the items that are true for you and your organization.[17]

Your Organization

The policies, procedures, and practices that define your organization's culture and structure may present huge barriers to your ability to display intellectual stimulation. How many of the following items are true for your organization?:

- Being a creative thinker is risky in my organization.
- Most new ideas don't get implemented in my organization.
- In the past, people in my organization have not been given credit for their innovative ideas.
- In my organization, there are standard assumptions for doing the work that must be followed.
- My organization most often wants innovation when it is looking to cut costs.
- My organization frowns on mistakes, so innovation and creativity are to be avoided.[18]

If your organization's structure, practices, and policies are a stumbling block, you must work with your colleagues to mobilize and build support to make appropriate changes. This involves championing innovation in strategic planning processes, building reward structures that support innovation, hiring creative people, and enlisting top management to identify and remove these roadblocks. What stumbling blocks do you need to get rid of? Who can you rely on when you initiate such changes? What can you do to jump-start such changes in your organization?

Your Leader

Your close or distant leader may put the brakes on your ability to display intellectual stimulation. How many of the following items are true for your leader?

- My leader expects everyone to think as he or she does.
- My leader believes only the leader is responsible for developing new ideas.
- My leader is unreceptive to new ideas.
- If I want to get ahead in my organization, I must avoid acting smarter than my leader.
- My leader discourages me and my staff when I try to be more creative.
- My leader often makes fun of other peoples' ideas.[19]

If your leader is a major stumbling block, short of a coup d'état, you must find ways to work around any roadblocks he or she presents. This involves entailing others to show how championing innovation leads to success, creating interest in problem-solving processes, creating demonstration projects to test out new ideas, and educating your leader about the folly of inhibiting creativity and innovation. What can you do to work around the roadblocks your leader builds?

Your Followers

Your followers may get in the way of your ability to display intellectual stimulation. How many of the following items are true for your followers?

- My staff relies on me to develop new ways for them to do their jobs better.
- My followers would feel silly if they were asked to brainstorm new ideas.
- My staff members avoid taking intellectual risks.
- My followers rarely initiate new ideas on their own.
- Most of my staff is afraid to show what they don't know.
- People who work for me lack creativity.[20]

If your followers represent a stumbling block, you can always train and reward them for displaying creative behavior. You can do this by matching their talents and skills with appropriate work. Teach them the intellectually stimulating behaviors described above. Enroll them in problem-solving and creativity courses offered through universities or consulting firms. Use traditional or electronic brainstorming (described below). And don't forget to "catch them being creative" and reward them for it. Which of your followers can you work with to change their attitude toward creativity?

Your Problem Orientation

Sometimes, the way you go about perceiving and solving problems hinders your ability to be intellectually stimulating. Do you agree with the following items?

- It is a waste of time to return to basic assumptions when trying to solve a problem.
- Everyone usually starts with the same basic assumptions about a problem.
- Usually there is only one right answer to a problem.
- It takes pure reasoning to solve problems. How you feel about a problem is irrelevant.
- Creative people are born, not made.[21]

The more items with which you agree, the more your problem orientation is getting in the way of your ability to practice intellectual stimulation. Nevertheless, your problem orientation can change if you attend problem-solving and creativity courses offered through universities or consulting firms.

For example, Penn State offers three courses that address problem orientation skills in our MLD program: Corporate Innovative Strategies, Developing Creative High-Performance Organizations, and Creativity and Problem Solving (see the appendix for details on these courses). Penn State also offers a four-course certificate program on problem-solving leadership that is popular with leaders in the field of engineering. Orientations can always change through education and practice. What will you do to improve your problem orientation?

Yourself

Jack Paar, a famous U.S. radio and television talk show host, once said, "All of life is an obstacle course, with myself being the chief obstacle." Indeed, so many of the wounds that maim or kill intellectual stimulation are self-inflicted. To assess your level of self-mutilation, count how many of the following items with which you agree:

- It makes me uncomfortable to question other people's assumptions.
- I feel I am lacking in creativity.
- Sitting around trying to generate new ideas is a waste of time.
- When I do something well, I stick to the basic ideas that support my approach.
- If I have the time, I can be far more creative on my own than with my followers.
- I will continue to use old methods that work for me.[22]

Again, the more items with which you agree, the more you are blocking your own ability to intellectually stimulate others. But of all the sources of roadblocks, this one is the easiest to fix (if you really want to change). All it takes is a positive attitude toward creativity and the habit of practicing the behaviors and tactics described in this chapter every day. Your learning partner can also help you a great deal by monitoring and reinforcing your practice.

Intellectual Stimulation and Pragmatic/ Problem-Solving Leadership

Problems are a part of everyday life. Leaders are responsible for developing creative and useful strategies for generating solutions to problems based on the functional needs of their organization. For example, Bavarian Motor Works (BMW), the world-famous German manufacturer, is known for its engineering prowess in producing high-performance luxury vehicles. BMW's executive leadership has a long tradition of challenging their engineers to create innovative yet practical cutting-edge designs that address important issues such as fuel efficiency and ecology-friendly emissions. They do this by stimulating the thinking of their employees, as described in Table 5.2.

BMW's practical approach to innovation is consistent with theory on pragmatic leadership. In Chapter 1, you read about pragmatic or problem-solving leadership theory and how it relates to Full Range Leadership Development. Now, let's consider how intellectual stimulation can be used to support pragmatic or problem-solving leadership.

In their conceptualization of pragmatic leadership, Professor Michael Mumford and his colleagues proposed that outstanding leadership does not always have to involve inspirational and idealized leadership (i.e., charisma), but instead may be associated with a more practical and functional search for solutions to problems confronting individuals and their organizations. Thus, pragmatic or problem-solving leadership is a process of collecting and using knowledge from problems, people, and their organizations to build and leverage higher levels of wisdom, experience, and perspective-taking capacity.[23]

Knowledge gained from problems is obtained through four processes: (1) defining the problem, (2) gathering information, (3) formulating understanding, and (4) generating trial solutions. You can use the intellectually stimulating behaviors described above to support these processes. Considering the problem from many different angles and perspectives can lead you to uncover hidden problems that are more fundamental to the situation and problem. Questioning deeply rooted opinions and assumptions can produce a solid understanding of the problem and alternate solutions. Creating demonstration projects to test out ideas can yield high-quality trial solutions.

Knowledge gained from people is obtained through three processes: (1) communicating, (2) initiating structure, and (3) implementing and revising plans. You also can use the intellectually stimulating behaviors described above to support these processes. Seeking different perspectives and challenging basic assumptions and premises can enrich the quality of the communication process. Intellectual stimulation can "establish a pattern or framework to explain a flow of events to reduce the complexity and diversity of those events,"[24] thereby providing structure to tasks followers must complete. Encouraging followers to revisit problems and reexamine assumptions can support the implementation and revision of plans.

Knowledge gained from organizations is obtained through four processes: (1) protecting outcomes and reactions, (2) identifying restrictions and requirements, (3) garnering support, and (4) formulating plans/visions. Displaying intellectually stimulating behaviors can help as well. Questioning deeply rooted opinions and assumptions can point out restrictions and requirements needed to solve problems successfully. Seeking varied perspectives can help to ensure that all opinions are communicated thoroughly so that consensus can be achieved more

Table 5.2   Leadership Profile: BMW and Technology Leadership

BMW, a company famous for manufacturing high-performance automobiles, can add another feather to its cap. It's now partnering with some of the world's greatest thinkers to spread intellectual thoughts throughout the world in the hope of shaping a better future for all of its citizens.

For many years, BMW has used several of the intellectually stimulating tactics discussed in this chapter to spur groundbreaking innovation. For example, BMW structures its work processes using network-based cross-functional teams that constantly discuss ideas and projects, both intensely and relentlessly. BMW realizes that the knowledge base for innovation resides in networks of workers, and that leadership is needed to meld their brainpower through intellectual stimulation.

Through cross-functional teams, lateral thinking and communication, balancing hierarchy and discipline within chaordic organizational structures, BMW has created an experimental learning-oriented environment where ideas come first and old-school rigidity is passé. According to BMW's top leadership, engineers working in this environment are exposed to a variety of rich information that allows them to perceive problems in new ways, and frame ideas more accurately. The speed and agility in creativity and problem solving that comes from this environment helps BMW to shift and adjust strategy so it can meet changing market demands.

More recently, BMW has joined forces with the TED (Technology, Entertainment, Design) Conference to share their belief that ideas can address many of the world's most pressing problems, such as global warming, poverty, sustainability, prosthetics, war, violence, alternate energy sources, and disease. Each year, over 1,000 great thinkers and performing artists are invited to TED. Speakers have included Al Gore, Tony Robbins, Nicholas Negroponte (One Laptop per Child founder), Amy Smith (MIT engineer), philosopher Daniel Dennett, and 11-year-old concert violinist Sirena Huang, among many other of the world's thought leaders. Through BMW-produced short movies and Web site distribution, TED provides people all over the world with intellectual stimulation. This form of mental exhilaration can drive the intersection of technology and social systems toward positive outcomes, just as a BMW can provide its customers with the ultimate driving experience.

Source: Edmondson, G. (2006, October 16). The secret of BMW's success. *Business Week Online.* Retrieved May 23, 2008, from http://www.businessweek.com/ magazine/content/-6_42/b4005078.htm; and http://www.bmwusa.com/Standard/Content/Uniquely/TVAndNewMedia/TEDTalks.aspx.

Table 5.3   Leader Profile: Lance Armstrong

Lance Armstrong is a cancer survivor, champion cyclist, hero, and leader. He may also be the most inspirational sports figure in the world today. In 1997, Armstrong launched Livestrong, the Lance Armstrong Foundation, whose mission is to inspire and empower people affected by cancer. The foundation works to reduce the stigma associated with cancer. They educate people all over the world about the disease. The organization's goal is to motivate national leaders and the international community to increase their commitment to fight the disease in their own countries.

A true role model, Armstrong overcame testicular cancer in the mid-1990s. He won the Tour de France seven times in a row before retiring from the sport in 2005. Through his brave recovery from cancer, Armstrong revitalized an international cancer awareness movement, raising $260 million for cancer research through his nonprofit foundation and personal example.

In 2004, Armstrong jump-started an international phenomenon when he initiated the wearing of yellow wristbands. These "live strong" bracelets signaled support for finding a cure for the deadly disease. The wristbands were an international sensation that intellectually stimulated and inspired many people to focus attention on cancer research. The simple rubber bracelets helped to raise unprecedented levels of awareness and millions of dollars for cancer research. In 2009, Armstrong made a run at an eighth championship as he returned to professional cycling and promoted the mission of his cancer foundation.

Source: Grabowski, J. F. (2005). *Lance Armstrong*. Chicago: Lucent Books; and retrieved January 30, 2009, from http://www.livestrong.org/site/c. khLXK1PxHmF/b.2661053/k.9207/Lances_Story.htm.

readily than if these perspectives were omitted or ignored. Imagining alternative states, considering absurd assumptions, and widening, shrinking, and splitting the leadership context can assist in formulating an evocative and compelling vision. Consider the unique and inspiring vision that Lance Armstrong has created for people battling cancer and other diseases, as described in Table 5.3.

In summary, you do not have to be a star athlete or rocket scientist to provide intellectual stimulation to your followers. It simply takes the ability and willingness to recognize and work to remove the things that get in the way of this rational approach to leadership. Once the roadblocks to intellectual stimulation have been removed, you can think about the problem-solving approach described above and how intellectual stimulation may apply in your specific leadership context. After carefully reflecting upon your strategy, you can display the behaviors of intellectual stimulation to solve your problems and develop your followers' ability to think for themselves.

Putting Intellectual Stimulation Into Practice
Display the Behaviors Described in This Chapter

This chapter presented six behaviors associated with intellectual stimulation. These behaviors emphasized the importance of seeking different perspectives and ways of analyzing problems, questioning assumptions that may no longer be valid, suggesting new ways to complete assignments, encouraging nontraditional thinking, and rethinking ideas that have never been questioned in the past. By displaying these behaviors with your followers, they will become more willing to think, generate creative and innovative ideas, and develop new perspectives about people, processes, and projects.

That's what Michael Lomax, an executive at Allstate Insurance, realized after he began to challenge his committee to produce a unique student recruiting event for the MLD program at Penn State. With the capable assistance of his co-chair, Patricia Bonner, Michael encouraged his committee to add new twists on the same old formulas for staging recruiting events. He scheduled meetings to solicit team members' ideas based on their personal experience. He encouraged them to collaborate with other students and university staff.

As a result of Michael's intellectual stimulation, the team produced an inspiring and innovative recruiting video for the MLD program. This video was debuted at the event. It is now included on the campus Web site and given to prospective students. The team also gave out leadership-related door prizes and certificates of recognition to participants. They also created a mini-conference atmosphere prior to the event, complete with tables highlighting how the MLD program contributes to areas such as corporate change initiatives, human resource management, social entrepreneurship, mentoring of children, strategic leadership, and community service projects. Through his encouragement of nontraditional thinking and inclusion of diverse individuals on the planning committee, Michael was able to produce an outstanding event that was widely attended and highly acclaimed by both current and prospective students and members of the business community as well.

Use Brainstorming

When you challenge followers the way Michael Lomax did, you expand their capacity to generate creative ideas together. The more ideas with which they have to work, the greater the base of raw material they have to build innovative solutions to their problems. One method for producing such a large range of ideas is *brainstorming*, a group creativity technique designed to generate a great number and variety of ideas. Traditional face-to-face brainstorming was developed in the 1930s by Alex Osborn, a marketing executive interested in enhancing the creativity of his staff. Today, many organizations use *electronic brainstorming* (EBS), which uses special software to encourage participation through anonymity, file sharing, and simultaneous input of comments from group members.[25]

Whether you choose face-to-face or electronic brainstorming methods, be sure to remember to apply the rules of brainstorming:

- *The more ideas, the better.* Encourage your group to produce as many ideas as possible because quantity is assumed to be related to quality.
- *No criticism is allowed.* There are no wrong or bad ideas in brainstorming. It is important for you to separate idea generation from idea evaluation because judgment of ideas by others can stifle creativity.
- *The wilder the ideas, the better.* The goal of intellectual stimulation is to encourage nontraditional thinking and ideas that are "off the wall." Some seemingly crazy ideas can actually lead to innovative breakthroughs. Remember when American Motors Corporation introduced the unsightly Pacer in the 1970s or when Toyota introduced the unusual Prius in 1997 in Japan? Both cars were funny looking when we first saw them. But with the painfully high cost of fuel these days, Toyota is laughing all the way to the bank.
- *Build on others' ideas.* By combining, modifying, and improving upon ideas offered, you can produce a wide variety of alternative solutions, some of which may be judged as useful when your group meets in a subsequent idea evaluation session.[26]

Brainstorming is a fun and effective way to intellectually stimulate your followers. Be sure to record all ideas generated by your group members either manually or automatically via EBS software. You should then evaluate, rank, and fine-tune all ideas on the list in a future meeting to transform the raw material of the brainstorming session into an action plan.

Promote the Use of Fantasy

John Lennon once quipped, "Reality leaves a lot to the imagination." Intellectual stimulating leaders, like Lennon, give themselves and their followers a reason to daydream and imagine an ideal situation or world. One way to encourage this is to promote the use of fantasy prior to or during decision-making meetings. *Fantasy* involves portraying in the mind something positive that is not the case or not present at this time. Many of the great inventors, such as Thomas Edison and Louis Pasteur, or famous movie directors, such as Steven Spielberg and Spike Lee, would imagine pleasant but unlikely events to jump-start their creativity. Fantasy is also used in corporate strategic planning methods such as *scenario planning*, in which alternative futures are envisioned as a way to give free rein to imagination.[27] We also find fantasy in role-playing exercises often seen in corporate training programs.

Fantasy provides us with several outcomes that can benefit our creative thinking. It can supply an experience that is optimal and free from real-life constraints and limitations that bind our ability to generate creative solutions. It allows us to try out various modes of action as potential solutions to problems without cost or risk. It also can be a rejuvenating distraction from the daily pressures and stresses in our lives. It also allows us to get away from it all via a "mental vacation." Even a brief respite can rejuvenate the mind and lead to more creative forms of thinking. In addition, fantasy allows us to dream in ways that are not allowed free expression in our real lives. Fantasy permits us to transcend these boundaries in ways that gain access to deeply stored information in the human psyche. This information can influence and create interest in problem-solving processes.[28]

Fantasy was used by the creators of the Educational Concern for Hunger Organization (ECHO) located in North Fort Meyers, Florida. ECHO uses science and technology to help feed the world's poor in 180 countries. By transcending traditional assumptions about agriculture, ECHO's founding leaders fantasized about and then developed a 50-acre farm that demonstrates how tropical food plants and innovative agricultural techniques can be applied to solve the real problems of world hunger and resource allocation. They do it by providing three services. They educate and train people through internships and workshops. They solve problems by sharing solutions through their bulletins and Web site, technical response unit, and seed bank. And they build networks of international community development workers through their annual conference and Web site. Next time you are in South Florida, visit this exemplar of intellectual stimulation that seeks "hunger solutions for families growing food under difficult conditions."[29]

Imagine Alternative States

Fantasy is helpful for intellectually stimulating your followers because it allows you to imagine alternative states. Many of our solutions are not optimal simply because we get bogged down in describing the current situation (and framing our problem) as things are or according to what we're used to, instead of how they *should* be. Rather than describing the current state of affairs, try envisioning the future state you are seeking for your problem solution.

Robb Most of Mind Garden, Inc., is excellent at imagining alternative future states. In April 2008, we met with Robb at the Society for Industrial and Organizational Psychology conference in San Francisco. Robb is a visionary who excels at seeing possibilities and opportunities through syntheses of ideas, people, processes, and technologies. Rather than seeing things as they are, Robb sees things as means for creating positive ends through alternative futures.

For example, as Robb showed us his iPhone, he talked of the possibility of running Mind Garden through his exciting new technology "toy." Robb also mentioned the need for intellectually stimulating leaders to step back and listen to the collective wisdom and life experiences that followers bring to the table. Robb has envisioned Internet-based tools to provide multiple self-surveys and assessments that can be administered to such leaders. Multiple observers could rate the leaders. Significant positive and negative events in the leaders' life context could be rated. All of these ratings could be repeated over time to track leadership development. By maintaining the focus on the leader, an unfolding of continuing understanding develops. With this information, a report could be generated and give leaders a comprehensive view of their beliefs, behaviors, feelings, and life context, and how these have changed over time.

Guided by ideas from his staff, Robb also imagined setting up Web pages based on Wikipedia technology that could capture the ideas and experiences of aspiring leaders and their followers. These Web pages could be used to illustrate FRLD concepts using unconventional media such as photography, music, art, and movie clips, along with commentary explaining their application. What a fun way to learn more about FRLD! How can you imagine alternate states in your leadership contexts?

Learn to Think Differently

International Business Machines (IBM) originated in Endicott, New York, only a few miles away from the Center for Leadership Studies at SUNY-Binghamton, where we received our doctorate degrees. IBM Endicott served as corporate headquarters for many years and was home to its education and training activities in the "IBM Schoolhouse." Employees trained at the IBM Schoolhouse were reminded everyday of the importance of thinking differently. As they entered into the schoolhouse, they walked up "the five steps of knowledge." Below each step, one of the following words was engraved: read, listen, discuss, observe, and think.[30]

Why? Because reading allows us to expand our knowledge base and exercises the mind. Listening allows us to enlarge our perspective by learning about different points of views and gaining knowledge from the world around us. Discussing permits us to exchange ideas and fine-tune our thought processes. Observing lets us learn by watching what other people do. Thinking allows us to synthesize all of this information into useful strategies and actions. By espousing these intellectual processes, IBM was teaching its employees that people learn and think differently and that this diversity is required to maximize the effects of intellectual stimulation. Without a doubt, IBM's learning-oriented culture and respect for diverse thinking has been one of the most fundamental reasons for its prolonged success. As an intellectually stimulating leader, you should be aware of several different approaches to thinking that you can use to influence followers.

Rationally oriented thinking uses logic and deduction to develop and articulate reasonable arguments supported by evidence. Use this form of thinking to convince followers by appealing to their reason, or when dealing with individuals who are more transactional in nature, such as colleagues from accounting, finance, and engineering, or with philosophical individuals.

Empirically oriented thinking uses data-gathering processes to weigh the evidence and test propositions offered by the self and others. Like rationally oriented thinking, empirically oriented thinking may be linear in nature and follows a systematic procedure of collecting and analyzing data to test the appropriateness of one solution at a time. Use this form of thinking with scientifically oriented people or technical types to justify your proposition or position developed through data-based decision making.

Idealistically oriented thinking bases its standards of evaluation on consistency with cherished virtues, values, and principles generally accepted by the community. If you value intellectual stimulation, you may have to adapt your standard of evaluation to include perspectives held outside of your community and those that change over time. Use this form of thinking to influence people who are ideological and find comfort in traditions and customs.

Existentially oriented thinking attempts to synthesize a variety of different perspectives and solutions through informal interactions with others. Because you are dealing with diverse opinions, you may have to use your intuition to access deeply held organizational assumptions, values, symbols, and emotions that you've learned through experience. Use this form of thinking when group consensus is important to moving your agenda forward.[31]

Ask Challenging Questions

Your followers and associates are more educated and technology-savvy than earlier generations. They enjoy being challenged intellectually. Another way to intellectually stimulate them is to ask what they find fascinating and what challenges them intellectually at work and in the community. Once they provide you with answers, you can ask them how they can respond to these challenges with your support.

This is what Professor Barrie Litzky does in her Social Entrepreneurship and Community Leadership course, the capstone course in the MLD program. She asks her students what they consider to be the most pressing social issues confronting their communities. Once they respond, Barrie challenges them to develop and initiate an action plan to address the issue. Students partner with and mentor high school students to work with local businesses to address important social issues, such as HIV/AIDS, as described in the Camp Dreamcatcher case at the start of this chapter. Next time you're struggling to intellectually stimulate your followers, think of the way Barrie challenges her students to solve important problems. The answers may already be there nesting in the hearts and minds of your followers. It's up to you to ask the right questions to get the answers out and into action.

Reverse the Figure and Ground

If you have ever taken a photography course, you probably learned the importance of the contrast between the foreground of your photo (i.e., the figure or subject) and its background (i.e., the ground). For example, the photographer must consider the color and lighting of the background in order to adequately highlight the subject of the photo. The notion of contrast was also used in Gestalt psychology by Edgar Rubin to illustrate the key role of shaping perception and how perception and cognition can change depending on whether one pays more attention to the figure or ground,[32] as illustrated in Figure 5.9.

Intellectually stimulating leaders use the notion of contrast as well. When evaluating problems, we often focus exclusively on the figure (i.e., the problem) without paying much attention to the details of the ground (i.e., the context of the problem). However, the intellectually stimulating leader will reverse

Figure 5.9 **Figure–ground reversal. The Canadian flag illustrates this perceptual process by focusing not on the maple leaf as figure, but instead on the background edge of the maple leaf as an image of two faces arguing.**

the figure and ground and focus on the ground to find interesting information that was originally overlooked. In the case of the university enrollment problem described above, increasing enrollments is the figure and the exclusive focus of many administrators. What these administrators fail to perceive is that the figure of the enrollment problem is set against a rich background of branding issues, program and school reputations, resources, etc. These branding issues may be the real drivers of enrollment and should be perceived as the figure set against the background of enrollment. This shift in perspective can allow administrators to collect data on the real drivers of enrollment and adjust their strategies using market research expertise.[33] What issues in your organization can be reevaluated by reversing the figure and the ground?

In summary, when you use intellectual stimulation, you get to change your followers' assumptions about people, processes, and Planet Earth and its resources. You also show them that you value their intellect and the power of their imagination by asking them to constantly challenge old ways of doing things. As a result, they are more likely to question the status quo, introduce change, champion innovation, and use reason along with the emotion you invoked with inspirational motivation. This powerful combination of effects helps develop followers' perceptional, cognitive, and intuitive skills required to become leaders.

We firmly believe that one of the biggest problems among many leaders (even successful ones) is that they do not utilize followers' intellectual capacity and creative potential fully. We found that this is due in part to leaders' arrogant thinking that they can't get anything useful and creative from their followers. This constant underutilization of creative potential among employees will eventually compromise your success as a leader and as an organization. Let's now turn our attention to individually considerate behaviors needed to further develop followers into leaders in the next chapter.

Summary Questions and Reflective Exercises

1. This exercise uses results of your Multifactor Leadership Questionnaire (MLQ) report to assess your level of intellectual stimulation behavior. Compare your intellectual stimulation ratings with the research-validated benchmarks. How did your self-ratings, ratings from subordinates, ratings from peers, ratings from superiors, and ratings from others compare against the benchmarks? On which specific MLQ items (i.e., questions) did you score highest? Lowest? What can you do to improve on the items where you scored lowest?

2. This exercise also uses results of your MLQ report to assess your level of intellectual stimulation behavior. Compare your self-ratings on *intellectual*

stimulation behavior with ratings provided by subordinates, peers, superiors, and others. Compute the difference score (d) as the difference between your self-rating score and the specific other rating source score of interest. If d is less than .5 and the other rating source score is less than 2.77, then you are considered to be *in agreement/poor*. If d is less than .5 and the other rating source score is greater than 2.77, then you are considered to be *in agreement/good*. If d is equal to or greater than .5 and the self-rating score is greater than the other rating score, then you are an *overestimator* on this dimension. If d is equal to or greater than .5 and the self-rating score is less than the other rating score, then you are an *underestimator* on this dimension. Consider the category under which you fall in terms of intellectual stimulation behavior. What are the implications of this categorization for you? Are there any things you can do to improve in this area?

3. Assemble a group of your associates for the purpose of brainstorming a list of the most pressing problems in your department or group. Spend a half hour identifying these problems using the rules of brainstorming listed above. Once your list is complete, ask your group to rank order the top 10 problems from the list. Assign the top five problems to specific group members to lead a series of brainstorming sessions using intellectually stimulating behaviors at your next meeting.

4. Building upon the results of exercise 3, assemble your colleagues to work on action plans for addressing the aforementioned top five problems. Make sure that your team uses intellectually stimulating behaviors to question underlying assumptions, examine problems from different perspectives and approaches, etc., during this meeting. Assign responsibilities for each step in the action plans to your colleagues and their staff. Follow up on their progress in weekly meetings.

5. Visit http://www.groupsystems.com/ and research the characteristics of electronic brainstorming (EBS) technologies. Summarize key product features and how they can support intellectual stimulation. How can this technology help your efforts to champion intellectual stimulation in your organization?

6. Building upon the results of exercise 5, perform a literature review using research databases such as ABI/INFORM, ERIC, Google Scholar, ProQuest, PsychARTICLES, and PsychINFO to identify articles on "leadership and advanced information technology," "e-leadership," or "leadership and group decision support systems." Summarize your findings and report to your group how leadership can be used with technology to promote creativity and innovation in your organization.

7. Find a popular movie that demonstrates intellectual stimulation by visiting your local video store, Netflix (http://www.netflix.com), local or school library, or YouTube (http://www.youtube.com). For example, we like to use several clips from Touchstone Films' *Dead Poets Society* (1989), starring Robin Williams, for this task. Present your findings to your associates at your next team meeting and teach them about the benefits of intellectually stimulating leadership. What roadblocks to intellectual stimulation will you face? How can you remove them?

8. Identify and adapt a popular game/toy or TV game show from the days of your youth to teach your associates about FRLD. For example, we often use the task of building an airplane with LEGO® building blocks to show FRLD training course participants how leadership styles influence group processes and outcomes. We assign this task to four groups, each guided by a leader displaying either laissez-faire, passive management-by-exception (MBE-P), active management-by-exception (MBE-A), or transformational leadership styles. Participants are amazed how different their planes turn out based on their group's leadership. How can you illustrate the differential effects of FRLD on group processes and outcomes in a fun-filled and intellectually stimulating way?

9. Invite your associates to a "Friday Afternoon Fantasy Camp" event in which you watch a fantasy movie such as *Star Wars*, *Lord of the Rings*, or *Chronicles of Narnia*. Provide refreshments and create a stress-free atmosphere during the film presentation. Immediately following the film, ask your colleagues to relate your organization and its leaders, followers, competitors, etc., to characters and situations in the film. After discussing these parallels, talk about the lessons learned from the film and how they can be applied to your leadership context. What assumptions underlying your situation and values may no longer be valid? What perspectives and new angles should be applied to address your most pressing issues? What is the value of fantasy and imagination in creating an intellectually stimulating culture in your organization? How can you use fantasy to improve your organizational processes?

10. This exercise teaches you how to apply intellectually stimulating and inspirationally motivating behaviors to solve a problem you are facing at work. Assemble a team of four or five associates and describe a problem that you have been working on together as concisely as possible. Start out by talking about the nature (not solution) of the problem with your team. Pay attention to differences in assumptions and perspectives of each team member and note them. Then apply methods of intellectual stimulation to help your team to

- Envision the *future state* you are seeking for your problem solution. What would it be like if the problem were solved? How would you and your followers feel? How would they benefit?
- Consider the problem's *current state* (i.e., the way you see the problem). You can begin discussing whether any of you have an intuitive or gut feel about the right ways to handle the problem.
- Based on your analysis of the problem, generate and list as many solutions as you feel are appropriate. In this brainstorming of solutions, be sure to list all of your ideas without censoring or evaluating any team member's ideas.
- Establish the criteria you will use to rank the solutions. Then modify and combine any solutions that you can and rank your solutions in the order of quality. Your criteria for ranking might include "It's doable" or "It has the greatest payoff."
- Record the insights and discoveries from using intellectual stimulation and inspirational motivation to solve your problem.[34]

Notes

1. Foote, A., Enterline, T., Egolf, P., & Kline, C. (2008). *Camp Dreamcatcher business plan.* LEAD 582: Social entrepreneurship and community leadership final report. Malvern, PA: Penn State Great Valley.
2. Retrieved May 16, 2008, from http://tinytearsdocumentary.com/. For a short trailer of the film, visit http://www.youtube.com/robertcornafilms.
3. Foote et al. (2008). As cited in Note 1; and Global Social Venture Competition *Social Impact Assessment Guides.* Retrieved February 15, 2008, from http://socialvc.net/index.cfm?fuseaction=Page.viewPage&pageId=96&parentID=58&nodeID=1.
4. Burns, J. M. (2003). *Transforming leadership.* New York: Atlantic Monthly Press.
5. Hock, D. (2005). *One from many: VISA and the rise of the chaordic organization.* San Francisco: Berrett-Koehler; and http://www.lap.org/Chaordic/. Retrieved May 16, 2008.
6. Deutsch, C. H. (2003, June 1). An apparent heir at Xerox. *New York Times,* p. 3.2; and Morris, B. (2007, October 15). Xerox's dynamic duo. *Fortune, 156,* 78–86.
7. Retrieved May 20, 2008, from http://www.well.com/~bbear/assumptions.html.
8. Adams, P., & Mylander, M. (1998). *Gesundheit! Bringing good health to you, the medical system, and society through physician service, complementary therapies, humor, and joy.* Rochester, VT: Healing Arts Press.
9. Dreachslin, J. L. (1996). *Diversity leadership.* New York: Health Administration Press.
10. Amabile, T. M., Conti, R., Coon, H., Lazenby, J., & Herron, M. (1996). Assessing the work environment for creativity. *Academy of Management Journal, 39,* 1154–1184.
11. Priore, D. (2005). *Smile: The story of Brian Wilson's lost masterpiece.* London: Sanctuary Press.

12. Retrieved January 25, 2009, from http://www.radiohead.com.
13. Retrieved May 22, 2008, from http://www.goldensphere.com/notraditional.htm.
14. Avolio, B. J., & Luthans, F. (2005). *The high impact leader: Moments matter in accelerating authentic leadership development*. New York: McGraw-Hill.
15. Gore, A. (2009). *The path to survival*. New York: Rodale Books.
16. Sosik, J. J., Avolio, B. J., & Kahai, S. S. (1998). Inspiring group creativity: Comparing anonymous and identified electronic brainstorming. *Small Group Research, 29*, 3–31.
17. Bass, B. M., & Avolio, B. J. (1990). *Advanced workshop: Full range leadership development*. Binghamton, NY: Center for Leadership Studies, SUNY-Binghamton.
18. Adapted from Bass & Avolio (1990). As cited in Note 17.
19. Adapted from Bass & Avolio (1990). As cited in Note 17.
20. Adapted from Bass & Avolio (1990). As cited in Note 17.
21. Adapted from Bass & Avolio (1990). As cited in Note 17.
22. Adapted from Bass & Avolio (1990). As cited in Note 17.
23. For a comprehensive overview and case study of pragmatic leadership, see Mumford, M. D., Zaccaro, S. J., Harding, F. D., Jacobs, T. O., & Fleishman, E. A. (2000). Leadership skills for a changing world: Solving complex social problems. *The Leadership Quarterly, 11*, 11–35; and Mumford, M. D., & Van Doorn, J. R. (2001). The leadership of pragmatism: Reconsidering Franklin in the age of charisma. *The Leadership Quarterly, 12*, 279–309.
24. Bass & Avolio (1990, p. 12.8). As cited in Note 17.
25. Sosik, J. J., Kahai, S. S., & Avolio, B. J. (1998). Transformational leadership and dimensions of group creativity: Motivating idea generation in computer-mediated groups. *Creativity Research Journal, 11*, 111–121.
26. Paulus, P. B., & Nijstad, B. A. (2003). *Group creativity: Innovation through collaboration*. New York: Oxford University Press.
27. Sosik, J. J., Jung, D. I., Berson, Y., Dionne, S. D., & Jaussi, K. S. (2004). *The dream weavers: Strategy-focused leadership in technology-driven organizations*. Greenwich, CT: Information Age Publishing.
28. Maccoby, E. E. (1954). Why do children watch television? *The Public Opinion Quarterly, 18*, 239–244.
29. American Automobile Association. (2008). *Florida tourbook* (pp. 85–86). Heathrow, FL: AAA Publishing; and http://www.echonet.org/. Retrieved June 3, 2008.
30. http://www-03.ibm.com/ibm/history/exhibits/vintage/vintage_4506VV2081.html. Retrieved May 29, 2008.
31. Bass & Avolio (1990, p. 12.9). As cited in Note 17.
32. Rubin, E. (2001). Figure and ground. In S. Yantis (Ed.), *Visual perception* (pp. 225–229). Philadelphia: Psychology Press.
33. Blumenstyk, G. (2008, January 18). Chronicle joins with Gallup to help colleges find out how they are seen by the public. *The Chronicle of Higher Education, 54*, A15.
34. Adapted from Bass & Avolio (1990). As cited in Note 17.

Chapter 6

Individualized Consideration
The Nurturing Side of Transformational Leadership

Leadership is unlocking people's potential to become better.

—Bill Bradley

Carolyn is executive director of development and annual giving for a large urban public hospital. When Carolyn joined the hospital, she inherited a diverse staff of 10 direct reports that did not see eye-to-eye on anything except ignoring her attempts at leadership. They considered themselves to be professionals who did not need her guidance and suggestions. That's because most of her staff were significantly older than Carolyn. Many had been with the hospital for over 20 years. Coupled with their close-minded attitude and sense of entitlement, the staff considered Carolyn's leadership attempts to be unnecessary and redundant sources of irritation. They disliked Carolyn's directive leadership style and her "big city" sophisticated mannerisms, which clashed with the staff's pedestrian style and attitudes. As a result, a storm was certainly brewing, and Carolyn felt she was losing control over the situation. She realized that she was in for many long and stressful days ahead. Does this sound familiar? What would you do to handle this situation successfully?

Carolyn first started to think about her leadership situation. She remembered two important ideas she learned in a Full Range Leadership Development (FRLD) training course. First, leadership is not a *power trip*, it's an *empowerment gift*. Second, leaders and followers can't move forward by taking a competing *firm stance*, but only through a kind of a *dance*, where partners take turns and the lead shifts back and forth until they become one. After pondering these recollections, Carolyn realized that her followers are part of her leadership system, and how she interacts with them will determine their collective success. She came to understand that her followers' individual differences in personality, self-concept, life experiences, knowledge, skills and abilities, and intelligence actually can empower her to achieve synergies. Now Carolyn's mindset was ready to start appreciating the unique differences of her followers and coach and mentor them to achieve their full potential.

Carolyn then took action. She set up a series of one-on-one meetings to get to know each of her staff members on a personal basis. They talked about where they grew up, their families, educational backgrounds, interests outside of work, and hopes and dreams. Then Carolyn asked each of her followers what they perceived their strengths to be and what type of work within her department they prefer to make the best use of their strengths. Carolyn's objective was to find a good person-job fit for each member of her staff. To confirm their suggestions, Carolyn arranged for her staff to complete Gallup's StrengthsFinder 2.0™[1] assessment tool. Based on the results of the assessment, Carolyn then restructured their jobs to be more in line with their talents and skill sets. She held weekly department meetings to hear what her staff had to say on important issues so that they could increase the amount of information flowing through their leadership system (see Chapter 2). In addition, Carolyn held quarterly career development meetings with each of her staff members to provide coaching and mentoring. In these meetings, she showed them how their individual and team roles were contributing to the success of the hospital and its patients. This allowed them to see a bigger picture of their work.

As a result of her evolution from a directive leader to a transformational leader, Carolyn has gained respect and admiration from her followers. They are much more engaged in their work as well. She is now able to motivate and encourage her followers to work together for the good of the hospital. She's no longer seen by her followers as a meddling and precocious boss, but as a leader who serves them by advancing their professional development. She has come to understand what it means to be individually considerate to followers.

Carolyn's story teaches us that individualized consideration recognizes the importance of followers to the success of the FRLD system. The goal of individualized consideration is to increase the engagement level of followers by providing necessary coaching and mentoring. This allows followers to actively take part in their personal and professional development, while they contribute to achieving organizational goals. Individualized consideration gets followers to become active participants in the leadership system.

Leadership researcher Barbara Kellerman recently identified a follower's engagement level as a way to classify followers who either contribute or detract from leadership systems. According to Kellerman, followers who detract from leadership systems are called isolates or bystanders. *Isolates* are followers who are completely detached from their work and organization. *Bystanders* go along to get along, but they do not actively participate in organizational initiatives.

In contrast, followers who contribute to leadership systems are participants, activists, and diehards. *Participants* are engaged in their work in ways that benefit them. *Activists* possess a strong emotional connection to their job and organization and are eager to contribute to almost all organizational activities. *Diehards* are zealots who are so enamored with their leader that they are willing to sacrifice themselves for the cause espoused by the leader.[2] Carolyn's staff members could be classified as ranging from isolates to participants and with time may evolve into activists. Therefore, your comprehension of the individualized consideration component of FRLD should begin with identifying your followers' level of engagement and motivation. By understanding where your followers are in terms of their level of engagement, you can better understand how to apply individualized consideration to help them reach their full leadership potential. Doing so also helps you enhance your organization's performance since individualized consideration is the component of transformational leadership most predictive of organizational effectiveness.[3]

This chapter shows you how to appreciate and tap into the unique variety of knowledge, skills, abilities, and engagement levels your followers bring with them to work every day. You will also learn how to develop your followers' talents into strengths that contribute to your organization's success. By coaching and mentoring your followers into transformational leaders themselves, instead of keeping them as your very own dependent underlings, you too can become an individually considerate leader. Let's start learning about this nurturing approach to leadership by considering the case of the most successful coach in the history of college basketball.

The Developmental Power of Pat Summitt

What does it take to accumulate 1,000 wins and 8 national championships over a 30-year coaching career? What leadership behaviors must you display to earn the title of "all-time winningest coach in the history of NCAA basketball"? Pat

Summitt, head coach of the Tennessee Lady Volunteers, knows the answers to these questions because she has lived the principles of FRLD almost every day of her life.

For the past 30 years, Summitt has coached some of the greatest athletes in women's college basketball, transforming them from maverick high school superstars into team players who go on to success in professional basketball, coaching, business, and life. Many of Summitt's recruits are "diehard" enthusiasts committed to their own personal agendas. Summitt breaks them down and rebuilds them into team players. They come to appreciate that success depends on interdependence rather than independence. Her legacy is not so much about the titles, trophies, or tournaments she has won, but the vast number of players who have achieved personal success in their own careers as a result of her magic touch.

How does she do it? Summitt has devised a leadership system that identifies the raw talents that players bring to the team and transforms them into strengths through a series of processes and principles she calls "the Definite Dozen." Actually, these methods are personal values that can be applied as life skills and include respect, responsibility, loyalty, discipline, hard and smart work, teamwork, positive attitude, competition, change, and humility.[4] Many of these values are aspects of idealized influence that Summitt ingrains into her players to guide their behavior on and off of the court. So, the first thing Summitt does is to teach and role model these values so that her players have clear expectations regarding what drives success. These expectations serve as important guidelines for their behavior.

Once Summitt sets these expectations, she then uses individualized consideration to pay special attention to each player on and off of the court. The heart of individualized consideration lies in treating each and every follower as a unique person, each with different needs and aspirations, and providing different development plans based on their strengths and talents. Thus, she does not treat all of her players the same. She administers personality tests to her players to learn how to best motivate each of them. She scrutinizes their behavior and playing styles at practice and studies game tapes to point out areas for development. She frequently meets one-on-one with her players to review their progress and make suggestions for improvement. She gives her players feedback that is both timely and direct. Because she is passionate about the game of basketball, Summitt uses a form of tough love on her followers. She constantly challenges them to improve and grow into team players. As a result, some players find her ways too demanding. In fact, she's been likened to Bobby Knight, her cantankerous counterpart in the men's collegiate game.[5]

Summitt's exemplary mix of individualized consideration and idealized influence shows that transformational leadership is not "feel good" or "touchy-feely" leadership. Many people have the misconception that transformational leadership is a soft form of leadership. This is not true. Rather, transformational leadership gets followers to move out of their comfort zones to develop to their full potential. Like exercise and weight training, this process can be painful or exhilarating, depending on the methods used and the attitude and maturity of the individual willing to make the effort. That's why transformational leaders often provoke strong emotional responses from their followers. During this process, individualized consideration should be used to make the developmental process more personal, nurturing, and compassionate. As Pat Summitt once observed, "It's OK to let down your guard and allow your players to get to know you. They don't care how much you know until they know how much you care."

Individualized Consideration: Definition and Behavioral Examples

Like Pat Summitt, you too can develop your followers into high-performing transformational leaders by displaying individually considerate behaviors. That's because *individualized consideration* involves dealing with others as individuals and considering their needs, abilities, and aspirations as you work together to further their development. Individualized consideration means being empathetic toward the follower, understanding what he or she is about, and being developmentally focused by encouraging continuous improvement. These characteristics of individualized consideration are achieved by being alert to each follower's needs and providing learning opportunities to them. Individualized consideration makes followers more willing to develop and grow as professionals and as persons. It makes them feel valued because you are paying special attention to them. It encourages a two-way exchange of ideas and personalizes your relationship with them. It also encourages individualism, which is required to promote creativity and prevent group-think that may occur from too much inspirational motivation or blind obedience to the leader. In essence, individualized consideration allows you to transfer your leadership capacity into the next generation of leaders. Individualized consideration is what makes transformational leadership more developmental than other types of leadership. To better understand these concepts, think about how displaying individually considerate behaviors comes naturally to Wendy Kopp (see Table 6.1).

Like Kopp, you can demonstrate individualized consideration by practicing behaviors that show care, concern, and empathy for your followers. Let's now examine six important leadership behaviors that allow you to display individualized consideration.

Table 6.1   Leader Profile: Wendy Kopp

Some of today's young people are turning away from the lure of lucrative salaries, prestige, and "job security" in corporations. Instead, they are increasingly becoming attracted by the ability to significantly influence the lives of individuals, one at a time, through the noble profession of teaching.

Wendy Kopp came up with an idea for a means for such people to realize their dreams and presented it in her undergraduate senior thesis paper at Princeton University. Kopp and her team went on to establish Teach for America, an organization that recruits and trains recent college graduates to teach for two years in disadvantaged urban and rural schools in the United States. The program is a type of Peace Corps for teachers. Over 5,000 members are now teaching 440,000 students in low-income regions. These members are working with 12,000 Teach for America alumni to introduce educational and social reform where it is most needed.

Kopp, who was named as one of the best leaders of 2006 by *U.S. News and World Report*, considers teaching to be leadership. Geographically and economically disadvantaged children across the United States represent a huge leadership challenge for teachers. Kopp's vision is to eliminate educational inequality plaguing the U.S. educational system. Her challenge is to put children on an equal playing field by giving them the individualized attention, passion, and expertise of the best and brightest college graduates. Her efforts are creating patterns of incremental successes within these pockets of disenfranchisement.

As an individually considerate leader, Kopp is interested in the well-being of others, especially the disadvantaged children her organization is helping. She is raising the hopes and aspirations of many of the United States' poorest children through the gift of education. She is also helping today's college graduates see the value of caring for the welfare of future generations, and raising their level of moral development along the way.

Source: Kopp, W. (2001). *One day, all children…: The unlikely triumph of Teach for America and what I learned along the way*. New York: Public Affairs; and retrieved June 16, 2008, from http://www.teachforamerica.org/mission/index.htm.

Consider Individuals as Having Different Needs, Abilities, and Aspirations From Others

We believe that the best way to start practicing individualized consideration is to recognize that your followers are not just a bunch of people who were hired to do their work. Rather, you need to realize that they have different needs, expectations, and aspirations. For example, John had an amazing teacher when he was a seventh grader who showed him what individualized consideration was all about, and it made a big impact on his life.

When John was in seventh grade, he transferred from public school to St. Vincent's parochial school in Plymouth, Pennsylvania, because he wanted to attend a private Catholic high school. It was easier for students to gain admittance to this high school if they came from a parochial middle school. After settling into his new school, John quickly mastered the academic subjects and found time to join the basketball team. He enjoyed the fun and camaraderie of training with his friends and classmates and learned much about leadership and teamwork along the way. Unfortunately, John's athletic abilities on the basketball court did not equal his academic prowess in the classroom. In class he was "the one with all the answers," but on the court, he was an average player, far from being "the answer," like Allen Iverson.

John's basketball team was coached by Anthony Saraceno, who was also his seventh and eighth grade science and math teacher. Mr. Saraceno was very demanding during practice and drilled each player based on what they needed to know to develop their playing skills. One day after practice, he came up to John and said he wanted to talk to him before school the next morning. "Oh no," John thought, "he must be cutting me from the team or will make me do more grueling drills." John dreaded coming to school the next day and worried about their meeting.

The next morning, with a sense of impending doom hanging over him, John approached Mr. Saraceno's office and slowly entered. Much to John's surprise, Mr. Saraceno did not lead him down to the gym or even mention the word *basketball*. Instead, he led John to the school's science supply room and asked if John would be willing to help him with a project. He wanted to inventory all of the materials (e.g., beakers, scales, microscopes, chemicals) stored in the supply room. Their job was to determine what materials and supplies could be salvaged or restored for use in teaching science and math topics in class. To a 13-year-old, entering this room was like coming into a mysterious cave filled with ancient artifacts and treasure chests. Many of the supplies dated back more than 50 years, to the school's inception. For a kid who loved history, being in this room was like going back in time through a magic time machine. The chance to bring these artifacts back to the present was both fascinating and motivating to John.

One day, while John was working on the project after school, Mr. Saraceno asked him a question: "John, do you know why I asked you to help me with this project?"

"Is it because you can count on me to get it done?" John asked in response.

He replied, "No, because I want you to realize that you, like everyone else, have different talents and skills that can be your ticket to a better life. For a very few, it will be basketball. In your case, education, not basketball, will be your ticket out of here because you have a love of learning, a keen mind, and the heart to persist. Recognize the gifts you were blessed with and work hard to make them stronger, just like we run drills to improve our basketball skills. But always remember that your priority should be your education. People who don't focus on the right priorities in life will end up like the old dusty beakers and chemicals that we're going through … useless and irrelevant."

Looking back now, John realizes that Mr. Saraceno was demonstrating individualized consideration with him. He recognized that John was a transfer student who wanted to fit in with the crowd by being on the team. More importantly, he took the time to recognize John's curious mind and need to learn and grow through education. By getting John involved in his special project, he leveraged John's unique talents and strengths and used them to set him on the path that would ultimately lead to his academic career. He also encouraged one of John's teammates to pursue his athletic aspirations. He recognized the different needs, abilities, and aspirations that his students all possessed and through his actions was able to help shape their futures in a significant way.

Don considers this an amazing story that teaches a timeless lesson: When you consider individuals in your organization as having different needs, abilities, and aspirations, you can make an equally profound impact on their life and career. As shown in Figure 6.1, you can assign them challenging tasks and high-visibility career assignments that are a good fit with their innate talents and skills.

Figure 6.1   Go for it. Individually considerate leaders assign challenging tasks appropriate for developing followers' potential to excel.

By focusing on developing their talents into strengths, you can give them the confidence to become their best possible self. When they become the best version of themselves, they can contribute to the best of their ability. Their contributions can help your organization achieve its collective goals by leveraging the uniqueness and special value that every human being possesses.

Treat Others as Individuals Rather Than a Member of a Group

Kristina works in the human resource department of television home shopping company QVC as a trainer. She is responsible for developing and delivering training modules on corporate leadership and culture. The employees who attend her training workshops come from a variety of functional areas, including accounting, finance, marketing, sales, information technology, and operations. Each group possesses its own leadership challenges, subcultures, and project requirements. They demand much of Kristina and often challenge her regarding training material content and the way she presents it to them.

Several participants complained to Kristina that her training was "too vanilla" and did not apply to their specific problems at work. Under the guise of fairness, she was treating all of her participants the same by force fitting her curriculum on them. Kristina soon realized that her use of an "average leadership style"[6] on all followers (i.e., training participants) was like a one-size-fits-all product offering or Henry Ford's ancient "any color you'd like as long as it's black" approach to marketing. This approach does not work today. With the increased diversity and educational levels of today's followers, leaders and managers must realize that they need to treat their followers as unique individuals rather than as just of group of people.

Kristina came to this realization by thinking about all of the ways her participants differed. After pondering this for some time, she recognized critical differences, such as cognitive abilities, moral development, self-confidence, attitudes, preference for teamwork, technology skills, task engagement, and developmental readiness among her participants. Some enjoyed learning and thinking about new ideas, while others liked to do the same old thing and test what they already knew against what she taught them. Some were interested in doing the right thing and developing character, while others considered such topics as condescending and preachy. Some possessed a positive attitude about their coworkers, jobs, and life in general, while others had a misanthropic view of humanity. Some enjoyed the give and take associated with teamwork, while others had a hard time of letting go of power and checking their ego in teams. Some got too caught up in the hectic pace of corporate life with emails, instant messaging, and role conflict, while others were able to set aside technology and talk face-to-face with others to solve conflicts. Some really enjoyed their work and had good friends at work, while others saw it only as a necessary means to pay the mortgage. Some sought to better themselves, while others were simply not interested in self-improvement. With all this diversity, it is no wonder Kristina's training was not being well received.

Once Kristina grasped the nature of their differences, she created an action plan to start treating them as individuals and not simply as members of a group with identical needs. She asked them to complete a survey that assessed the above-mentioned factors and list their leadership challenges and expectations regarding her training sessions. She then asked them to identify a specific work-related problem that they would turn into a class project and solve using the knowledge, skills, and abilities she imparted upon them in her training. Based on ideas she learned in graduate school, she created the following set of principles that she shared with her training program participants:

- *Rule 1: Rattle your righteous mind.* Introduce new ideas that challenge your worldviews and the way you are used to doing things. While we may believe that we are righteous and think accordingly, we may fall victim to self-righteousness that can only be cured with a healthy dose of diverse thinking.
- *Rule 2: Believe.* Believe in yourself. Believe in your team. Believe in your leader. Believe in God. Research has revealed positive relationships between self- and group confidence and performance. So believing leads to performing well, and can help to reduce the amount of stress and anxiety in our lives.[7]
- *Rule 3: Attitude is everything.* A negative attitude is poisonous and contagious. It ruins not only your life, but also the lives of those around you. It often ruins your day and makes you miserable. It makes your associates miserable. Fortunately, life is all about choices. You can choose to be positive! Next time you fall victim to negativity, stop to talk with a person who is in failing health or is dying. Chances are, they will tell you that every day is a gift and that we have the choice to perceive things either positively or negatively. Life is 10% of what happens to us and 90% of how we choose to react to it. Make the positive choice, and you will be happier and more successful.
- *Rule 4: There is a* me *in* team. Some people will tell you that there is no *me* in *team*. We believe this is false. Anyone can see that the letters *m* and *e* appear in the word *team* and that they spell *me*. However, notice what happens to the word *me* that is part of *team*. The *m* gets separated from the *e*. The *me* is changed when it is part of *team*. And that's what happens when you become part of a team. A part of you changes when you join a team. You start to lose some, but not all, of your egocentric ways as your individual qualities are melded into the collective force of the team. But it

is your unique individual qualities that complement those of other team members and help to build high-performing teams. This is what leadership scholar Bruce Avolio meant when he talked about the vital forces within teams and the way that individualized consideration is required to reconcile the power of diversity with the collective synergies produced with inspirational motivation.[8]

■ *Rule 5: Break out of your virtual prison and start talking.* Organizational researcher Phil Bobko of Gettysburg College was once asked how he solves faculty conflicts that often arise over issues of curriculum development or resource allocation. Phil responded by saying that the first thing he does is to move people away from email communication and get them talking face-to-face. How many times have you felt imprisoned by the unnatural pace and stress that our technology-driven society places upon us? Have you noticed the propensity for people to argue more forcefully and "flame" others when they communicate through email? Phil recommends taking time to talk things out until the conflict is solved. If such talking takes a lot of time, so be it. As shown in Figure 6.2, the relationships that you save by solving the conflict is priceless compared to the cost of the time it takes to talk.

Figure 6.2   Let's talk it over. Talking one-on-one helps leaders treat followers as unique individuals rather than members of a group. This makes followers feel special and appreciated.

- ▪ *Rule 6: That which does not kill you makes you stronger.* Kristina often shows her students a clip from the *Rocky Balboa* film (2007, Columbia Pictures). In the clip, Rocky shares a life lesson with his son. Rocky tells him that life is tough and will knock you down often. Successful people get knocked down as much as those who are less successful. But the difference is that successful people keep getting back up and trying again. They never give up. They never stop believing. Life's hard knocks often teach us the most important lessons. We often learn more from our failures and disappointments than from our successes. So, whenever you feel that life just betrayed you, go back to Rule 3 and rejuvenate yourself with positive attitudes.

- ▪ *Rule 7: Become the best version of yourself.* Master of Leadership Development (MLD) alum Jay Wischum recommended to Kristina and us one of his favorite authors, a talented motivational speaker and writer named Matthew Kelly.[9] We were intrigued by his work because it paralleled findings that we reported in a series of studies on the self-concept and positive forms of leadership.[10] Kelly's message is that your true purpose in life is not about what you do (e.g., teach at a university) or what you have (e.g., a red BMW and big new house). Rather, it should be about *what you become* over your lifetime. In other words, your purpose in life should be to grow into your best hoped-for possible self through constant self-improvement. Individually considerate leaders use this philosophy when they build upon each follower's unique talents and strengths and encourage them to grow through inspiration, character development, role modeling, perspective taking, and coaching and mentoring.

Listen Attentively to Others' Concerns

For the U.S. troops fighting in Iraq during the Second Gulf War, winning the peace has been more difficult than winning the war. Nevertheless, the troops occupying Iraq have found that paying attention to the input and concerns of the Iraqi people is the best way to help improve their situation after the fall of Saddam Hussein.

In June 2008, John received an email from MLD student Sgt. Darrell Davis, who was deployed as part of a U.S. Army Special Forces unit somewhere in Iraq. Darrell volunteered to serve in Iraq because of his firm belief that fighting Al-Qaeda terrorists is the right thing to do. Despite all the negative news coming out of Iraq, Darrell reported that on numerous levels the U.S. military presence is having a positive impact on the people of Iraq. He noted that some of what you hear on the news is true. However, there is a lot going on that is either not being reported or is being reported inaccurately.

According to Darrell, an increasing number of Iraqi people are informing on the terrorists every day. U.S. forces are targeting and eliminating numerous terrorist leaders nightly. At the same time, U.S. forces have one team that is putting together an energy project that will give a town of 250,000 people electricity for the first time since the war began. The United States has also rebuilt schools and provided medical care to hundreds of thousands of people in Iraq. As the U.S. forces win the hearts and minds of the Iraqi people, Iraqis are giving up the terrorists at ever-increasing rates. Much of this success is because the U.S. forces are meeting daily with the Iraqis and listening to their concerns and helping to address their needs.

Why bother with such griping sessions, either in war or in corporations? Why should we care about hearing what is on the minds of others? The answer is simple: We need to listen because followers and others, such as customers, competitors, and suppliers, are part of the leadership system described in Chapter 2. They provide important sources of information and serve as partners that facilitate the operation of the leadership system. Simply put, they want to be heard by their leader, and as a leader, you have the responsibility of listening to them.

For example, one of the first things that Lou Gerstner did when he joined IBM as its CEO was to visit key customer accounts and listen to their concerns. He realized that customers are an important part of the leadership system. By meeting with customers, Gerstner was able to detect changes in customer preferences and demand, areas for product and service improvement, and information about competitors. By displaying individually considerate behavior with his customers, Gerstner was able to jump-start one of the greatest corporate turn-arounds in history.[11] IBM's current CEO Sam Palmisano is hoping to follow in Gerstner's footsteps in adapting to a more service-oriented industry.

When you attentively listen to followers' concerns, you are able to empathize with them. You can recognize their state of mind and emotion, as shown in Figure 6.3. You are able to "put yourself in their shoes." This can make your communication very effective. Most of the time, we're so busy that we ignore what followers say. Or we pretend to listen to them, but we're really thinking about something else. Other times, we listen only to what we want to hear and screen out the rest of the message. But when we practice individualized consideration with active listening, we devote our full attention, and our heart and mind, to what they have to say. This allows us to achieve what leadership consultant Stephen Covey identified as one of the seven habits of highly effective people: "Seek first to understand, then to be understood."[12]

Figure 6.3 I'm listening. The individually considerate leader listens empathically to the concerns of the follower by cuing in on her emotions and the subtext of her message.

Help Others Develop Their Strengths

A team of MLD students recently interviewed American entrepreneur, sports team executive, and television personality Pat Croce. In the Philadelphia area, Croce is a celebrated maverick leader whose adventurous lifestyle has made him an entertainment and business icon. He has led companies ranging from physical therapy firms to Internet start-ups to the Philadelphia 76ers professional basketball team. One visit to his Web site (http://www.patcroce.com/; you have to see it to believe it!) shows the wide range of business initiatives and community events that Croce leads. With his high-energy and charismatic personality, Croce provided the students with an up close and personal view of inspirational motivation and individualized consideration.

One of the questions they asked Croce was whether he focuses on identifying and developing followers' strengths or aims to eliminate their weaknesses through training and development. Croce bemoaned that some of the Internet technologists (i.e., programmers) in his companies have no personality,

> but their strengths come into play when you put them in front of a keyboard and they are wickedly good! Or a receptionist may have a great personality. She can welcome your customers in the front door,

but she can't add two and two together. So what you do is that you expand on the strengths and you pair her weakness with someone who is strong in her area of weakness because it takes too much time and energy to try to make her weakness strong. I'd rather take someone and match them up instead of saying "you can't add, so I'm going to send you to a math class." Nah. Tell her, "You just make sure you smile and tell that person 'hello,' bring them in, book them, make sure the date's right, but you make sure your next door neighbor here does all the billing" … you spend too much time and energy training to train people who don't already have the talents and skills….[13]

Once Croce identifies strengths in his people, he puts them in jobs and assignments that build their strengths to the level of champions. Then he spends time getting to know about their likes and dislikes and what they find motivating. He finds out about their passions and what they need to accomplish their "game plan." Some need reminders to stay positive. Some need to unlock their minds and think differently. Some need to be reminded that if you don't ask, the answer will always be no. Others need to do more listening and less talking. By providing motivational feedback along the way, Croce stretches his people to develop their innate talents into strengths. And he encourages them to stretch their muscles with his daily exercise routine that he calls "freakin' fitness."

You may not be as extreme as Pat Croce, but you also can demonstrate individualized consideration when you help others develop their strengths. Sometimes, your followers may not have any clue as to what their strengths are. Or, they are not confident enough to believe that they are talented. You have to help them identify their strengths and utilize them. This takes a lot of encouragement and assurance from you. By helping them to accentuate the positive, you build your organization's collective skill set and can match them up with other team members whose skills can complement each other. As shown in Figure 6.4, that makes for a potent one-two punch when tackling complex and difficult tasks. It also builds a high degree of mutual respect because followers typically appreciate the time and effort you expend investing in their personal and professional development.

Spend Time Teaching and Coaching

Outside of meetings, much of the time spent by transformational leaders involves teaching and coaching followers. That's certainly the case for Ashley Schneider of Wyeth Pharmaceuticals. On account of her unusually astute and critical mind, Ashley often reports to multiple bosses from several cross-functional teams. She's frequently called upon to bring new team members up to speed on new drug

Figure 6.4   Bringing out the best. The speaker is receiving elocution tips from the individually considerate leader.

trials and product tests. Due to her extensive background in research methods and experimental design, Ashley spends a majority of her time teaching colleagues about the benefits and drawbacks of new statistical procedures and designs that they can use. These teaching sessions are typically delivered one-on-one on an *ad hoc* basis. Ashley enjoys the deep level of understanding she gains by teaching others the concepts she has learned. However, proper training takes time, and Ashley faces many demands for training from all levels of the organization.

Ashley has developed a few tactics that make teaching and coaching more efficient across organizational levels. First, she explains why the topic is important to the trainee and the organization. Second, she asks a lot questions and uses the Socratic method and critical questioning to probe the trainee's level of comprehension. Third, she uses colorful diagrams to illustrate difficult concepts. And she makes herself available for follow-up tutoring sessions or to answer any questions they may have. All of these tactics enhance trainees' level of interest, comprehension, and ability to apply their new knowledge, skills, and abilities as soon as possible.

Figure 6.5 Just a few pointers. Individually considerate leaders spend time teaching followers about work processes and procedures. They are good coaches and mentors.

When you take the necessary time to teach and coach others like Ashley, you expand your power base as you influence others. As shown in Figure 6.5, you become a trusted source of knowledge and information as you share your wisdom with others. You also contribute to the organization by passing on essential wisdom and knowledge. Indeed, an essential aspect of transformational leadership is the development of followers into leaders themselves. So it seems that this individually considerate behavior may be mandatory for effective transformational leadership.

Promote Self-Development

In Chapter 2, you read about Aimee Firth, who managed a group of associates in the revenue analytics department at DaVita, the largest independent provider of dialysis services in the United States. Aimee is also a strong advocate of promoting the self-development of her staff. While at DaVita, Aimee met with each of her 11 teammates on a biweekly basis or once a week if they were new to the team. During their meeting time, they explored their successes and challenges since their last meeting, and Aimee provided them with coaching and support. She also promoted self-development and encouraged her teammates to pursue stretch assignments that would help them to develop their career opportunities. With teammates who have a great interest in self-development, she worked with them on creating and working on an individual development plan (IDP). By crafting and following up on their IDP, Aimee's teammates can focus on specific behaviors or attributes associated with high performance and identify ways to develop in identified areas.

Aimee feels that building on strengths is important, but ignoring areas of weakness can blindside associates down the road. She quipped, "You can ignore your weaknesses and fail to address them, but I guarantee that your competitors or adversaries will not ignore them. They will exploit them. That's why it's important to build on your strengths and address your weaknesses through transformational leadership." Aimee's comment reminds us of the concept of *confident vulnerability*[14] discussed by Bruce Avolio and alluded to by Mother Theresa, who said that "we must come to terms with the hole in our heart." All of us have holes in our heart, mind, and soul that we need to recognize and mend in the spirit of continuous personal improvement in order to become the best version of ourselves. What vices do you and your followers possess that are puncturing your heart, mind, or soul? How will you eliminate them?

Promoting self-development involves getting your associates to possess a love of learning. They must become enthralled by the process of learning from feedback from others, self-reflection, and discussions with others who also value self-development. Feedback from surveys such as the Multifactor Leadership Questionnaire (MLQ) promotes self-development because it points to strengths and areas for development in specific areas. As shown in Figure 6.6, self-reflection promotes self-development through quiet time and thinking deeply about leadership issues in a setting devoid of external stimuli, noise, and interruptions. Discussions with others can enrich and expand understanding of strengths and areas for development through stories and life experiences that bring humanity back into the leadership process. Isn't that what individualized consideration is all about?

Thinking About Individualized Consideration

You are now familiar with the concept of individualized consideration. Now it's time to start thinking deeply about what implications this concept has for you in terms of four concepts related to leadership: individuation, mentoring, empowerment, and developing followers through delegation. A good understanding of these topics will help you to identify areas in your leadership context to apply individualized consideration to bring out the best in your followers and associates.

Figure 6.6   Some quiet time. Individualized consideration motivates followers to study and reflect on their own as they discover a love of learning.

Individuation

When leadership scholar Bernard Bass first conceptualized the idea of individualized consideration, he identified two main subcomponents: individuation and mentoring.[15] *Individuation* refers to the process of recognizing important individual differences in followers that can influence their levels of motivation and performance and promote their development. This process is perhaps more important than ever given the increased workforce diversity in organizations today. For example, women are assuming more leadership positions in U.S. corporations than ever before. By the year 2011, 48% of the total workforce in the United States will consist of women. Unfortunately, women typically receive only 77% of men's earnings for similar positions.[16]

To overcome this injustice, women are working very hard to navigate through their complex labyrinth-like career paths. They are also striving to shatter the glass ceiling, which presents an invisible barrier that blocks women and minorities from top management positions. They do this by exceeding performance expectations, and therefore transformational leadership can help in this regard. They are also developing a leadership style with which male leaders are comfortable (i.e., a blend of transactional and transformational leadership). They are seeking out difficult or challenging assignments through individualized consideration displayed by their leaders. They also benefit from learning from influential mentors.

Another trend that illustrates the need for individuation is the growth of racial minorities in the workforce. For example, between the years 2010 and 2020, the percentage increase in U.S. population for Asians is projected to be 27%, and 26% for Hispanics, compared to 13% for African Americans and 3% for Caucasians.[17] In order to stem the growing charges of perceived discrimination within minority groups, leaders should learn to individuate between followers. This allows for tailoring their leadership styles to followers on a personal basis and addressing issues related to diversity leadership. This will make your leadership more appropriate and effective in the highly diversified work environment.

Diversity Leadership Issues

Our colleague Janice Dreachslin teaches a popular course in Penn State's MLD program based on her research on diversity leadership. Dreachslin sees diversity as multidimensional, including all of the similarities and differences that together make each of us unique. In addition to our individual personality or temperament, we each belong to a variety of identity groups. Some of these groups, such as our profession or religion, are chosen, while others are assigned by society based on visible characteristics, such as gender, age, race, and ethnicity. We respond to one another's visible (i.e., gender or race) and, once known, invisible identities (i.e., sexual orientation or religion) based on our assumptions about each of these identity groups. We each experience our own group identities differently, depending on the meaning that the group has to us in our lives. How we experience our own and others' group identities depends on the cognitive map or worldview that we operate from vis-à-vis that group, even when our worldview operates outside of our own conscious awareness.[18]

Without well-developed diversity leadership skills, it is not possible to give ourselves or others individualized consideration. Dreachslin identified a five-part transformation process that organizations and their members must follow to move from awareness to understanding to action on diversity leadership:

- *Step 1: Discovery.* Hold events that grow awareness of diversity as an important leadership and organizational strategic imperative. This step helps individually considerate leaders be alert to the individual needs of followers.
- *Step 2: Assessment.* Systematically review the organization's culture, climate, and practices from the perspective of diverse stakeholders. This step assists individually considerate leaders to recognize differences among people in their strengths, weaknesses, likes, and dislikes.

- *Step 3: Exploration.* Deploy targeted and ongoing training and professional development, including executive coaching, to build on the strengths and address the challenges identified through the assessment phase. This step helps individually considerate leaders provide learning opportunities for followers.
- *Step 4: Transformation.* Introduce fundamental change to people, policies, procedures, culture, and climate to better address the needs of a diverse workforce and customer base. This phase establishes a pattern of incremental successes for elements of the leadership system.
- *Step 5: Revitalization.* Pursue continuous renewal of the organization's commitment to diversity leadership as a distinctive competence and strategic imperative. This phase institutionalizes diversity leadership into the organizational culture.[19]

A large number of organizations have established such diversity leadership processes to introduce their members to the benefits and disadvantages of diversity (visit http://www.diversityinc.com for detailed examples). Theories of information processing and decision making highlight the advantages of diversity. Heterogeneous (diverse) groups use better task-relevant processes that lead to higher-quality decisions and creative or innovative products and services. However, diversity also has its downside, such as conflict and confusion among group members.[20] Social categorization theory proposes that similarity leads to liking and attraction of group members. Such appeal can lead to fewer interpersonal conflicts, cooperation among members, and cohesiveness in homogenous groups.[21] So, the focus should be on how to manage diversity properly so that you can enjoy benefits associated with diversity while minimizing its potential challenges.

Proper management of diversity first requires proper perspective. For example, the melting pot metaphor illustrates the traditional view of diversity. Perhaps you have seen video clips from the popular ABC television series entitled *Schoolhouse rock*! first televised in the 1970s. One of the classic songs from this show is "The Great American Melting Pot," written by Lynn Ahrens and sung by Lori Lieberman. (Please view this short video on YouTube.com.) At that time, diversity was considered to be a form of assimilation where "you simply melt right in" and blend into American "collective" culture. FRLD trainees often chuckle with a mix of nostalgic sentimentality and skepticism every time we play the video clip for this song to illustrate this perspective. With today's emphasis on globalization and political correctness, most people experience a discomfort with focusing on assimilation to describe diversity. They are also uncomfortable with focusing solely on differences. Fortunately, a new paradigm that can update the notion of individuation has gained some attention.

Diversimilarity and Transformational Leadership

Today, diversity can be expressed in the phrase "We are different but we are the same." This alternative view of diversity recognizes and respects differences between people while highlighting similarities and is called *diversimilarity*.[22] To understand diversimilarity and practice it through transformational leadership, we must first review several layers of diversity that represent individual differences in followers.[23]

We can individuate between followers and associates by considering four layers of diversity: personality characteristics, internal dimensions, external dimensions, and organizational dimensions.[24] In terms of personality, there are many ways we can understand an individual's social reputation and innate nature. However, most individuals vary greatly on the degree to which they possess the Big 5 personality characteristics: openness to experience, conscientiousness, extraversion, agreeableness, and neuroticism/emotional stability.[25]

Openness to experience is a trait associated with being intellectually curious, imaginative, and broad-minded. Followers with high levels of this trait would respond well to intellectual stimulation. *Conscientiousness* is associated with being dependable, responsible, achievement oriented, and persistent. Conscientious followers are open to self-development and other individually considerate behaviors. *Extraversion* involves being outgoing, talkative, and social as opposed to being reserved and introverted. Extraverted followers typically respond well to inspirational motivation and individualized consideration. *Agreeableness* describes being trusting, good natured, cooperative, and soft hearted. Agreeable followers respond well to the transformational behaviors described in this book. *Neuroticism/emotional stability* describes whether a person is more inclined to being very anxious, nervous, and apprehensive as opposed to being relaxed, secure, and unworried. Emotionally stable followers respond well to idealized influence and the coaching and mentoring provided by individualized consideration.

Another important personality trait that transformational leaders work to strengthen is a follower's *self-efficacy*. Donny Deutsch, a top executive at marketing powerhouse Deutsch, Inc., describes the idea of self-efficacy in the following quote, "Once you realize there are no geniuses out there, you can think, '*I can do that.*' One reason I've succeeded is I have that naïve sense of entitlement." Self-efficacy refers to a person's belief that he or she is capable of performing a specific task. Research indicates the higher a follower's self-efficacy, the better his or her performance.[26] Followers can increase their self-efficacy levels by learning from past experiences and celebrating their success on similar tasks. Behavior models, such as leaders who display idealized influence and individualized consideration, boost followers' self-efficacy levels. Verbal persuasion and encouragement from these leaders also make followers feel more efficacious. In addition, followers can raise their level of self-efficacy by assessing their physical and emotional state and working to improve it.

Locus of control is another personality trait of followers that transformational leaders influence. Individuals with an *external locus of control* (i.e., externals) think that events in their life are influenced by environmental factors, such as luck or fate. In contrast, those with an *internal locus of control* (i.e., internals) believe that they can control key events and consequences in their life. Research has shown that internals perform better and are more satisfied with their jobs, earn better salaries and more promotions, and experience less anxiety than externals.[27] Transformational leaders who use individually considerate behavior empower their followers to take control of their lives and job responsibilities in the hope of increasing their level of internal locus of control.

Beyond individual differences in personality, diversimilarity recognizes other internal dimensions that can represent differences or similarities. These include age, cognitive/emotional intelligence, sexual orientation, physical ability, ethnicity, and race. Individually considerate leaders appreciate the unique talents, knowledge, and experience that both older and younger followers bring with them. They tailor their interactions and motivational approaches to match followers' level of intelligence and emotional states. They recognize and respect individual differences in followers' sexual orientation. They accommodate and respect individuals with disabilities, both physical and mental. They also appreciate and celebrate the traditions, values, and customs of the race and ethnicity of their followers.

Diversimilarity extends beyond internal dimensions to reflect dimensions outside of the workplace. These external dimensions include followers' geographic location, income level, personal and recreational habits, religion, educational background, work experience, appearance, and parental and marital status. Individually considerate leaders learn about where their followers came from, where they live, and their cultures. They recognize that followers differ in their socioeconomic status; some must work to make ends meet, while others are more financially secure. They find out what followers like to do in their spare time, how they relax, and what their hobbies are. They are sensitive to followers' right to practice the religion of their choice and exercise their religious obligations. They find out where followers went to school and how their university degrees can help them better contribute to the organization. They talk to followers about their prior work experience so they can match them in appropriate jobs. Within reason and organizational culture, they tolerate differences in appearances in terms of dress codes and personal expression. They also recognize and facilitate work-family balance for followers with and without families.

Diversimilarity also considers differences and similarities that organizational structures, policies, and culture place on individuals. These include followers' functional area, work content or field, division/department/unit or work group, seniority, work location, and management status. Individually considerate leaders are aware of the functional area in which their followers work, such as accounting, finance, human resources, marketing, or operations. They learn about the professional fields of their followers. They know where followers fit on the organization chart in terms of their business unit or work group. They track followers' tenure with the organization by recognizing work anniversaries. They know the geographic work locations of followers. They also recognize differences in whether followers are management, professional, or staff. In this regard, they do *not* practice "rankism," in which they give individuals at a higher rank more respect or perks than individuals lower on the organizational totem pole.[28] By considering the many ways followers can differ (or be similar), you can become more sensitive to followers and use common sense to adapt your leadership behaviors to better fit the motivational and developmental needs of today's diverse workforce.

Mentoring

In addition to individuation, mentoring represents the other major subcomponent of individualized consideration. *Mentoring* occurs when a more knowledgeable and senior individual (i.e., mentor) shares wisdom and experience with a more junior individual (i.e., protégé) for the purpose of advancing the junior individual's career and professional development.[29] Think about the relationships you have been in at work over the course of your career. Who were your mentors? Who have you mentored? What did you think was an effective way to be mentored? As a mentor or protégé, what did you get out of your mentoring relationship?

Benefits of Mentoring

Research indicates that mentoring relationships benefit mentors and protégé and their organizations. Individuals with mentors (i.e., protégés) receive more promotions and compensation than individuals without mentors. They also experience higher levels of job satisfaction, career satisfaction, life satisfaction, and commitment than those without mentors. Mentors reap benefits such as feelings of prestige, satisfaction that they are shaping a younger version of themselves, and knowing that they are passing on their legacy to another generation or cohort. In addition, the organization reaps benefits from mentoring relationships, including higher levels of organizational commitment and engagement, retention, better managerial succession planning, institutional memory, perceived justice, and enhanced productivity and performance.[30] These benefits occur through the display of mentoring functions by the mentor and perception of them by the protégé.

Mentoring Functions

Mentors provide two main functions: career development and psychosocial support. *Career development* involves several task-related actions that help advance the protégé's career. Examples include sponsoring the protégé in organizational events and championing her cause politically. Providing protégés with high exposure and visibility opportunities gets protégés noticed by top management and sets them up for promotions. Coaching the protégé with performance feedback and strategies for success is another important career development function. Also important is protecting the protégé from nasty organizational politics and advising the protégé of potentially dangerous adversaries in the organization and industry. In addition, providing the protégé with challenging and intellectually stimulating assignments can develop skills sets and knowledge bases essential for career advancement.[31] All of these career development mentoring functions use tasks and information to develop the full potential of the protégé and therefore reflect aspects of individually considerate behavior.

In addition to career development functions, good mentors provide *psychosocial support* to address the psychological and emotional needs of protégés so that they stay satisfied and engaged in their careers. These functions address the personal needs of the protégé. They include role modeling of idealized influence behavior by the mentor so that the protégé can emulate appropriate behavior for career success. Mentors also provide acceptance and confirmation behaviors when they compliment and encourage protégés to continue along despite struggles and challenges. When needed, mentors counsel protégés on the best approaches for dealing with setbacks or failures. Most importantly, mentors form friendships with the protégé. As time progresses, the mentoring relationship often evolves from a teacher–student association to a collegial association, and ultimately to the protégé's independence from the mentor.[32] All of these psychosocial support mentoring functions use relationship building and diver-similarity concepts to develop the full potential of the protégé and therefore reflect aspects of individually considerate behavior.

Mentoring and Transformational Leadership

Mentoring and leadership are separate and distinct concepts. Not all leaders are mentors and not all mentors are leaders. However, when you use individually considerate behaviors, you are actually forming mentor-protégé relationships with your followers. Once again, one key difference we've found between transformational and other types of leadership is follower development and leader's active involvement in the process. As a transformational leader, you should take time to get to know your follower/protégé and work with her to achieve developmental and career-related goals. The above-mentioned mentoring functions illustrate ways that you can use individualized consideration to develop followers' talents into strengths and promote the self-development of followers. Research indicates that mentoring and transformational leadership are "complementary forms of development that can help organizational members to achieve high levels of professional and personal development."[33] Learn to enjoy the process of mentoring and you will become a more individually considerate leader.

Two Faces of Transformational Leadership: Empowerment and Dependency

It is important to point out that individualized consideration, coupled with idealized influence, can have unintended effects on followers. FRLD scholar Boas Shamir (see Table 6.2) and his colleagues pointed this out in an interesting study.[34] When followers receive specialized treatment and careful attention from a leader whom they deeply admire, they can become dependent on the leader rather than empowered. Indeed, there can be two faces of transformational leadership: empowerment and dependency.

Empowerment occurs when followers develop into confident and capable independent-minded leaders in their own right, who may or may not share exactly the same ideals, values, and beliefs as the leader. Empowerment stems from a follower socially identifying with the vision for the organization that the leader espouses and followers support. Empowerment is known to improve followers' self-confidence and their commitment toward their organization. Empowerment also makes followers more independent.

In contrast, *dependency* occurs when followers become emotionally attached to the leader in a way that they cannot separate themselves from the image and ideals of the leader. We often see dependency occur in followers of personalized charismatic leaders such as David Koresh, Ken Lay, or Ted Haggard. The outcome of personal identification with the leader is that the follower develops an unhealthy dependence on the leader. This is inconsistent with the fundamental goal of transformational leadership espoused by James MacGregor Burns, namely, to develop followers into leaders themselves. Therefore, be careful not to get too close to followers when using individualized consideration. Be cognizant of excessive levels of dependence that followers may develop and place upon you as a leader. And encourage their independent thinking.

Table 6.2   FRLD Scholar Profile: Boas Shamir

Boas Shamir is currently dean of the faculty of social sciences at the Hebrew University of Jerusalem and is a giant in the field of leadership. Shamir considers importing James McGregor Burns's concepts of transactional and transforming leadership into the organizational studies sphere and developing them further to be vitally important. According to Shamir, relating them to the construct of charisma, developing research instruments to study them, and drawing their implications for leadership development have probably been the greatest contributions to the leadership literature and the field of leadership studies in the last 30 years.

Because charisma is a central component of the FRLD theory in its original form, Shamir's self-concept–based theory (with Robert House and Michael Arthur) has contributed significantly to the understanding of how transformational leaders affect followers. A more direct contribution is the article noted in the text (with Ronit Kark and Gilad Chen) that transformational leadership may create both empowerment and dependence among followers. Shamir also played a key role in demonstrating the power of FRLD by a field experiment that showed how transformational leadership can be trained and have an impact on the followers' development and performance.

Bernard Bass's seminal 1985 book, *Leadership and Performance Beyond Expectations*, was one of the major reasons for leadership becoming Shamir's main focus of research in the last 20 years. In 1993, Shamir spent a semester with Bass and Bruce Avolio at SUNY-Binghamton and taught the authors of this book in a PhD seminar. Since then, Shamir developed an affiliation with FRLD research and with Bernie and especially Bruce. They reviewed each other's research and were enriched by each other's work.

The above-mentioned experimental study by Dvir et al. played a role in the decision to adopt the FRLD model for training cadets at the Israeli Defense Force's School of Leadership. The model has also been adopted by Reuven Gal, Micha Popper, and Giora Ayalon in their Center for Quality Leadership in Israel and used for many years for the development of managers who were identified by their organizations as having particularly high leadership potential.

Developing Followers Through Delegation

One way to promote followers' independence is by delegating appropriate tasks to them so you can build their talents into strengths.[35] That doesn't mean dumping the work on them you don't want to do yourself. Rather, it means carefully matching the delegated task to the follower based on his talents, needs, and aspirations. For followers who need to learn to make decisions independently, try sharing problems with them and soliciting their suggestions on how they would solve the problem. If necessary, you can coach them by suggesting appropriate alternatives to their solutions.

Another delegation tactic is appropriate for followers who need help in staying focused and completing tasks in a timely manner. For these followers, try requesting progress reports over specified intervals and provide feedback to guide their progress. Make sure that you explain to followers why you have chosen them to perform the delegated task and how they will benefit from completing it. When delegating, always assign tasks that are meaningful, interesting, and challenging to them based on their unique personalities and skill sets.[36] That's what individualized consideration is all about.

Putting Individualized Consideration Into Practice

Display the Behaviors Described in This Chapter

This chapter presented six behaviors associated with individualized consideration. These behaviors emphasized the importance of (1) recognizing and appreciating the different needs, abilities, and aspirations followers possess; (2) personalizing interactions with followers; (3) being an active listener with followers; (4) developing followers' talents into strengths; (5) effectively coaching, counseling, and mentoring; and (6) promoting self-development and love of learning. By displaying these behaviors with your followers, they will become more willing to develop, express their individuality, learn to enjoy the process of continuous personal improvement, and eventually develop into transformational leaders themselves.

That's what Gregory Lowe found with his work with the Westtown School located in Chester County in Southeastern Pennsylvania. The Westtown School is a Quaker college preparatory day and boarding school for grades pre-K to 12. A core Quaker philosophy guides the educational process and curriculum at Westtown: There is an aspect of God in each person—the Inner Light. The Inner Light allows for a personal, direct relationship with God where the Truth can be revealed. Part of this revelation is that faith should be exercised in daily life and that God's creations (nature and humans) must be respected, nurtured, and preserved.[37]

Lowe has provided executive coaching to John Baird, the Westtown School's charismatic top administrator. Together they have encouraged teachers and staff to provide appropriate challenges and learning opportunities for students based on their individual needs. They challenge their students to realize their individual talents while learning and living together in a diverse community. They have developed a culture that celebrates their school's rich diversity of its members and prepares them to live and lead in a diverse and complex world. This example teaches us that individualized consideration is both timely and relevant for leaders wishing to foster inclusiveness and fellowship within the ranks.

Become Interested in the Well-Being of Others

Individually considerate leaders show real care and concern for their followers and associates. Consider the example of Reverend Stan Stycharz, PsyD. Father Stan is pastor of St. Leo the Great Catholic Church in Bonita Springs, Florida. While on vacation, John had the pleasure of attending a mass celebrating the groundbreaking for expansion of Father Stan's parish. At the reception for the event, several parishioners told John how much they love and admire Father Stan. One parishioner told John that she appreciates the way he genuinely cares for people and that his inspiring homilies often bring her to tears. Father Stan's charismatic effects on his parishioners have helped to accumulate over $7 million in pledges for the church expansion project, with $3 million collected as of June 2008.

During the reception John introduced himself to Father Stan and asked him about his successful approach to leadership. In response, he identified three elements of his leadership style. First, he makes sure that he does not take people for granted. He lets them know they are appreciated. Second, he listens to people who come to him with a need and does his best to help them. And third, he said it is important to be humble. We believe that Father Stan has practiced individualized consideration without knowing the FRLD theory!

We want to challenge you to follow Father Stan's example by looking out for the best interests of your followers. Build trust and rapport with them by getting to know them on a personal basis. Let them know you appreciate what they do. Talk to them about what is going on in their lives. Get to know their challenges and needs. Once you possess this knowledge, you will be able to identify developmental opportunities and resources that you can provide them to show that you are looking out for them.

Celebrate Diversity

Armando Johnson supervises training for a group of technicians at a large regional power company. His associates come from all walks of life, a large range of ages, and several different ethnic and racial groups. Instead of demanding conformance to his directives across the board, Armando realizes that there is an infinite number of ways to do a job. So Armando takes the time to explain to his associates the intent of his objectives. Then he leaves it up to his associates to find the best ways to complete their tasks.

Armando uses personal recognition to highlight and share success stories that illustrate his associates' participation in his leadership process. For each individual who gets involved, he celebrates diversity by sponsoring various ethnic food lunches, favorite music genre days, and other cultural events. A similar practice is implemented companywide at Qualcomm, where employees with different ethnic backgrounds take turns hosting a party to introduce their unique culture and cuisine. Through these cultural events, employees learn to appreciate cultural diversity and develop global insights for their work. By making as many people as possible feel appreciated, Armando and leaders at Qualcomm are able to highlight the benefits of diversity described previously in this chapter.

Establish Mentoring Programs in Your Organization

Several students and alumni in Penn State's MLD program are employed by the Vanguard Group, a prestigious provider of no-load mutual funds. Lara Dushkewich and Gary Generose have established an informal group of MLD students and alumni at Vanguard. The group meets to mentor other Vanguard employees who are interested in becoming better leaders. The group uses one-to-one, peer, and network-based mentoring relationships to build the leadership skills of interested associates.

This informal mentoring program, along with Vanguard's formal mentoring program, builds a strong learning community. Promoting a love of learning and culture that embraces change is paying off big dividends for Vanguard. The company is yielding a smarter and more diverse portfolio of aspiring leaders, reducing turnover, and enhancing employee engagement and satisfaction levels. Isn't it time for you to grow your human resources through mentoring programs to maximize your return on investment as well?

Create Strategies for Continuous Personal Improvement

Vicki Ferguson, SPR, is a former manager of human resources at a large insurance and investment firm. Vicki's job was to grow the talent pool at her company. Vicki was successful in her role for many years prior to moving on to other opportunities. Part of her success comes from her ability to get associates excited about personal development and continuous improvement of the self. Through reward programs, celebrations, fun events, and relevant training, Vicki created a culture of continuous improvement that senior management supported with resources. With proper organizational support, you, like Vicki, can get your associates in the right frame of mind when it comes to building their best possible self. If you accomplish this feat, you have truly mastered the essence of transformational leadership.

But effective transformational leadership is built upon a solid foundation of transactional leadership to satisfy both the intrinsic and extrinsic needs of your followers. We turn our attention to this essential element of FRLD in the next chapter.

Summary Questions and Reflective Exercises

1. This exercise uses results of your Multifactor Leadership Questionnaire (MLQ) report to assess your level of individually considerate behavior. Compare your individualized consideration ratings with the research-validated benchmarks. How did your self-ratings, ratings from subordinates, ratings from peers, ratings from superiors, and ratings from others compare against the benchmarks? On which specific MLQ items (i.e., questions) did you score highest? Lowest? What can you do to improve on the items where you scored lowest?

2. This exercise also uses results of your MLQ report to assess your level of individualized consideration behavior. Compare your self-ratings on *individualized consideration behavior* with ratings provided by subordinates, peers, superiors, and others. Compute the difference score (d) as the difference between your self-rating score and the specific other rating source score of interest. If d is less than .5 and the other rating source score is less than 2.79, then you are considered to be *in agreement/poor*. If d is less than .5 and the other rating source score is greater than 2.79, then you are considered to be *in agreement/good*. If d is equal to or greater than .5 and the self-rating score is greater than the other rating score, then you are an *overestimator* on this dimension. If d is equal to or greater than .5 and the self-rating score is less than the other rating score, then you are an *underestimator* on this dimension. Consider the category under which you fall in terms of individualized consideration behavior. What are the implications of this categorization for you? Are there any things you can do to improve in this area?

3. This exercise is designed to make you more aware of the wide variety of worldviews and perspectives in today's diverse workforce. Think of a social, ethnic, racial, generational, or sexual orientation group that you are *not* a part of, or would be considered a minority if you were among its members. Then attend an event or meeting of the group as a visitor. While you are at the meeting, strike up a conversation about the group's core values, beliefs,

and practices. Reflect upon what you learned based on your conversation and observations. How do their beliefs differ from your convictions? How are they similar? What strengths did this group possess? How did your attitude about this group change as a result of your experience?

4. Select a high-potential associate in your organization who you would feel comfortable mentoring. If possible, take this person to the area where you were raised or to your hometown. Show this person a few aspects of your culture and the area that shaped your development. After a few weeks, ask if this person would return the favor by taking you to his or her hometown so you can learn more about him or her. What do you have in common? What are your differences? What do each of your want out of your lives and careers? How can you look out for each other at work?

5. Establish the practice of holding a weekly or monthly "town meeting" with your staff. At this meeting, be sure to share the group's accomplishments and allow each member to report on activities since the last meeting. Then ask them to voice any concerns or questions they might have. Be sure to concentrate on listening empathetically to their issues. Take note of their concerns. Work diligently to identify potential solutions to their issues and continue this process to strengthen your individually considerate leadership.

6. Purchase the rights to administer Gallup's StrengthsFinder 2.0™ assessment (https://www.strengthsfinder.com/) or a personality test such as the Myers–Briggs® Type Indicator (MBTI; http://www.myersbriggs.org/my-mbti-personality-type/take-the-mbti-instrument/). Administer this instrument to your followers and provide them with feedback on their innate talents, skills, or preferences. Identify jobs or tasks where they can best develop their strengths or use their personality traits in a way that is a good fit with tasks that need to be completed. What did you and your followers learn after completing this exercise?

7. Identify an individual in your organization who is neglected or ignored by others. Make time to meet with him or her. Ask what he or she does at work. Inquire what he or she hopes to achieve over the next five years? Ask how you can help to achieve this goal? Check in periodically with this person to follow up on his or her request. What did you achieve by paying special attention to this person?

8. With permission of top management, establish a Diversity Action Council (DAC) in your organization. The mission of DAC should be to create a more inclusive culture and educate your associates about the concepts of

diversity, diversimilarity, and individualized consideration. Hold meetings and events to inform your associates of culture, history, individual differences, and the benefits of diversity for your organization. Introduce intellectually stimulating concepts such as Robert Fuller's notion of rankism (http://breakingranks.net/). Be sure to hold discussion sessions after these events so that others can learn from the DAC events. Report your activities to others interested in leadership development.

9. On your next business or personal trip, take time to learn about the city, region, or country you visit. Read about its people and their history and culture. Travel through its regions. Strike up conversations with the locals to learn about their preferences, worldviews, and aspirations. How are the culture and history of this locale similar and different from your hometown? What useful information from this experience can you use to help others in your organization? Use your newfound knowledge to highlight what you learned in your next business meeting, presentation, or social gathering.

10. Imagine that you have four employees in your work group. Your four employees are

   Miles—Miles is out for himself. He always seeks to maximize his personal goals, regardless of whether they are at the expense of others. His goal is to become the youngest manager in the history of your company to be promoted to director of a business unit. Miles thinks of people as either those who can help his cause or those that will get in his way. He sees people as having motives similar to his and therefore judges people on that basis. Miles is a very effective manager, but he has a hard time cooperating with others, unless it advances his own personal agenda.

   Flint—Flint likes to please other people. He considers the personal interests and attitudes of others and recognizes that the needs of others are different from his own. He attempts to coordinate his needs with the needs of others. Flint is well known for sacrificing his personal needs and goals to maintain good relations with his coworkers. He generally has high regard and respect for his associates. Flint's problem is that he has trouble taking a hard stand on issues. He walks away from the tough fights that need to be dealt with at work. It's not his style to confront or challenge others. He's afraid of hurting the feelings of others.

   Sam—Senior management considers Sam to be a high-potential manager and future top-level director. He likes to place others in challenging assignments that stretch them to the limits of their capacity. Sam believes in stretching people, rewarding them for their performance, and working with them toward a common goal. He is highly motivated to do his best on every job. People who work with Sam place a great deal of trust in his ability to overcome difficult challenges. Sam has a high level of energy that gets others to work harder. When you work with Sam, you feel like he gives you his undivided attention and that you really matter to him.

Perry—Perry has worked for your company for over 15 years but has become increasingly alienated and unengaged in his work. He only puts in the minimum amount of effort to slide by on his job because he feels like the organization owes him. He has not kept up on changes in technology and is the last one to get up to speed on changes in new performance standards. He could care less about learning new and better ways to perform his work. Perry was once a very capable manager when he was promoted into management many years ago. Today, Perry's skills have deteriorated to a point where he is not very effective. Perry thinks that if he stays within the minimal bounds of acceptable performance he will not lose his job.[38]

Due to budget constraints, you can only select one of the four employees to develop through delegation. Your objective is to *maximize the amount of transformational leadership in your work group*. Who will you choose? What tasks will you delegate to this person to raise his level of moral development and performance? Why? What will your preliminary performance improvement plan look like for this person? Which three employees will you *not* choose to develop through delegation? Why?

Notes

1. Rath, T. (2007). *StrengthsFinder 2.0*. New York: Gallup Press.
2. Kellerman, B. (2008). *Followership: How followers are creating change and changing leaders*. Boston: Harvard Business School Press.
3. Most, R. (2008, September 11). Personal communication.
4. Summitt, P. H., & Jenkins, S. (1998). *Reach for the summit: The definite dozen system for succeeding at whatever you do*. New York: Broadway Books; and Summitt, P. H., & Jenkins, S. (1998). *Raise the roof: The inspiring inside story of the Tennessee Lady Vols' undefeated 1997–98 season*. New York: Broadway Books.
5. Smith, G. (1998, March 2). Eyes of the storm. *Sports Illustrated*, *88*, 88–106.
6. Dansereau, F., Graen, G., & Haga, W. J. (1975). A vertical dyad linkage approach to leadership within formal organizations: A longitudinal investigation of the role-making process. *Organizational Behavior and Human Performance*, *13*, 46–78.
7. Peterson, C., & Seligman, M. E. P. (2004). *Character strengths and virtues: A handbook and classification*. New York: Oxford/American Psychological Association.
8. Avolio, B. J. (1999). *Full leadership development: Building the vital forces in organizations*. Thousand Oaks, CA: Sage.

9. Kelly, M. (1999). *The rhythm of life: Living every day with passion and purpose.* New York: Fireside Books. Retrieved June 19, 2008, from http://www.matthewkelly.org/mkf_index.html.
10. Sosik, J. J., Jung, D. I., & Dinger, S. L. (2009). Values in authentic action: Examining the roots and rewards of altruistic leadership. *Group & Organization Management, 34*(4),395–431; Sosik, J. J., Avolio, B. J., & Jung, D. I. (2002). Beneath the mask: Examining the relationship of self-presentation attributes and impression management to charismatic leadership. *The Leadership Quarterly, 13,* 217–242; and Sosik, J. J., & Dworakivsky, A. C. (1998). Self-concept based aspects of the charismatic leader: More than meets the eye. *The Leadership Quarterly, 9,* 503–526.
11. Gerstner, L. V. (2002). *Who says elephants can't dance? Inside IBM's historic turnaround.* New York: Harper Business.
12. Covey, S. R. (1989). *The seven habits of highly effective people: Restoring the character ethic.* New York: Simon & Schuster.
13. Interview with Pat Croce conducted February 5, 2008, by Brian Kovatch, Andrea Laine, Robert Eidson, and Shawn Minnier.
14. Avolio, B. J. (1999). As cited in Note 8.
15. Bass, B. M. (1985). *Leadership and performance beyond expectations.* New York: Free Press.
16. Dychtwald, K., Erickson, T. J., & Morison, R. (2006). *Workforce crisis: How to beat the coming shortage of skills and talent.* Boston: Harvard Business School Press; Clark, H. (2006, March 8). Are women happy under the glass ceiling? *Forbes.* Retrieved February 20, 2007, from http://www.forbes.com/ceonet/2006/03/07/glass-ceiling-opportunites-cx_hc_0308glass.html; and Treftz, D. Women post job gains, data show. *The Wall Street Journal,* p. A8.
17. Retrieved July 8, 2008, from http://www.census.gov/ipc/www/usinterimproj/.
18. Dreachslin, J. L. (1996). *Diversity leadership.* Chicago: Health Administration Press.
19. Dreachslin (1996). As cited in Note 18.
20. Pearsall, M. J., Ellis, A. P. J., & Evans, J. M. (2008). Unlocking the effects of gender faultlines on team creativity: Is activation the key? *Journal of Applied Psychology, 93,* 225–234.
21. Thompson, L. (2000). *Making the team: A guide for managers.* Upper Saddle River, NJ: Prentice Hall.
22. Ofori-Dankwa, J., & Julian, S. D. (2004). Conceptualizing social science paradoxes using the diversity and similarity curves model: Illustrations from the work/play and theory novelty/continuity paradoxes. *Human Relations, 57,* 1449–1477.
23. Bass, B. M. (1997). Does the transactional/transformational leadership paradigm transcend organizational and national boundaries? *American Psychologist, 52,* 130–139.
24. Gardenswartz, L., & Rowe, A. (1994). *Diverse teams at work: Capitalizing on the power of diversity.* New York: McGraw-Hill.
25. Barrick, M. R., & Mount, M. K. (1991). The Big Five personality dimensions and job performance: A meta-analysis. *Personnel Psychology, 44,* 1–26.
26. Bandura, A. (1997). *Self-efficacy: The exercise of control.* New York: Freeman.
27. Rotter, J. A. (1978). *Personality.* Glenview, IL: Scott Foresman.

28. Fuller, R. W. (2004). *Somebodies and nobodies: Overcoming the abuse of rank.* New York: New Society Publishers.
29. Kram, K. E. (1985). *Mentoring at work: Developmental relationships in organizational life.* Glenview, IL: Scott, Foreman & Co.
30. Wanberg, C. R., Welsh, E. T., & Hezlett, S. A. (2003). Mentoring research: A review and dynamic process model. *Research in Personnel and Human Resource Management, 22,* 39–124.
31. Kram (1985). As cited in Note 29.
32. Kram (1985). As cited in Note 29.
33. Godshalk, V. M., & Sosik, J. J. (2007, p. 172). Leadership and mentoring: Standing at the cross roads of theory, research and practice. In B. R. Ragins & K. E. Kram (Eds.), *The handbook of mentoring at work: Theory, research, and practice* (pp. 149–178). Los Angeles: Sage.
34. Kark, R., Shamir, B., & Chen, G. (2003). The two faces of transformational leadership: Empowerment and dependency. *Journal of Applied Psychology, 88,* 246–255.
35. Kuhnert, K. W. (1994). Transforming leadership: Developing people through delegation. In B. M. Bass & B. J. Avolio (Eds.), *Improving organizational effectiveness through transformational leadership* (pp. 10–25). Thousand Oaks, CA: Sage.
36. Bass, B. M., & Avolio, B. J. (1990). *Basic workshop: Full range leadership development.* Binghamton, NY: Center for Leadership Studies, SUNY-Binghamton.
37. Retrieved June 24, 2008, from http://www.westtown.edu/.
38. Adapted with permission from Bass and Avolio (1990, pp. 6.21–6.22). As cited in Note 36.

Chapter 7

Contingent Reward and Management-by-Exception Active

The Two Faces of Transactional Leadership

> The first responsibility of a leader is to define reality. The last is to say thank you.
>
> **—Max DePree**

Leaders of today's corporations are challenged to operate in ways that solve rather than contribute toward environmental and social problems. A growing number of organizations are monitoring and reporting the actions of corporations for compliance with socially responsible and "green" business practices. For example, Co-op America's (www.coopamerica.org/) mission is to "harness economic power—the strength of consumers, investors, businesses, and the marketplace—to create a socially just and environmentally sustainable society."[1] Co-op America works to ensure that corporations operate in ways that promote fair labor practices and environmentally responsible business initiatives. They work hard to make corporations more accountable for attaining these goals that protect people and our planet, in addition to meeting financial goals that maximize wealth for shareholders.

We were surprised to see that Co-op America identified the Vanguard Group as investing in many of the least sustainable companies, financing companies operating in war-torn areas such as Sudan, and failing to use proxies to support climate resolutions.[2] The Vanguard Group was founded in 1975 by John C. Bogle, a visionary on corporate social responsibility.[3] As CEO, Bogle helped Vanguard to become one of the largest investment companies in the world with more than $1 trillion of assets under management. They focus on selling no-load mutual and index funds where the buyer pays no sales commission. Our students who work at Vanguard tell us that they do not offer socially responsible funds because they are too expensive to run. Vanguard's strategy is to be a low-cost investment management company that provides products and services based on what their clients desire. As clients become increasingly committed to a more balanced approach to corporate success (profit + people + planet issues), we suggest that Vanguard establish goals, action plans, and reward systems that harness returns from more socially responsible and environmentally sustainable investments.

Vanguard is well positioned to make this strategic move based on its goal-setting and reward systems. Vanguard strives to accomplish these goals through a two-pronged approach to goals. There are goals that relate to employees' personal development that are reviewed on a semiannual basis. And there are strategic goals around what top management wants to achieve as a business. These are also set on a semiannual basis and discussed monthly. Their senior leaders meet at least once every other week with each of their direct reports. They talk about what they're doing and how they're getting things done. They also talk about development opportunities and where things are headed. This helps to prevent big surprises by the time year-end rolls around, when they discuss bonus rankings or merit pay increases. We believe that this mentoring-based developmental approach gives direct reports a more meaningful opportunity to learn something important and relevant to their growth compared to a more traditional program-based approach.

Vanguard's strong work ethic culture and reward systems can also help. In the Vanguard culture, it is assumed employees come to work with the expectation that they will work hard every day. That expectation gets even stronger the higher one is in the company. For associates in the upper echelons of the company, it is expected that they are going to work very hard, and that will yield positive results because they're in the office, more available, and giving maximum effort. At lower levels of the organization, associates look for some type of reward, something to satisfy those who say, "What's in it for me to work harder?" That's where reward systems are vitally important and Vanguard continually explores both monetary and nonmonetary ways to reward their associates. They have reward and recognition mechanisms in place to motivate their associates on a wide range of initiatives. And when senior leaders see their associates step up and do a great job, they reward them for meeting performance expectations.[4]

But what happens when there is someone on the crew (i.e., team at Vanguard) who is not performing as she should, and the other members of the crew are very aware of that? The others look to their leader and say, "Why aren't you doing something about Sharon? She doesn't seem to be doing her part. She's not getting things done over here the way she should." In some ways, that is not for them to know because there may be personal reasons for why Sharon might not be meeting their expectations. People often open up and talk about these situations. If associates see a Vanguard leader get more actively involved with someone who isn't performing as well, then they will have a sense that the leader is taking care of them. Therefore, it can help the team dynamic and overall organization by dealing with someone who may not be performing as well as they should be. This requires a leader's active involvement in monitoring their behavior and performance and providing honest and accurate guidance for making improvements.

This chapter shows you how to use goal setting and contingent rewards to pave a path for your followers to reach their performance goals. It also shows you how to actively monitor and control your followers' performance and redirect their focus and effort when they get off the path to success. By monitoring their progress and exchanging contingent rewards for their achievement of agreed-upon goals, you can become a leader who helps followers attain expected levels of performance. Let's start learning about this transactional approach to leadership by considering the case of one of today's most successful CEOs.

The Transactional Leadership of Sam Palmisano at IBM

A quiet confidence exudes from the imposing frame of Sam Palmisano, president and CEO of the IBM Corporation since 2003. Unlike the charismatic CEOs of many other corporations, Palmisano doesn't like being the center of attention. Instead, he has gained his confidence by learning from his employees and customers, who provide a wellspring of ideas for managing in today's global business environment. He respects the expertise and knowledge his associates bring to work with them every day. He listens carefully to his associates because they are closer to customers and suppliers than he is. And he uses an interesting blend of transactional leadership because that style best reflects who he is as a person.

Palmisano loves to dig into the details of planning and speed up the reporting cycle to match the pace of business in the information technology (IT) industry.

Goals guide Palmisano's strategic thinking, and he holds his associates responsible for reaching those goals. When things get dicey, he makes his sales goals by holding conference calls at the beginning *and* end of 14-hour workdays. He advocates using sales forecasts with a time horizon of only one week—and no longer. He holds weekly operating meetings, instead of the traditional monthly meetings. IBM's old 90-day sales forecasts are a thing of the past. Instead, Palmisano asks managers to provide reports on what they plan to close within the week. His focus is on the short term, and he operates with a sense of urgency. He lives in the now.

Never a fan of long meetings, Palmisano tries to keep meetings to only 15 minutes instead of the traditional 1-hour or longer meetings in other organizations. He would much rather spend the time accomplishing tasks that get things done. That is why he schedules meetings in the early evening, when they do not interfere with the business day. We've seen Palmisano's logic shared by task-oriented leaders with a high need for achievement, who often get frustrated with meetings because they see them as interruptions of work. Indeed, one of our MBA students humorously suggested that meetings are "good for the lonely, those who don't like working on their own, or for those who hate making decisions." According to this student, meetings allow employees to see other people, draw flowcharts, feel important, and impress colleagues all on company time. This makes meetings sound like a handy alternate to work! And Palmisano might smile and perhaps agree.

When IBM employees meet their performance targets, Palmisano rewards them with personal visits, compliments, coffee, handshakes, and bonuses. He goes out of his way to visit plants and offices that were integral to successful achievements of project goals. He makes employees around him feel comfortable. He tells them they are valued members of IBM. And in return, they give Palmisano their very best.[5] This completes the business transaction Palmisano has entered into with his associates when he helps them to set goals and work toward their attainment. His transactional leadership style gets things done to meet Wall Street's expectations, and that's what IBM's board of directors expects of him.

Contingent Reward—Definition and Behavioral Examples

Like Sam Palmisano, you too can pave a path for your followers to reach their performance targets by displaying contingent reward leadership behaviors. That's because *contingent reward* involves a constructive transaction between the leader and the follower. It is constructive because the leader sets goals for followers that clarify expectations for what needs to be achieved to meet expected levels of performance. It is also constructive because it uses rewards to reinforce the positive behaviors the follower displays to meet performance targets. Followers typically like receiving rewards because they are positive affirmations of their value as a professional and a good organizational citizen.

Over the many years we have been teaching Full Range Leadership Development (FRLD), one *inaccurate* perception we have found over and over again among our MBA students and even executive audiences is that transformational leadership is the only positive way to lead. Some have wrongly concluded that transactional leadership based on contingent rewards is inferior to transformational leadership and therefore should be discouraged. However, we believe that contingent reward could be an equally effective and powerful way to motivate people since it creates consistent expectations between the leader and followers.

Contingent reward is based on an implied transaction between the leader and the follower. Think of contingent reward as a type of contract. A contract spells out what is expected for the parties involved in the transaction. With a constructive transaction, the leader's side of the deal involves setting goals, identifying potential pathways for meeting the goals, and supporting followers for meeting performance expectations. The follower's side of the deal involves performing the tasks required to meet the goals and reaching those goals. When the follower does this, the leader then completes the deal by providing an agreed-upon extrinsic reward to the follower for her satisfactory performance. *Extrinsic rewards* come from outside of the follower, such as a bonus or recognition provided by the leader. These are financial, material, or social awards given by the leader or organization to the follower. In contrast, *intrinsic rewards* come from inside of the follower from performing a task without external incentives. These are self-granted or psychic rewards internally given by the follower.[6]

Contingent reward leadership establishes instrumentality and valence for followers. It suggests for followers how they can achieve their targets. By clarifying what management wants to achieve and values, followers become well positioned to achieve what's deemed important by their organization, which will create more meaningful and relevant outcomes. Through these processes of clarifying mutual expectations, followers typically possess satisfactory levels of trust and commitment toward their leaders and organization. This is how contingent reward leadership becomes an important foundation of effective leadership (sometimes as much as inspirational leadership we discussed throughout this book). To better understand contingent reward leadership, consider how Michael Bloomberg has led in many different situations over his lifetime (see Table 7.1).

Like Bloomberg, you can display contingent reward leadership by practicing behaviors that guide, monitor, and reward your followers. Let's now examine

Table 7.1   Leader Profile: Michael Bloomberg

When you think of superstar businessmen, chances are Michael Bloomberg comes to mind. Born to a middle-class Jewish family of Polish and Russian descent, Bloomberg was raised to value hard work and social responsibility. He worked his way through school to pay for his undergraduate education in engineering at Johns Hopkins University. He then went on to earn an MBA from Harvard University and land a job on Wall Street at Salomon Brothers.

While at Salomon Brothers, Bloomberg gained experience in information technology that led to his eventual founding of Bloomberg LP, the successful global financial news and information services company. Bloomberg's education and life experiences taught him the importance of transparency in financial matters, accountability, and innovation by applying technology systems to enhance the efficiency of social systems in organizations. As a result of his successful business ventures, Bloomberg is considered to be one of the world's richest men and most generous philanthropists.

Then the call for public service beckoned. Bloomberg ran for mayor of New York City and was elected in 2001, reelected in 2005, and plans to run for a third term in 2009. Bloomberg's leadership style is a mix of pragmatic problem solving and transactional planning and control—a style he used effectively in his business career. He has a data-driven approach to decision making. He loves to balance budgets, cut waste, and increase the efficiency with which programs are delivered to the citizens of New York. Finding ways to do more with less in a fiscally conservative manner is a Bloomberg value.

Bloomberg uses this transactional leadership style to advance his agenda on important issues facing the citizens of New York. He advocates delivering high-quality education to help children achieve their dreams. He champions a variety of public health programs to improve quality of life for his constituents. His economic development programs have helped to create new jobs and reduce unemployment. He has partnered with Mayors Against Illegal Guns to crack down on criminals who have easy access to guns. To promote affordable housing, he has created the largest program seen in U.S. cities. To reduce poverty, he has created a program that rewards people for working and promotes the power of education. His "PlaNYC: A Greener, Greater New York" is an innovative strategy to protect the environment and sustain its resources. Through his philanthropy, Bloomberg has funded many nonprofit organizations offering arts and culture in New York. His story teaches us that money talks, but without a noble vision, it can't promote prosperity and serve the common good.

Source: Bloomberg, M. (1997). *Bloomberg by Bloomberg.* New York: Wiley; and retrieved August 26, 2008, from http://www.mikebloomberg.com/.

four important leadership behaviors that allow you to establish a constructive transaction with your followers.

Set Goals for and With Followers

Daniel is department manager of a training group within a corporate university. His staff consists of trainers and support staff. Every April he asks his staff members to complete an activity report. This report summarizes their achievements in terms of the number of courses they have taught and developed and the ratings and comments they received from participants in their courses. It also includes a list of job-related goals for the upcoming year as well as a comparison of last year's goals to their actual performance achieved during the current year. After staff members complete these reports, Daniel meets with each of them to review their goals for the upcoming year. They discuss how the individual goals fit into the overall goals for the department. Daniel often revises his staff's goals to direct their attention to the most important goals that will contribute to the department. He also uses "stretch goals" that elevate his staff's performance expectations because some of his staff members get lazy and set goals that can be easily achieved.

As shown in Figure 7.1, setting goals strategically is an important aspect of contingent reward leadership because it directs your followers' attention to

Figure 7.1   Making the grade. Parents can set goals for their children's academic achievement and reward them for getting good grades.

what needs to be achieved. If they know what to shoot for, they can regulate the amount of effort they exert. Goals motivate followers by increasing their persistence to try and try again. Goals also get them to strategize ways to best achieve the objective or develop action plans to meet their target.[7]

Do you play golf? The sport of golf is a great way to understand the power of goals in motivating your followers. When you tee up your shot at the beginning of a hole, you know the par for the hole. *Par* represents the normal or standard number of shots it takes to hit the golf ball into the hole. Therefore, par is a type of goal. The par tells you what you need to achieve for the hole. With this knowledge, you can strategize how many shots you'd like to take and which golf clubs you will use to achieve par. You get a good sense of the amount of effort you need to put into your shots. Even if you don't make par, knowing what par is gives you the incentive to make par next time you play that golf course.

Whatever your golf game is, you can win the "master's cup of leadership" by setting goals with your followers and encouraging them to be more persistent. This helps you to reframe their perspective of work into a challenging game. This change in perspective will increase their focus, drive, and commitment to achieving desired results because they, like you, love to be a winner.

Suggest Pathways to Meet Performance Expectations

Setting goals is one thing. But knowing how to accomplish them is another. Followers often want some ideas on how they can attain the goals they agree to achieve. That's why clarifying your expectations by suggesting ways to accomplish tasks is important to initiate a constructive transaction with your followers. This contingent reward leadership behavior is something that Dina practices every chance she gets.

Dina heads up the human resource management group with her colleague Cherie at the Autobahn Automobile Mall (AAM). One of Cherie's former customers, Visha, expressed an interest in building better relationships between her company and AAM by meeting to discuss a possible large sale. While Visha, Dina, and Cherie were meeting, Ben, AAM's sales manager, happened to walk into Dina's office. As luck would have it, Visha identified the Lexus RX 350 as a potential fleet car for her company. This is a type of car that Ben sells. Dina connected Visha's needs (demand for the Lexus) with Ben's potential to satisfy her need (supply of the Lexus). Following the meeting, Dina told Ben that he could make his sales goal by sealing the deal with Visha. In essence, Dina was paving a pathway for Ben to meet his performance obligations, thereby adding to her constructive transactional relationship with Ben.

Another example of this contingent reward behavior is found in the school systems of Canada. Pathways to Education™ is a charitable organization that is based on the principle of providing pathways to reach performance targets. Its goals are to reduce poverty and lower high school dropout rates by increasing access to college education for disadvantaged children. It is not enough to simply focus children's attention on the need to earn a college degree through goal setting. Children need support for their goals to ensure that they persevere in reaching them. Pathways to Education provides four supports or pathways so the children can attain their goals: (1) academic tutoring in five subjects, (2) social group mentoring, (3) financial assistance for tuition and transportation fees, and (4) advocacy where workers connect students, parents, schools, and community agencies to meet specific needs. Results of this program include significant reductions in dropout rates, 95% enrollment in the program of all eligible children, reduced absenteeism, and significant increases in college enrollment of program graduates. In addition, the social impacts of this program, as computed by the Boston Consulting Group, include a return on investment of 25 times the initial investment, a $400,000 cumulative lifetime benefit for each student in the program, and a net present value for each student of $50,000.[8]

Both of these examples show that followers need support from their leaders and organization to meet their goals. By suggesting ideas and providing resources to attain the goal, you can provide the well-defined pathway followers need to reach your performance targets. This contingent reward leadership behavior helps to initiate a structure that supports followers' efforts to be successful. Meeting performance expectations is an increasingly difficult task because expectations from organizational stakeholders are higher than ever. We believe that most of your followers will do their very best, as long as, in return, you support them through the many trials and tribulations they face in working to achieve their goals.

Actively Monitor Followers' Progress and Provide Supportive Feedback

Parenting is one of the noblest forms of leadership. One of the great things about FRLD is that almost everything you learn in this book can be applied to your role as a parent. That's what Jackie Sharifi did when she used a combination of transactional and transformational leadership on her 21-year-old son, Oliver. Like many children his age, Oliver is at a crossroads in his life where he is reluctant to leave adolescence and move into adulthood. Jackie has been watching the progress Oliver is making in transitioning into a new chapter in his life. She took the time to write a supportive letter to provide him with feedback on where he is in life, where he needs to go, and how she will help him get there.

Jackie told Oliver that he is now a man and that he is facing some daunting challenges that she is confident he will overcome. She emphasized her intent of helping him with some tools that he can use to succeed in whatever it is that he chooses to do in life. She went on to praise him for his friendship with Sam.

> You have been spending a lot of time with your friend Sam, which is a terrific example of reaching out to a friend for help and advice. Sam has set some goals for himself, has a vision of what he wants to become, and a plan for how he is going to achieve his goals. You don't have to follow Sam's path but you can use some of his strategies to get you going in the direction you want to go, like envisioning your future a year or two from now and setting goals to get there and maybe even keeping a daily log of your progress.[9]

In her letter, Jackie outlined six suggestions for Oliver to consider in successfully transitioning into adulthood. These included meeting with her to consider his options for a career, reading a book on career paths for college graduates, studying money management topics, identifying a mentor or life coach for him, reflecting upon Coach John Wooden's "pyramid of success"[10] as an inspirational guidepost, and watching a video of Steve Job's speech at the 2005 Stanford University graduation ceremony. Jackie gave her son these suggestions as specific guidelines for what needs to be done to succeed in life. Oliver read the letter and told his mother that it was motivating when they sat down to talk about it. She will continue to follow up with her son to see if he is willing and ready to take the steps she outlined in her letter. Jackie certainly showed what constructive transactional leadership is all about.

Whether in the role of parent (like Jackie) or leader at work, it is important for you to monitor your followers' progress toward goals proactively, and provide resources that empower them physically, psychologically, and intellectually. Your role here is to be supportive—to catch them if and when they fall. Be careful not to be too overbearing or controlling. The only time you should look down on them is to help them back to their feet. By doing this, you are building a base level of trust with transactional leadership. Remember that transactional leadership is an important foundation before you can practice transformational leadership.

Provide Rewards When Goals Are Attained

Exchanging extrinsic rewards and recognition for meeting performance targets is the hallmark behavior in contingent reward leadership. This is the payoff that followers expect from leaders when they follow through on their side of the deal. And they expect rewards that they value and find personally appealing. That's why it is important to personalize the type of reward you use to the follower's needs and preferences.

For example, Vicki likes the finer things in life and loves to show off her material possessions. With this in mind, Ernie (the boss) rewards her with salary increases or stock options when she meets her sales targets. In contrast, Pierre is financially secure from wise investment of some "old money" from his family. But his financial security fuels his big ego. Therefore, Ernie rewards Pierre with compliments and public recognition that make him feel special and important to the company. Ernie also recently assigned Betty, his gregarious project manager, to a nice corner office after she successfully sealed an important deal. He used this type of extrinsic reward because she spends a lot of time at work and is responsible for building relationships with many people both inside and outside of the company. After Ernie gives his followers their rewards, he often hears them say, "Now, that's what I like!"

Such extrinsic rewards can also enhance the level of intrinsic rewards your followers perceive. For example, when your followers are promoted, get recognition, or get a pay increase, they will feel pride in themselves and a sense of accomplishment and joy in their jobs. These feelings are likely to increase their self-esteem. There are also many people who enjoy their job or service even without a high level of salary or public recognition. Such people include social activists, nonprofit or social service workers, artists, poets, "starving" musicians, or painters. However, some researchers argue that extrinsic rewards diminish intrinsic motivation and rewards (we elaborate on this point below). Nevertheless, you have to remember that reward systems need to allow followers to grow and develop as people, but at the same time realize the power of pay and benefits as strong forces for motivating action.[11]

Management-by-Exception Active—Definition and Behavioral Examples

We now turn our attention to a more severe face of transactional leadership. If contingent reward leadership is the cordial and civil face of FRLD, then *management-by-exception active* (MBE-A) is its stern face. The MBE-A leadership style seeks to monitor and control followers through forced compliance with rules and regulations and expectations for meeting performance standards and behavioral norms. It is based on an old concept of exception management dating back to Fredrick Winslow Taylor and the scientific management school. This school of thought aims to improve organizational efficiency through structured systems, detailed instruction, careful observation, and active supervision. One of their tenets suggests that leaders should focus their attention on the special cases (e.g., noncompliant people or processes, inaccurate data, mistakes, poor performance) that need to be addressed because they deviate from normal business operations, expectations, or performance.[12] Based upon this philosophy, MBE-A leadership behavior actively seeks to find and eliminate exceptions prior to or immediately after they occur.

MBE-A leadership aims to keep people and processes in control. Leaders can use elements of control to renew their organizational strategies and harness their followers' willingness to contribute and achieve performance goals. At the strategic leadership level, such systems can reduce strategic uncertainties, avoid unnecessary risks, and ensure that important goals are being achieved. For individual followers, control systems can reduce uncertainty about purpose, reduce temptations to shirk duties or act unethically, refocus attention to what needs to be achieved, and define opportunities to meet performance objectives.[13]

MBE-A leadership behavior involves a *corrective transaction* between the leader and the follower. It is corrective because the leader tends to focus on deviations from predefined standards. In other words, the leader swiftly fixes the problem whenever the follower's performance deviates from standard. If used only occasionally or in critical situations, we believe that MBE-A is OK, and followers might even appreciate the MBE-A leadership style. However, if used too frequently or inappropriately, followers will despise MBE-A leadership behaviors because they focus on what is wrong (punitive), rather than what is right (developmental). This focus can be de-motivating and disheartening to followers if it is repeated over time or applied out of context, as Carly Fiorina found out at Hewlett-Packard (see Table 7.2). In other cases, it can produce positive results. For example, Lee Kuan Yew has used this leadership style to turn a Third World nation into one of the economic powerhouses of Asia (see Table 7.3).

Like Lee Kuan Yew, you can display active management-by-exception leadership by aggressively searching for errors, micromanaging, and correcting problems before they occur. Let's now examine three important leadership behaviors that allow you to establish a corrective transaction with your followers.

Closely Monitor Work Performance for Errors

Herman delivered the interoffice and postal mail at a financial service center of an international foods company. Although Herman was not one of the most efficient workers, coworkers loved him because of his outgoing personality. During his daily mail delivery runs, Herman would stop and chat with almost anyone. He could ably strike up a conversation on a wide variety of topics, such as how well the Philadelphia Phillies were playing, what was on television the night before, office gossip, and even the quality of food at local church bazaars and festivals. These conversations brightened many days for his coworkers and boosted their morale. When the long conversations ended, Herman would cheerfully meander to his next stop in the office.

Table 7.2 Leader Profile: Carly Fiorina

Carly Fiorina had a hard-edged, top-down leadership style, which by all accounts rubbed many a Hewlett-Packard employee, shareholder, industry analyst, and HP board of director the wrong way. During Fiorina's tenure as chairman and CEO, the market value of HP dropped by over half and the company incurred heavy job losses. Always a highly visible CEO, Fiorina traveled extensively and made numerous public appearances analogous to a political candidate on the campaign trail. In 2002, Fiorina, in one of many highly debated and questionable moves, forced a controversial merger with tech industry rival Compaq. She went against the wishes of many board members, including Walter Hewlett, son of the company co-founder, who strongly opposed the deal. The merger did nothing to solidify HP as a technology company, and in fact, it caused HP stock to lose significant value. Industry experts classified the merger as a colossal failure.

Once dubbed by *Fortune* magazine as the most powerful woman in business, Fiorina was dismissed in early 2005 after six years. The board presented her with a four-page list of issues regarding her inadequate performance. Fiorina tried to introduce change too forcefully, focusing too much on the wrong details with MBE-A behavior, while ignoring issues that the board of directors viewed as more important. Fiorina was credited with transforming the organizational culture at HP, and her charismatic leadership style built a loyal following with some. However, she failed to gain support of the larger constituent groups required to drive the successful execution of her vision for HP.

Once news of Fiorina's dismissal hit the press, HP stock jumped 7%. After leaving HP, she has continued her leadership role through writing, serving as a business news commentator, and political activism. In 2008, Fiorina was actively involved in advancing the Republican agenda and supporting John McCain's failed bid for U.S. president.

Source: Burrows, P. (2003). *Backfire: Carly Fiorina's high-stakes battle for the soul of Hewlett-Packard.* New York: Wiley; and Fiorina, C. (2006). *Tough choices: A memoir.* New York: Portfolio.

One day, Herman's manager, Kim, returned from a seminar on "management-by-walking-around."[14] Kim was a well-respected manager and, at the time, the only woman in the upper echelons of company management. As such, she felt compelled to exceed performance expectations and instill a high level of motivation in all of her employees. She pondered how she could apply what she learned at the seminar to satisfy her compulsion. After thinking about this for some time, she identified Herman as an obvious target.

Table 7.3   Leader Profile: Lee Kuan Yew

In *Meditation XVII*, English poet John Donne wrote that "no man is an island." But he never met Lee Kuan Yew of Singapore, the stern and self-assured man who helped to create the island nation and became its first prime minister. In fact, Lee is Singapore. Trained as a lawyer, Lee used his intelligence, work ethic, integrity, and political skills to transform Singapore from a poor country to one of the economic powerhouses of Asia. In fact, many of Lee's personal characteristics and values, such as high energy, pugnacity, clannishness, and frankness, are recognized by citizens of Singapore as national virtues worthy of emulation. He is considered to be one of the greatest statesmen in Asia, even today in his current governmental role as minister mentor.

Lee's status as an idealized leader in Singapore is built upon a strong foundation of transactional leadership. Those who supported him were often rewarded with governmental posts. Those who opposed him were either jailed or forced into bankruptcy. Lee is famous for his knowledge of the law and his willingness to use it to advance his agenda, and crush his opponents.

While prime minister from 1965 to 1990, Lee was responsible for setting many lofty goals for Singapore and its citizens after Singapore's independence from Great Britain in 1959. Today, Singapore's infrastructure, public housing system, national security, tightly controlled economy, Corrupt Practices Investigation Bureau, family planning policies, and relations with neighboring countries are the result of Lee's insightful planning and domineering control systems. Lee's penchant for control comes from his strong influence by the British culture and education, his country's domination under British colonization, and its occupation by Japan during World War II. Given this history, it is no wonder why some of Lee's critics label him an autocrat.

Despite such criticisms, Lee's leadership of Singapore and its ascent to economic prosperity are no less than amazing. In a small nation with limited land space and natural resources, Lee has used goal setting, rewards, and punishments to propel his nation from a developing country to one of the most developed countries in Asia. He achieved this by convincing the citizens of Singapore that their only natural resources are their people and strong work ethic. He told them that they and future generations will achieve a great destiny for Singapore through relentless development: "So there must be this continuous renewal of talented, dedicated, honest, able people who will do things not for themselves but for their people and for their country." This certainly sounds like a call for the kind of leadership fostered through FRLD.

Source: Barr, M. D. (2000). *Lee Kuan Yew: The beliefs behind the man.* Washington, DC: Georgetown University Press; and retrieved August 25, 2008, from http://www.time.com/time/asia/asia/magazine/1999/990823/lee1.html.

The next day, Kim snuck behind a cubicle and watched Herman as he lollygagged along, philosophizing about how the New York Yankees are the most overpaid team in major league baseball. After listening to five minutes of Herman's sermon, Kim sprang into action and shouted, "Aha! Is that how you add value to our company, Herman? By working at a snail's pace while the rest of us have our nose to the grind? You better get cracking!" Scared half out of his wits, Herman picked up the pace and started chanting "Speedy delivery! Speedy delivery!" as he moved to the next mail drop. Herman's exclamation conjured up images of Mr. Speedy McFeeley (David Newell), the nervous mailman on the classic PBS television show *Mr. Rogers' Neighborhood*, in the mind's eye of a nearby group of coworkers. They broke into laughter as they witnessed the hilarity of the situation.

Kim used management-by-walking-around to closely monitor Herman's work performance for errors, and he certainly gave her a lot of material with which to work. This type of MBE-A behavior motivates followers through intimidation. Because they fear the repercussions of not complying with standards, they typically will change their behavior to get back in line. Their behavior modification is often swift and may remain in the short run. However, it is unclear whether these changes are long lasting. What Kim got from Herman was mere compliance, not commitment—she needs to create sustainable motivation. By monitoring the work of your colleagues as shown in Figure 7.2, you can help to control their work habits, eliminate deviations from work processes, and improve your organization's efficiency.

Focus Attention on Mistakes, Complaints, Failures, Deviations, and Infractions

Mickey loved his job as executive director of corporate training. His position gave him the power and opportunity to control almost everyone in his department. A born problem solver, Mickey enjoyed fixing as many problems that he could find with his staff. He did this with information gathering sessions veiled as social gatherings, interrogations of associates, and heavy-handed approaches to micromanaging his direct reports. Even though he was an executive responsible for building relationships with his clients, Mickey spent most of his day in the office monitoring email, editing copy for print ads, and even editing the email grammar of coworkers. Mickey's frequent display of MBE-A behavior led others to believe that he had a "God complex."

One morning Mickey sat at his desk drinking coffee from his cup that read "He who must be obeyed." As he sipped from the cup, he thought about his approach to leadership. Always a pragmatic type, he reasoned that leadership is all about solving problems for others. He felt confident that he was helping

Figure 7.2 Waiting to strike. The male manager in the background stands by ready to put an end to his subordinates' gossiping during work hours. He's heard complaints that they are wasting valuable company time.

others by "fixing what was wrong with them." After all, a little tough love never hurt anyone. Right?

Dead wrong! This example teaches us that there is a fine line between the pragmatic problem-solving approach to leadership described in Chapter 1 and focusing your attention on mistakes, complaints, failures, deviations, and infractions to the excess, like Mickey did. Mickey's tough love approach to leadership, when used too frequently, can have extremely negative consequences on followers, such as anxiety, inhibition, and damage to self-esteem and self-efficacy. When you break people down as much as Mickey did, some never are able to come back. Instead, why not build people up when they are broken? The only reason you should look down on people is because you are going to pick them up.

When you actively focus on exceptions, you need to quickly turn the negative message to a positive one by framing it as a developmental experience. Mickey missed out on a great opportunity to use intellectual stimulation to help his followers solve their own problems instead of dictating to them what is wrong and how they should go about fixing their problems. By moving from the display of MBE-A to the display of intellectual stimulation, Mickey could have created a great mentoring moment for many of his followers. Learn a lesson from Mickey and temper your focus on exceptions with transformational leadership. That way you will not end up being the one who must be obeyed due to fear and retaliation, but instead the one who must be respected and admired.

Arrange to Know If and When Things Go Wrong

Janet is a big believer in systems as sources of control because they let people know if and when things go wrong. Coming from the IT department, Janet had seen the power of technology in monitoring and recording communications, tracking employees' forays on the Internet, and capturing interpersonal interactions through hallway surveillance cameras. This technology, when coupled with her knowledge of internal auditing and fraud detection, is a powerful force to ensure that employees comply with rules and regulations. It provided Janet with the documentation she needed to justify disciplinary action against violators. She considered this to be a great source of leadership power since she believed the political philosopher Machiavelli was correct in saying "It is better to be feared than loved."

Once in her new role as director of internal audit, Janet felt confident in her ability to lead. Her IT systems and auditing knowledge gave her many ideas for designing activities to "keep her people in control." Her philosophy stems from the accounting and auditing profession's emphasis on using a system of *internal controls* to keep an organization on track toward meeting its objectives and minimizing the risks that things will go wrong. The purpose of internal controls is to keep people and things in control because of what can happen when things get out of control. Fraud, deception, and financial loss are just some of the outcomes that Janet wanted to avoid.[15]

Janet uses a variety of control activities to monitor employees and ensure that the strategic initiatives set by the senior leadership team are efficiently executed. We believe that auditing might be one area where MBE-A leadership behavior might be most beneficial. Here is how Janet uses disciplined approaches to actively monitor deviations from standards. First, her staff conducts performance reviews of the operational and financial aspects of the departments within her organization. For example, her staff reviews monthly reports comparing budgeted to actual dollars spent and activities performed by the department. They investigate any unusual differences or deviations from standards and ensure that department managers take corrective action. Second, she reviews IT systems to ensure that the accounting and reporting of financial transactions are accurate. She also leads her staff in protecting physical assets and records through inventory counts and reconciliations to records. Third, she makes sure that a segregation of duties exists by assigning different individuals to the recording of transactions and physical custody of the actual assets. This helps to reduce the risk of fraud.[16]

Like Janet, you also can establish a system of internal controls to know if and when things go wrong. By consulting with your associates in the accounting and IT departments, you can leverage auditing knowledge and the power of technology to provide you with the information to monitor and control the people and processes in your department. A solid understanding of organizational policies and their clear communication to your followers helps them understand what you are policing through MBE-A leadership.

Thinking About Transactional Leadership

You are now familiar with the concept of the two faces of transactional leadership. Now it's time to start thinking deeply about what implications these concepts have for you in terms of three topics related to FRLD: identifying when MBE-A leadership is appropriate, goal setting, and extrinsic rewards and punishments. A good understanding of these topics will help you to identify areas in your leadership context to apply transactional leadership to help your followers reach performance expectations.

When Is MBE-A Appropriate?

After reading the section above on MBE-A, you may not particularly care for this style of leadership. We agree with you that MBE-A is not the most effective way to lead people. It is similar to what Travis Bradberry has dubbed the "seagull manager." These managers swoop down out of the blue to solve problems by dumping their solutions on followers only when there is a fire to put out. They do this without carefully thinking about alternate solutions or how their abrupt and impersonal interactions affect followers. As a result, they frustrate and alienate their followers and only make the problem worse through their dumps.[17] Have you ever felt that you need to wear a protective cap that reads "Damn Seagulls!" when you come to work?

No one likes being bombed by a seagull manager. The seagull manager is especially problematic now because your biggest challenge is to find a way to harness creativity and commitment from your employees. Few people enjoy working for a micromanager. And fewer can constantly deal with MBE-A leadership that dwells on fixing problems. Does this suggest that there is no place for MBE-A leadership? Is this something you need to avoid at all costs? In what situations is MBE-A appropriate?

Actually, MBE-A leadership can be quite effective in a number of situations. When working on tasks or in industries that are regulated, such as the accounting or pharmaceutical industries, MBE-A is essential for ensuring compliance with rules and regulations. Or consider the IT group in your organization. IT systems are critical for the collection and analysis of organizational data and knowledge and for our basic means of communication these days. These systems cannot go down. MBE-A leadership may be required to ensure that they are up and running. Another place where MBE-A leadership is appropriate is in life-and-death situations. Military operations often rely on MBE-A to support the command and control function that protects the lives of our soldiers. Individuals managing nuclear power plants use MBE-A to ensure safe operations and prevent meltdowns or accidents such as those we witnessed at Three Mile Island in Pennsylvania or Chernobyl in Russia.

So, the bottom line for you is to figure out what are appropriate situations in which you can selectively practice MBE-A. It's interesting to note that there is a fine line between MBE-A and intellectual stimulation. Both use rational decision making to solve problems. Both take an active approach to solve problems. These similarities give you a great opportunity to quickly shift from MBE-A behavior to the more effective intellectual stimulation behavior. Once you identify problems to fix, why not *collaborate* with your followers to solve the problem, instead of *commanding* them to do as you say. The difference here is subtle, but the outcome in terms of followers' commitment and attitude toward their work will be significantly different. By getting your followers involved in the decision-making process and using their ideas and proposed solutions, you can improve their engagement level and accelerate their development as well. We firmly believe that this will help to free the skies of seagull managers in your organization.

Goal Setting

Goal setting is an integral aspect of contingent reward leadership. When leaders set goals for their followers, they must make the goal attractive to followers *and* increase the amount of effort they exert toward attaining the goal. Neil Bryant of Siemens Medical Solutions excels at both of these tasks. Neil makes goals attractive to his followers by illustrating to them how attaining the goal will have a positive impact on their professional and personal development. He does this by explaining how their success in achieving the goal is one small step toward where they want to be in a year or two in their career. He shows them how they can attain personal goals in their life by successfully achieving the tasks required to meet the goal at hand. This helps them to see that the outcome they are striving for is valuable to their growth and success in the future and maintains a balance and connection between professional and personal objectives.

To increase the amount of effort his followers put into their work, Neil raises their expectations of attaining performance goals if they work hard. He does this by pointing out other colleagues who have achieved their goals by working hard and tells them how alike they are. He also points out similar situations where followers were successful in the past and how their success was based on exerting a high level of effort. Another important element is challenging an employee to create her plan for how to achieve objectives within the larger goals so that individual creativity and commitment are ensured. Regardless of how you practice goal-setting processes, it is very important to do it consistently. Otherwise, your followers will get confused. Be as persistent as you can be. That's why Neil constantly preaches discipline and persistence, knowing you will face challenges, by embracing a philosophy of "adversity does not build character—it reveals it!" How persistent are you and your followers when you face difficult situations?

Neil also gets his followers to work harder by increasing their perception of the attractiveness of reaching the performance goal. He does this by highlighting the prestige associated with reaching the goal for followers with a high need for achievement or big egos. For those with a high need for affiliation, he emphasizes the professional and social connections that can come from attaining the goal. And for those with a high need for power, he calls attention to the influence they can exert on others by hitting their target. In essence, Neil makes the goals attractive to his followers by showing them how, by reaching their goals, they can satisfy their personal needs.[18] How do you use goals to motivate your followers to meet performance expectations? How can Neil's example help you to do a better job at using goal setting to influence your followers?

One of the most important aspects of successfully using goal setting in contingent reward leadership is holding high expectations for followers. This is what psychologists call *self-fulfilling prophecies* and the Pygmalion effect. In ancient Greek mythology, Pygmalion was a lonely sculptor who carved a statue of a woman out of ivory based on his expectations of the perfect woman. The statue was so beautiful that he fell in love with it. He offered it as a gift as he prayed to the goddess Venus, who brought the statue to life because she pitied him. This myth is the basis for George Bernard Shaw's famous play in which Professor Henry Higgins refines a lower-class flower girl named Eliza Doolittle into a society lady. Both of these stories show us that the power of expectations cannot be overestimated.

These stories are supported by a growing base of research that indicates that your high hopes for another person can result in high performance and that a person's self-expectations can also lead to high performance. In leadership contexts, a leader's high hopes coupled with supportive leadership can increase a follower's positive self-expectations. High hopes that followers self-impose make them more persistent and oftentimes lead to superior levels of performance, which in turn reinforces followers' positive self-expectations and those of the leader. Over time, this sequence of events can spiral into higher and higher levels of confidence and performance.[19]

All of this suggests the following takeaways to apply in your leadership situation:

- Develop high hopes for your followers and communicate them actively. These expectations fuel their positive expectations and performance and, over time, can allow them to top their previous achievements. However, if you don't communicate your high expectations to your followers, they won't know anything about them.
- Find out what your followers want in their personal and professional lives. Then link their current work to these outcomes so that they will see value in achieving the goals.
- Build your followers' confidence levels by pointing out their previous success stories and identify good performance so that they can connect the behaviors they used to meet their goals with the value you both place on achieving the goal.

Set SMARTER Goals

Goal setting is a method that works well with contingent reward leadership. But not all goals are effective motivators. Have you ever tried to motivate someone with goal-setting techniques but they did not work? What happened that got in the way of goal setting's effectiveness? What could you have done better?

Perhaps your goals did not work for you because they were not "smart" enough. If so, then you need to make your goals smarter. The most effective goals meet the following characteristics that spell out the mnemonic SMARTER:

- Specific—Goals need to be precise and clear. "To purchase a BMW X5" is a specific goal, while "To purchase a vehicle" is not.
- Measurable—Goals need to matched with metrics to assess the degree to which they are attained. "To increase my contingent reward leadership behavior score by .5" is a measurable goal because contingent rewarding can be measured with the Multifactor Leadership Questionnaire (MLQ). In contrast, "To increase my display of Zen by .5" is not a measurable goal because Zen is a philosophical concept that cannot be measured with a valid and reliable instrument such as the MLQ.
- Attainable—Goals need to be difficult, but not impossible to meet. "To decrease my MBE-A score by 1" is attainable, while "To decrease my MBE-A score to 0" may be unattainable in an auditing department.
- Results focused—Goals need to focus on outcomes, not processes. "To increase my annual sales dollars generated by 20%" is results oriented, while "To increase my level of concentration during interactions with

customers by 20%" is not because it focuses on processes used to achieve a sales goal.

■ Time-bound—Goals need a specific time period that they cover so that deadlines can be set. "To increase my level of annual sales dollars by 20% for the fiscal year ending December 31, 2011" is time-bound. In contrast, "To increase my level of annual sales dollars generated by 20%" sets no deadline or time period for achievement.

■ Evaluated—Goals need to be reviewed to determine the extent of progress made toward their attainment. Use contingent reward or MBE-A leadership behaviors to monitor the progress followers make toward their goals.

■ Rewarded—Recognize and reward those who meet your goals. Of course, contingent reward leadership behavior helps to make your goals SMARTER because it exchanges an extrinsic reward for successful achievement of the goal.[20]

Next time you have to create a budget or strategic plan or action plan for a project, create goal statements that possess these qualities. What goal statements in your work can you improve by applying these guidelines? How can you help others in your organization to make their goal statements SMARTER and help them achieve expected levels of performance with transactional leadership?

Extrinsic Rewards and Punishments

Contingent reward leadership behavior is based on a tenet from educational psychology that people tend to repeat behavior that has favorable consequences or is rewarded. In contrast, they tend to avoid behavior that has unfavorable consequences or is punished.[21] Rewards and punishments are an effective way to shape a follower's behavior by systematically reinforcing each successive step that moves her closer to the desired action. Such reinforcement may be required to change a follower's behavior, as shown in Figure 7.3.

Recall that some reinforcers are more effective than others because followers place different values on the reinforcers. For example, a follower who is punished for not meeting standards may not change his behavior because the sanction is not severe enough or does not carry with it serious repercussions. In general, *positive reinforcement* (e.g., providing rewards or recognition) strengthens positive behavior. This makes the behavior occur more often by contingently presenting something positive. *Negative reinforcement* (e.g., withdrawing a negative condition) also strengthens positive behavior. This makes the behavior occur more often by contingently withdrawing something negative, such as nagging or hazing. *Punishment* (i.e., administering a negative consequence) weakens or eliminates negative behavior. This makes the behavior occur less often by contingently

Figure 7.3   Good going. The woman on the right is receiving a well-deserved hefty bonus for meeting her annual sales goal. Because she's been rewarded for her hard work, she is likely to repeat her positive behavior in the future.

presenting something negative (e.g., MBE-A) or by contingently withdrawing something positive. And *extinction* (i.e., the lack of any consequence following a behavior) also weakens negative behavior. This makes the behavior occur less often by ignoring or not reinforcing it. For example, laissez-faire behavior shows no interest even in positive results and therefore can be applied as a form of extinction.[22]

These approaches to shaping your followers' behavior give you a wide array of possible actions you can use with contingent reward leadership. But one critical issue that you should always remember is that you need to reward and punish your followers *contingently* upon their performance. In other words, you need to reward them for successful attainment of an agreed-upon goal consistently. And you should punish them contingently only when appropriate and in a consistent manner. If you reward for no reason at all or if you reward based on personal favoritism, they will not be able to make the connection between the effort they put into their work and their performance. They will also fail to see the connection between their performance and the outcomes that you value.

It is even worse if you punish your followers for no reason at all. Were you ever the victim of noncontingent punishment? What did it feel like to be on the receiving end of this kind of punishment? How did it affect you and those around you? Did you ever dole out punishment for no reason at all? If so, what happened to you and your followers as a result? It probably caused much confusion in the minds of those punished. It may have produced a number of unintended results. It may have caused them to dislike or even hate you. They might have become anxious or aggressive toward you or others. As a result, there might have been total breakdowns in communication and the destruction of trust in your relationship. That's why it is important for you to use your reinforcers contingently and consider the timing of their application. We believe that you now have a potentially powerful tool in contingent rewards and punishments, but the potency of such a tool is totally dependent upon how you use it. Think carefully and use it wisely.

Timing of Rewards

Research indicates that the timing of reinforcement affects the follower's learning speed and performance. Ideally, rewards and punishments should be administered as close as possible to the behavior associated with them. That will allow your followers to make the connection between what they did and the results it generated.[23]

Several options exist for the distribution of rewards. Consider weekly or monthly paychecks. These are rewards given at fixed time intervals. The reinforcement is the receipt of the paycheck. In contrast, some rewards are given at variable time intervals, such as occasional praise given by your boss or her unexpected visits to your office. The reinforcement is the praise you receive for being present on the day your boss visits.

Other rewards are given based not on time periods, but rather on relationships between one event and another. These are called ratio rewards. Fixed ratio rewards are given based on a fixed amount of output, as seen in piece-rate pay. For example, the reinforcement is the earning of $10 for each 100 widgets a factory worker produces. Other rewards are given at variable amounts of output, as seen with commissioned salespeople. The reinforcement is the making of the sale and the associated percentage of sales price earned on account of the sale.

When and how do you motivate your followers with rewards? Do they see the connection between their effort, performance, and the rewards they receive? What can you do to help them make these connections?

Advantages and Disadvantages of Extrinsic Rewards

Indeed, extrinsic rewards are integral to contingent reward leadership. However, there are pros and cons of administering extrinsic rewards. They are important for you to consider because they may influence whether or not you should use contingent reward leadership or shift into your transformational leadership mode and use intrinsic rewards to motivate your followers.

Let's consider the advantages of extrinsic rewards first. Many people are motivated by money. Some are more motivated by money than others. Money helps us to buy the things we need to live the way we deem best. The amount of money we earn is an indicator of how much value society places on our work. However, not every job is extremely valuable, nor interesting nor challenging. Money can make up for the lack of intrinsic satisfaction that may be missing in some jobs. Adults who work do so for different reasons than college students. Adults often work to make ends meet, whereas students often study subjects from which they derive intrinsic satisfaction. In many industries, monetary rewards work well to motivate performance quantity, but not necessarily quality. In these cases, extrinsic rewards do not necessarily erode intrinsic motivation.[24]

On the other hand, extrinsic rewards may get in the way of intrinsic motivation by lowering the performance level requiring creativity and innovation. Extrinsic rewards tend to be instrumental. This means they motivate performance because such performance is expected to lead to a desired outcome, such as more money. If you wave dollar bills in front of people, it may lead them to think of themselves as doing work *only* for the reward. As a result, they may only exert minimal effort to just get things done fast. This may serve to buy off their intrinsic motivation because they feel they are being controlled by the reward.[25]

This conflicting evidence suggests that it is important to emphasize intrinsic rewards with transformational leadership, especially to promote high-quality work that is needed for today's knowledge-based business activities. It's also important for you not to rely on monetary incentives exclusively because doing so might cause your followers to focus too much on the extrinsic reward at the expense of the intrinsic nature of the task and your overall vision for the project. If a follower's job is boring, you should take the time to explain how the task fits into the overall vision for the project by displaying a little inspirational motivation. What can you do in your organization to balance your followers' need to be extrinsically rewarded with their need to derive satisfaction from their jobs?

Answering this question allows us to draw a conclusion regarding the role of contingent reward leadership: Contingent reward leadership matters and is key to achieving desired levels of performance. However, it is not sufficient to inspire your followers for achieving performance beyond expectations. That's because extrinsic rewards tend to shift your followers' attention from their work itself to potential rewards they will get for the work they do. It can diminish intrinsic aspects of their work motivation.[26]

Additionally, extrinsic rewards have temporary motivational effects on followers who easily can acquire a sense of entitlement toward the rewards. In other words, it may take more and more extrinsic rewards to satisfy their needs. Contingent reward leadership assumes that followers are driven by lower-order needs, such as food, money, and safety. However, many followers are also driven by higher-order needs, such as socializing, thinking highly of themselves, and being the best they can be in their personal and professional lives. Today, professionals work in complex organizations that cannot solely rely on extrinsic rewards like the ones used in the early to mid-1900s based on the tenets of scientific management.

Extrinsic rewards also have the potential to destroy followers' motivation to work as a team. Suppose that the annual salary increase allowed to a team is limited to $100,000. This is a limited and fixed amount. Each individual team member may compete to get a bigger pay increase and more of the total amount. They will perceive the situation as win-lose or zero-sum. Under the team-based structure, where each member's knowledge, skills, and abilities are complementary and synergistic and collaborative effect is critical, emphasizing financial incentives exclusively may impede cooperation among team members. That's why adding inspirational motivation to the foundation of contingent reward is needed to stem the competition and promote cooperation within the team.[27]

Putting Transactional Leadership Into Practice

To be fluent in FRLD, you should be able to apply both corrective and constructive forms of transactional leadership. To establish the corrective form of transactional leadership, apply MBE-A behavior to the situation. To establish the constructive form of transactional leadership, apply contingent reward behavior to the situation.

Applying Contingent Reward Leadership

Display the Behaviors Described in This Chapter

This chapter presented four behaviors associated with contingent reward leadership. These behaviors emphasized the importance of (1) setting goals for and with your followers, (2) suggesting pathways to meet performance expectations, (3) actively monitoring followers' progress and providing supportive feedback, and (4) providing rewards consistently when goals are attained. By displaying these behaviors with your followers, they will become more willing to exert the effort needed to attain goals, become focused on their work, understand what is expected of them, and be satisfied with your leadership.

That's what a vice president of customer service at Verizon has found. This executive told us that goal setting starts at the strategic level by looking at different areas of the market. At Verizon, they do this geographically as well as by looking within market segments while maintaining reliable service goals. They then align these goals with departmental goals. Each employee needs to understand the part he or she plays in reaching these goals. Verizon conducts a series of planning sessions for both individuals and teams so that their efforts are well aligned toward accomplishing organizational objectives.

When it comes to rewards, top management at Verizon spends a fair amount of time thinking about how to recognize and reward people. Each year they find more creative ways to do that. They are careful not to always reward people just for doing their job because this creates an unhealthy sense of entitlement. But sometimes this is necessary, especially with Verizon's employees right out of college. Verizon gives out free lunches or other small rewards to those who meet their performance goals. This helps to keep up good morale with employees. This example teaches us that goal setting coupled with contingent rewards is an effective way to provide leadership.[28]

Give Praise When It Is Deserved

Transactional leaders recognize their followers when they meet agreed-upon objectives. Sometimes, this means that you should be willing to give constructive criticism toward the work that your followers just completed. Consider the example of a student who submitted a poorly written and incomplete personal leadership development plan to Don. After receiving negative feedback from Don, the student said he was "very concerned that there was not one positive comment on the paper." The student justified his reaction based on Tom Rath and Donald Clifton's book *How Full Is Your Bucket?* This book espouses that leaders should keep things positive when interacting with followers. The student wanted his professor to "fill his bucket" with some positive comments written on his paper, despite the poor quality of the work.[29]

Don responded by citing research on FRLD that indicates that rewards should be given in exchange for meeting performance expectations. If rewards or compliments are given to all students, regardless of the quality of their performance, such rewards will lose differentiating power and students will not see the connection between their effort, performance, and outcome. And it would discount the effort and performance outcome associated with a student who truly earned an A on the assignment. That's why it is important for you to give proper recognition to your followers when they perform to levels that meet agreed-upon objectives. But be sure to be fair and equitable in giving earned praise only when it is deserved.

Provide the Resources Needed by Followers to Reach Their Goals

Transactional leaders physically empower their followers by giving them the time and resources at their discretion to get the job done. This sets followers up for success. Consider the example of Kirk Fleming, who is a training manager working in a team in a large, global pharmaceutical company. Kirk's operating company is responsible for drug safety and regulatory reporting of adverse events possibly related to his company's products. His team is tasked with introducing and training flexible standards that meet the needs of the over 200 independent operating companies, while also promoting the efficient processing of events on time and within quality standards. The team also monitors and assesses complex medical situations.

Much of what Kirk's team does is to promote organizational change. But most people do not like change and are stuck in their ways. That's the case with Sally, who Kirk has recently spent much time with establishing a plan to help her adapt to change. Sally says that she wants to try new things at work, but she does not take any action to make any change. She spends much of her time saying that she will "have to take a look at the possibilities and make a plan." She gets spurts of energy to investigate possibilities and asks Kirk for advice, but never gets beyond information gathering. Sally is frustrated that her efforts so far to help shape organizational culture have either been dismissed or generated hostile reactions from other colleagues.

Kirk addressed Sally's need for leadership by highlighting the talents and strengths that she possesses. Then he offered her specific support and advice for goal setting to take action. He discussed in specific terms what Sally needs to accomplish, suggested some ways she could meet her goals, and got her to agree with their objectives. Kirk complimented Sally along the way as she took small steps toward acting on her plan. This example illustrates that effective leaders balance the energy they spend on building both transactional and developmental relationships with others to create positive outcomes.[30]

Use Rewards to Support Six Sigma and Total Quality Management Initiatives

Quality is not a trend. It is a much valued characteristic of individual, team, and organizational effectiveness that will never go out of style. The U.S. National Institute of Standards and Technology established the Malcolm Baldrige National Quality Award to support quality initiatives in manufacturing. This award was the U.S. government's attempt to use contingent rewards to jump-start the quality movement. Over the years, award winners have come from a wide variety of types and sizes of organizations, ranging from Motorola to the Ritz Carlton Hotel Company to the Pearl River School District in Pearl River, New York.[31]

Today, many organizations are using Six Sigma programs and other quality initiatives to improve the quality of their products and services. These initiatives are a natural application for contingent reward leadership because they rely heavily on goal setting, planning, and measuring progress toward goals. These goals include customer satisfaction relative to competitors, customer retention, and market share gains. Building and maintaining organizational and technology systems to reach these goals requires clarification of effective pathways for desired outcomes and the exchange of rewards and recognition for their accomplishment.

Contingent reward leadership can provide a foundation for supporting these requirements by rewarding with bonuses followers who have the lowest error rates in production, or best supporting continuous, employee-driven, customer-focused improvement. Be sure to make continuous improvement an everyday matter, not a daylong event. Listen to and learn from customers and employees. Use teams to foster cooperation, trust, and mutual respect. And reward associates for doing it right the first time to eliminate costly rework. What opportunities for improving quality through constructive transactions lie dormant in your organization?

Applying MBE-A Leadership

Display the Behaviors Described in This Chapter

This chapter presented three behaviors associated with MBE-A leadership. These behaviors emphasized the importance of (1) closely monitoring work for performance errors; (2) focusing attention on mistakes, complaints, failures, deviations, and infractions; and (3) arranging to know if and when things go wrong. By displaying these behaviors with your followers, they will become more focused on what you are paying attention to, control any maverick impulses, develop a more cautious attitude, and take corrective actions to bring their work in line with organizational norms and policies.

Results from our research support what the Verizon executive told us about his experience with MBE-A leadership. At Verizon, employees and managers alike know that people are accountable for their own actions. We've found that a lot of managers in technology-driven companies use MBE-A as a way not to meddle with their highly educated subordinates' work processes.[32] They use MBE-A to step in only when necessary. Managers and individuals need to make sure the tasks are clear. If this turns out to be a problem, corrective action is taken. Warnings for failing to comply with policies and procedures are given as often as necessary. Many discussions take place in the human resource department concerning how this needs to be done and rules that need to be enforced. This is one way Verizon keeps things in control.

Set Standards

Transactional leaders use benchmarks to set standards for followers' performance. These predetermined standards allow leaders to assess the level of effectiveness and efficiency in their organization. When standards are not met, leaders can coach followers to adjust their behavior or increase their efforts to meet the standard. Over time, leaders typically raise these standards to reflect best practices and encourage continuous improvement.

Consider how Leah sets standards for her faculty's performance in teaching and research. In evaluating teaching effectiveness, Leah collects teaching evaluation scores, rated on a 7-point scale, for both course quality and instructor quality. She collects these data for each course her faculty members teach. She then computes a departmental average for both metrics and uses them as standards to compare against scores for each faculty member. In evaluating research effectiveness, Leah counts the total number of faculty publications and computes a departmental average. She uses this average as a standard to compare against each faculty member's output. She also assesses the quality of the faculty's journal publication based on its impact factor and reputation. Her faculty has commented that they are now aware of what constitutes unsatisfactory versus satisfactory performance in the department. Leah's example illustrates how MBE-A's focus on standards can promote efficiency and effectiveness in your employee's work processes.

Preach Accountability and Responsibility

Transactional leaders guide their followers along the path to achieve expected results by clearly communicating mutually accepted expectations. Leaders do the guiding while followers do the work. This implies that you must ensure that your followers understand how their actions impact the organization and that they are being held accountable for making progress toward achieving their goals. A sense of accountability often motivates followers to be conscientious and dedicate focused attention to their jobs. These motivational effects often lead to desired levels of performance. For these reasons, take the time necessary to communicate your expectations to your followers regarding the awesome responsibility that comes with the prized position power of their job.

Assess Risk and Be Alert

Transactional leaders identify ahead of time any threats that can seriously affect individual, team, and organizational performance. They actively monitor events inside and outside of their organization and work to assess and minimize risk.

Once identified, these leaders use MBE-A to pick up quickly on these risks and take steps to mitigate their effects. As a result, followers pay attention to activities, processes, and performance metrics that leaders monitor.

After returning from his auditing seminar, Andy became worried about the volatile economic and business environment. He reasoned that the constant changes in the market can introduce uncertainty and risk in his company. Being risk averse, Andy needed some strategies to help him keep things in control. He needed ways to keep up on the trends and changing events so he could reduce the amount of his perceived risk.

The auditing seminar provided Andy with some ideas on how to deal with such risk by being alert to things that might create any risk-related concerns. First, competition and regulation often introduce unforeseen changes in customer demands and business processes. To successfully field these changes, Andy set up a task force that uses environmental scanning techniques to identify and monitor important trends and create strategies for dealing with them.[33] Second, rapid growth can strain an organization's workforce and internal controls. New staff members, who are unfamiliar with corporate values and expectations, also present a potential liability to the organization. Andy tasked his internal audit group with periodically assessing workload demands and the effectiveness of internal controls. Third, new technologies and revamped IT systems are often saturated with problems that can destroy operational efficiency and productivity. To stem these potential disasters, Andy met with his director of IT services to develop several automated controls, systematic testing plans, and disaster recovery plans. Andy's efforts to use MBE-A leadership to assess risk have helped him to maintain more control in his organization and get a better night's sleep as well.[34]

These practices suggest that building corrective transactions with followers seeks to keep them in control and prevents any possible disaster from happening in advance. However, we firmly believe that absolute control is unattainable. Trying to attain it relentlessly with MBE-A leadership can break down your followers, who might develop a feeling of helplessness. Such helplessness comes from a situation where people are under constant tight control and think that there is nothing they can do about the way they work. Therefore, be sure to temper your corrective transactional leadership with a healthy blend of constructive transactional leadership and the 4Is of transformational leadership. If you fail to do so, your followers may perceive your leadership to be "hyperactive leadership on steroids." They will stress or burn out and leave you for greener pastures where they perceive leadership to take on a more passive role. In the next chapter, we turn our attention to more passive forms of leadership that are sometimes needed.

Summary Questions and Reflective Exercises

1. This exercise uses results of your Multifactor Leadership Questionnaire (MLQ) report to assess your level of contingent reward behavior. Compare your contingent reward ratings with the research-validated benchmarks. How did your self-ratings, ratings from subordinates, ratings from peers, ratings from superiors, and ratings from others compare against the benchmarks? On which specific MLQ items (i.e., questions) did you score highest? Lowest? What can you do to improve on the items where you scored lowest?

2. This exercise also uses results of your MLQ report to assess your level of contingent reward behavior. Compare your self-ratings on *contingent reward behavior* with ratings provided by subordinates, peers, superiors, and others. Compute the difference score (d) as the difference between your self-rating score and the specific other rating source score of interest. If d is less than .5 and the other rating source score is less than 2.84, then you are considered to be *in agreement/poor*. If d is less than .5 and the other rating source score is greater than 2.84, then you are considered to be *in agreement/good*. If d is equal to or greater than .5 and the self-rating score is greater than the other rating score, then you are an *overestimator* on this dimension. If d is equal to or greater than .5 and the self-rating score is less than the other rating score, then you are an *underestimator* on this dimension. Consider the category under which you fall in terms of contingent reward behavior. What are the implications of this categorization for you? Are there any things you can do to improve in this area?

3. This exercise uses results of your Multifactor Leadership Questionnaire (MLQ) report to assess your level of active management-by-exception behavior. Compare your active management-by-exception ratings with the research-validated benchmarks. How did your self-ratings, ratings from subordinates, ratings from peers, ratings from superiors, and ratings from others compare against the benchmarks? On which specific MLQ items (i.e., questions) did you score highest? Lowest? What can you do to improve on the items where you scored too low or too high?

4. Announce to your staff that you are now using the management-by-walking-around technique. Explain to them that you will visit them during the day to assist them in identifying and managing their problem areas. Present yourself as a problem solver. When you make your rounds, pay attention to mistakes, errors, and deviations from standard operating procedures. Work with your staff members to correct these problem areas. Note how your staff responds to your active management-by-exception

leadership behavior. What areas and staff members respond favorably? What areas and staff members respond unfavorably?

5. Make a list of staff members whose performance or attitude requires monitoring. Pay special attention to these individuals and work to ensure that they improve their problematic performance or attitude toward work and the company. Note which employees respond favorably and unfavorably to your active management-by-exception leadership behavior. Determine which situations in your work unit are appropriate for displaying active management-by-exception leadership behavior.

6. With the assistance of your accounting or IT group, design an exception report that monitors variations in dollars, units, etc., from standards, goals, or operating norms. Compute the difference between what is expected (the standard or budget) and what is actually achieved (the actual). This difference is called a *variance*. Require the person accountable for the variances on this exception report to explain in writing the reasons for all variances that exceed 5% of the standard or budget. Note the areas in your work group where these exception reports are effective and ineffective.

7. Write or revise five goal statements for your work unit or personal leadership development plan. For each goal statement, be sure that the goal is SMARTER—specific, measurable, attainable (but difficult), results oriented, time-bounded, evaluated, and rewarded.

8. For each of the goal statements developed in exercise 7, identify an appropriate measure or metric to assess whether the goal is attained. Present your goals and their measures to your learning partner or a colleague for their consideration. Based on their feedback, determine the validity and reliability of the measures you have identified. A valid measure assesses what it is supposed to assess, while a reliable measure provides a consistently true score across situations and time. How is this process helpful in providing feedback to you and your colleagues?

9. Work with your superior or human resource department to identify the types of rewards you can use to motivate your staff to achieve your goals. Make a list of these rewards. Which of these goals are intrinsic motivators? Which of these goals are extrinsic motivators? Match the rewards shown on this list with the names of individuals in your work group who would respond well to the reward. What motives, needs, or personal characteristics should you consider when matching each type of reward to these individuals?

10. Create a Six Sigma or Total Quality Improvement program in your work unit or organization. Ask project teams to document the amount of dollars saved from their efforts in monthly, quarterly, and annual reports. Request a committee of senior managers to review these reports and provide rewards to the team that makes the greatest contribution based on cost savings or revenue enhancement through their efforts. Hold an annual awards banquet as another form of reward for those teams making the greatest contribution and to build a culture of quality with transactional leadership.

Notes

1. Retrieved October 8, 2008, from http://www.coopamerica.org/about/.
2. http://www.coopamerica.org/programs/responsibleshopper/company.cfm?id=303. Retrieved October 8, 2008.
3. Bogle, J. C. (2005). *The battle for the soul of capitalism.* New Haven, CT: Yale University Press.
4. Adapted from interview with Robert Snowden conducted by Gary Generose, July 1, 2002.
5. Ante, S. E., & Sager, I. (2002, February 11). IBM's new boss: Sam Palmisano has a tough act to follow; Here's what to expect. *Business Week, 3769,* 66–68; and Hemp, P., & Stewart, T. A. (2004). Samuel J. Palmisano: Leading change when business is good. *Harvard Business Review, 82,* 6073.
6. Deci, E. L., & Ryan, R. M. (1985). *Intrinsic motivation and self-determination in human behavior.* New York: Plenum.
7. Locke, E. A., & Latham, G. P. (2002). Building a practically useful theory of goal setting and task motivation: A 35-year odyssey. *American Psychologist, 57,* 701–717.
8. Retrieved October 22, 2008, from http://www.pathwaystoeducation.ca/about.html and http://www.pathwaystoeducation.ca/results.html. *Net present value* (NPV) represents the difference between the present value of cash flows and outflows for the program. For more details, see Atkinson, A. A., Kaplan, R. S., Matsumura, E. M., & Young, M. S. (2007). *Management accounting* (5th ed.). Upper Saddle River, NJ: Pearson/Prentice Hall.
9. Sharifi, J. M. (2008). *Analysis of Leadership Potential Assessment Center.* Malvern, PA: Pennsylvania State University, School of Graduate and Professional Studies at Great Valley.
10. Retrieved October 22, 2008, from http://www.woodencourse.com/woodens_wisdom.html.
11. Tuckman, B. W., Abry, D. A., & Smith, D. R. (2008). *Learning and motivation strategies: Your guide to success.* Upper Saddle River, NJ: Pearson/Prentice Hall.
12. Drucker, P. (1974). *Management: Tasks, responsibilities, practices.* New York: Harper & Row; and Montgomery, D. (1989). *The fall of the house of labor: The workplace, the state, and American labor activism, 1865–1925.* Cambridge, UK: Cambridge University Press.

13. Simons, R. (2008). *Control in the age of empowerment: How can managers promote innovation while avoiding unwelcome surprises?* Boston: Harvard Business School Press.

14. Peters, T. J., & Waterman, R. H. (1988). *In search of excellence: Lessons from America's best-run companies.* New York: Harper & Row.

15. Thompson, R., & Letcher, G. E. (2007). *Ethics and the attest function: A practical update for CPAs in public practice 2007.* Philadelphia: PICPA Foundation for Education and Research.

16. Thompson and Letcher (2007). As cited in Note 15.

17. Bradberry, T. (2008). *Squawk! How to stop making noise and start getting results.* New York: HarperCollins.

18. Maslow, A. H. (1970). *Motivation and personality* (2nd ed.) Upper Saddle River, NJ: Prentice Hall; and Vroom, V. H. (1964). *Work and motivation.* New York: John Wiley & Sons.

19. Eden, D. (1990). *Pygmalion effect in management: Productivity as a self-fulfilling prophecy.* Lexington, MA: Lexington Books; and Shea, C. M., & Howell, J. M. (2000). Efficacy-performance spirals: An empirical test. *Journal of Management, 26,* 791–812.

20. O'Neil, J., & Conzemius, A. (2005). *The power of SMART goals: Using goals to improve student learning.* New York: Solution Tree.

21. Thorndike, E. F. (1913). *Educational psychology: The psychology of learning.* New York: Teachers College Press.

22. Smith, D. L. (2002). On prediction and control. B.F. Skinner and the technological ideal of science. In W. E. Pickren & D. A. Dewsbury (Eds.), *Evolving perspectives on the history of psychology.* Washington, DC: American Psychological Association.

23. Domjan, M. (2003). *The principles of learning and behavior* (5th ed.) Belmont, CA: Thomson.

24. Gupta, N., & Shaw, J. D. (1998). Let the evidence speak: Financial incentives are effective!! *Compensation & Benefits Review, 30,* 26–32.

25. Kohn, A. (1988). Inner and outer rewards. *Across the Board, 22,* 11–13.

26. Deci and Ryan (1985). As cited in Note 6.

27. Tuckman et al. (2008). As cited in Note 11.

28. Interview with key executive at Verizon, conducted April 29, 2003, by Michelle Dearwater.

29. Rath, T., & Clifton, D. O. (2004). *How full is your bucket? Positive strategies for work and life.* Omaha, NE: Gallup Press.

30. Fleming, K. D. (2008). *Analysis of Leadership Potential Center (LPAC).* Malvern, PA: Pennsylvania State University, School of Graduate and Professional Studies at Great Valley.

31. Retrieved October 27, 2008, from http://www.nist.gov/public_affairs/factsheet/mbnqa.htm.

32. Sosik, J. J., Jung, D. I., Berson, Y., Dionne, S. D., & Jaussi, K. S. (2004). *The dream weavers: Strategy-focused leadership in technology-driven organizations.* Greenwich, CT: Information Age Publishing.

33. Sosik et al. (2004). As cited in Note 32.

34. Thompson and Letcher (2007). As cited in Note 15.

Chapter 8

Management-by-Exception Passive and Laissez-Faire
Inactive Forms of Leadership

> Laissez-faire, supply-and-demand, —one begins to be weary of all
> that. Leave all to egoism, to ravenous greed of money, of pleasure, of
> applause: it is the Gospel of Despair!
>
> **—Thomas Carlyle**

Lisa was bristling with excitement as she drove north along Interstate 81 through
the beautiful Endless Mountains region of Pennsylvania. She was returning home
to Binghamton, New York, after visiting PhillyCarShare™, a nonprofit organization that provides its members with access to a fleet of cars on an hourly basis.
This organization has won numerous awards for its environmentally friendly
and sustainable approach to reducing dependence on automobiles through the
sharing of community resources. This ecologically sound and financially smart
business model caught Lisa's attention when she discussed with her community group ways to make businesses in the triple cities of Binghamton, Johnson
City, and Endicott more ecologically aware. Students and others in the academic
community at Binghamton University were doing their part. By now it was time
for yearlong residents to make their contributions.

Lisa was quite impressed with the environmental movement that Philly CarShare had spawned. According to its Web site, "Over 30,000 Philadelphians (to date) have traded in car ownership for PhillyCarShare, walking, biking, and public transit. Members, after joining, report driving 53% fewer miles, consuming nearly one million fewer gallons of gas, owning 8,000 fewer vehicles, and saving $33 million annually—money that gets reinvested largely into Philadelphia's local economy."[1] Philadelphians have embraced PhillyCarShare as part of their city's culture and its transportation system. Based on Philadelphia's success, Lisa wondered, why couldn't she work with community leaders to establish a similar project in her community? This idea inspired her as she took the Conklin/ Kirkwood exit off I-81 and headed straight for the home of Pat, a key community leader in her group.

Once at Pat's home, Lisa made a compelling case that the status quo of green initiatives in Broome County needed a jump-start. Lisa argued that with the information gained from her trip, they now had a viable business model to introduce a great idea to their own community. They might even join the growing list of organizations that have received the Green Initiative Award from the Broome County Legislature for their efforts at social entrepreneurship.[2] To Lisa, doing good things for people and the planet, while doing good business, is something that made a lot of sense.

After sharing some beverages, Nirchi's pizza, and spiedies[3] with Lisa, Pat sat quietly and grinned after thinking about what Lisa told him. Pat then advised Lisa to wait until there was more of a call from local officials to address the issue of car pollution. Pat argued that Binghamton does not have the infrastructure or environmental problems that big cities do, and therefore it would be a bit premature to establish an organization like PhillyCarShare in Broome County. He also claimed that no prominent political figures are calling for such an idea at the present time. In Pat's opinion, it was a pretty good idea, but the time wasn't right to put it into action in their region. It wouldn't hurt to be just a bit more safe and careful. As Pat reached for another slice of pizza, he told Lisa that things are fine just the way they are. After their visit was through, Lisa left feeling somewhat discouraged as she headed home through the snow and heavy rush-hour traffic along the Vestal Parkway.

Have you ever felt like Lisa after someone rejected an idea you were excited about? Have you ever tried to introduce positive change only to be dismissed by somebody higher up who prefers the status quo? Ever been frustrated by someone who likes to take a passive approach to leadership? How did you feel? How did it affect your energy level and subsequent performance? On the other hand, were there times when you acted like Pat and saw your followers react like Lisa? Take a few minutes to reflect upon the causes and consequences of such passive forms of leadership based on your life experiences.

Chances are your experiences with passive leadership were not positive. Leadership is about action rather than inaction. It's about change, not maintaining the status quo. It's about taking risks, not about being risk averse all the time. Nevertheless, we've found that there are times when taking a passive approach to leadership is more appropriate. In fact, in our previous research, many leaders in top executive positions told us that there are times when they prefer *not* to take action and simply let things settle naturally.[4] Their leadership experiences suggest that you should understand when and how to display passive forms of leadership selectively, but also to be aware of the advantages and disadvantages of doing so.

This chapter presents the pros and cons of passive leadership. It shows you how to let things settle naturally and take a passive approach to leading by avoiding unnecessary change. It also shows you how to passively monitor and control your followers' performance and enforce corrective action when necessary. By reacting to mistakes and refraining from intervening in your followers' work initiatives, you can keep things quiet and in order. Let's start learning about this passive approach to leadership by considering some of the most inactive leaders in history.

The Legacy of Lazy Leaders

Inactive forms of leadership, while sometimes appropriate, often result in predictable and negative consequences. Consider the following examples:

- King Louis XVI of France lost his head for spending most of his time tinkering with clocks and ignoring France's social and economic problems. During the 1792 French Revolution, he was arrested, found guilty of treason, and executed by a guillotine.
- America's 30th president, Calvin Coolidge, was reported to have slept 11 hours a day while in office. "Silent Cal's" passive presidency prompted a movement away from laissez-faire government styles of the 19th century.[5]
- In the early 1990s, John Sculley, then CEO of Apple Computer, was criticized for spending too much time helping Bill Clinton get elected U.S. president and not enough time on Apple's strategic initiatives. By 1993, Apple's stock was plummeting due to a number of poor strategic moves. Later that year, Sculley resigned and turned his attention to politics full-time.[6]
- In 2005, Federal Emergency Management Agency (FEMA) chief Michael Brown showed a lack of concern for the tragic events following Hurricane Katrina's massive devastation of the New Orleans, Louisiana, region. Employees and the general public looked to Brown for leadership after the disaster hit. Instead, he showed indifference and provided little if any support. After receiving information from his staff that the situation was past

critical, Brown responded by saying "thanks for the update" and offered to only tweak the already ineffective federal response. Email records indicate that Brown made several flippant remarks concerning his responsibilities at FEMA. Ironically, his notes ranged from "Can I quit now? Can I come home?" to "I'm trapped now, please rescue me." By September 2005, Brown was forced to resign due to the huge public outcry over his passive style of leadership.[7] His inaction might have cascaded down from his boss, then-president George W. Bush, who was dubbed by political satirists as "Do Nothing Bush" for his initial lack of leadership and avoidance of action during the Katrina tragedy.[8]

- Terry Rook created a Web blog where lazy leaders all around the world can unite. It teaches leaders shortcuts that can make their lives easier. It prescribes tactics such as dumping work on followers, avoiding putting things in writing, valuing fun over work, and holding a carefree attitude about things. Predictably, the volume of blogging on the Web site at the time of this writing was modest.[9]

These examples teach us that leadership requires conscious efforts and proactive actions. A lack of effort on the part of the leader typically results in a lack of effort from followers, which leads to lousy results. As the old saying from the information technology field goes, "garbage in, garbage out." When leaders take a passive approach to their roles and responsibilities, they often leave situations behind that are worse than when they first arrived on the scene. Even if leaders produce some positive outcomes during their tenure, people tend to remember the negative things they did. They let memories of bad events overtake the good. Unfortunately, it's human nature to do so. When leaders fail to take the initiative to actively manage situations and proactively introduce positive change, followers have no incentive to forgive and forget. When leaders are too passive, things can quickly get out of control. Therefore, you need to carefully consider if and when you should display passive leadership. The benefits of doing so are small, but the detriments and risks from things getting out of control can be devastating to your reputation and to the future of your organization.

Management-by-Exception Passive—Definition and Behavioral Examples

After thinking about the above-mentioned examples of passive leadership, you probably would never want things to get as out of control as in these situations. Fortunately, you can rely on organizational processes and systems to help you keep things in control. With *management-by-exception passive* (MBE-P), you choose to sit back and wait for things to go wrong before taking action. The MBE-P leadership style allows you to intervene only if standards are not met because of the controls you have in place. It permits you to hold the attitude "if it ain't broke, don't fix it." It works when you let your followers know that if you happen to catch them doing something wrong or not complying with rules and regulations, you will hold them accountable for their actions and force them to comply with your directives. This helps them to see you as policing their behavior and performance. As a result, your followers will pay attention to what you deem important. It will make them comply with policies and procedures. However, they will not identify with you as their leader all that much. They will not trust you as much as if you took a more active approach to your leadership. And they will show little commitment to you or your organization and exert little effort beyond what it takes to not be caught by you. In other words, all you will get from your followers with such a passive form of leadership is their passive compliance.[10]

To better understand MBE-P leadership, consider how the infamous Idi Amin Dada exercised brutal leadership to keep his followers in line in the police state he established in Uganda (see Table 8.1). Amin's tyrannical leadership became a model for many of today's worst dictators, such as Robert Mugabe of Zimbabwe, Kim Jong-il of North Korea, and Than Shwe of Myanmar.

Most leaders who display MBE-P are not nearly as brutal as Amin. But like Amin, their leadership behavior can promote fear and complacency among followers. You can display MBE-P leadership by practicing behaviors that wait for deviations from policies and then react aggressively to mistakes that your followers make. Let's now examine four leadership behaviors that allow you to set standards, wait until things go wrong, and then spring into action to get things back in control.

Intervene Only If Standards Are Not Met

A dean at a small college was notorious for his MBE-P leadership style. He would hold two faculty meetings per year—one at convocation (in September at the beginning of the academic year) and one at graduation (in May at the end of the academic year). This is unusual since most college faculties meet once a month during the nine-month period. At the end of the first meeting, the dean would quip, "See you at graduation." For the most part, he would remain in his office during this time. He would emerge only if there was a serious problem that needed to be addressed. This caused his faculty and staff to become anxious every time they saw him. They became conditioned to fear him because they linked his appearance with some punitive action that awaited them. Whenever he came around, they smelled trouble.

Table 8.1   Leader Profile: Idi Amin Dada

Idi Amin Dada is one of the most peculiar and brutal leaders in history. Amin received little or no schooling, but excelled in sports such as boxing. He was a large man with a formidable frame that was both powerful and intimidating, much like his ruthless charismatic leadership style. Amin worked his way up the military ranks of Uganda while and after Uganda was under British rule. After a coup in 1971, he became a despot military dictator of Uganda. Some say that Amin proclaimed his title to be: "His Excellency President for Life, Field Marshal Al Hadji Doctor Idi Amin, VC, DSO, MC, Lord of All the Beasts of the Earth and Fishes of the Sea, and Conqueror of the British Empire in Africa in General and Uganda in Particular."

He was an eccentric megalomaniac who had extravagant tastes. His leadership behavior was extremely threatening. He established brutal military rule. He sought to eliminate his opponents. He disregarded basic human rights of his citizens and those of other African nations. He killed people without trials. Modeling himself after Hitler, he relished in ethnic cleansings and persecutions, and expelled Asians from Uganda. He sought out to eliminate any voice of opposition, actively searched for variation in thought and ethnicity, and became closely aligned with nations and groups that sponsored terrorism. In the British and American press, Amin was known as the "Butcher of Uganda" due to claims from some human rights organizations that he slaughtered up to 500,000 Ugandans.

Amin eventually lost his power base in 1979. Following the Tanzanian-Ugandan war, Amin fled to Libya and then settled in Saudi Arabia, where he died in 2003. While some view Amin in a comic light due to his unpredictable and clownish behavior and idiosyncrasies, his murderous legacy must not be forgotten. To learn more about Idi Amin through film, please view *The Rise and Fall of Idi Amin* (1980, Twin Continental Films) and *The Last King of Scotland* (2006, Fox Searchlight Films).

Source: Foden, G. (1998). *The last king of Scotland.* New York: Knopf; and Orizio, R. (2003). *Talk of the devil: Encounters with seven dictators.* New York: Walker.

The dean relied on systems of controls to monitor student enrollments and faculty performance in the areas of teaching, research, and service. These systems were based on notions of control employed by the finance and accounting industries. Controls represent policies, procedures, and activities designed to make sure an objective is achieved. They are created so that functions and processes run smoothly according to a plan. Some are created to prevent fraud or errors from occurring. Others are set up to detect fraud or errors that have already taken place.[11] The dean displayed a leadership style that focused on negativities, substandard performance, and irregularities. By displaying this MBE-P leadership behavior, he felt confident that he could run a tight ship.

By relying on a system of financial and operational controls, the faculty viewed the dean as passively maintaining the status quo, focusing only on what was wrong, and failing to recognize what was going right in the school. He was correct in considering systems of controls to be useful in monitoring critical processes and outcomes. However, the dean failed to recognize that people are *the most important part* of any organizational system. People require active attention, direction, and coaching. To be successful, you must learn a lesson from the dean's blunder. Rely on control systems to manage processes, but use them sparingly with people. Instead, work on building the true "internal controls" within your followers that we discussed in the chapters on transformational leadership—trust, value congruence, and commitment.

Wait for Things to Go Wrong Before Taking Action

Stephanie worked as an internal auditor at Crowley Foods, a U.S. East Coast producer and distributor of dairy products. She was comfortable with her company's system of controls that indicated the time to take action to prevent financial fraud and errors. Her comfort level was high because her director of internal audit made effective monitoring systems a priority. Senior leadership emphasized the importance of control in Crowley's production and distribution systems. Their human resources staff worked hard to place the right people in the right jobs. HR was quick to communicate any deviations from standards to their associates. They let associates know when things went wrong and insisted on prompt remedies to fix any problems. Any time a change or variation was introduced into their systems, they managed the change effectively by introducing a new standard or by fixing the problem that led to the deviation. In other words, they focused their attention on areas of change. This gave Stephanie the opportunity to wait until the time was right to introduce more proactive change with transformational leadership.

Waiting for problems to arise before addressing them can only work in organizations that have effective monitoring systems and predefined plans for addressing contingencies (see Figure 8.1). Effective monitoring systems integrate controls with their operations. They provide objective process and performance measures. They include associates who understand how their systems work. They use feedback from their systems to improve processes. And they communicate control issues efficiently and effectively. If you decide to use this form of MBE-P leadership, be sure that the size of your organization is not large and the complexity of your operational processes is not high. Relying on controls as a foundation

Figure 8.1 Big brother is watching. Leaders who display MBE-P behavior can rely on computer systems to monitor people and processes for compliance with standards when things get out of control.

for your MBE-P leadership in these cases can place you and your organization at a level of risk that is unacceptable to your organizational stakeholders.[12]

Believe That "If It Ain't Broke, Don't Fix It"

Howard and Al anxiously awaited the big local high school football game between the Binghamton Patriots and their long-time rivals, the Union-Endicott Tigers. In their mind, it was going to be a classic. Snow was in the forecast as the temperature plunged through the 30s. Al quipped, "This is what *Friday Night Lights* is all about." They got to the game early to buy hot chocolate and good seats to see Al's nephew quarterback for the Patriots. Their expectations were met as the first half of the game was a knockdown drag-out brawl, with the Patriots leading by only a field goal. But in the second half, Al and Howard noticed that the Patriots were on to something. Coach Mike Ramil realized that if his offense kept running the ball to the left side, they could make at least six yards per carry. So the Patriots kept running sweeps or traps to the left. "If it works, keep doing it!" yelled Al. With a wink of the eye, Howard smiled and replied, "If it ain't broke, don't fix it. Sounds like good old MBE-P leadership from our training sessions at the Center for Leadership Studies. Ha!"

As the coach realized, there are times for leaders to take a passive stance and let things settle naturally by maintaining the status quo. This type of MBE-P behavior rests on the assumptions that there is no evidence of a problem with the current system, and trying something new would not result in a better outcome. In these cases, it is better to not waste followers' time and energy trying something new that would result in some fruitless outcomes. Leaders with this attitude believe that change is necessary only when a better and surer alternative becomes available or when the processes they use no longer work. We believe that this attitude is appropriate only when proper monitoring and control systems are in place, and they allow leaders to sense potential trouble early. You can rest assured in these assumptions only when (1) your control systems operate effectively; (2) you can identify changes in people, processes, and situations that put you at risk; (3) your control and leadership systems can manage change as needed and produce intended results swiftly; and (4) independent appraisals of your control systems confirm their effectiveness.

React to Mistakes Reluctantly

In our Full Range Leadership Development (FRLD) courses and training programs, we show students a cartoon depicting a staff assistant peeking her head into the boss's office as he sits quietly upright in his chair. His desk is perfectly clean except for a penholder, a picture of his family, and an unintelligible piece of equipment sitting on the desk. The cartoon's caption reads: "Is everything all right? I heard the motion detector go off."

It's a strange and funny image. But oftentimes, truth is stranger than fiction. Do you know anyone like the boss depicted in this cartoon? Chances are you have worked for or with someone with this hands-off approach to leadership. We certainly have. Consider the example of Betty, who was director of academic affairs for a small college. Betty rose through the ranks to her current position because of her friendly disposition and "go along to get along" attitude. In mentoring sessions with junior faculty, she advised her protégés to "learn to play the game" and "know what it takes to keep *everyone* happy." Unfortunately, Betty's closest friend was Trent, a tenured faculty member who had a reputation for bullying the untenured junior faculty. Trent would use a combination of threats, uninvited office visits, innuendo, and slander to intimidate junior faculty not to publish more than he did and not to create new courses. Michael was one victim of Trent's misbehavior.

Then one day, Michael had enough of Trent's antics, hired an attorney, and told Betty to tell Trent to knock it off and threatened legal action. Betty responded by saying that she didn't want to come across as being heavy-handed. She intended to sit back and not get involved in the situation. It was not until

Michael told her that legal action would implicate Betty and bring her down as well that she agreed to intervene. She reluctantly told Trent to knock it off and ordered human resources to resolve the conflict with a face-to-face meeting between the two opponents. If it were not for Michael's threat to bring Betty into the fray, she would not have been involved.

Betty learned the hard way about the perils of being reluctant to take timely actions or respond to inappropriate behavior displayed by followers. As Jesse Jackson once said, "Leadership cannot go along to get along. It must meet the moral challenge of the day." As a leader just beginning to understand the key tenets of FRLD, Betty realized that sometimes the challenges she must meet will have moral implications. Other times, they will represent run-of-the-mill challenges of keeping her systems operating efficiently and effectively. More often than not, Betty's challenges are also about keeping her followers motivated and performing to standards.

To meet either type of challenge, Betty has now established and uses a control system to set key objectives for being successful. Then she works with her followers to identify any risks that might get in the way of achieving these objectives. They prioritize risks that will have the most adverse effects on their school. For each risk, they have designed appropriate responses to reduce their likelihood of occurring and mitigating their negative effects if undetected. They now take a more active approach to monitoring their processes and procedures, especially when it comes to creating a more collegial culture. They communicate the importance of creating a collegial culture and the procedures they created to take corrective action to bring things back in line. Betty now pays much more attention to what matters most—her followers and their development.

Laissez-Faire—Definition and Behavioral Examples

Leaders who display MBE-P behavior enforce corrective action when mistakes are made. However, they can become complacent with their monitoring systems and grow to accept a wide range of errors and deviations. This complacency prompts them to police any actions that rock the boat, and therefore followers maintain the status quo. If MBE-P behavior leads to complacency, then laissez-faire behavior is a catalyst for outright indifference. When leaders display laissez-faire behavior, they really don't care whether or not followers maintain standards or reach performance goals. That's because they are rarely involved in their followers' work. They avoid taking a stand on issues and evade solving pressing problems at all costs. They are often absent from important meetings and sometimes find excuses to circumvent their daily work responsibilities. Therefore, laissez-faire leadership behavior is not really leadership at all.

It is nonleadership since it involves absolutely no exchange between the leader and the follower.

Research has shown that laissez-faire behavior is associated with the lowest levels of follower, team, and organizational performance. Followers become confused over their roles. Their confusion often leads to conflicts with their coworkers and the leader. Eventually, followers become totally detached from their leader as much as (or even more than) their leader is detached from them. Some may view their leader more as an idiot than a source of influence. In desperation, followers may make up for their leader's laziness by substituting for his leadership with their own knowledge, skills, abilities, and professional experiences. They may also look to others to provide them with guidance and support. In the end, they become frustrated, and this leads to low levels of satisfaction with the leader, their job, and organization. Some even leave the organization for better job opportunities elsewhere.[13]

Consider Imelda Marcos, who seemed to care more about collecting shoes and real estate properties than caring for the social and economic problems of the Philippines. Her laissez-faire approach to leadership is described in Table 8.2. Marcos' passive approach to leadership can also be seen with Omar al-Bashir of Sudan, Muammar al-Gaddafi of Libya, and Rod Blagojevich, former governor of the U.S. state of Illinois.

Be careful not to hold an attitude toward leadership like Imelda Marcos did. It's easy to become complacent and direct your attention to the wrong things. Let's now examine four key aspects of laissez-faire leadership that you should typically avoid.

Avoid Getting Involved, Making Decisions, or Solving Problems

Oliver was manager of the internal audit group of a financial service center within a large manufacturing company. His beautiful mahogany desk and cabinets were always tidy. They were stacked with neatly piled working papers to give the impression that he was very busy with work. However, Oliver would delegate all tasks and meeting responsibilities to the department's supervisor. This allowed Oliver to sit with his back to the door reading the *Wall Street Journal* and keeping track of his personal handgun inventory.

Oliver's staff came to know this because the department shared a computer printer. They sent their documents to this printer so they could get hard copies of their work. However, this particular kind of Hewlett-Packard printer required pressing the form-feed button. If someone forgot to do this, the last page of the printout would remain in the printer. When Oliver sent his spreadsheet list of handguns to the printer, he forgot about this requirement and the last page of his

Table 8.2   Leader Profile: Imelda Marcos

Ferdinand Marcos and his wife, Imelda, ruled the Philippine islands from 1966 until 1986, when they were ousted following the People Power Revolution led by Corazon Aquino. One of the first things Aquino did as president of the Philippines was to investigate and restrict the amazingly large amount of wealth that the Marcos family had amassed during their administration.

Imelda played a central role in governing the Philippines during her husband's dictatorship. Even in her early days, Imelda always possessed a sense of entitlement. After graduating from college, Imelda gained prominence as a beauty queen in several pageants in the Philippines. She desired the finer things in life and loved to accumulate prized possessions of the rich and powerful. Her husband's position as supreme leader of the Philippines helped satisfy her needs.

Imelda and Ferdinand led an extravagant lifestyle and accumulated their vast fortune at the expense of their citizens. Imelda was known for her $5 million shopping trips in New York and Rome, her purchases of multi-million-dollar sky rises in Manhattan, 508 gowns, 888 handbags, and 1,060 pairs of shoes. As a ruler of an impoverished nation, her lifestyle seemed most selfish and inappropriate. She justified her profligacy by saying that the poor in the Philippines needed her to be a role model of success, to point the way for them.

Imelda lived this lifestyle while her husband used intimidating and heavy-handed approaches to leadership. When uprisings occurred, he would wait until the right moment and intervene with brutal force to crush the opposition. The Marcos regime worked to preserve the status quo. This afforded them with a gold mine of funds derived from natural and labor resources sold abroad. But ultimately, their passive and self-centered approach to leadership led to their eventual exile to Hawaii. If only they had used their fortune to address the Philippine's economic and social problems, their legacy may have been positive.

Source: Ellison, K. W. (1988). *Imelda, steel butterfly of the Philippines.* New York: McGraw-Hill; Lico, G. (2003). *Edifice complex: Power, myth, and the Marcos state architecture.* Quezon City, Philippines: Ateneo de Manila University Press; and Morrow, L. (1986, March 31). The shoes of Imelda Marcos. *Time.* Retrieved August 26, 2008, from http://www.time.com/time/magazine/article/0,9171,961002,00.html.

printout stayed in the printer. It was later discovered by two of his staff members. Talk about shotgun management!

Oliver's followers reacted in a way that is typical for followers of laissez-faire leaders. If Oliver didn't get involved in work-related events and instead put his

Figure 8.2   Glued to the tube. This husband is ignoring his wife's request for help moving a table upstairs. It's only a matter of time before his laissez-faire attitude will result in negative consequences.

personal pursuits ahead of the department's, then why should they? Performance levels dropped. Staff became frustrated and started using their time at work for personal matters. The department took on an atmosphere of a country club. There was little overtime and most associates left the office by 4:30 p.m.

Oliver's laissez-faire behavior created a wide range of negative outcomes in his department. This story teaches us that followers look to the leader as a role model whose words and actions guide their own behavior at work. As shown in Figure 8.2, you need to be very careful not to be perceived as indifferent or uninvolved in decision-making and problem-solving processes. If you are not actively engaged in your work, your followers may reduce their own commitment toward work and the organization.

Be Absent When Needed

Jack was not looking forward to getting back to the office. But his department had a 10:00 a.m. Monday morning meeting with the boss. They had to review a presentation for a big client. The image of presenting at this meeting held little appeal to Jack. It was far less interesting than the four golf games at the En-Joie Country Club that Jack played with his clients over the past two weeks. Not to mention his recent travel to the Technology, Education and Design conference in Hawaii. It certainly was back to reality for Jack.

Then his direct reports started sending him a flurry of emails and text messages. They had no idea what was required for the meeting because he didn't keep them in the loop during his frequent absences over the last two weeks. As Jack started to panic, Laura, his ace salesperson, knocked on his door. She came in and sat down to talk with him.

"What are we supposed to do at today's meeting? I have no idea what to expect. I wish you could have spent some time giving us some guidance, Jack," said Laura.

"Ah, well ... we've certainly been out of town a lot lately. And we've got too many irons in the fire. Look, Laura, just follow my lead and work off of this canned template sales presentation we made last time. Things will work out just fine. Don't worry, be happy. By the way, Laura, could you whip up the PowerPoint slides for me in the next hour? Thanks!" responded Jack. Laura left the room looking both angry and defeated.

How well do you think Jack and Laura will fare at the meeting? How did Jack's frequent absences affect Laura? How did Jack's work habits and interaction with Laura illustrate laissez-faire behavior?

Delay and Fail to Follow Up

During his graduate school days, Don lived in a nice apartment complex in Johnson City, New York, just north of the local shopping mall. It provided comfortable accommodations and was generally well maintained. From time to time, there were minor problems with heating or plumbing that required the attention of the maintenance staff. The winter weather in the southern tier of New York gets very cold and snowy. Problems with heating or plumbing can cause big headaches for tenants.

After one long and hard day on campus, Don looked forward to relaxing at home listening to some music on radio station 680 WINR. As he drove home around the traffic circle, Don turned on the radio and smiled as he heard Andy Williams sing "The Most Wonderful Time of the Year." Don couldn't wait to spend time at home with his family during the upcoming holidays.

But when he got home, there was no heat, despite the fact that it was a freezing cold day in December. Don's wife, Sin, called the office repeatedly during the day, but every request for service seemed to be ignored. The maintenance man waited until almost 5 p.m. to come to look at the heating system. Finally, by 6 p.m., the heat was back on and restored to its normal operation. But the damage was already done because Don's family suffered through the cold day with no heat. They were frustrated, tired, cold, and angry from the lack of appropriate and timely response.

This is a problem that almost everyone might have experienced in the past. A one-hour delay means one hour more pain to somebody. However, many leaders just do not realize how their inaction or delayed reaction might hurt their followers. Consequently, leaders (and followers) who delay in responding to requests or fail to follow up on issues get similar reactions. A lack of proper attention and timely response to issues is de-motivating. It destroys trust. It decreases the credibility that you must develop as a leader. And it demonstrates a lack of caring and concern for others. Followers require attention and feedback so they can adjust their level of effort and approach to work. Whenever possible, respond to followers' inquiries and requests as promptly as possible and always with the highest level of sincerity, lest you be perceived as laissez-faire like, Don's old maintenance man.

Avoid Emphasizing Results

Jack Welch, the iconic former CEO of General Electric, once wrote a column in a business magazine about lousy leadership.[14] One of the awful leaders he bemoaned was what he called "the wimp." These are leaders who can't make a hard decision. They are the consensus builders who avoid emphasizing results. They are unwilling to give candid and rigorous performance evaluations. They give everyone the same "good job" review regardless of their actual performance results. This does little to differentiate the star performers from the mediocre ones, and offers little developmental feedback and improvement opportunities for followers. What feedback they do give is vague and meaningless.

Have you ever noticed how most politicians, when asked questions about tricky issues, purposely keep their responses vague? They provide little details on what their position is on the issue or how they plan to achieve the results people are hoping to achieve. That's because they don't want to be held accountable for failing to meet predefined goals.

Some leaders are even worse. They avoid emphasizing results. They fail to set standards for key financial performance measures such as sales growth, market share, net income, or return on investment. Likewise, they avoid any responsibility for achieving these results. Their lack of responsibility allows them to loaf around and do their own thing. The illusion that they are not responsible for outcomes persuades them to persist in being passive.

Unlike leaders who display contingent reward leadership, laissez-faire leaders are not motivated by goals. They actually try to avoid setting specific goals due to a fear of not achieving them. They also believe that they can always delegate or dump their responsibilities on their followers. They may be working behind the scenes to advance their personal agenda or next career move. They have already checked out of their current leadership position. Have you ever avoided your leadership responsibility? What was a consequence of your inaction? What do you think your followers can gain by avoiding the emphasis on results? What are some obvious downfalls of this laissez-faire behavior?

Thinking About Inactive Forms of Leadership

You are now familiar with the two types of passive leadership in the FRLD model. Now it's time to start thinking deeply about what implications passive leadership has for you in terms of four topics related to leadership: social loafing and free riding, letting things settle naturally, empowerment versus laissez-faire, and exception reporting. A good understanding of these topics will help you to identify areas in your leadership context to apply passive leadership when appropriate.

Social Loafing and Free Riding Are Outcomes of Passive Leadership

When leaders are consistently passive, followers respond in kind. Because fairness is something all individuals typically value, followers will seek an equitable behavioral response to their leader's laziness. Two typical responses followers working in groups have for their leader's passive behavior are social loafing and free riding.

Consider the case of a group of three employees who were high-performing individuals, but were social loafers when they worked as a group. Every time Steve, Eddy, and Vee Jay got together, they acted silly and goofed around instead of working hard. *Social loafing* occurs when group members put less effort into their collective work than when they work alone. They are able to hide their inactivity in the group since there is no mechanism for their individual accountability. This causes them to loaf. Followers will loaf when they feel their inaction or lack of contribution can go unnoticed. Because passive leaders role model loafing themselves, followers typically feel justified in withholding their own effort. In essence, passive leaders create a norm signaling to their followers that it is OK not to take any action.

With MBE-P leadership, followers see little importance in the work they do, except avoiding being corrected by the leader and her systems of control. They also may perceive that there is a chance that their contributions will not be evaluated by the control systems in place. In other words, they think there is a chance that the leader will not catch them loafing. They think they can get away with it. This motivates them to engage in social loafing. The case is even worse with leaders who display laissez-faire behavior. Followers of these passive leaders perceive less of a chance of being detected and don't understand the importance of their task, so they loaf.[15]

Have you ever noticed your followers loafing on account of your passive leadership? What can you do to avoid this undesirable outcome? Fortunately, you can evade this undesirable result by limiting your display of passive leadership. Increase your followers' level of motivation by getting them involved in performing separate but equally important group tasks. Let them choose what tasks they will perform based on their innate talents, strengths, or preferences. Spend time explaining why the tasks they perform are important and how the tasks contribute to the overall goals of the project. Here, a combination of inspirational motivation and contingent reward leadership (goal setting) can do wonders to eliminate any desire to loaf.

Another undesirable result of passive leadership is *free riding*. Unfortunately, we have seen this phenomenon occur when a lazy colleague gets involved in one of our research projects, but contributes little if any effort and value to the published paper. Sound familiar? In many organizations, this can occur when followers substitute for their passive leader's lack of initiative and influence by usurping the leader's role and responsibility. In other words, they pick up their leader's slack. The lazy leader benefits unfairly from the leadership effort exerted by the followers and not his own effort. To use an old metaphor, the leader "hitches his cart to the followers' horse" and catches a free ride to desired outcomes. It is the "Doing Nothing Bush" example we discussed earlier when he didn't do anything but dump his leadership responsibilities down to people below him during the Hurricane Katrina disaster in New Orleans. Once the situation becomes stable or the problem is eliminated, the free-riding leader tends to receive more benefits for his "leadership" than he deserves. However, continued free riding by the leader can create resentment among followers when they get tired of carrying the leader's weight for him.[16] Have you ever had a temptation to get a free ride or take a credit away from your followers? Do you know of any passive leaders who have used free riding to advance their careers? How did their free riding come to an end? Remember, there is no free riding in cultures built with transformational leadership.

Should You Let Things Settle Naturally?

In studying the effects of FRLD in high-tech firms, we once asked a group of executives the following interview questions: "How often do you prefer not to take action and let things settle naturally?" and "Can this policy be effective sometimes?"[17] We were somewhat surprised to find several top leaders making a case for displaying passive leadership from time to time. But most executives said they use passive leadership only in moderation. For example, a top executive at the San Diego-based wireless telecommunication innovator Qualcomm told us:

> It depends on the individual and the circumstances. It can be effective with motivated employees and the challenge of orienteering their way out of a tough spot. Orienteering is the use of a map and a compass. Some people like the freedom to come up with the full draft document with the full analysis. We can't always do that because of schedules and needs that may not allow that.... I don't really believe in being passive. If you want a passive boss, I'm not the guy to work for. At the same time, I'm not a micromanager. I am detailed-oriented and I am a good follow-up person. And a good way to get me off your back is if you could give me specific answers as to when, where, what, who, and how the project is coming along. What are the big issues? How are we approaching them? ... So it is always a judgment call, but I try not to be passive in any of the areas I am responsible for.[18]

Research on *substitutes for leadership* supports this executive's response. It suggests that passive leadership may be appropriate when characteristics of the followers, the task, and organization can effectively substitute for the leader's lack of initiative. Regarding followers' characteristics, a passive approach to leadership may be appropriate when the level of ability, training, experience, and knowledge of followers is very high. In addition, followers who like to work alone or those who work in highly regulated professions may not need very active forms of leadership. Similarly, aspects of the task that a follower performs can substitute for leadership. Tasks that are somewhat routine and unambiguous, provide their own feedback, or are intrinsically satisfying are good candidates for MBE-P leadership. Regarding the organization, passives forms of leadership may be OK in formalized or inflexible settings with clear plans, rigid rules, and procedures. When leadership is shared within a team, it may be best for the formally designated leader to take a passive approach and simply provide support when needed.[19] However, it is equally important for you to put your antenna up so that you can actively monitor work progress your followers make and be ready to intervene when necessary.

While some leaders may see a role for passive leadership, others do not. For example, Joe, an executive of a global accounts payable business unit in a large international IT company, told us he had never heard the term *passive leadership*.

> I know what it's getting at but I'm not sure I buy it. [For] every situation that comes up to me and requires me to do something, I'll do something. That may mean that I have to do something quickly or I

may decide, because there are cases where the best immediate action is no action. Some situations will resolve themselves, but that's a decision like deciding to do something quickly. I don't know that it's a passive style, and it probably doesn't happen that frequently.

Joe went on to say that his followers react negatively when he is less involved in their work. He told us that there are times, due to their organization's size, that he will spend less time with his accounts payable managers. Although, there are times when over the course of a conversation Joe might seem less engaged than normal. That's when his staff senses that something is wrong, and that concerns them. They even mention it to him sometimes. Joe believes that they like to see him getting involved because it validates that what they are doing at work is important. They don't need constant validation, but if they see a change in his behavior or a drop in his level of interest and activity, it truly concerns them.[20]

These examples suggest that you need to be very selective in displaying passive forms of leadership. There is a time and place for everything, but using passive leadership too frequently can be a big turn-off with today's followers who hold high expectations for leaders. Take a few moments to assess which of your followers, jobs, and organizational units may be able to get by with passive leadership.

Is It Empowerment or Just Laissez-Faire?

One thing that we have found in our consulting is that many successful business-people oftentimes get confused between empowerment and laissez-faire leadership. For example, Susan's community group has put the issue of global climate change on its agenda. They are convinced that the carbon emissions and greenhouse gases that business and industry produce are ruining our natural environment. They also feel that most corporations can do much more to increase the use of energy-efficient technologies. Invigorated by these beliefs, Susan has met with Jim to identify ways to empower a group of community members with information that can help address these issues. Jim assured Susan that at their next meeting he would use his leadership post to empower their group.

One week later, Susan was disappointed by Jim's behavior. As he started the meeting, he said that the new green initiative "is anything that you all want it to be." Then he sat back and said, "I'm hereby empowering you to come up with a plan and do whatever it takes to make it work. I'll never get in your way." Then he turned the meeting over to Susan.

This was much less than what Susan expected. When she heard Jim use the word *empowerment*, she visualized him giving the group more than decision-making authority. She expected an overall mission and vision for the group, along with some key objectives and suggestions for getting started. And she expected Jim to create a short- and long-term timeframe, specific responsibilities assigned to each member, and some metrics to assess outcomes. Where was Jim's encouragement of learning more about carbon emissions? Why didn't he talk about carpooling and combining trips? Why didn't he mention the need for better fuel economy or ways they could switch to "green power" or electricity generated by low routine emissions of carbon dioxide? And why didn't Jim offer resources to support their efforts? In Susan's opinion, Jim was more laissez-faire than empowering. And, she believed that Jim either was a lousy leader or did not have a genuine commitment to make their green initiative happen.

Empowerment means much more than delegating decision-making authority to others. It involves the leader getting actively involved in providing resources and support for the ideas that followers generate. It also involves psychologically empowering followers by boosting their confidence levels through inspirational motivation and individualized consideration, as discussed in previous chapters. Jim failed to do all of these things, and Susan and the group viewed his attempt at leadership to be laissez-faire, instead of empowering, as he originally intended.[21]

Next time you attempt to empower your followers, be careful not to fall victim to the same trap that Jim did. Take an active rather than passive role in supporting and encouraging your followers. To be a truly empowering leader, you need to be there for them when they need you. And don't smother them with too many control systems that can inhibit their creativity and ability to introduce innovation into your organization.

Exception Reporting and Reactive Leadership

MBE-P relies on finding mistakes after they occur and then fixing the problem that caused the mistake. This FRLD leadership style forces leaders to react to situations that get out of control. The key to success with MBE-P is knowing what problems and issues to look out for in advance in order to spot them. Fortunately, the accounting and auditing literature provides several suggestions.

There are at least four problems with the design of organizational controls that can lead to failure in operations. First, many organizations do not keep adequate documentation of their policies and procedures. This can result in a control system that does not protect from misappropriation of funds or resources. A periodic review of policies and procedures can identify areas at risk. Second, some organizational cultures are not conscious about the need for controls. This can lead to a failure to reconcile reports with actual assets. Top leadership that emphasizes the importance of control systems can set an appropriate tone for all members of the organization.

Third, weak controls for safeguarding assets open up the organization to the risk of fraud or theft. These risks force leaders to react to crises and fight fires on a continual basis. Working with internal and external auditors to design, test, and maintain strong controls can remedy this potential problem. Fourth, some organizations have poor monitoring of their control systems and no processes to report deficiencies in these systems to senior leadership. These issues can result in deficiencies in the collection and reporting of relevant and reliable data for generating financial and operational reports. A more active examination of systems of control can reduce the risks associated with these inadequacies and the susceptibility of assets to fraud.[22]

Take a few minutes to consider how you can improve your systems of exception reporting so that you can take a more proactive approach to control. Which types of control problems are you dealing with in your organization? What can you do to eliminate them?

Putting Passive Forms of Leadership Into Practice

To be fluent in FRLD, you should be able to apply both forms of passive leadership. To react to problems after they occur, apply MBE-P behavior to the situation. To avoid intervening when your leadership is not necessary, apply laissez-faire behavior to the situation.

Applying MBEP Leadership

Display the Behaviors Described in This Chapter

This chapter presented four behaviors associated with MBE-P leadership. These behaviors emphasized the importance of (1) intervening only if standards are not met, (2) waiting for things to go wrong before taking action, (3) believing that "if it ain't broke, don't fix it," and (4) reacting to mistakes reluctantly. By displaying these behaviors with your followers, they will become more willing to comply with rules and regulations in the future, work to maintain the status quo, or fix problems.

Finding solutions to problems is an outcome that Nancy Dart Orlando of the Vertex Corporation achieved in a grass-roots leadership initiative. Nancy waited until the time was right to help solve a problem. After reading about efforts to enhance the productivity of low-income workers overseas where reliable and environmentally friendly transportation is scarce, Nancy decided to get involved. She became concerned about the millions of people in developing countries who have no means of transportation other than their feet. Each year, Americans buy 22 million new bicycles and discard millions of old ones. Most of these end up in already overburdened landfills. Meanwhile, many poor people in underdeveloped countries need cheap, nonpolluting transportation to survive.

Bikes provide a reliable and environmentally sound form of transportation at low cost and represent a green solution to a common problem.

Nancy built a partnership between Penn State's Master of Leadership Development students and her coworkers at Vertex to support Pedals for Progress (P4P), an organization that provides used bicycles to people in developing countries throughout the world. Nancy organized a site where bicycles were donated, disassembled, and prepared for shipment to the Republic of Moldova, a land-locked country in Eastern Europe located between Romania and Ukraine.[23] Nancy's example of responding to a pressing global problem teaches us that an interesting blend of MBE-P and inspirational motivation behaviors can sometimes make a real difference in the lives of the less fortunate.

Place Energy on Maintaining the Status Quo

The global economic crisis that emerged in 2008 brought many challenges to Carl as he assumed a top leadership position at a public high school in a rural part of the state. His school was under increasing pressure to figure out how to make their programs tighter and encourage more students to excel on the state's advanced placement exams in science and math. But his budget was being cut by 6% and enrollments were down. The drop in the housing market and rise in food prices were hitting families hard. For everyone, it was difficult to make ends meet. Given these conditions, belt tightening and risk aversion became key aspects of Carl's strategic plan. It was time for the school to proceed with caution.

Carl's situation illustrates a time when MBE-P leadership may be appropriate. When it's time to pull in the reins on spending and risk, a passive approach to leadership can be effective. That's because it focuses followers' attention on performing within constraints and maintaining the status quo. It also reduces risk because it does not encourage followers to try new things, but to play it safe by complying with rules and regulations. By displaying MBE-P behavior and relying on the professionalism of his faculty, Carl shifted his leadership into a conservative mode that was right for the times. He hopes that when economic conditions improve he can once again display transformational leadership to show his faculty that they can work together to implement growth and change in their school. Carl's combination of MBE-P and transformational leadership illustrates the need to display flexible leadership under tight economic conditions.

Enforce Corrective Action When Followers Make Mistakes

Kathryn enjoyed working in the clinical trials group of a large international pharmaceutical company. Her group was responsible for testing the effects of new Alzheimer's drugs on the elderly. These drugs would eventually be used to save the elderly from this form of dementia. In clinical trials working toward this ultimate goal, the need for precision and care in systematic testing is essential because results of such tests influence whether drugs receive further research and development dollars. The work of Kathryn's group was very important, and its funding depended upon tests that produced good results.

To facilitate the process of testing, Kathryn used an interesting blend of intellectual stimulation and MBE-P leadership behavior. To ensure compliance with federal regulations for testing, Kathryn frequently briefed her group regarding what to do and how to do it to ensure compliance with protocol. But when it came to analysis of the data, she wanted her followers to develop alternative approaches and use new data analytic techniques that might improve their chances of detecting the effects they were hoping to achieve. She saw this as a way to build her followers' confidence and make them feel good about their own ideas, talents, and strengths.

Kathryn's mix of FRLD behaviors allowed her to build better brains within the constraints of complying with the hedgerow of legal constraints. Kathryn's example of adeptly shifting between behaviors on the FRLD model teaches us that the most effective leaders cannot be labeled either transformational, transactional, or nontransacting leaders. Instead, the most effective leaders can modify their display of FRLD behavior to fit the situation, as long as they spend most of their time displaying transformational and contingent reward leadership, while displaying passive forms of leadership selectively. So, your challenge is not just to develop transformational leadership style, but to develop a blend of leadership styles within FRLD and use them wherever and whenever appropriate.

Fix the Problem and Get Back to Coasting Along

Leaders who are fortunate enough to have knowledgeable, skilled, or professional followers can rely on them to set and work toward lofty goals, and take appropriate risks as necessary. Such empowered followers typically do not like leaders to get in their way when it comes to creative tasks, weighing pros and cons, and making complex decisions. As shown in Figure 8.3, too much direction can inhibit followers' creativity and entrepreneurial efforts. These are processes that are needed to move contemporary organizations forward. We have seen some leaders, who after empowering their able followers, support their efforts only if problems arise that the followers don't feel comfortable addressing themselves. When called upon, these leaders use MBE-P behavior to fix the problem and then get out of their followers' way. Even Jack Welch practiced this passive form of leadership and admitted it.

Figure 8.3 Watch it! Overbearing parents who display MBE-A behavior too frequently can inhibit their children's creativity and make them anxious.

> My job is to put the best people on the biggest opportunities, and the best allocation of dollars in the right places. That's about it. Transfer ideas and allocate resources and get out of the way.[24]

Sometimes, leaders like Jack Welch spend their time maintaining the systems that support their followers' creative processes. Not all followers and jobs require active forms of leadership. It's up to you to determine when you need to get involved and when you can sit back and assume a support role.

Applying Laissez-Faire Leadership

Please Avoid the Behaviors Described in This Chapter

This chapter presented four behaviors associated with laissez-faire leadership: (1) avoiding involvement and not making decisions or solving problems, (2) being absent when needed, (3) delaying and failing to follow up, and (4) not emphasizing results. Please note that we *do not* advise you to display these behaviors. But you need to be aware of these passive leadership behaviors so you don't fall victim to their outcomes. By displaying these behaviors with your followers, they can get confused over their roles at work, fight with each other over their responsibilities, look to others for guidance, and put little or no effort into their work. Their performance will suffer and their satisfaction with your leadership will decline.

Unfortunately, that's what Tom experienced when he hired Perry to help their local library save money by going green. Perry was a recent graduate from a business entrepreneurship program taught at a prestigious private university. During his days in school, Perry spent some time at an elite public university as a transfer student. There he learned how the public university developed and implemented policies, practices, and academic courses that promoted effective sustainability efforts. These included "energy management systems, extensive recycling efforts, organic gardening and composting … energy saving contests in residential communities, faculty expertise on watershed management, solar energy, flexible electronics, and environmental policy and biochemical sensors used in environmental studies."[25] While in school, Perry saw these efforts result in ecologically friendly solutions and real cost savings. Perry promised Tom he would generate the same results at the library.

Perry was smart, but he also had a sense of entitlement that made him lazy. He never provided the right guidance to the library staff to implement these programs. He failed to build connections in the community to get volunteers involved. He didn't seem to care about the project. He spent most of his time surfing the Internet or chatting up the young ladies in the library. Nothing got done. As a result, Tom lost faith in Perry and reassigned him to the job of maintaining the library's computer systems. Perry could have been a "green giant" of change in the library. Instead, he let his opportunity spoil.

Perry's folly teaches us a valuable lesson: These are the days of our lives. We are given a limited supply of days to make a difference in the world. Spend your days wisely. Never waste opportunities to do great things by being a passive leader when circumstances call for a more active form of leadership. Make a difference in your world one opportunity at a time. This will increase your credibility as a leader. Leadership writer John C. Maxwell considers leadership and credibility as pocket change (i.e., coinage). Whenever you do something good to your followers, you are adding one more piece of change to your pocket.[26] Your passive leadership will eventually deplete the change in your pocket and reduce your credibility.

Talk About Getting Things Done, But Let Others Take the Lead

Jay was always quite the talker. He loved to chase big ideas and was sure to tell you about them. He would brag about all of his successes, pontificate about his lofty plans for his department's future, and exude confidence that his vision was the only one to follow. He would boast that he was working on 10 huge projects at once. He would always take on more work for his staff without considering their current workload. Yet, when push came to shove, Jay never got involved in the details of the plans he constantly made for others without their consent. He would dump the details of his far-flung plans on his unlucky followers in the name of empowerment. As a result, they performed well below expectations because Jay's plans were just pipe dreams.

Consider this example as a warning to be careful not to assume the role of a pseudotransformational leader[27] like Jay, who, as the saying goes, could sing for his supper, but just couldn't make it. The danger of big talking without active involvement and support is being perceived as nothing more than a laissez-faire leader.

Show Lack of Interest When Things Go Wrong

Every day Barbara drove to work from her home in Kirkwood through a rough section on the south side of Binghamton. The local park where she played as a child had deteriorated into a run-down shambles. It had become a haven for drug dealers and gangs. No one dared to spend much time in the park. Barbara remembered many good times she spent there during its better days. She was amazed how things had changed for the worse. Although Barbara had a special place for the park in her heart, she wrote it off as a victim of urban decay. She had many more important things to worry about in her life. Her lack of interest made Barbara a kind of laissez-faire leader.

One day Barbara gave Sharon a ride to work and commented on the sad fate of the park. Always the community activist, Sharon responded by saying that things didn't have to be that way. She spoke of many examples of urban renewal projects around the country that were changing things for the better. She convinced Barbara to volunteer with her community group to do something about the park. They planned to rally a group of workers and partner with the local police department and university to help restore the park. Six months later, the partnership resulted in significant improvements for the park. Their group picked up the garbage littered around the park. They planted new trees, flowers, and shrubs. They put down new mulch under the swing sets and rides. They painted the walls of the park buildings and installed new security systems and picnic tables. They restored the park to its past glory so that people could take pleasure in it today and also look forward to enjoying it tomorrow.[28]

Barbara's laissez-faire attitude offered no help for the park until Sharon got her to do something about it. Don't look the other way when you see persistent problems like Barbara did. The only way they will go away is if leaders and their followers look at them through the filter of a positive vision and then do something about them. Indeed, the difference between laissez-faire and inspirational leadership is much smaller than you might imagine. You can always change yourself into a transformational leader if you make the time for change and have support from other people.

Let Things Settle Naturally

Leaders need to carefully decide which issues they will get involved in and which issues they will avoid. For example, a CEO of an IT security company told us when it comes to problems workers have with each other, he lets things settle naturally. He tends just to help them get back to the "coffee house" and work it out themselves. But he's not passive in affairs relevant to his turf and job responsibilities. In those areas, he asks his followers to work closely with him. He is quite involved in the company side of what they do. He is less involved in the social aspect of the job. That is an area he doesn't mind being viewed as a slacker. He walks around and asks followers how they are and what's on their mind, but for the most part he deals with things at the strategic level of the company as a whole, and not at the personal or micro level. Learn a lesson from this CEO and choose your battles wisely, especially when dealing with contentious groups of followers with competing agendas.

In such group situations, the potential for destroying followers' trust and commitment is more likely to occur. In groups, it is often hard to promote individual accountability and motivate members with passive leadership. We consider the role of FRLD in influencing group members to share leadership responsibilities in the next chapter.

Summary Questions and Reflective Exercises

1. This exercise uses results of your Multifactor Leadership Questionnaire (MLQ) report to assess your level of laissez-faire behavior. Compare your laissez-faire ratings with the research-validated benchmarks. How did your self-ratings, ratings from subordinates, ratings from peers, ratings from superiors, and ratings from others compare against the benchmarks? On which specific MLQ items (i.e., questions) did you score highest? Lowest? What can you do to improve on the items where you scored highest?

2. This exercise uses results of your MLQ report to assess your level of passive management-by-exception behavior. Compare your passive management-by-exception ratings with the research-validated benchmarks. How did your self-ratings, ratings from subordinates, ratings from peers, ratings from superiors, and ratings from others compare against the benchmarks? On which specific MLQ items (i.e., questions) did you score highest? Lowest? What can you do to improve on the items where you scored too high?

3. Assemble a team of colleagues to review the work procedures or standards in your work unit. Announce to your entire staff that a review team will be conducting a compliance review of a randomly selected area in your work unit. What areas need monitoring? How did your staff respond to your announcement? How motivated were the review team members to conduct the compliance review? How can this form of passive management-by-exception leadership be used effectively in your organization?

4. Leaders who use passive management-by-exception leadership typically apply a wide acceptance range for deviations from the standard. How should you determine the range of exceptions that you are willing to tolerate before taking corrective action in your work unit?

5. Leaders who use passive management-by-exception leadership typically reinforce their followers' behaviors with corrections, criticism, negative feedback, and punishment. In what circumstances can these methods be effective? In what circumstances can they be ineffective?

6. Punishment is sometimes required to help shape expected behavior of individuals. Unfortunately, punishment can have unintended effects on those to which it is applied and on those around them. Based on your experience, describe five situations where punishment led to unintended effects.

7. Visit www.youtube.com and search for scenes from popular television shows depicting life in the office. Or visit your local library to borrow DVDs with episodes of these or similar shows. Identify scenes that illustrate passive management-by-exception and laissez-faire leadership and their effects on followers' motivation and performance. Present these scenes to your staff members as an icebreaker at your next meeting. Use such video clips to start a discussion about the perils of relying too much on passive forms of leadership.

8. Based on your experience, identify ways that laissez-faire leadership can be mistaken for delegation. How should effective delegation be used to avoid being misinterpreted by others as laissez-faire leadership?

9. Identify five situations where laissez-faire leadership can be appropriate and effective. What do these situations have in common that contribute to their being suitable for laissez-faire leadership?

10. Review the management literature on the concept of empowerment. Based on your research, define *empowerment* and list five ways you can promote empowerment of your associates without being perceived as laissez-faire.

Notes

1. Retrieved November 7, 2008, from http://www.phillycarshare.org/28/vision/history. php.
2. Retrieved November 7, 2008, from http://www.gobroomecounty.com/legis/Legis GreenBusinessInitiative.php.
3. Spiedies are a unique regional cuisine originating from the southern tier of New York State. They are sandwiches made of grilled pieces of chicken, lamb, veal, or venison marinated in a special sauce that resembles Italian salad dressing. For more details, see http://www.spiedies.com/spiedies.htm. Retrieved November 7, 2008.
4. Sosik, J. J., Jung, D. I., Berson, Y., Dionne, S. D., & Jaussi, K. S. (2004). *The dream weavers: Strategy-focused leadership in technology-driven organizations.* Greenwich, CT: Information Age Publishing.
5. Ebert, J. C. (Director), Bass, B. M., & Avolio, B. J. (Writers). (1992). *The full range of leadership* [Training videotape]. Binghamton, NY: Center for Leadership Studies, State University of New York at Binghamton.
6. Linzmayer, O. W. (2004). *Apple confidential 2.0: The definitive history of the world's most colorful company.* San Francisco: No Starch Press.
7. Retrieved November 9, 2008, from http://www.cnn.com/2005/US/11/03/brown. fema.emails/.
8. Retrieved November 24, 2008, from http://politicalhumor.about.com/library/ images/blbushdonothing.htm.
9. Retrieved November 9, 2008, from http://lazyleaders.blogspot.com/.
10. Bass, B. M., & Avolio, B. J. (1994). *Improving organizational effectiveness through transformational leadership.* Thousand Oaks, CA: Sage.
11. Allen, C. (2008). *Management's assessment of internal control over financial reporting.* Lewisville, TX: American Institute of Certified Public Accountants; and American Institute of Certified Public Accountants. (2005). *Management override of internal controls: The Achilles' heel of fraud protection; the audit committee and oversight of financial reporting.* New York: American Institute of Certified Public Accountants.
12. Allen (2008). As cited in Note 11.
13. Bass, B. M., & Avolio, B. J. (1990). *Full range leadership development: Advanced workshop manual.* Binghamton, NY: Center for Leadership Studies, SUNY-Binghamton.
14. Welch, J., & Welch, S. (2007, July 23). Bosses who get it all wrong: Blowhards. Jerks. Wimps. How inept leaders can derail a thriving enterprise. *Business Week, 4043,* 88.
15. Karau, S. J., & Williams, K. D. (1993). Social loafing: A meta-analytic review and theoretical integration. *Journal of Personality and Social Psychology, 65,* 681–706; and Rothwell, J. D. (2004). *In the company of others.* New York: McGraw-Hill.
16. Tuck, R. (2008). *Free riding.* Cambridge, MA: Harvard University Press.
17. Sosik et al. (2004, p. 243). As cited in Note 4.
18. Interview with Rich Sanders conducted by Don I. Jung in June 2002.
19. Kerr, S., & Jermier, J. M. (1978). Substitutes for leadership: Their meaning and measurement. *Organizational Behavior and Human Performance, 22,* 375–403; and Pierce, J. L., & Newstrom, J. W. (2008). *Leaders & the leadership process: Readings, self-assessments & applications* (5th ed.). New York: McGraw-Hill.

20. Interview with executive conducted by Roseann MacDonald and Val Zimmerman, submitted December 20, 2002.

21. Thomas, K. W., & Velthouse, B. A. (1990). Cognitive elements of empowerment: An 'interpretive' model of intrinsic task motivation. *Academy of Management Review, 15,* 666–681.

22. Thompson, R., & Letcher, G. E. (2007). *Ethics and the attest function: A practical update for CPAs in public practice 2007.* Philadelphia: PICPA Foundation for Education and Research.

23. Lash, K. (2008, November 12). *Vertex hosts bicycle collection drive for global charity.* Berwyn, PA: Vertex, Inc. press release; Lord, M. (2008, November 17). *Leadership in action at Penn State Great Valley.* Malvern, PA: Penn State Great Value press release; and retrieved November 13, 2008, from http://www.p4p.org/.

24. Slater, R. (2003). *29 leadership secrets from Jack Welch.* New York: McGraw-Hill.

25. Anonymous. (2008). A "green" giant. *Binghamton University Magazine, 4,* 7.

26. Maxwell, J. C. (2007). *The 21 irrefutable laws of leadership.* Nashville, TN: Thomas Nelson.

27. Bass, B. M., & Steidlmeier, P. (1999). Ethics, character, and authentic transformational leadership. *Leadership Quarterly, 10,* 181–217.

28. Adapted from Anonymous. (2008). Scholars beautify city park. *Binghamton University Magazine, 4,* 4.

Chapter 9

Sharing Full Range Leadership Within Teams

Snowflakes are one of nature's most fragile things, but just look at what they can do when they stick together.

—Vesta Kelly

A group of people sit down around a table at the local Whole Foods Market and contemplate what items should be on sale during the weekend. They are extremely intent about the data they have regarding the weather forecast, customers' buying patterns, special events, inventory levels, and even the national economy. Based on these data, they project what items should be "eye catchers"—products that will create lots of foot traffic to their store. The team also decides what products they want to stock in order to meet local customers' demands. The next item on the agenda is to evaluate Jerry, the new guy on the team. Jerry has been working for the team for the past four weeks and it is time for team members to carefully assess his personality, work ethic, commitment, and contribution. If a two-thirds majority of team members agree that Jerry is a good fit for the team, he gets to stay. Otherwise, he is out. The last item they need to discuss is the team's performance in relation to other teams in the store and similar teams in charge of the same section in other stores across the country. Their performance is measured by the profit per labor hour and is available to them along with comparative data for other teams. Their bonus is directly and immediately tied to these comparative performance data.[1]

The team's decision-making process at Whole Foods Markets is quite intense, somewhat like a military operation. Does it sound like a Navy SEALs team working on a special mission? You got it right! There are a lot of commonalities between how this team at Whole Foods Market and a Navy SEALs team work together with their team members. In both teams, it is all about freedom, accountability, and sharing leadership within the team. Just like a Navy SEALs team, every team member is empowered to make many important and mission-critical decisions on his or her own. Even if they have a formally designated team leader, leadership on the team is shared with everyone. This is how Whole Foods Markets enables its employees to become profit-conscious and highly empowered self-managing team members. And this is how the company's stock grew almost 3,000% since its IPO in 1992, and averaged about 11% annual growth over the last five years, which is three times greater than the industry average.[2]

Contemporary businesses operate in an era in which work has become too complicated to be performed by single individuals. Collective intellectual capacity and firm's intangible assets count more than tangible assets, such as buildings, factories, and technology.[3] Therefore, a great deal of interest has been generated in the United States and abroad in recent years, regarding the utilization of teams to build and rebuild organizations. Pressures to downsize and restructure organizations to make them flatter have led to a reduction of hierarchical levels, with more emphasis now being placed on creating flexible forms of work, greater degrees of empowerment, and more interdependence among workers to accomplish their tasks.

As more and more organizations are becoming team based, the role of leadership becomes increasingly important. One reason is that the role of leadership in building and maintaining effective teams has often been identified as a common cause of failures in implementing teams in organizations.[4] How many of you have witnessed basketball players on the Los Angeles Lakers or your favorite NBA team confessing after a losing game that they didn't play as a team due to a leadership failure? Yet, only a few researchers have explicitly considered leadership as one of the determinants of team performance in models of team effectiveness.[5]

Team performance can depend upon an individual's leadership capability. That's why much of the prior research that has focused on leadership in teams has assessed leadership by focusing on a single individual leading the team. However, as employees become more autonomous and empowered, and as self-managing teams like the one described earlier at Whole Foods Markets become more prevalent, we believe that collective or distributed leadership *within* teams or leadership *by* teams (rather than leadership *of* teams) becomes more critical to a team's success. This chapter shows you what team leadership is and how to use the FRLD concept to develop leadership shared by the team. Let's start learning about team leadership by considering a case about arguably the most famous and influential rock band in history.

Team Leadership Lessons From the Beatles

The Beatles are the most commercially successful and important rock band in the history of popular music. Their music, hairstyles, clothes, interests, and social and political commentary influenced not only those who grew up in the 1960s, but subsequent generations as well. Their music has influenced countless artists over the years, including Bruce Springsteen, Elvis Costello, Oasis, the Kooks, and the Zutons. The Beatles consisted of band leader John Lennon, his songwriting collaborator Paul McCartney, their younger schoolmate George Harrison, and fellow Liverpool music journeyman Ringo Starr. The Beatles are an example of a high-performing rock group whose leadership was first driven by John Lennon, but later was shared by members of the group. They have sold over a billion albums worldwide and have been ranked as the number one rock group of all time by both *Rolling Stone* and *Billboard* magazines. Their phenomenal international success has passed the test of time and provides us with at least five lessons for effective team leadership using FRLD.

Carry That Weight

Performing at peak levels of effectiveness can be exhausting, and the Beatles experienced this firsthand (see Figure 9.1). For team leadership to be effective, the team must consist of the right members whose knowledge, skills, and abilities complement each other. This allows teams to bear the heavy burden of striving for and maintaining success over long periods of time. The Beatles' lasting influence comes from the complementary composition of their group. Lennon's drive, sarcastic wit, playfulness, and imaginative lyrical prowess were perfect foils for

Figure 9.1 The Fab Four look exhausted during the height of Beatlemania. Paul McCartney, Ringo Starr, John Lennon, and George Harrison's stamina and synergy helped them become the most successful rock group in history and an excellent example of a highly developed team.

McCartney's ego, sentimentality, technical expertise, and ability to write beautiful melodies. Both Lennon and McCartney loved to rock out in the style of Elvis Presley and Little Richard, just as many of today's bands like to imitate the Beatles. Based on their common interests, they frequently shared bits of their own compositions with each other as they collaborated. They valued each other's feedback on demos of each other's songs. In a form of friendly competition, they challenged each other to raise the level of quality for their music. No matter who was the primary songwriter, they always credited the songs as "Lennon–McCartney" compositions. These behaviors show the Beatles using forms of intellectual stimulation and individualized consideration in their creative processes.

The Lennon–McCartney partnership was enhanced by the support of Harrison and Starr. Harrison provided a distinctive lead guitar sound. His interest in Indian culture and religion led the Beatles to use unusual instruments, such as the sitar, in their recordings. Harrison's deep spirituality also influenced the core message of the Beatles' songs: love, peace, and life as worth living. While the introspective Harrison provided a positive musical direction for the Beatles, Starr was an extroverted member who held the band together with his unmistakable drum rolls and his laid-back and friendly personality. Starr was the group's peacemaker, who intervened when tempers flared or members felt unappreciated or out of sync with the others. These examples show the Beatles once again using intellectual stimulation and individualized consideration to move the band forward and flourish under stressful conditions.

Don't Let Me Down

Highly developed teams have members who possess high levels of drive and commitment to achieving their goal. When the Beatles were initially turned down by several record labels, Lennon never gave up. Instead, he rallied the group with a war cry veiled in the question: "Where are we headed, boys?" The other group members would chant in return: "To the toppermost of the poppermost!"—meaning they were aiming for the Top the Pops. In other words, their goal was to be the very best. The Beatles backed up their bravado by working extremely long hours, practicing constantly, and fine-tuning their act. Their talent, passion for their work, and commitment to being the best paid off in 1963 when they made it big in the United Kingdom. By 1964, Beatlemania crossed the Atlantic to America and began to spread around the world. The Beatles displayed inspirational motivation and idealized influence by aiming for and working toward excellence in their music.

Come Together

Members of highly developed teams find common ground in their shared vision. This vision helps them put aside their self-interests and focus on advancing the best interest of the team. By 1969, the Beatles were practically torn apart by internal strife, low levels of drive, conflict between group and personal roles, and individual projects that took them away from the group. The *Let It Be* sessions and film were evidence of the group falling apart. During those sessions, McCartney and Harrison can be seen having a verbal fight. With the interest level of Lennon, Harrison, and Starr waning, McCartney assumed leadership, but he failed to instill the high level of motivation and creativity for which the Beatles were known. It seemed as if the Beatles as a group had breathed their last.

But the band and their producer, George Martin, felt that they had "one more good album in them," and they worked during the summer of 1969 to record *Abbey Road*. They agreed that this would probably be their last recording, so they set aside their differences and decided to give it their all so they could end on a positive note. *Abbey Road* is where Harrison came into his own with his classic songs "Something" and "Here Comes the Sun." Lennon contributed several hard-rocking tunes, while McCartney's beautiful suites of compositions on side 2 added to the album's majestic allure. Even Starr contributed with the charmingly quirky "Octopus' Garden." As producer, Martin did an excellent job integrating these pieces into a comprehensive whole that was greater than the sum of its parts. Here the Beatles created team synergy from Martin's inspirational motivation, and they displayed idealized influence by agreeing to reach for the summit of collective success despite their individual differences.

Tell Me What You See

Highly developed teams use life experiences and ideas from their members to identify exciting new directions for the team. Disillusioned and worn out by touring, the Beatles officially retired from the road in 1966. Later that year, they returned to the studio to begin work on their magnum opus, *Sgt. Pepper's Lonely Hearts Club Band*. McCartney suggested the album's concept for the Beatles to portray fictitious characters in this imaginary band. This would allow them the room to experiment with different types of songs and instruments. Each member contributed ideas, thoughts on album cover design, and songs based on their experiences. Starr imagined himself as "Billy Shears" and sang lead vocal on "With a Little Help From My Friends." Harrison contributed Indian culture and music for the album. Lennon wrote "A Day in the Life," based on a newspaper account of an automobile accident. McCartney penned the quaint "When I'm Sixty-Four" that appealed to the older generation. The album was a huge international hit and today is ranked as the greatest album of all time by *Rolling Stone* magazine.[6] This example shows the Beatles using intellectual stimulation and individualized consideration to foster teamwork and create perhaps the most influential rock album of all time.

Within You Without You

Highly developed teams seek leadership from all members and help from others outside of the team. Leadership roles shift between team members, depending on the situation and the tasks at hand. During their rise to fame and fortune coming from Beatlemania, Lennon was the strong driving force within the band. McCartney exerted more leadership influence when Lennon's interests shifted toward Yoko Ono. When things got very tense during the recording of *The Beatles* (White Album), Harrison collaborated with guitar god Eric Clapton on "While My Guitar Gently Weeps" and contributed this work to the project. Starr briefly left the band during this time and McCartney played drums on several tracks. This is when McCartney took on a more dominant role in the group.

To help ease conflict in the band during the *Let It Be* sessions, Harrison brought in soul musician Billy Preston to play keyboards. To paraphrase Harrison, it is amazing how people change when you bring someone new into a group; "people don't act so bitchy" when they know they are being judged by an outsider. And at different points in time, the Beatles relied on their producer, George Martin, and manager Brian Epstein to make important decisions for them that were outside of their areas of knowledge and expertise. These examples show the Beatles using idealized influence to rise above adversity by allowing the best person, both within and outside of the group, to provide ideas and leadership when necessary.[7]

Team Leadership Defined

The members of the Beatles demonstrated all aspects of transformational leadership while they worked together to produce some of the best rock albums in history. One important issue that we would like to emphasize is that the role of leadership shifted from one member to another whenever circumstances were changing. For instance, when Lennon's passion and drive toward music cooled down, other members, such as McCartney and Harrison, came in with different qualities and talents to substitute for Lennon's leadership role. In other words, their leadership was shared by the team.

Several attempts have been made by a few scholars to define leadership at the team level in the past. For example, while summarizing the Harvard Laboratory Studies on leadership, Robert Freed Bales, a noted social psychologist, created a new term, co-*leadership*, suggesting that it might be beneficial in groups to allocate the task and relational leadership roles to different individuals.[8] Another group of scholars headed by Robert Waldersee and Geoff Eagleson found empirical evidence supporting Bale's position, concluding that the implementation of major change programs in hotel settings was more effective when the task and relational roles were divided among two individuals on the change management

Figure 9.2   All together now. Captains of this football team share leadership by partnering with each other to take on the responsibility for leadership.

team.[9] These studies suggest that leadership can extend beyond an individual person to behaviors shared by members of a team.

Team leadership can be defined as a form of leadership in which team members share roles and responsibilities of a leader. In other words, in team leadership, leadership roles are distributed among, and stem from, team members as shown in Figure 9.2.[10] Therefore, team leadership is different from traditional top-down leadership or leadership *of* the team in several different ways.

First and foremost, team members share the responsibility for group performance. In a shared leadership situation, the team leader does not bear the responsibility for team performance alone. Team members are collectively responsible for the team's performance. This is evident in the two examples we discussed earlier. Members of the self-managing team at Whole Foods are responsible for revenues and profits of their team, which is independent from the performance of other teams, even in the same store. Similarly, the four members of the Beatles were responsible for their collective success. It was not their manager or their band leader, Lennon, who was solely responsible for their success.

Second, since team members are responsible for their own performance, they are almost always fully empowered to make key decisions that affect team performance. In other words, control over the final decision is always left to the team. While this may create a higher level of conflict, which was pretty evident among members of the Beatles, this is a very critical part of creating team leadership. We consider this a "growing pain" during which shared leadership is being developed. To facilitate team leadership development, members should be allowed to make all of the critical decisions that would affect their performance. That's the way teams at Whole Foods Markets are empowered to make many critical decisions such as hiring/firing new members, selecting/pricing/ordering goods, and promoting different product mixes.

Third, interpersonal processes and interactions become much more prominent in team leadership settings. Since all members are expected to carry out team responsibilities jointly, they are likely to interact with one another much more actively and comprehensively than in traditional team situations. They tend to raise expectations not only for themselves but also for the others, as the Beatles did when they worked hard to make it very big. These common expectations held among team members are called *norms*. In a traditional team situation, the team leader oftentimes establishes and enforces team norms. However, members share a collective responsibility to develop and use their norms as a governing mechanism in a shared leadership context. This implies that members should voice their needs and feelings so that they get a chance to understand others and be understood.

Now that we have formally defined team leadership and discussed its unique characteristics, let's turn to some important issues on teams and think about how the FRLD model can be applied to these team concepts.

Thinking About FRLD in Groups and Teams

It is quite interesting to watch how people tend to consistently use the terms *groups* and *teams* for different situations. Nobody taught us when to use groups and teams selectively. However, we use these terms for different purposes. Think about some examples. What do you call a gathering of people playing basketball together? Group or team? Without a doubt, it is called a basketball team. The same is true for an NFL football team, a major league baseball team, and an NHL hockey team. It would sound somewhat strange to call them groups. How about people getting together to share a common hobby? You would probably call them a group. If a business school is not departmentalized, then we use the term *group* to designate a collection of professors who belong to a certain discipline, such as the organizational behavior group or the finance group.

As organizations increasingly use group- and team-based work structures to get things done, it is important for you to understand the distinction between the concepts of group and team. This is because the nuances between groups and teams have important implications for improving the dynamics through leadership of these work structures.

What's in a Name? Differences Between Groups and Teams

Groups and teams do not appear to be much different if one thinks of them causally. After all, they consist of two or more individuals, interacting and interdependent, who have come together to achieve specific goals. So, what makes teams different from groups? We can differentiate teams from groups in a number of aspects.

Information and Workflow

Group members merely share information and interact with one another to make decisions, which will help them fulfill their own responsibility. In contrast, team members not only share information but also work together to increase their collective performance. In other words, teams must have shared purposes. Therefore, contingent reward and active management-by-exception leadership would be a more frequent norm in groups.[11]

People are often ready to blame others for lack of performance in groups. Or they become quite transactional in that they are willing to work hard as long as others agree to do so. Group members constantly contemplate whether it would be better off if they jump ship and do things on their own to create a bigger and more positive outcome. In groups, social loafing or free riding is quite common because members are not committed to take their responsibility. Self-interest often supersedes collective interest. This often leads to personal conflicts, and that's why many people generally prefer not to work on things in a group context.

In our consulting work, we have seen the distinction between groups and teams become blurred because the client merely named a particular collection of people a team. But in reality, the behaviors of its members resembled a group. For example, individuals first come together in a disorganized fashion and lack a sense of purpose. They set no clear agenda and do not assign specific tasks to their members. As a result, they experience high levels of conflict within the group and are confused about their responsibilities. In essence, they are an *unstructured group* of individuals with a *laissez-faire* attitude about leadership.

Some individuals work in a *semistructured group* and display *passive management-by-exception* (MBE-P) leadership behaviors. They react to the circumstances that surround them and accept a wide range of deviations from standards before taking action. They wait for problems to arise and intervene reluctantly with each other only when absolutely necessary. They are uncertain about their roles and hesitate to offer ideas.

Somewhat more effective are the *structured groups* that use a combination of *active management-by-exception* (MBE-A) and *constructive transaction* (CR) leadership styles. When in the MBE-A mode, the group closely monitors processes for deviations from standards and takes immediate action to correct problems when detected. Members of structured groups strictly enforce rules to guide their work processes. However, they may be unwilling to take risks and may engage in struggles to influence others. When in the CR mode, the group specifies its purpose, defines roles for each of its members, and recognizes their accomplishments. By taking this active approach to group leadership, members of the structured group create an agenda describing what goals needs to be accomplished, and what tasks need to be completed to meet the goals. Members follow up with each other to ensure that tasks are completed as well.[12]

In contrast, teams are designed to achieve collective objectives through a shared purpose. Through idealized influence, team members develop a shared vision for their existence and set clear expectations for themselves. They are ready to sacrifice their self-interest if doing so would facilitate the process of achieving collective objectives. They show an intense commitment to the team's vision. At the individual level, such idealized influence behavior is displayed by a leader, but is shown at the team level in shared team leadership situations, like the member of Barack Obama's political movement shown in Figure 9.3.

Consider the 2008 Major League Baseball World Series champion, the Philadelphia Phillies. They are a good example of a potent team that held together with idealized influence. Team manager Charlie Manuel was careful to select, develop, and retain players with big bats and big hearts instead of big egos. Players like "the Gentle Giant" Ryan Howard, Pat Burrell, Jimmy Rolins, and Cole Hamels put in long hours of practice and shared responsibility to rally to become world champions. They let their collective performance speak for them, and that's the essence of idealized influence.

Synergy

Another key difference between teams and groups involves the level of synergy. *Synergy* means individual efforts create a level of performance that is greater than the sum of individual inputs, such that $1 + 1 + 1 = 4$. Through inspirational motivation, team members elevate expectations by setting extraordinarily high standards. They show enthusiasm and confidence and constantly emphasize interdependence among members of their team. They achieve synergy by collaborating and committing to reach the highest levels of performance goals, as demonstrated by the Beatles.

Due to personal conflicts present in groups, members are not likely to create an outcome that exceeds even their own expectation. The main purpose of their collaboration is getting things done fast and efficiently, not necessarily creating

Figure 9.3 Shared leadership and idealized influence. Team members who believe, talk about, and act in ways that are exemplary foster shared purpose in teams.

a better and bigger outcome. This might be due to the problem of poorly articulated expectations among group members. Since they are transactionally oriented, group members do not get a chance to idealize their influence with one another.

In contrast, team members are keenly aware of their collective and individual sense of purpose, and therefore, they talk about a positive future that they will be able to enjoy by working collaboratively. This shows their idealized influence within the team. Through inspirational motivation, team members also discuss what needs to be done in order to create synergy and share their collective confidence about achieving their stretched targets. We have emphasized personal confidence called self-efficacy in this book so that you can practice FRLD successfully. Collective efficacy or group potency refers to group members' collective perceptions about how efficacious their group is.[13]

This team-level confidence increases team performance in a variety of settings. The importance of having collective confidence has been demonstrated particularly well in various sports settings, where players and coaches oftentimes attributed their success or failure to the fact that they worked (or didn't work) as a team. For example, team members' collective confidence was positively related to team cohesion among 92 volleyball players participating on elite and recreational teams, which oftentimes would lead to a higher level of team performance.[14] Likewise, perceived team confidence assessed prior to the opening season among hockey players from six teams in a midwestern college hockey league contributed toward team performance.[15]

Pete Carroll, head coach of the University of Southern California (USC) football team, has created a dynasty of confidence and victories for his teams. He selects large, smart, and fast players. Instead of breaking them down and building them back up like Pat Summitt, Carroll takes a different approach. He simply builds up his players by focusing on their strengths. He keeps things positive and boosts his players' levels of confidence, hope, optimism, and ability to bounce back. As a result, his players become less interested in their personal star power and more interested in creating team synergy. In the 2009 Rose Bowl, Carroll's USC Trojans defeated Joe Paterno's Penn State Nittany Lions.

As another example, consider the New York Jets famous upset victory over the heavily favored Baltimore Colts in 1969's Super Bowl III. NFL films and many sport commentators have described this "David versus Goliath" contest as one of the most important professional football games in history. Prior to the game, the Jets practiced hard and smart for many hours so they could execute their plays perfectly. During the game, the Jets were led to victory by a charismatic young quarterback by the name of "Broadway" Joe Willie Namath. In his induction speech into the National Football League's Hall of Fame, Namath pointed out the essential role of collective efficacy in contributing to his team's stunning victory, noting that "the help we get on the field by other teammates is so important … the guys on the team, we believed in ourselves sure … we believed in one another and that's what got us over the hump … we won the championship."[16] This example teaches us that it takes confidence, collective efficacy, hard work, and poise in execution of roles to produce championship levels of performance.

We believe that the several examples we described above in various sports settings illustrate the importance of building shared leadership practices in order to overcome challenging odds and win the game. Through inspirational motivation, team members can encourage one another to raise their own expectations and passionately talk about visions of victory. That will surely build a high level of shared leadership and collective confidence in your own team.

Individual Versus Mutual Accountability

Accountability lies with individuals in the group, whereas it lies at both individual and mutual levels in the team. Since group members are primarily concerned about their own work in the group, their focus is on how to finish their own work. This transactional attitude can lead to tension and personal conflict if they see that all members are not contributing equally. Mutual expectations are rarely examined and articulated in groups. There is not much consideration as to how their own work contributes to overall performance of their group. As long as they do their work, group members perceive that their responsibility is over.

In contrast, team members believe that they not only are accountable for their own performance, but also hold mutual accountability for collective objectives. They develop a high level of trust, and every member encourages others to look at their work from a larger perspective. There is no slacker who contemplates how he could maximize his outcome by goofing around. Team members exhibit idealized influence to challenge one another so that they can exceed their own expectations. Common outcomes of highly developed teams where members share leadership together include a high level of trust and cohesion.[17] We see these levels of trust and cohesion in high-performing college football teams, such as University of Florida, University of Oklahoma, USC, and Penn State.

Overlapping Versus Complementary Skill Sets

Another difference that distinguishes teams from groups is skills that members bring to the table. Groups are usually put together without explicit consideration given to individual skill sets. In this way, skills of group members tend to be random and overlapping. Group work process rarely becomes an opportunity to learn each other's skills.

In contrast, each team member is fully aware of each other's strengths and weaknesses. Through individualized consideration, team members provide coaching to others so as to develop new skills continuously. They are alert to the needs of other team members and are empathetic about each other's strengths and areas for development. Since they know that these complementary skill sets are vital to their collective success, team members have a genuine interest in each other's development. We illustrate this phenomenon to our students by showing them the movie *Remember the Titans*, starring Denzel Washington. It's a great story of how a coach uses intellectual stimulation to build unity in a football team torn apart by racial strife. When the players finally come together, they recognize that their individual strengths and weaknesses can complement each other and make their team strong.

Through such intellectual stimulation, team members challenge the way that they work together. They encourage imagination and challenge assumptions underlying the team's processes and goals. By questioning assumptions, they expand the boundaries of what is appropriate to discuss. As a result, team members feel free to offer new ideas.

As in the case of the Beatles, team members take turns to lead the team whenever their skills and expertise become critical in achieving their goals. Members have enough trust in their current leader to become equally contributing followers. However, there is an implicit assumption that, when circumstances are changing, anyone from the team with a different set of skills can emerge as a temporary leader. This makes complementary skills such an important foundation to developing shared leadership. The key differences between groups and teams are summarized in Table 9.1.

Table 9.1   Differences Between Groups and Teams

Group	Team
Strong, clearly focused leader (of the group)	Shared leadership roles (leadership by the team)
Individual accountability	Individual and mutual accountability
Purpose same as that of the broader organizational mission	Specific team purpose reflecting the collective work products the team delivers
Runs efficient meetings	Encourages open-ended discussion and active problem-solving meetings
Individual work products	Collective work products
Measures effectiveness indirectly by its influence on others outside of the group	Measures effectiveness directly by the collective products
Discusses, decides, and delegates tasks with a "split the work" approach	Discusses, decides, and works interdependently to complete tasks together
Emphasis on "star player" or best individual in group	High level of pride and collective identity in the team
Potential for social loafing and free riding of slackers, off of highest performers in group	Developmental vehicle for all team members

Source: Belbin, R. M. (2004). *Management teams: Why they succeed or fail.* Oxford: Butterworth/Heinemann; and Katzenbach, J. R., & Smith, D. K. (1992). *The wisdom of teams: Creating the high-performance organization.* Boston: Harvard Business School Press.

Shared Leadership and the Miracle on Ice

One of the best ways to illustrate these differences between teams and groups and the importance of shared leadership in overcoming big challenges is to consider the 1980 U.S. Olympic hockey team, which won a gold medal against all odds. The story of their remarkable victory was made into a movie entitled *Miracle*, featuring Kurt Russell. The "Miracle on Ice" is the nickname given to their victory. A team of U.S. amateur and collegiate players, led by coach Herb Brooks, defeated the Soviet Union 4–3 in the semifinal round. The Soviets were considered to be the best international hockey team in the world. The United States went on to win the gold medal by beating Finland (4–2) in their final game. For those of you who are not familiar with it, the story goes like this:

> The United States team, composed of young collegiate players and amateurs, entered the competition seeded seventh in the final round of twelve teams that qualified for the Lake Placid Olympics. The Soviet Union was the favored team. Though classed as amateur, Soviet players essentially played professionally (the players were active-duty in the Red Army) in a well-developed league with excellent training facilities.... A year earlier the Soviet national team had routed the NHL All-Stars 6–0 to win the Challenge Cup....
>
> As in several previous games, the US team fell behind early. Vladimir Krutov deflected a slap shot by Aleksei Kasatonov past US goaltender Jim Craig to give the Soviets a 1–0 lead, and after Buzz Schneider scored for the United States to tie the game, the Soviets rallied again with a Sergei Makarov goal.
>
> Eruzione teed up the go-ahead goal. Down 2–1, Craig improved his play, turning away many Soviet shots before the US team had another shot on goal.... In the waning seconds of the first period, Dave Christian fired a slap shot on Tretiak. The Soviet goalie saved the shot but misplayed the rebound, and Mark Johnson scooped it past the goaltender to tie the score with one second left in the period.
>
> In the second period, Aleksandr Maltsev scored on a power play to make the score 3–2 for the Soviets, but Craig made numerous saves to keep the US in the game. Johnson scored again for the US, 8:39 into the final period, firing a loose puck past Myshkin to tie the score just as a power play was ending. Only a couple shifts later, Mark Pavelich passed to US captain Mike Eruzione, who was left undefended in the high slot. Eruzione fired a shot past Myshkin, who was screened by his own defenseman. This goal gave the US a

4–3 lead with exactly 10 minutes to play in the contest. Craig with-stood another series of Soviet shots to finish the match…. As the US team tried to clear the zone …, the crowd began to count down the seconds left. Sportscaster Al Michaels, who was calling the game … picked up on the countdown in his broadcast, and delivered his famous call: "… Eleven seconds, you've got ten seconds, the count-down going on right now! Morrow, up to Silk … five seconds left in the game … Do you believe in miracles? Yes!"[18]

Can you feel the energy of this exciting event? If you've never seen this amazing story of perhaps the greatest victory in sports history, we encourage you to view *Miracle* on demand, DVD, or YouTube.com. Without a doubt, the main driving force behind this incredibly played game was the team's coach, Herb Brooks, who coached with his tough love so beautifully (see Table 9.2). However, the players on the U.S. hockey team clearly demonstrated how teams differed from groups and what shared leadership is all about. So, let's go back to the four key differences we discussed earlier and now apply these to the Miracle on Ice.

First, the U.S. team's sole interest was about how they could work together to beat their Russian opponent. There was no "I" on the U.S. team. It was all about how "we" worked together to beat the best hockey team in the world. They weren't thinking about a fat NHL signing bonus they could enjoy after they won the Olympic game.

Second, the U.S. team consisted of young collegiate players and amateurs who had limited experiences playing at the international level. In contrast, Russian players were mostly professional hockey players who were serving in the military. Therefore, almost everyone speculated that it would take a miracle for the U.S. team to beat the Russians. However, what the U.S. team had was synergy. They became much larger than the sum of individual players. They played as a team, not as a bunch of collegiate and amateur players. The high level of synergy and shared leadership gave them the collective confidence they needed.

Third, each player felt a full responsibility to achieve their collective success. Thus, there was a sense of team accountability, not just individual accountability. Each member was not interested in criticizing the other members for their mis-takes. Instead, their interest was in figuring out how they best worked together to increase their team performance. In their minds, there was only "we" and "our" performance.

Fourth, since they weren't superstar NHL hockey players, everyone was interested in developing the skills they needed to win the game. They were also keenly aware of the expected role they should play to increase their collective performance. In contrast, the Russian team had many star players, such as Boris

Table 9.2   Leader Profile: Herb Brooks

The Soviet Union's national hockey team's dynasty ended at the 1980 Winter Olympic games in Lake Placid, New York, at the hands of Herb Brooks's novice U.S. team. The timing of this miraculous event was critical. America's collective self-concept was reeling from an array of bad events, including the fall of Saigon, Watergate, President Nixon's resignation, and poor economic conditions. Sensing that the United States needed an event to help restore American pride, the U.S. Olympic commission selected Brooks to coach the American hockey team.

Brooks was a no-nonsense, tough-as-nails taskmaster with passion and dedication to hockey as long and hard as a Minnesota winter. Brooks was born in St. Paul and played hockey for his high school team, which won the state championship in 1955. He went on to play for the University of Minnesota and U.S. Olympic teams. During the 1970s, Brooks coached the University of Minnesota hockey team to three national championships before his glorious moment in 1980. Brooks was on the verge of leading his team to a miracle.

In less than one year of preparation for the games, Brooks transformed a rag-tag group of maverick collegiate players into a disciplined and cohesive team. They exploited weaknesses in the Soviet team by using their speed to stay with the Soviet players and aggressively challenge them. They were proactive instead of reactive. Before the game with the Soviets, Brooks told his players, "You were born to be a hockey player. You were meant to be here. This moment is yours." Brooks got his team to believe in themselves and execute well. His blue-collar work ethic, intelligence, drive, and tough love inspired Team USA to defeat the Soviets and win the gold medal. Team USA's victory was dubbed the "Miracle on Ice" and is one of the most inspiring tales of sports team leadership in history. Brook's miraculous story teaches us to pursue our dreams knowing that passion, dedication, and a strong work ethic can make dreams come true.

Source: Bernstein, R. (2003). *Remembering Herbie: Celebrating the life and times of hockey legend Herb Brooks.* Cambridge, MN: Adventure Publications; and retrieved August 29, 2008, from http://www.herbbrooksfoundation.com/.

Mikhailov, who was considered one of the best right-wingers in the world, and Vladislav Tretiak, who was considered by many to be the best ice hockey goalie in the world at the time. These famous players were more interested in *their* ways of playing the game rather than thinking about developing complementary skills as a coherent team. Therefore, even if the Russian team had many more talented players, they couldn't generate synergy like their U.S. counterpart.

For these reasons, we believe that shared leadership is one of many important reasons that the U.S. Olympic team had such a memorable experience and achieved what many people believed to be the unthinkable game. Later, this victory was voted the greatest sports moment of the 20th century by *Sports Illustrated*.[19]

Levels of Team Development

The Miracle on Ice illustrates a team at the peak of its performance and development. Research indicates that groups and teams go through various stages of development, and the leadership displayed by their members changes depending upon the stage. These stages of development are also associated with different levels of performance, as shown in Table 9.3.

Social psychologist Bruce Tuckman provided the classic description of the stages of group development: forming, storming, norming, performing, and adjourning.[20] Additional scholars have considered these stages using different labels. In Table 9.3, we highlight models created and trained at the Center for Creative Leadership[21] and by leadership scholar Bruce Avolio to explain the dynamics and leadership styles associated with these stages.

Early in their life, groups form in an unstructured fashion. Members of groups at this stage ask the questions "Why am I here?" and "Do I want to be part of this group?" These questions highlight the members' need to maintain

Table 9.3   Levels of Team Development

Stage/Performance Level	Tuckman (1977) Concept	Center for Creative Leadership Concept	FRLD Concept (Avolio, 1999)
Early in group life/ lowest	Forming	Undifferentiation	Unstructured group (LF)
When deadline approaches/low	Storming	Differentiation	Semistructured group (MBE-P)
When deadline is imminent/ mediocre	Norming	Integration	Structured group (MBE-A + CR)
Due date/high	Performing	Synergy	Team (IC + IS)
Due date and beyond/ excellence	Excelling and then adjourning	Synergy squared	Highly developed team (II + IM)

their individuality. They frequently experience excitement, anticipation, and optimism along with confusion over roles, fear about outcomes, and anxiety over how they fit in the group. They take a laissez-faire approach to leadership of the group, and their performance is typically poor.

When the group's deadline for completing its project approaches, group members start to storm through confrontations with each other over expectations and roles. Members of groups at this stage ask the questions "Who are you?" and "Who's in charge?" These questions also highlight the members' need to assert their individuality. They typically begin to argue among themselves, choose sides, and become defensive. They posture for specific roles in the groups and start to become acquainted with each other's strengths and weaknesses. They take an MBE-P approach to leadership of their semistructured groups, and their performance level is typically low.

When the group's deadline is imminent, groups become structured by establishing norms and roles for their members and rewarding performance that meets expectations. The members of groups in this stage ask the question "How will we get the work done?" This question highlights the group members' shift in perspective taking from independence to interdependence and their need to integrate the knowledge, skills, and abilities of their members. They typically define roles more clearly, establish norms, and accept their members as part of the group. They reward each other with compliments and financial incentives when they meet goals. They become more cohesive and communicate more frequently and effectively, but may fall victim to groupthink. They use MBE-A and CR leadership behaviors to add structure to their work processes and interactions, and their performance reaches mediocre to acceptable levels.

When the group's deadline arrives, it is "show time." Groups at this stage morph into teams that no longer ask questions, but instead exclaim, "We've got it!" This expression of confidence highlights the synergy and optimal experiences achieved by members because they are part of the potent and cohesive team. These teams are very interactive in terms of both communication and collaboration. They thoroughly understand each other's strengths and areas for development. They are energized by the team's mission and take great pride in being part of their team. Their team becomes part of who they are as an individual. They take a transformational approach to leadership, and their performance is typically very high and exceeds all expectations.

You can now see how as groups develop into teams, their members progress up the FRLD model by becoming more active and willing to share their leadership with their colleagues. In the next section, we discuss how you can put FRLD into practice in your own team and build shared leadership. As more and more organizations use teams as their basic unit of operations, developing shared leadership through FRLD can give you a very important core competency you need to create sustainable growth in the future.

Putting FRLD Into Practice in Teams

We strongly believe that the behaviors associated with FRLD will put you in the front line of leaders who establish shared leadership and create high-performing teams. Therefore, we will highlight some behaviors that can be instrumental in building shared leadership. These behaviors include: (1) instill pride in team members for being associated with the team, (2) go beyond self-interest for the good of the team, (3) emphasize the importance of having a collective sense of mission, and (4) help my team members to develop their strengths.

Although every behavior associated with transformational leadership could potentially help you develop shared team leadership, we believe that these are more relevant and make the process more effective. Let's carefully examine each behavior with some examples.

Instill Pride in Team Members for Being Associated With the Team

Don taught two teams of U.S. Navy SEALs several years ago. SEALs are one of the most elite military units in the world. They distinguish themselves as an individually reliable, collectively disciplined, and highly skilled maritime force. Because of the dangers inherent in their mission, prospective SEALs go through what is considered by many military experts to be the toughest training in the world.[22] By working with the SEALs, Don got to know their beloved creed. We encourage you to carefully read the edited SEALs creed shown below (we italicized passages that we felt are especially relevant) as a way to reflect upon your own team and find a sense of pride associated with that of the SEALs:

> In times of war or uncertainty there is a *special breed of warrior ready to answer our Nation's call.* A common man with uncommon desire to succeed. Forged by adversity, *he stands alongside America's finest special operations forces* to serve his country, the American people, and protect their way of life. I am that man.
>
> *My loyalty to Country and Team is beyond reproach.* I humbly serve as a guardian to my fellow Americans always ready to defend those who are unable to defend themselves.
>
> *We expect to lead and be led. In the absence of orders I will take charge, lead my teammates and accomplish the mission.* I lead by example in all situations.

We demand discipline. We expect innovation. *The lives of my teammates and the success of our mission depend on me*—my technical skill, tactical proficiency, and attention to detail. My training is never complete.

Brave men have fought and died building the proud tradition and feared reputation that I am bound to uphold. In the worst of conditions, the legacy of my teammates steadies my resolve and silently guides my every deed. I will not fail.[23]

As the italicized sections of the above SEALs creed reveal, being a SEAL is all about pride. A pride that they are the toughest warriors in the world. A pride that they are the most elite military organization in the world. A pride that they defend their country at the front line of a battle ground. Since they instill the highest pride in being associated with the SEALs, everyone is expected to lead and be led at the same time. We believe that SEALs are an excellent example of shared leadership and pride is at the center of their operation. When was the last time you tried to instill pride in your team or organization? Do you think that your team members are proud of working in your team? What can you do to increase their sense of pride?

Go Beyond Self-Interest for the Good of the Team

Recall the Penn State Nittany Lions football team and their legendary coach Joe Paterno that we highlighted in Chapter 3. What makes the Nittany Lions strong is Paterno's aggressive effort to temper individual players' big and strong egos. One way he does this is by eliminating players' last names from the back of their jersey. This kind of de-individuation process is absolutely necessary for a leader to create shared leadership in a team. Such symbolic action shifts the attention of team members from their self-interest to the critical needs for the team to succeed.

When people work as part of a team, it is always tempting to maximize their personal outcome by engaging social loafing, as shown in Figure 9.4. When team members observe one or two people on the team doing this, it can create anger and betrayal. Soon, such feelings lead to a very common reaction like, "If she does it, I think I should be doing it too!" Then, it is a matter of time for the team to create a very negative norm signaling that it is OK to goof around or get a free ride. Therefore, it is important for you as the team leader to highlight the importance of teamwork and urge team members to put their self-interest behind them and work their hardest for the good of the team.

When team members begin thinking about their self-interest, it is impossible to develop shared leadership. Make the best interest of the team part of your team's culture. If necessary, create a symbolic action or event through which

Figure 9.4   Slacking off. Many hands make the work lighter. But many hands also make it easier for this group member to not carry her fair share of the workload.

team members are constantly reminded that they should put their self-interest behind them just, like what Joe Paterno does for his players.

Emphasize the Importance of Having a Collective Sense of Mission

As we have emphasized throughout this book, the best way to describe the current business environment is uncertainty. Several factors that have contributed to this high level of uncertainty include global economic downturns, housing market declines, credit crises, fluctuations of crude oil prices and currency exchanges, record-breaking trade deficits, and crises on Wall Street. As the outside environment becomes more uncertain, leaders in organizations need to instill a collective sense of mission through shared vision and leadership. According to leadership authors James Kouzes and Barry Posner, who wrote *The Leadership Challenge*, collective mission creates a sense of belonging in the times of uncertainty.

> This communion of purpose, this commemoration of our dreams, helps to bind us together. It reminds us of what it means to be a part of this collective effort. It joins us together in the human family. This sense of belonging is particularly key in tumultuous times, whatever the cause of the tumult.[24]

We are currently living in tumultuous times. Consider the threats of terrorism, economic collapse, a depleted environment, housing crisis, and businesses led to ruin. As Barack Obama assumed presidential leadership of the United States, he was dubbed "the Great Uniter." His success in leading a diverse nation and world will depend, in part, upon his ability to create a collective mission. That collective mission must go beyond building hope to addressing the causes of the tumult with pragmatic solutions to the world's problems.

Collective mission was key to the renowned NFL coach Vince Lombardi's success in building a dynasty for his legendary Green Bay Packers. According to Lombardi, "Teamwork is what the Green Bay Packers were all about. They didn't do it for individual glory. They did it because they loved one another." He considered individual commitment to a team effort to be what makes a team, company, society, and civilization work.[25]

How often do you emphasize the importance of having a collective mission when you attend a team meeting? Do you only emphasize personal benefits and interests that your team members would enjoy when their project is completed successfully? When you focus on personal benefits rather than collective benefits and accomplishment, members are not likely to develop shared leadership and put the team ahead of their self-interest. Sharing leadership is a time-consuming process to develop, and your team members are not likely to commit themselves if they do not share a common mission and vision. So, next time when you have a team meeting, put aside everything you have on your agenda. Spend time on the collective mission and make sure that every team member is fully committed to it before anyone does anything.

Help Your Team Members to Develop Their Strengths

Leadership icon Jack Welch, the former CEO of General Electric, is well known for his leadership philosophy regarding how to use company talent. He believes that his most important job is to recruit the best people, give them the best opportunity, allocate resources they need to perform their job, and then get out of their way.[26] How could he empower people to the level he did? His belief was that when you are surrounded by A-level employees, all you need to do is to give them lots of opportunities to develop their strengths so that they become self-motivated. We believe that this is a form of shared leadership. When team members identify a set of skills they must develop and are committed to take full responsibility for their collective work, they are leading and being led at the same time, just like the Navy SEALs.

Now, the important question becomes: "How do you go about helping your team members develop their strengths?" The trick is for you to conduct astute observations and identify team members' potential that they may not even realize themselves. Do you remember the science and math teacher who gave John one of the most motivational moments in life when he was in the seventh grade? All he did was to observe John for a while, recognize his strengths and weaknesses, and give John work he would be enjoying and doing well. The rest of the story is straightforward. So, we want to challenge you do the same to your team members so that you can become the next great teacher and developer of talent in your teams.

When team members have enough skills and talents, are self-motivated through empowerment, and are given the opportunity to work together toward a common goal, your role as a leader can be helped significantly. We advise you to become more comfortable with your newly defined role in the context of shared leadership. Forget about a sense of control. Avoid having nightmares that your team project is out of control. Don't panic. The less you have a desire to manage, the greater the chance you can develop shared leadership in your team. Trust your judgment and that of your team members. They will do well. All you need to do is to nurture their strengths. That is essential to practicing FRLD and building shared leadership. It is also essential to using FRLD as a strategic intervention in organizations, which we will discuss in the next chapter.

Summary Questions and Reflective Exercises

1. This exercise uses LEGO™ or similar building block toys to demonstrate how behaviors in the FRLD model influence group/team processes and outcomes. Four groups compete to design and showcase a new jet airplane: the Boeing 777½. First, separate the LEGOs into four bags, each with an equal amount of colored blocks. In this exercise, each block has a corresponding price:
   a. Black and white = $ 0
   b. Red = $1
   c. Blue = $2
   d. Yellow = $3

   Each block (regardless of color) has an additional $1 labor assembly cost. Next, each team has five team member roles:

   Team leader—Each team leader portrays either laissez-faire, MBE-P, MBE-A, or transformational leadership behavior. Leaders should display their appropriate FRLD behaviors based on their personality and preferred styles. For example, the laissez-faire leader should simply hand the bag of LEGOs to the team members and leave the room. The

MBE-P leader should sit back and only respond when asked questions. The MBE-A leader should micromanage the task using a drill sergeant style. The transformational leader should energize, challenge, coach, and help the team accomplish its task.

Accountant—Team member responsible for costing out the final product in terms of labor and materials. A $24 budget restriction has been imposed by the client, although the last plane assembled cost $35.

Design engineer—Team member responsible for making sure the plane meets certain technical specifications. All planes must have the following parts: two wings, a fuselage, and a tail. The plane must resemble a real airplane and be proportional.

Production engineer—Team member responsible for listing step-by-step assembly instructions to pass on to manufacturing. Directions must be clear enough that anyone could duplicate your plane.

Marketing associate—Team member responsible for creating an attractive advertisement poster for the jet airplane, complete with artwork and a catchy slogan.

Once team members have selected their roles, the teams have 20 minutes to complete their jet airplanes. Once 20 minutes have passed, each team leader makes a formal presentation to the entire group of the team's final product, accounting costs, engineering plan, and marketing advertisement. Team members can then comment on what it was like working under their leader. How did each of the FRLD behaviors used in these teams relate to the quality of the final product and the satisfaction level of the team?

2. Teams that share leadership often begin by committing to a common goal for a project and agreeing on how it will be best achieved. One way to accomplish this is to create a *team charter*. Begin by assembling your team and discussing the nature of the project. Discuss and agree upon the following items that will comprise your team charter:

   a. Define the *mission* or fundamental purpose of your project.

   b. Identify the *shared vision* or image of what your team would like to see happen as a result of your project.

   c. List and define the *shared values* that will guide the key behaviors and work values of your team.

   d. Agree upon the *shared goal* that the team members would like to achieve as a result of the project.

   e. List the *shared objectives* or important milestones that the team must reach in order to achieve its goal.

   f. Identify the *shared tasks* that need to be performed in order to achieve the objectives and goal.

    g. List the *shared assignments*, identifying who is responsible for completing each task and when each task is due.

    h. *Evaluate* the progress made on the shared assignments by agreeing upon the performance metrics/measures to be used to gauge progress.

    Assemble this information and draft your team charter. Share the team charter with the team members for their review. Based on their feedback, revise as necessary. When you reach final consensus, ask each team member to sign their names to the team charter to indicate their commitment to the team project.

3. List five characteristics you associate with a team. Think of the last team you worked on and explain whether or not the team displayed these characteristics. Describe how the leadership of that team helped or hindered these characteristics.

4. Explain the general characteristics, actions of the members, and reactions of members in unstructured groups of individuals, semistructured groups of individuals, structured groups, teams, and highly developed teams.

5. For the stages of group/team development, identify the behaviors in the FRLD model that are associated with each stage of development. Explain why these behaviors are associated with the stage being discussed.

6. Create a DVD or video clip illustrating unstructured, structured, and team leadership. Each example clip should be no more than five minutes. In your role playing and videotaping session, be careful to carefully plan and illustrate the leader's and team members' verbal and nonverbal behavior, their interaction, the context or situation, and the outcome or degree of effectiveness of the team. Which FRLD behaviors did the leader and team members display in each stage of development?

7. Review the group and team dynamics literature to determine how each of the following factors influences the stage of development of your group/team. How does your group/team measure up on these factors? What specific FRLD behaviors can you use to influence each of these factors?

    a. Drive and cohesiveness

    b. Self-efficacy of the team members

    c. Balance between individual and group roles

    d. Conflict resolution procedures/policy within the team

    e. Social loafing or free riding within the team

    f. Competition within and between teams

    g. Cooperation within and between teams

    h. Types of power and influence tactics used in the team

    i. Styles of decision making in the team

    j. Individualism versus collectivism of the team

    k. Task versus relational focus within the team

    l. Group potency or team efficacy level

    m. Trust level within the team

    n. Shared purpose

    o. Performance/productivity level

    p. Satisfaction of members within the team

8. Identify and reflect upon the three most significant positive and negative critical incidents that occurred in your group/team during the last three months. What did you learn from each incident? What FRLD behavior influenced the incidents? For each of the negative critical incidents, think about what you would have wanted to occur instead. How would you use FRLD behaviors to create an optimal outcome in the future?

9. After reviewing the group/team dynamics factors listed in exercise 7, select the ten most relevant and important factors for your team(s) given your organizational and leadership context. Clearly define each of these factors in a clear, crisp, and short sentence. Then create a team *peer review form* that assesses how each team member is perceived by other team members regarding these factors or is effective in helping the team reach its goals. Each item you choose can be rated as simply as yes or no, followed by some space to provide additional written comments.

10. Identify a famous and successful group or team from business, entertainment, sports, or the performance arts. What is their stage of group/team development? Why? What FRLD behaviors do they use in their interactions? Is leadership shared within the team or is it provided by one individual? If possible, demonstrate their team behavior and leadership using film or Internet video clips. What lessons from your example can you apply to the teams in which you currently work?

Notes

1. Hamel, G. (2007). *The future of management.* Boston: Harvard Business School Press.
2. Hamel (2007). As cited in Note 1.
3. Schmitt, B. H. (2007). *Big think strategy: How to leverage bold ideas and leave small thinking behind.* Boston: Harvard Business School Press.
4. Katzenbach, J. R. (1997). *Teams at the top: Unleashing the potential of both teams and individual leaders.* Boston: Harvard Business School Press.
5. Dirk, K. T. (2000). Trust in leadership and team performance: Evidence from NCAA basketball. *Journal of Applied Psychology, 85,* 1004–1012.

6. Retrieved September 8, 2008, from http://www.rollingstone.com/news/story/6595610/1_sgt_peppers_lonely_hearts_club_band.
7. Lennon, J., McCartney, P., Harrison, G., & Starr, R. (2000). *The Beatles anthology.* New York: Chronicle Books; and Turner, S. (2005). *A hard day's write: Stories behind every Beatles song* (3rd ed.). New York: Harper.
8. Bales, R. F. (1954). In conference. *Harvard Business Review, 32,* 44–50.
9. Waldersee, R., & Eagleson, G. (1996). *The efficacy of distributed leadership in implementing change.* Unpublished manuscript, Australian Graduate School of Management, University of New South Wales.
10. Pearce, C., & Sims, H. (2002). Vertical versus shared leadership as predictors of the effectiveness of change management teams: An examination of aversive, directive, transactional, transformational, and empowering leader behavior. *Group Dynamics: Theory, research, and practice, 6,* 172–197.
11. Avolio, B. J. (1999). *Full leadership development: Building the vital forces in organizations.* Thousand Oaks, CA: Sage.
12. Avolio (1999). As cited in Note 11.
13. Jung, D., & Sosik, J. (2003). Group potency and collective efficacy: Examining their predictive validity, level of analysis, and effects of performance feedback on future group performance. *Group & Organization Management, 28,* 366–391.
14. Spink, K. S. (1990). Collective efficacy in the sport setting. *International Journal of Sport Psychology, 21,* 380–395.
15. Feltz, D., & Lirgg, A. (1998). Perceived team and player efficacy in hockey. *Journal of Applied Psychology, 83,* 557–564.
16. Sportsline.com. (2004). *Joe Namath's hall of fame induction speech.* Retrieved October 8, 2008, from http://ww1.sportsline.com/u/fans/celebrity/namath/super/hallfame.htm.
17. Avolio (1999). As cited in Note 11.
18. Wikipedia.com. (2008). *Miracle on ice.* Retrieved October, 7, 2008, from http://en.wikipedia.org/wiki/Miracle_on_Ice.
19. Wikipedia.com. (2008). As cited in Note 18.
20. Tuckman, B. W., & Jensen, M. A. C. (1977). Stages of small group development revisited. *Group & Organization Management, 2,* 419–427.
21. Retrieved October 19, 2008, from http://www.ccl.org/leadership/programs/LTIOverview.aspx.
22. Retrieved October 8, 2008, from http://www.seal.navy.mil/seal/.
23. Retrieved October 8, 2008, from http://www.seal.navy.mil/seal/PDF/Seal.Creed.pdf.
24. Kouzes, J. M., & Posner, B. Z. (2002). *The leadership challenge.* San Francisco: Jossey-Bass.
25. Lombardi Jr., V. (2003). *The essential Vince Lombardi: Words and wisdom to motivate, inspire, and win.* New York: McGraw-Hill.
26. Slater, R. (2003). *29 leadership secrets from Jack Welch.* New York: McGraw-Hill.

Chapter 10

Full Range Leadership Development for Strategic, Social, and Environmental Initiatives

> Show me the business man or institution not guided by sentiment and service, by the idea that "he profits most who serves best," and I will show you a man or an outfit that is dead or dying.
>
> **—B. F. Harris**

It was summer 2008. As the bright morning sun rose on the shimmering Philadelphia skyline, the City of Brotherly Love was once again coming back to life. Hawkers, walkers, and workers were hustling and bustling on its busy streets, filled with the flurry of buses, cabs, trucks, and cars. Echoing in the distance were the sounds of trains, bringing in tired workers, scrambling for their morning coffee, while their bleary eyes were glued to their Blackberries and PDAs. For one downtown resident, the city's morning flurry brought on a rush of enthusiasm and energy. Robert Lockwood emerged from his Center City home invigorated by his new strategic initiative to produce profound change in higher education.

As a partner at the Gallup Organization, Lockwood worked to help schools, such as Harvard University, Nova Southeastern University, and Drexel University, enhance their strategic planning processes through better brand imaging. His job involved building strong relationships with college constituents, including students, alumni, faculty, administration, community leaders, and local government. Lockwood asked these groups about the brand image of their schools and examined what respondents perceive their school's identity to be. In this way, Lockwood solicited input and opinion, thereby pulling constituents into the school's leadership system. Lockwood worked to tear down the traditional silos of isolation to instead promote communication and collaboration among these constituent groups. This enables school leaders to reach consensus on what brand image they aspire to and build a strategy to reach that goal.

Lockwood is an excellent communicator who uses inspirational motivation to woo his audiences with his vision of change. He argues that achieving an excellent brand image requires dramatic institutional change. Of course, bringing about such fundamental change is no easy task because it involves capturing people's hearts, minds, and souls. According to Lockwood, rational persuasion is not good enough. He believes people need to become emotionally committed to change to generate the passion, trust, engagement, and collaboration associated with effective organizations. While intellectual stimulation may help with the rational side of promoting change, Lockwood acknowledges that inspirational motivation is the key to success when it comes to organizational change efforts. In fall 2008, Lockwood left Gallup and moved on to start princetongreen.org, a strengths-based organization that helps others save energy.

Robert Lockwood's story underscores the belief that an organization's reputation is a valuable intangible asset. This asset has to be built through the emotional and psychological commitment from people within the organizations. When employees are committed to their jobs, it is reflected in their attitudes and dedication toward customers, which in turn makes their customers happy and satisfied. When customers are satisfied, they become repeat customers who spread positive word-of-mouth advertising about your organization. When customers do this, they become evangelists for you.

Many successful companies, such as Harley-Davidson, Apple, Best Buy, and Lexus, know exactly how they can make their customers loyal. For example, Lexus provides luxurious dealerships that treat customers as VIPs and surveys its customers about their experiences during service visits. From a strategic standpoint, this is one way organizations can differentiate themselves from others and stand out as something special.[1] Because emotional and psychological processes are key motivational mechanisms of Full Range Leadership Development (see Chapter 2), it makes sense to apply FRLD principles to strategic initiatives in your organization and community. This chapter shows you how to do this. Let's start learning about this process by examining the case of a giant in the field of information technology.

Steve Jobs and the Resurrection of Apple

Building brands is a task Steve Jobs knows well. In the early days of Apple, Jobs and co-founder Steve Wozniak succeeded in creating a unique personal computer that was wholeheartedly embraced by school students and computer enthusiasts. Emboldened by his masterful salesmanship and showmanship, Jobs proclaimed that Apple was on a "mission from God." They believed that their work was vitally important for improving life for humanity. This motivated Apple engineers to work tirelessly to create computers that were technologically sophisticated and elegant—what Jobs refers to as "insanely great." He also tried to appeal to customers by communicating his personal vision of "computers for everyone," thereby creating customer loyalty. This egalitarian edict sparked the hearts and imaginations of businesspeople and school students alike. Apple's customers have always loved its products, to the point of being cult-like fanatics hopelessly smitten by Apple products' design features and performance. This intense brand loyalty is what the Gallup Organization refers to as a high level of customer engagement.[2]

Following its initial success competing against IBM and its PC, Apple lost market share with what some believed were overpriced Macintosh or Mac products. Apple had difficulty meeting market demands, which left a bad impression on customers. Internal strife then began to brew within the Apple boardroom. A struggle between Jobs and then-CEO John Scully resulted in Jobs being forced out of Apple in 1985. Over his career, Jobs has been well known for his domineering and sometimes dictatorial style, complete with forceful intimidation of employees, temperamental behavior, and no tolerance for people, processes, or products that were not "insanely great." Jobs' complex personality illustrates the point that charismatic leaders can be directive or participative, collaborative or controlling, manipulative and even narcissistic.

After leaving Apple, Jobs went on to start NeXT Computer while Apple continued to flounder under a succession of ineffective CEOs who led with a transactional style. With a low stock price and an unhealthy financial position, Apple was in serious trouble and needed a charismatic savior. In 1996, Apple purchased NeXT and Jobs returned to the helm as its CEO. It is then that he led a number of brilliant strategic moves. First came integration of NeXT technologies to develop lightening-fast operating systems. Then Jobs turned his attention to expanding Apple's products and service lines by reframing his business into more than simply a computer company. Its new domain now includes telecommunications and music as well as computers. For the next 10 years after returning as CEO of Apple, Jobs inspired the company to introduce eye-catching products such as the iMac, iPod, and iPhone, and its stock price rose from about $5 to $150 per share. Eventually, Apple topped the "Most Admired Companies in the

U.S." ranking by Fortune. Apple's partnership with rival Microsoft opened the door for more applications to be run on Apple's products. Jobs emphasized not only innovation, performance, and design elegance, but also delivering work products on time. Jobs also initiated a "green" initiative to promote environmentally friendly shipping and recycling of Apple's products.[3]

These strategic shifts resulted in unprecedented success for Apple and its shareholders. And they illustrate the use of several aspects of FRLD concepts. We see inspirational motivation in Jobs' ability to envision and recreate Apple as a telecommunications products company. He achieved this by foreseeing and setting trends with his vision. As he stated in his keynote speech at the 2007 Macworld Conference and Expo, "There's an old Wayne Gretzky quote that I love. 'I skate to where the puck is going to be, not where it has been.' And we've always tried to do that at Apple. Since the very very beginning. And we always will."

Perhaps Steve Jobs' most defining behavior as a transformational leader is his ability to challenge his employees intellectually. His intellectual stimulation has been a key success factor in Apple's consistent introduction of new and cutting-edge technology products and services that wow its customers. In 2003, Jobs was diagnosed with pancreatic cancer and has recently struggled with subsequent health issues. At the time of this writing, Jobs appears to have mellowed a bit and has moved away from his aggressive leadership style. By sharing life lessons with the audience, he even displayed individualized consideration in his graduation speech given at Stanford University in 2005. Apple's newfound embracing of environmentally friendly ways of shipping and disposing of its products is further evidence of individualized consideration deployed as a socially responsible strategic initiative.

Strategic Leadership Defined

Top corporate leaders like Steve Jobs are responsible for creating wealth for their shareholders. They do this by increasing profits and stock price and by creating a sustainable growth plan for the future. Of course, they can't do this alone. They have to motivate organizational members to create the strategies, structures, markets, processes, and talent pools required to achieve their financial goals. However, these exceptional CEOs possess a special set of perceptional and thinking abilities, along with a vast relevant knowledge base, and excellent interpersonal competencies and leadership behaviors. These resources combined enable the most effective leaders to predict trends among customers and in the market and then create products and services that satisfy these new needs. The capacity to orchestrate complex business processes and to leverage these opportunities into financial rewards for shareholders is called *strategic leadership*. It involves the abilities, skills, behaviors, and processes required to anticipate and prepare an organization for its future and add to its prosperity.

We have written elsewhere that top leaders often focus on achieving these goals by applying aspects of FRLD.[4] In this chapter, we explain how top leaders, such as Indra Nooyi (see Table 10.1), use aspects of FRLD to enhance customer relationships and engagement, promote employee learning and growth, and improve operational efficiency. As a result of these leadership effects, an organization's financial performance should increase.[5]

Strategic Leadership and the Balanced Scorecard

A useful framework for understanding how FRLD can be applied in strategic leadership initiatives is the balanced scorecard. Professors Richard Kaplan and David Norton developed the *balanced scorecard* as a performance management tool to plan, execute, and monitor organizational strategy. It works by encouraging organizations to measure their success from customer, employee, operational, and financial perspectives. Similar to the assumption that leaders are much more likely to influence bottom-line performance indirectly through followers and processes influencing profits, the balanced scorecard assumes that organizations should focus on planning for and measuring things that influence financial outcomes over time (e.g., customer engagement, employee engagement, cycle time, waste, production and management efficiency). These factors influence financial outcomes and are called *lead indicators* of performance, while the financial outcomes themselves are *lag indicators* because they are a direct result of the lead indicators.[6]

We believe that strategic leadership should involve identifying and communicating a vision that can be translated into several organizational objectives and more specific goals that are attained. These goals can be measured and monitored by sorting them into the four perspectives of the balanced scorecard:

- *Customer perspective*—Objectives, goals, and measures indicating the quality of relationships with customers and their view of the organization's products and services. Sample measures include market share, market growth, and customer engagement. The Gallup Organization's CE11 survey measures customer engagement by assessing customers' perceptions of confidence, integrity, pride, and passion related to an organization's products or services.[7]
- *Innovation and learning perspective*—Objectives, goals, and measures indicating the quality of relationships with employees and how they view their development of knowledge, skills and abilities, motivation, and commitment. Sample measures include trust, skills inventory, innovation and

Table 10.1   Leader Profile: Indra Nooyi

Indra Nooyi, CEO of the global giant PepsiCo, Inc., is a prime example of down-to-earth charm, frankness, and business savvy that makes for effective strategic leadership. She is listed on the *Time 100* and *Fortune* and *Forbes* lists of most influential and powerful leaders. As Pepsi's first Indian and female CEO, Nooyi is a role model for minorities hoping to attain top positions in organizations. Her strategic leadership skills were honed through graduate work at Yale University, and a swift career progression at Boston Consulting Group, Motorola, ABB (the huge multinational Asea Brown Boveri), and Pepsi. She joined Pepsi in 1994 as head of corporate strategy.

Nooyi blends transformational and transactional leadership to maximize her firm's performance. She introduced change in the lineup of subsidiaries owned by Pepsi by spinning off its restaurant businesses. The popular press reported that Pepsi's annual revenues rose 72% under her leadership as CFO, and net profit more than doubled between 2000 and 2007 due to her brilliant strategic moves as CEO. Now she's focusing on international sales growth.

In a speech she gave to students of Dartmouth University, Nooyi offered several tips for successful global leadership:

- Use change proactively to create your environment, rather than using it to merely adapt to your environment (this philosophy is essential to inspirational motivation in many multinational firms).

- Identify and leverage your core competencies (these strengths can be built through individually considerate strategic and HR initiatives).

- Set clear financial goals and make decisions rationally—not emotionally (transactional contingent reward leadership is based on this principle).

- Plan, plan, and plan again, with a healthy dose of hope (goal setting + inspirational motivation is a powerful leadership mix).

- Finance and accounting numbers are important, but people are the most important factor for shaping your success (always build upon a base of transactional leadership with the 4Is of transformational leadership).

These are good lessons to remember when thinking about using FRLD as a strategic intervention in your organization.

Source: McKay, B. (2008, September 11). PepsiCo CEO adapts to tough climate. *Wall Street Journal*, pp. B1, B6; retrieved August 29, 2008, from http://www.tuck.dartmouth.edu/news/releases/pr20020925_nooyi.html.; and Sosik, J. J., & Jung, D. I. (1994). A theoretical consideration of leadership and the global heterarchy. *Journal of Leadership & Organizational Studies*, *1*, 10–27.

creativity measures, attitude surveys, and employee engagement. Gallup's Q^{12} survey measures employee engagement from self-reports of employees' perceptions of what intrinsic rewards they get from their job, what effort they put into their job, whether they belong in their organizational role, and how they can grow in their role.[8]

- *Internal business process*—Objectives, goals, and measures indicating the efficiency and effectiveness of the organization's processes, practices, and manufacturing/service systems. Sample measures include cycle time, waste, and sundry efficiency metrics. At Ann Taylor Stores Corporation, computer programs display salespersons' performance metrics for average sales per hour, unit sales, and dollars per transaction. These metrics help managers schedule who should work when and for how long.[9]
- *Financial perspective*—Objectives, goals, and measures indicating how accountants and financial analysts view an organization's cash flow, financial condition, and investment rating. Sample measures include net income, return on investment, assets, debt, stock price, and economic value-added (EVA™). Companies like Ford, General Motors, and Disney use EVA™, a metric developed by Stern Stewart & Company, to assess after-tax profit less the cost of capital used to generate profits.[10]

We believe that the best starting point for the balanced scorecard process is an organization's vision. Companies differ in their vision. For example, BP's vision is "beyond petroleum." Nike's is to "crush the enemy." Microsoft's is "a personal computer on every desk in every home." Even the engineering department of the Ritz Carlton on Amelia Island, Florida, has a vision: "To go boldly where no hotel has gone before—free of all defects." While all of these visions are interesting and somewhat grandiose, we see them as being pretty vague. This limits their usefulness.

The balanced scorecard process begins by translating the vision into more specific organizational objectives from the perspectives shown in Figure 10.1. Top leaders communicate the vision and its importance to all employees. In developing strategy, a leadership team should connect each of the objectives and their specific goals within these perspectives to the organization's vision and its mission. They then drill down these goals through the business units to divisions to departments to teams to individuals. This aligns the goals across organizational levels, encourages coordination and collaboration, and promotes accountability. One thing that CEOs sometimes forget often is the importance of *shared* vision. They tend to believe that once they communicate their vision, employees accept and cherish it immediately. However, to make your vision a collective and shared commitment of the overall organization, you must communicate it and reinforce it through various means, such as socialization, evaluation, and compensation.

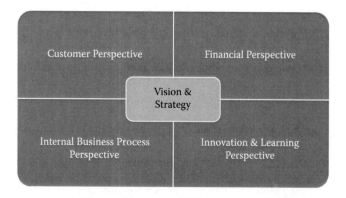

Figure 10.1 Strategic leadership tool. Transformational leaders use a balanced approach to strategic planning that considers perspectives of the customer, employees, operations experts, and financiers.

As part of their strategic business planning, the leadership team then works with associates to map out *cause-and-effect relationships* between the goals. They create a strategy map in the form of a flowchart. This map charts organizational strategy for achieving the vision, as illustrated in Figure 10.2. The links on the strategy map represent hypothesized relationships between measures within and between the four perspectives of the balanced scorecard. Once appropriate measures are identified for the goals, the leadership team collects data from these measures over time. These data can be used in linear regression models to test the causal assumptions in the strategy map. This process allows leaders to examine the validity of their assumptions supporting their strategic initiatives and revise their strategy map whenever necessary.

For example, the leadership team may wonder whether employee engagement, depicted in the strategy maps shown in Figure 10.2, actually leads to customer engagement and a higher level of employee participation in ideas generation for continuous improvement. Results of the statistical analysis testing relationships between these measures can determine whether money should be spent on improving employee engagement. This process could squeeze speculation out of decision-making processes. Only carefully collected and analyzed data can provide an objective answer to such questions. Therefore, leaders should use data-driven decisions and integrated strategic planning models to align their strategy and vision. This process provides a feedback loop that allows the top leadership to learn from the feedback and adjust their strategy appropriately to maximize their financial outcomes over time.

Mutual of Omaha has successfully used this process in its strategic planning. According to the late Jack Weekly, former chairman and CEO of Mutual of

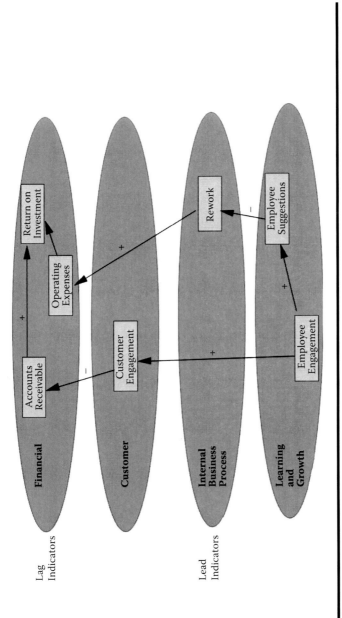

Figure 10.2   Cause and effect. Strategic maps present hypothesized relationships between key metrics within and between the customer, innovation and learning, internal business process, and financial perspectives.

Omaha, his top leadership team first talked about what it would require to reenergize the company and attain their vision. As a service company, they identified five key objectives to meet: growth and customer loyalty (customer perspective), profitability and financial discipline (financial perspective), and accountability (innovation and learning perspective). They fleshed out their key objectives with more specific goals and then determined how to measure progress on each of these goals. For example, they partnered with the Gallup Organization to use Gallup's Q^{12} survey to assess accountability through employee engagement.

Mutual of Omaha's balanced scorecard "was designed so that operating units at all levels with targets and measures could then develop their own scorecards that were in sync with larger corporate goals and objectives." This alignment strategy allowed employees across all business units to see their contributions and responsibility for working toward the overall corporate goals. This helps employees see how their daily work contributes to the overall vision of the company in terms of the five objectives.[11] This strategic process accomplished for Mutual of Omaha what inspirational leaders do when they show followers the importance of their work. Indeed, FRLD can augment strategic leadership in many ways.[12]

How FRLD Enhances This Process

Kaplan and Norton originally designed the balanced scorecard as a performance management and strategy tool that uses principles of management-by-objectives (MBO).[13] This strategic management approach involves aligning a company's objectives at various levels of an organization and monitoring progress toward meeting those objectives. You're probably thinking that this sounds very much like a transactional approach to strategic leadership. If so, you're correct. That's because MBO's emphasis is on goal setting (contingent reward leadership) and actively monitoring progress toward achieving these goals (active management-by-exception leadership). However, transformational aspects of the FRLD model also can be applied to maximize benefits of the balanced scorecard system as a strategic leadership tool.

When you translate the vision into organizational goals, you need to understand the essence of the vision to make the translation process more effective. You should use aspects of inspirational motivation and intellectual stimulation to inspire and challenge your associates to define what objectives are most important to achieve as they work toward attaining the vision. Your vision should be about where your company wants to be in the future. It reflects the future environment and works in concert with your organization's mission (i.e., core values, purpose, and reason for existence).

When you are tasked with communicating the vision and linking it to individual performance, idealized influence, inspirational motivation, and contingent reward leadership are appropriate. Through idealized influence, leaders should talk about the importance of organizational values, trust, personal sacrifice, and commitment. You have to show to your employees that these elements are essential to achieve the high level of performance required to attain the vision. Through inspirational motivation, leaders should present the vision in a clear and evocative way—one that energizes followers to work diligently to achieve the vision.

Providing contingent rewards is another great way to motivate associates to begin working hard toward the goal. Contingent reward leadership also provides feedback and learning through a cycle of goal setting, monitoring of results, giving advice derived from results, providing rewards or punishments as necessary, and fine-tuning aspects of strategy, including goals and the actions needed to attain them.

Aspects of FRLD are also helpful in coordinating the people, processes, and resources required to attain objectives and goals across the four perspectives of the balanced scorecard. In regard to the *customer perspective*, you may be interested in providing perceived value to the most desired customer groups and keeping them satisfied and engaged. You can attain this goal via one or some combination of three strategic approaches: operational excellence, customer intimacy, or product leadership. You can promote operational excellence by displaying inspirational motivation behavior that raises the bar on performance levels and contingent reward behavior that compensates associates for meeting elevated performance standards. You can create customer intimacy by encouraging sales staff to display individually considerate behaviors that ask customers what they value in a product or service and use this feedback in improving products or services. You can promote product leadership by displaying intellectually stimulating behaviors that promote creativity and innovation in research and development and deliver new products and services that are cutting edge and cost-effective.

Regarding the *internal business process perspective*, you need to create sustainable processes that develop and deliver your products and services more efficiently and effectively. You can attain this goal by examining all the activities and processes, eliminating those that do not add value to the product or service, and expanding those that do. You should examine the following functional areas: operations management, customer management, innovation, and regulatory/ social responsibility. For operations management improvement, you can use intellectual stimulation to question assumptions regarding asset utilization and supply chain management processes. Ask your associates, "What do we need to eliminate to make our operational processes more efficient and effective?" For customer management improvement, you can encourage salespeople to use individually considerate behavior with their customers. For innovation, intellectual stimulation is the obvious choice. And for regulatory and social responsibility initiatives, you can use active management-by-exception behavior to enforce compliance with laws, and intellectual stimulation to think of new ways to produce and deliver products and services in an environmentally friendly manner, much like Steve Jobs did at Apple.

In regard to the *innovation and learning perspective*, you may be interested in developing the internal skills and capacities required to support your organization's internal business process functions. You can attain this goal via job design, systems development and maintenance, and organizational development (i.e., addressing culture and climate issues). You can promote innovative job design initiatives through individually considerate behavior that identifies talent and fits it into the right role in the organization, and provide coaching and mentoring to turn associates' talents into strengths. Or, you can use intellectual stimulation to redesign jobs to offer more task variety, task meaningfulness, feedback, and autonomy.

You can support systems development and maintenance with a combination of active management-by-exception, contingent reward, and intellectually stimulating leadership. Intellectual stimulation is helpful when creating new systems and fine-tuning them over time. Active management-by-exception leadership may be necessary to ensure that critical systems do not fail by identifying and correcting problems before they occur. Contingent reward leadership is useful in planning for, monitoring, and rewarding systems development projects that are often burdensome to manage due to their size and lifestyle.

You can help develop a positive organizational culture and climate by displaying idealized leadership that role models high expectations for performance and ethics, inspirational motivation that champions teamwork, and individualized consideration that values diversity and builds a supportive work environment. After all, it's your employees who make most things happen. As Herb Kelleher, charismatic co-founder and former chairman and CEO of Southwest Airlines once said, "Who comes first? The employees, customers or shareholders? That's never been an issue to me. The employees come first. If they are happy, satisfied, and energetic …" Herb's thoughts teach us that it is *your* responsibility to build a positive culture and climate that values your employees and keeps them happy.

Regarding the *financial perspective*, you may want to see if your strategy and the processes for its execution are indeed creating wealth for your shareholders. Here the focus is on bottom-line improvement of the organization. However, you need to consider this outcome to be long term in nature since it results from the activities described in the customer, innovation and learning, and internal business process perspectives.

Because of its long-term timeframe, you need to recognize whether your organization is in a period of rapid growth, sustenance, or harvest. For the *development and growth period*, you should emphasize sales growth and volume, and acquisition of new customers. Here the building of relationships with customers is critical. You should use individually considerate behavior to understand their unique needs and keep them engaged. Contingent reward leadership can be used to motivate your sales force. For the *sustenance period*, you should emphasize managing operations and controlling costs by examining return on investment and operational efficiency metrics. Here forms of transactional leadership, namely, management-by-exception active and contingent reward, are appropriate for identifying errors in systems, fixing them, and rewarding behavior that meets performance goals. For the *harvest period*, you may wish to reap the benefits from the strategies you have sowed. Your focus should be on cash flow, payback periods, and sales volume. Here the analysis of the degree of success of the strategic initiatives is imperative.[14] At this point, you should display a blend of management-by-exception active and intellectual stimulation. Carefully analyze the results of your strategic implementations, with the expectation that your people, plans, and processes have added to your organization's bottom line and the accumulated wealth of your shareholders.

Triple Bottom Line

In 2007, the United Nations ratified the notion of a *triple bottom line* as a standard for urban and community accounting. This approach to public sector accounting is a way to expand the traditional notion of organizational effectiveness beyond measures of economic success to include environmental and social measures as well. The triple-bottom-line approach seeks to include measures of success for people (e.g., development of human potential; fair and beneficial treatment of labor, community, and region), planet (environmental protection and sustainability), and profit (economic benefit) to promote corporate social responsibility.[15] The triple bottom line offers leaders a new way of defining organizational success and provides many new opportunities to apply FRLD principles.

Many of the world's top companies have embraced the triple-bottom-line philosophy. Consider Robert Lockwood's princetongreen.org new venture; Toyota's fuel-efficient Prius automobile; General Electric, with its revenue-boosting Ecomagination green technology; BP's reduction of greenhouse gas emissions from its production processes, or Unilever's Project Shakti, which provided training for 13,000 women to distribute its products across India, thereby greatly increasing their families' income while expanding Unilever's market share.[16] These examples teach us that boosting profits through innovative green initiatives and improving the lives of all organizational stakeholders are not mutually exclusive. Instead, these desired outcomes can become sustainable when socially responsible leaders find opportunities for them to intersect with FRLD behaviors. We believe that FRLD can help organizations to boost profits, develop people, and protect the earth.

Thinking About Full Range Leadership Development as a Strategic and Social Intervention

We can do good while we do business. The advent of the balanced scorecard and triple-bottom-line concepts provides you with many opportunities to do "good business" by applying FRLD to address strategic, social, and environmental issues. In this section, we offer some thoughts on social entrepreneurship, safety issues, and environmental challenges for you to reflect upon. As you read on, think about ways you can apply FRLD behaviors to address these issues in your personal leadership situation.

Social Entrepreneurship

James MacGregor Burns wrote, "Transforming leadership begins on people's terms, driven by their wants and needs, and must culminate in expanding opportunities for happiness."[17] We believe that expanding opportunities for people's happiness should be one of the most critical missions for today's business enterprises. However, it requires a renewed entrepreneurial spirit that expands its aim beyond the accumulation of wealth to solving the world's most pressing social problems. Entrepreneurship involves starting new business ventures or revitalizing mature organizations based on perceived opportunities to create wealth. Entrepreneurs excel at recognizing opportunities, exploring innovative approaches, mobilizing resources, managing risks, and building viable, sustainable enterprises. Entrepreneurial skills are just as valuable in the social sector as they are in business because both social and business opportunities involve risk taking and building connections with people. Some entrepreneurs use their skills to craft innovative responses to social needs, such as Patty Hillkirk's work with children with HIV/AIDS described in Chapter 5 (see Figure 10.3). These individuals are called *social entrepreneurs*.

Social entrepreneurs work to improve the world's social conditions while they accumulate economic wealth in the traditional entrepreneurial sense as well. In other words, they do good while they do business. Even during prosperous economic times, numerous social problems remain, and some seem to

Figure 10.3   From dream to reality. Visionary social entrepreneur Patty Hillkirk inspires an audience as she explains the genesis of Camp Dreamcatcher.

always get worse.[18] Countless opportunities for social entrepreneurship can be found in helping the homeless, the poverty stricken, the mentally and physically challenged, victims of domestic violence, survivors of natural disasters, troubled children, those suffering from diseases, the elderly, abused animals, gardens lost due to floods, and other disadvantaged groups. Social entrepreneurship, therefore, gives us the opportunity to address these challenges by *connecting with people who are in need and expanding their opportunities for happiness*. We must and can do this, not only through the training of FRLD, but also by role modeling FRLD behaviors in our interactions with others.

These challenges require us to be proactive and innovative social entrepreneurs, who introduce radical positive change to organizations and society, monitor progress toward goals, and avoid being bystanders. FRLD behaviors offer social entrepreneurs ways to introduce reforms, set goals for reform and reward people for progress made toward them, and take action to improve the environment around them.[19] You can do these things by creating and communicating a clear entrepreneurial vision (inspirational motivation), providing ample rewards and recognition for socially responsible achievements (contingent reward), and encouraging experimentation, challenges, and education (intellectual stimulation) that promote the entrepreneurial thinking of others.

We feel that FRLD can help social entrepreneurs be more effective in their pursuits by

- Adding to their practical knowledge of the alternative behaviors and methods for turning good social ideas into viable business options
- Defining new possible roles and strategies with which entrepreneurs and established companies can address social needs and contribute to sustainable development
- Capitalizing upon the social value that can result through the collaborative efforts of businesspeople, government agencies, and educators

Our claim is based upon evidence derived from Penn State's Master of Leadership Development (MLD) program, which attracts and educates many social entrepreneurs. MLD students conclude their program by completing a capstone course in social entrepreneurship and community leadership. This course applies graduate students' accumulated knowledge of FRLD to address the social needs of communities on a local and global scale. MLD students lead teams of high school and undergraduate students as they work on a wide range of social entrepreneurship projects.

Social Entrepreneurship in Action

Since 2003, MLD and MBA students at Penn State have completed over 40 social entrepreneurship projects benefiting communities in the United States and abroad. Examples of such projects include producing marketing plans, planned giving and capital campaigns, brand recognition studies, strategic planning and strength, weaknesses, opportunities, and threats (SWOT) analysis, product development processes, product pricing studies, publicity campaigns, public relations assistance, feasibility studies, fund-raising research, and documentation of leadership strengths of women. By providing such business services to social entrepreneurs, these students develop their FRLD competencies, while they help satisfy important social needs across a wide variety of organizations and communities (see Table 10.2 for a sample of organizations that have benefitted from these efforts). We have observed that student leaders frequently display inspirational motivation to keep everyone motivated. This was necessary even when everyone knew that they were working on something important and valuable to the community. We believe that people need to be continually energized and motivated, even at the height of success. That's why FRLD is so critical.

As you examine Table 10.2, think about ways that you can work with entrepreneurs to address a pressing social need in your community and expand opportunities for happiness for those in need. For example, we were particularly

Table 10.2 Sample of Social Entrepreneurial Ventures Aided With FRLD

Organization	Web site	Overview of Project Mission
Camp Dreamcatcher, Inc.	www.campdreamcatcher.org/	Developing a business plan for buying land to establish an all-season facility that can be used by Camp Dreamcatcher, a nonprofit organization serving 170 HIV/AIDS-infected/affected children for the past 12 years, and also be available for other nonprofit organizations serving all children with diverse and special needs.
PainBeGone™ Central	www.painbegonevillage.com/	Develop a business plan for PainBeGone Central. PainBeGone Central offers products and services for individuals in chronic pain. Write a well-conceived business plan for PainBeGone Central that describes the proposed venture to an audience of investors.
George Fox Friends School	www.bym-rsf.org/gfschool/	Investigate feasibility of proposed expanded programming—after school program, adult evening classes, "specials" for homeschooled and cyber-schooled children.
Ray of Hope Children's Hospital of India	n/a	Strategy development to establish a state-of-the-art pediatric network to provide low/no cost health care; prioritize core service lines, identify funding and partnership opportunities.
Selene Whole Foods Cooperative, Inc.	www.selenecoop.org/	Build a publicity campaign to attract more members/customers, and build a strong involved membership in the community of Media (recently voted as the first fair trade town in the United States, beating San Francisco). We represent locally grown organic food, community orientation, environmental responsibility, contributing strongly to the town's sustainability, and support its members and citizenry with strong values.

(continued)

Table 10.2 Sample of Social Entrepreneurial Ventures Aided With FRLD (Continued)

Organization	Web site	Overview of Project Mission
West African American Trading Company	www.waatco.com/	Develop five-year strategic plan.
La Comunidad Hispania, Inc.	www.lacomunidadhispana.org/	Develop a marketing plan for an established endowment that was created through Chester County community foundation.
Pennsylvania Home of the Sparrow	www.homeofthesparrow.org/	Prepare a planned giving plan.
Friends Association for the Care and Protection of Children	www.friendsassoc.org/	Prepare a marketing plan to bring attention to the need for more foster families.
The ARC of Chester County	www.arcofchestercounty.org/	Develop a marketing plan and collect marketing research.

impressed by our colleague Sue Kershner's volunteer work through Calvery Fellowship Church in Downingtown, Pennsylvania. Sue's church partnered with Michelle Henry of Faith Bible Church in New Orleans immediately after Hurricane Katrina struck in August 2005. They were called into service to assist with the coordination of the teams of volunteers that were showing up at Faith Bible Church after Katrina hit. This group has also reached out to assist the needy of the U.S. Gulf region when Hurricanes Gustav and Ike struck in 2008.

Sue's work has inspired a group of our students to consider social entrepreneurial ventures in New Orleans and other regions affected by natural disasters. Even after several years, the New Orleans area is still reeling from the devastating flooding. Homes must be built or rebuilt; there are needs for land donations, labor, trucks, and forklifts. Cheap transportation must be provided; there are needs for bicycles, tools, and labor. Hungry people must be fed both physically and mentally; there are needs to establish cafes, kitchens, literacy programs, life skills training, and job placement in the hospitality and construction industries. Animals must be cared for; there are needs for rescue and adoption programs, supplies, food, and newspaper. The natural environment requires restoring; there are needs for farm and gardening expertise, seeds, and tools. Each of these challenges provides opportunities for inspiring resilience, role modeling compassion, challenging the status quo, and coaching people to come back as a community reborn. Opportunities for social entrepreneurship are all around us. Look around, find one, and work hard to bring about positive change and help people realize their human potential.

Environmental, Health, and Safety Issues in the Workplace

We found that there has been a sharp increase in attention being paid in organizations to environmental, health, and safety (EHS) issues in the workplace. Several of our manufacturing clients have requested training that utilizes aspects of FRLD to help reduce the number of injuries and fatalities on the job, promote safe work practices, and create a culture that promotes both safety and quality. We believe that these three goals are not mutually exclusive, and with FRLD, they can be sustained over a long-term period. In Table 10.3, we illustrate our belief with thoughts gleaned from an engagement at a large multinational manufacturing firm.

While preparing for this consulting engagement, colleagues came across the work of leadership scholar Julian Barling and his associates. Barling and his students are pioneering some interesting work that examines the intersection of transformational leadership and workplace safety outcomes. Their preliminary research indicates that executives who take a passive approach to workplace safety actually create a dangerous environment for their employees. Employees

Table 10.3   Environmental, Health, and Safety Application of FRLD

EHS issues have evolved over time to meet the safety requirements of government policy and standards organizations. In the early 1900s there were few, if any, safety rules and regulations. Authors such as Upton Sinclair exposed the wretched conditions that existed in American plants and factories. This created a public outcry that resulted in government intervention with safety standards, etc. Over the years, the role of government in EHS grew and evolved into what we today know as the Occupational Safety and Health Administration (OSHA).

Throughout the decades, corporate management dealt with the safety requirements on a transactional basis by reacting to rules and regulations as they were issued by governing bodies. As a result, the management of EHS remains in the lower and less effective styles listed in the FRLD model. For example, laissez-faire or management-by-exception leadership would go into effect when an incident occurs or when rules are broken. In other words, management deals with the problem after it happens. Typically, this involves filling out OSHA forms, figuring out who is to blame, and how this type of accident could be prevented in the future. This method of EHS management is quite prevalent; there is no true leadership—it is a reaction to a negative event. Here exists an opportunity to reengineer the management and leadership style to change the way corporations approach EHS that will result in a triple win situation.

Suppose the employees were to take the initiative prior to EHS incidents, and led EHS policies and procedures because it was the right thing for them to do, not because it meets OSHA requirements. This is a major philosophical and attitudinal change similar to the one experienced in the United States regarding seatbelts. Initially people used seatbelts "because it's the law," and some used them because they were a good idea to protect themselves from harm in an accident. They did it because it was the right thing to do. Today most individuals automatically clip their seatbelt without considering the law, it is the correct action. In this case, a cultural and attitudinal change has taken place in America.

A similar attitudinal change by employees and management regarding EHS in the workplace would produce significant positive results, i.e., safety for safety's sake. The employees would experience fewer accidents, less bodily harm, and better health; thus, they reap real, personal benefits. Management would spend less time with incident investigations, reviews, and the administrative work (paperwork) that accompanies every EHS incident. The corporation receives an additional benefit in the form of reduced insurance premiums, which are directly impacted by the company's accident rate. The government and society benefits in that less policing would be required, thus reducing costs, and the citizens would enjoy a safer environment. Here we have a triple win: the individual, the company, and the country.

Table 10.3   Environmental, Health, and Safety Application of FRLD (Continued)

In order to accomplish the required attitudinal change, top management must reengineer its practices and philosophy from the lower, less effective styles in the FRLD model to the transformational style. If you examine successful plants, those with very few if any EHS incidents, you'll typically find a manager who displays transformational leadership. The 4Is are noticed and reported by the subordinates during interviews we've conducted. The leader's philosophy reflects the desired attitudinal change regarding safety, and all subordinates, management and employees, follow the lead. Clean workplaces, accident prevention policies, and protective equipment and clothing are incorporated into everyone's daily practice. This results in very few, if any, accidents; thus, all are winners.

Many firms can point to a single department or plant with an outstanding and exemplary OSHA record. The problem is that their other facilities are unable to replicate the successful model. In our leadership consulting engagements, the managers are introduced to transformational leadership focused on their EHS environment. The leadership training targeting EHS attitudinal change is necessary to demonstrate the direct connection between leadership and EHS success. Now that management understands how leadership makes the difference, they are able to visualize the correct style. They also recognize it in the manager with the outstanding record—he or she is a transformational leader. Comprehending the importance of leadership, the managers are in a position to modify their personal styles, typically of the lower order, and become a more transformational leader.

Cultural change is not a short-term project, but rather a long-term commitment to a vision of the desired future state. The seatbelt attitudinal change took several years to become a reality, and so it will be in the EHS arena, and the benefits will accrue for many years to come.

—John Juzbasich, DEd (c), MLD

who work for such leaders actually take on the same lazy attitude toward safety, pay little attention to safety issues, and therefore raise the risk of serious injuries on the job. These results suggest that the passive approaches to FRLD (i.e., laissez-faire and passive management-by-exception) can actually make your workplace more dangerous. Much more active forms of leadership are necessary to reduce such risk and raise levels of safety awareness. If action is taken after an incident occurs, active forms of management-by-exception may not be sufficient. The monitoring aspect of management-by-exception does have a place in EHS concerns, especially when leaders manage by walking around. It is amazing how the lazy and passive attitudes of some current leaders toward worker safety can be transmitted to the next generation of leaders. We can do much better by using the active behaviors in the FRLD model. What can you do to actively lead safety initiatives in your organization?

To become more actively involved in the safety arena, you should use a mix of transactional and transformational leadership. When safety conditions are high risk or involve life-and-death situations, you should use active forms of management-by-exception to monitor circumstances that may be hazardous and nip the problem areas in the bud. For example, management-by-walking-around and complimenting those who practice or exceed EHS expectations are likely to work well because they put positive psychology into action. You should use contingent reward leadership to set four or five safety goals and work each day to make incremental progress toward each goal. You should provide feedback on progress made on the goals. And when the goals are reached, you should distribute appropriate rewards to those who helped achieve the goal to recognize their active contributions. Awarding those that exemplify the desired behavior will demonstrate management's commitment to EHS. These awards are forms of positive reinforcement.

You should then build upon these contingent rewards by displaying the 4Is of transformational leadership. You can display *idealized influence* by talking about workplace safety as an important organizational value, consider implications for safety in your decisions, and role model best safety practices. You can display *inspirational motivation* by setting high safety standards and clearly communicating them to associates in a way that is interesting and meaningful. You can display *intellectual stimulation* by urging associates to identify potential safety hazards and risks and thinking about causes of injuries as well as ways to eliminate them. And you can display *individualized consideration* by coaching and mentoring associates on safety issues, and listening to a wide variety of associates to get their perspectives on ways to improve safety. The good news is that training leaders at all organizational levels on these transformational leadership behaviors often results in future positive changes in their associates' attitudes toward safety and safety programs and fewer incidents and injuries.[20]

Environmental Leadership Initiatives

The environmentally conscious Beatle George Harrison once wryly sang, "We've got to save the world. Someone else may want to use it."[21] Soon after, scientists told us that there was a hole in the earth's ozone layer above Antarctica. Despite the advent of the ecology movement in the 1960s and more recent green initiatives, the number of problems facing our natural environment has been expanding rapidly. As mentioned in Chapter 1, the land has been excessively concreted over, and our human activities have produced a litany of environmental problems that need our immediate attention and proactive actions.

If business leaders are going to "save the world," they must view our many environmental problems as opportunities to create a better place for all of us while generating new sources of revenue. But often, environmental and societal interests are at odds with each other. In these cases, FRLD is needed to achieve a solution that balances these competing agendas and values. Today more than ever before, top executives need to partner with governmental agencies and the general public to empower people in their green initiatives and demand more socially responsible behavior from corporations. Intellectual stimulation is certainly critical in generating creative solutions that not only protect the environment but also create sustainable business opportunities. This process requires us to question old assumptions, consider alternative points of view, and rethink tried and true practices and policies. Once ideas are agreed upon, leaders should use inspirational motivation to achieve consensus and rally employees, volunteers, and others to put their ideas into action.

One interesting study of CEO transformational leadership offers some hope in finding ways to lead the process of making corporations more socially and environmentally responsible. Leadership scholar David Waldman and his colleagues studied the FRLD behaviors and corporate strategies of CEOs of 56 U.S. and Canadian companies. They found that those CEOs who displayed intellectual stimulation most frequently led companies that were more likely to engage in strategic corporate social responsibility initiatives.[22] These results suggest that the more top executives get their associates to "think green" and focus on the triple bottom line, the more environmentally responsible they will become. Ecomagination, a recent successful green initiative launched by GE and its CEO Jeff Immelt, illustrates this point very nicely.

Contingent reward leadership offers another avenue to lead such environmental initiatives. Since 1992, New York State's Agricultural Environmental Management annual awards program has recognized the outstanding efforts of farmers who preserve the environment through cutting-edge conservation and innovation. For example, the 2008 award winner was Tim Fessenden of Fessenden Dairy. Fessenden created a unique set of environmental tools to boost his farm's profits. He designed a polymer lagoon cover to trap methane gas and its odor. This reduced the manure odor as the methane gas was piped off the top. This process reduces greenhouse gases at little or no cost to Fessenden and has been replicated at five other farms in upstate New York.[23] This example shows that you don't have to be a corporate executive to use intellectually stimulating strategic initiatives. FRLD behaviors can be used by leaders in all walks of life to save our precious Planet Earth and its natural resources.

Putting Full Range Leadership Development Into Practice at the Strategic Level

While conducting research for this book, John made a nostalgic pilgrimage back to the Center for Leadership Studies (CLS) at the State University of New York at Binghamton in July 2008. The CLS is where the great leadership scholar Bernie Bass was inspired to develop the notion of transformational leadership, and where we forged our passion for teaching and conducting FRLD research in our doctoral program. Although John had gone back to Binghamton many times since graduating in 1995, his return to the CLS after 13 years was still very much a refreshing homecoming.

As John perused the CLS library, he was filled with the same sense of wonder and excitement that he experienced as a student. The library contained many books from Bernie's personal collection, along with his publications and working papers. These items were moved into the CLS library after his death in October 2007. To peruse the personal effects of a leadership research legend and mentor was indeed thrilling for his student and admirer. One item that caught John's eye was an unpublished early working paper with implications for strategic leadership. In this paper, Bernie argued that transformational leadership should be fostered with appropriate organizational policies, practices, and strategies.[24] In honor of our esteemed mentor and "intellectual father," we draw upon this paper to provide you with six ways to apply transformational leadership to your own strategic initiatives.

Use Transformational Leadership Measures for Promotion and Transfer

To support the innovation and learning perspective of the balanced scorecard, consider using the Multifactor Leadership Questionnaire (MLQ) to select, screen, assess, and place leaders into higher-level or lateral positions for managing talents more effectively. This helps to ensure that your associates are in the most appropriate organizational roles or what the Gallup Organization refers to as an "appropriate fit" along the Gallup path.[25] Human resources staff can administer the MLQ on a yearly basis to facilitate the development of aspiring transformational leaders. By providing feedback from the MLQ report to these managers, the quality of mentoring and coaching typically increases, and you can accelerate your associates' leadership development. Remember that transformational leadership is all about creating a larger leadership capacity for the whole organization through active mentoring and developmental opportunities.

Recruit and Select the Best

Your search for new leadership talent should be constant. Today, the key to success is recruiting and retaining the best and the brightest. Google is a great example of building a highly successful company through the recruitment of the best human talents available. When an intelligent prospective recruit is interviewed, she will pay attention to your organization's climate, culture, and reputation. When she sees that the climate is friendly, collaborative, energetic, and intellectually stimulating, she will be attracted to your organization. If the human resource managers conducting the interview treat her with individualized consideration, the candidate is likely to walk away from the interview with a positive attitude. We have witnessed these practices at successful organizations such as Southwest Airlines, Sanofi Aventis, and the Vanguard Group.

Use Transformational Leadership as a Career Development Tool

Your organization's training and development processes can benefit from FRLD. As we described in Chapter 5, the first supervisor of a new trainee can either make or break his potential to succeed. Research from the mentoring field indicates that the support and challenges provided to subordinates by superiors goes a long way in determining subordinates' future promotions, salaries, and career paths. In order to move up the organizational ranks, subordinates often take on the behaviors and attitudes that their superiors display.[26] Therefore, it is important for supervisors to role model idealized leadership, show individualized consideration, and provide intellectually stimulating, challenging, and highly visible assignments. These behaviors can enhance the career development and psychosocial support you give your associates through mentoring and reduce their perception of job-related stress.[27] You might feel a lot of pressure to know that it is you who may either make or break the career of your new subordinate. But, you should also consider it to be a privilege to have such a big responsibility.

Reengineer Jobs and Processes

To support the internal business process perspective of the balanced scorecard, those responsible for operations management should consider introducing challenge, intrigue, and problem solving into jobs, processes, and systems. Our experience is that employees working in research and development, manufacturing, and engineering like to be constantly challenged. They enjoy taking on more responsibility in their jobs. People love being challenged so much that they are spending their personal time working on many public projects on the Internet, such as Wikipedia and Linux. And they seem to love finding solutions to problems even if they don't get paid a dime.

So, use intellectual stimulation to design jobs with more challenge built into them. And get your associates excited with tasks that appeal to them. Use individualized consideration to review workflows and operational procedures from the production, engineering, and sales points of view. Be sure to design jobs with the talents, skills, and developmental needs of your associates in mind. This will keep them actively engaged in their work, generate interest in Six Sigma and continuous process improvement, and determine which activities add value to your products and services.

With the advent of advanced information technologies such as smart phones and PDAs, leaders are being challenged to find time to think and perform creative tasks. There are simply too many interruptions these days with 24/7 operations and the electronic leashes that email, voicemail, and instant messaging place upon us. You can be an intellectually stimulating leader only if you are able to design your jobs to be relatively free of interruptions and constant demands. As we spend more time on communication than ever before, we need to make our communication process far more efficient and effective. If you can, take the time to design your own job so that it gives you time to think. This will free you up to examine new strategic opportunities for your organization, learn from the past, solve problems that need fixing, come up with new ideas, and think ahead to envision a brighter future.

Build a Strong Brand and Corporate Image

To support the customer perspective of the balanced scorecard, consider developing strategies that project images of quality, excellence, and vision to your customers, like Robert Lockwood used at Gallup and princetongreen.org (see Table 10.4). Your customers need to see value in what they buy, appreciate what is created and sustained over time by your organizational culture and top management. Create an image of your organization as having its eyes on the future, confidence in its strategic direction, collaboration, and teamwork, and valuing its intellectual capital, innovative processes, and development of its associates. A blend of inspirational motivation, idealized influence, intellectual stimulation, and individually considerate behaviors displayed by individuals and teams at all levels of the organization can help you attain this goal. Their passion can create strong emotional connections with your customers and a reputable brand for your product and services.[28]

Table 10.4   Princetongreen.org: Applying FRLD for People, Profit, and Planet

Today's leaders face increased pressure to create sustainable business practices leading to profit, while operating in very challenging economic conditions. Robert Lockwood and his partners saw this trend as a great opportunity to start a socially-responsible business based, in part, on FRLD concepts. In 2008, Lockwood formed Princetongreen.org as an association of entrepreneurs, who work in a virtual workspace and paperless environment, to help other organizations find innovative ways to save natural and environmental resources. The founders strive to boost profits, while saving precious natural resources.

Princetongreen.org has created an image of a research- and educationally-based grassroots organization with a very timely vision. Their lofty goal is to build a "community that believes that we can be both environmentally conscious and fiscally responsible, thus conserving both natural and economic resources...to simply save energy, every day." They teach their clients about environmental issues and energy efficiency through product offerings and practices that help to conserve more energy.

Lockwood and his associates leverage FRLD and human psychology concepts to strengthen their clients' organizational cultures in several ways. They blend marketing know-how with inspirational motivation to enhance their clients' brand image as an environmentally-conscious organization. They use intellectual stimulation to get their clients to apply state-of-the-art technologies, research, and education to find solutions for environmental and energy problems. They employ individualized consideration to enhance their clients' employee engagement, customer engagement, and diversity initiatives supporting environmentally-conscious living. They also encourage fiscally responsible practices and monitoring of costs to boost their client's return on investment. By role modeling these FRLD practices, princetongreen.org hopes to create transformational changes in the thinking and behavior of individuals and organizations responsible for the stewardship of our planet Earth.

Source: Retrieved January 30, 2009, from http://princetongreen.org/

Periodically Examine and Redesign Your Organizational Structure

Conditions change, and your organizational strategies and the structures required to carry them out change as well. To adapt to market conditions, organizations conduct strategic planning sessions and design an appropriate organizational structure to support the execution of the plan. In most industries, business markets are fraught with turbulence, uncertainty, risk, competition, ill-structured problems, and unforeseen opportunities and ever-lurking threats. Organizations fight with competitors to secure limited financial, intellectual, technological, and material resources. Such vexing environmental conditions demand constant renewal and change. Many companies, such as General Motors, Motorola, and Xerox, have faced crises due to organizational inertia, which prevents these big companies from reinventing themselves as the market changes constantly.

To overcome these challenges, you should use transformational leadership to create an *organic organizational structure* with little hierarchy and specialization of functions and a fluid and flexible network of highly skilled associates. Organic structures provide you with the ability to forecast trends using intellectual stimulation and individualized consideration. They allow you to consider a broad array of issues over both short- and long-term time horizons, meet new challenges, and embrace new opportunities as they arise. Recognizing the implications of these trends for your organization requires you to also inspire your colleagues with a compelling vision that unifies them to execute the objectives laid out in the balanced scorecard. If this vision is communicated effectively, it can add clarity to the purpose and meaning underlying your objectives and goals.

Making progress toward these goals involves creating product/service value, improving the activities that create value, and developing the knowledge, skills, and abilities of people who enable these processes. These are the leading indicators of organizational success that can result in your financial success down the road. We believe that promoting transformational leadership in your organization through high-quality recruiting, selection, training, job design, and organizational structuring will pay off in increased economic and market value over time.[29]

More Evidence That FRLD Promotes Prosperity and Well-Being

Bernie Bass would have been most pleased to see how people from all walks of life are embracing and benefitting from FRLD. Whether promoting the prosperity of colleagues, building companies and communities, or working to save our precious planet, these people are helping FRLD to become what sociologists call "part of the culture." To further illustrate this phenomenon, we leave you with some testimonials from individuals compelled to share their experiences with you. They are our clients, associates, and adult graduate students. They work in the education, government, for-profit, and nonprofit sectors. They are not famous CEOs of global companies. They are people just like you—ordinary people capable of doing extraordinary things and making a truly remarkable difference in the world. They are able to accomplish great and exciting things because they have made FRLD part of who they are. May their words guide you on your own fantastic journey of leadership development throughout your life. May they inspire you to help others to reach their full potential as both leaders and human beings.

Empowering Women With FRLD

Two years ago, I spent a life-changing month as an international volunteer in Tanzania, Africa. Tanzania is the eighth poorest nation in the world and, similar to other developing nations, faces significant cultural obstacles to providing even basic human rights for women. Assigned to work at a national women's organization near the base of Mt. Kilimanjaro, I arrived ready to help the women develop the economic resources needed to improve their lives and the lives of their families.

According to FRLD theory, transformational leadership is the process whereby leaders develop followers into leaders. In my de facto role as leader, I hoped to offer my expertise in a way that would enable the women to effectively market their handmade items at their small shop, thereby elevating their status as businesspeople and leaders in their community.

As a volunteer, my effectiveness depended on my ability to exhibit the behaviors of a transformational leader. I spent time learning about the women who worked at the shop—their challenges, lifestyles, and the context of their work. I asked questions to understand what motivated them and what inspired them. At the same time, I had to expose some of my vulnerabilities—my limited knowledge of the language, the culture, and the business environment in Tanzania. We learned about each other, built trust, and worked together to set challenging goals that would move their business forward. In our limited time together, we remerchandised the store, developed new marketing materials, created a training guide, and doubled the income of the store over the same time period the prior year. These accomplishments led to enormous satisfaction, both personally and professionally, for all of us.

Napolean Bonaparte once said that "leaders are dealers in hope." My greatest wish is that my work with the women in Tanzania not only empowers them in business, but also opens the door to hope.

—Patricia Enright, social entrepreneur

Life-Changing Experience

Since I began my journey to develop my leadership skills as a sales leader through FRLD, I found myself being transformed as a person, a father, and a husband. It was through FRLD and the transformational leadership process that as my leadership development grew, so did my effectiveness in leading others, especially leading my family.

Transformational leaders behave in ways that result in being role models for their followers. In the absence of confidence, followers will gravitate toward a concern for existence or a lack of purpose. Through my behaviors, I now display confidence and self-control during times of crisis, and humility during times of accomplishment. I now offer a transformed perspective and specify a purpose for my actions and the interactions that I have as a sales leader, father, and a husband.

As a sales leader, my mission is to have others believe the purpose of their work is to make a difference in someone else's life, while leading to outstanding results. I am now achieving this through engagement and attributions of idealized influence. My number one goal as a sales leader is to develop my people. My mission is to have a fully engaged team while developing their skills, knowledge, and leveraging their talents. I believe my open-mindedness has allowed me to process diverse ideas and opinions and help lead my teams to greatness.

My children are ages 10 and 7, respectively; they are at a tipping point of becoming industrious and initiative. As a father, my mission is to make sure my daughters know that I believe in them; children are likely to live up to what you believe of them. As with my sales team, I now utilize attributions of idealized influence to build my children's self-confidence and to respect others. I now discuss the importance of values and beliefs and specify the importance of having a strong sense of purpose. It is through my own FRLD that I am building their identity.

As a husband, I have grown more supportive of my wife and her role as the mother of our children. It is through individual consideration that I pay special attention to her needs. I am now more in touch with her needs and her aspirations as she is the primary care giver while I am at work and school. My wife and I now discuss how our family values, such as integrity, fairness, and open-mindedness, will guide our family's behaviors to greatness.

Now that I have grown as a transformational leader, I have been able to lead my sales team, my children, and my family to be open-minded. I have been able to stimulate their interest to new perspectives and motivate them to do more than they expected. I have been able to motivate others more than I expected.

—Larry Hinson, Astra Zeneca

Creating Sustainable Changes With FRLD

Allstate Insurance Company has been going through a variety of changes simultaneously that could be classified separately as developmental and transitional. For much of its 75 years, Allstate has been considered a market leader and rewarded for this leadership. Despite our many successes and the recognition that has accompanied them, we find ourselves in transition between who we are and who we are becoming. The transformation is being forced on the organization by rapid changes in technology, demographics, competition, consumer habits, and deregulation. My perspective is that the organization is responding to the changes it recognizes are occurring, and has proactively chosen to adapt to those changes.

Since no organization can change without people changing themselves, I consider it part of my leadership responsibilities to embrace change, anticipate change, and, in many respects, initiate change. The skills required to effectively lead the type of disruptive change encountered by Allstate are embodied in FRLD, especially transformational leadership. I have used these skills and personally seen their effectiveness.

Providing a compelling vision of the future and inspiring others are critical aspects of successful leadership, and FRLD has provided me with these skills. Embracing the FRLD model has enabled me to apply the behaviors of transformational leadership in my role as a territorial leader and as chairman or president of a number of community organizations.

FRLD and the MLQ gave me a chance to measure and compare my leadership behaviors through self-evaluation and independent assessment as perceived by my subordinates, peers, and supervisors. I then designed a leadership plan of action and applied it in my various leadership roles, at home, at work, and in my community. Having been exposed to Gallup's StrengthsFinder™ as part of my leadership curriculum, I have embraced the concept of developing my own unique talents and strengths, and understanding those of the people I manage, thereby enhancing my individualized consideration. Doing so and embracing all of the behaviors of the FRLD model has made a tremendous difference in their performance and my own career progression.

—John G. Wischum, Allstate

Raising Funds and Lifting Spirits With FRLD

When I decided to join Penn State's Master of Leadership Development program, I knew that I had already done well as a leader, but I did not understand why and consequently how to improve myself. This program, with its strong research-based FRLD foundation, has given me an understanding of my own leadership style as well as leadership in general. I enjoyed the Social Entrepreneurship and Community Leadership capstone course, which concluded the program by putting what we had learned about FRLD into practice. It gave me the opportunity to close the circle of using what I learned about transformational leadership in a socially responsible manner. This was a most gratifying experience—a sort of eureka moment!

As a fund-raiser/volunteer, I had at times had some concern that the program was mostly geared toward those who planned to work in the for-profit sector. Realizing the overlap of transformational leadership with social entrepreneurship, I experienced a newfound burst of energy, and felt an urgent responsibility to share with others in the volunteer sector some of the tools available for all of us to improve our work. I have already started employing concepts such as social impact assessment as we give new priority to turning annual fund-raisers into more sustainable models.

We can all become change makers. I may be a very small part of a very big picture, but I believe that we can all benefit from working and learning together and supporting each other at all levels. We can only truly improve our society by improving every little part of it. I believe that FRLD has given me some great tools to become a more effective change maker as I pursue my volunteer fund-raising work.

—Grete Greenacre, The Franklin Institute

Developing Righteous Minds Through FRLD

My experience as a middle-level leader in a top Fortune 50 corporation is that many agency owners I consult with are not aware of or committed to personal self-improvement plans. These business owners find themselves so absorbed in the action of closing the next deal that they lack a sense of the legacy they may leave behind.

The FRLD model has provided me with a unique platform of skills and tools to help these business owners develop a broader vision than the day-to-day business transaction. Recently, one of the large tenured agency owners called to thank me for helping him through what he described as a four-month period of self-imposed paralysis due to his frustration with senior management's direction for the company. He acknowledged my work with him on a continuous personal improvement plan was extremely valuable. He also stated my assistance in redefining his business objective to focus on consumer relationships and not just profit was a tremendous personal awakening for him. He told me that he now has a game plan that keeps him focused and personally motivated. He is less troubled with corporate decisions over which he has no control.

That agency owner's call gave me an adrenalin rush and I was reminded of a phrase from the award winning movie *The Great Debaters*. The leading character, Professor Melvin Tolson, comments to a student that his job, as is the job of every professor at the university, is to "help you to find, take back, and keep your righteous mind." That is what I did for this agency owner, and it was refreshing.

Using the continuous personal, people, and process improvement concept within FRLD, I have stretched the minds and the abilities of these owners to achieve results they did not believe were possible. They no longer look at problems as insurmountable obstacles but as creative opportunities.

—**Michael W. Lomax, Allstate**

Negating the Naysayers With FRLD

"I'm sorry, I can't give you one. I just don't think you'll be successful." As I heard these words from my favorite high school teacher when I asked her for a college recommendation, I was not quite sure if I should laugh or cry. I cried. Always social in high school, I hid the stress of medical issues that were ongoing. Suffering through them in college as well, I fought for every grade, and barely made it through. My mistakes were glaring, and my goal became to prove to the world that I could be successful.

Deciding to work with adolescents with behavioral and psychological disorders, my advice from those around me was "I just don't think you'll be successful in the long run." I worked for five years in the field, attempting to prove everyone wrong. After my attempt to enter a graduate program for adolescent counseling failed, due to an insufficient undergraduate GPA, I left.

As time went on, I discovered that FRLD and the Master of Leadership Development program encompassed all that I was looking for—a positive approach to leadership and the belief that people can achieve great things. After expressing my decision to apply, I began to hear from some people around me, "I don't think this is the time," and "You don't need this to be successful." I was accepted on provisional status, requiring a 4.0 average GPA for the first three classes to continue. Feeling the need to prove myself once again, I began to question if everyone around me was right.

When I got acquainted with the FRLD theory, my heart, mind, and soul became inspired. When asked to picture our idealized leader, I realized that I, myself, did not have one. Perhaps I could become an idealized leader myself for others by learning the 4Is of transformational leadership. Incorporating the 4Is of transformational leadership into my life was my goal. Over the past two years, I have abandoned the need to prove myself, and have simply enjoyed learning. More importantly, I have embraced the desire to help others believe that they can always be successful. My 4.0 GPA has since dropped to a 3.96, and I received an award for academic achevement at graduation. Life is for living and learning, and for saying "yes you can."

—**Kate McKinnon, Verizon Wireless**

A Most Noble Form of Transformational Leadership

As a parent, I find the FRLD model useful in monitoring the leadership style that I apply with my daughter. I can easily point out when I am on the one extreme, approaching transformational, as well as those times when I am just too tired and drift toward laissez-faire.

With children, a transactional approach can have such a big impact. My daughter loves stickers. I can get her to do just about anything by waving a sticker in front of her. And her blanket? Threatening to take that away has an even bigger effect. But, if used too much, those transactions will not have a long-lasting effect. The model serves as a reminder that I must work toward transformational interactions, despite the short-lived results of a transactional approach.

Analyzing my leadership style with my daughter is pretty simple when so much of the focus is on her personal development. This is in sharp contrast to a work environment, where leaders have the responsibility to develop several people and also accomplish a variety of tasks. The day-to-day routine can often make it easy to focus on the tasks and ignore their development.

Being more aware of my leadership style in a focused one-on-one environment has helped me to translate that awareness into the work environment. Rather than thinking of my leadership style in terms of a one-to-many relationship, I have started to analyze my style with respect to each person in our group. The key measurements I use are the amount of time I devote to each person and my ability to set aside tasks and deadlines to focus on individual development. I benefit by getting better feedback on how I can apply transformational principles to each person I work with. The team benefits through each individual getting a focused period of development. With FRLD, it's a win-win situation for the entire team, my family, and myself.

—Richard Pomager, large defense contractor firm

* * *

If you have followed the pathways we have paved throughout this book to becoming a transformational leader, you will be able to make a similar testimonial in the future. We hope that your story will be about the changes you initiate at home, work, and in your community. You now have the potential to be a brand new leader who embraces FRLD to create positive change in your life and the lives of others. Remember that *leadership is all about change*. If you are not creating change in your life and others' lives, you are not leading. So be a champion of change! You have been empowered, and you now have what it takes. Your journey as a leader that champions positive change in people, profits, and planet begins this very minute. Godspeed!

Summary Questions and Reflective Exercises

1. Interview a member of the senior leadership team at your organization or an organization that you admire. This person should be a C-level executive (e.g., CEO, CFO, CIO, COO). Inquire about the organization's vision, mission, core values, and major objectives. Summarize your ideas regarding how aspects of FRLD can be used to support these elements of organizational strategy. Present your findings to your learning partner, team, or class.

2. Building upon your response to exercise 1, identify how specific aspects of FRLD can be used in the organization you selected to support or enhance each of the following strategic initiatives:
   a. Leveraging core capabilities
   b. Building a foundation for future growth
   c. Addressing an unmet need in the market
   d. Establishing a strong, differentiated position in the market
   e. Improving process efficiencies and effectiveness
   f. Developing new businesses
   g. Penetrating a large new market[30]

3. Review the accounting and organizational literatures for information on the *balanced scorecard*. This strategic leadership concept describes how an organization's mission drives the major strategic objectives in the customer, employee, operational, and financial functional areas of an organization. What are your organization's major strategic objectives in these four areas? What metrics or measures can be used to assess the progress made toward these major strategic objectives? How can specific FRLD behaviors be used to help achieve each of these objectives in your organization?

4. Identify ways that specific FRLD behaviors can drive innovation processes in your organization. How can you get your customers and markets to provide information for your innovation processes? How can FRLD behaviors be used to prompt your customers to provide inspiration, design, testing, and product/service enhancement ideas? How can you use FRLD behaviors to leverage your core competencies and technology to accelerate your rate of innovation?

5. Summarize your FRLD leadership strengths as indicated by your Multifactor Leadership Questionnaire (MLQ) report. Assess how these strengths help or hinder your current leadership role/responsibilities and your organization's mission. How well do you currently fit into your leadership role based on your MLQ report?

6. Conduct an external environment assessment for your organization. List the top three most relevant trends pertaining to the following areas for your organization:
   a. Economic
   b. Sociocultural
   c. Global
   d. Technological
   e. Political/legal
   f. Demographic
   g. Competitors
   h. Industry (e.g., threat of new entrants, power of suppliers and buyers, product substitutes, intensity of rivalry)

   For each of the above factors, how can you use specific FRLD behaviors to help shape or adapt to the trends you identified?

7. Identify a local nonprofit organization that is in need of leadership, management, or operational assistance. Volunteer at the organization for a few hours a week to provide assistance. How can you use your leadership strengths as identified in your MLQ report to best help this organization? Provide a weekly report to your learning partner, team, or class on your activities.

8. Work with a local group to develop green or environmentally responsible initiatives in your community. How can you use specific FRLD behaviors to motivate your group to prepare a plan for being more eco-friendly? (*Hint*: Intellectual stimulation and inspirational motivation work well here.) Present your plan to your learning partner, team, or class for feedback as you develop it.

9. Lead a team advocating improved workplace safety in your organization. Remember that the key to success here is reducing the amount of exposure to hazards for your associates. What changes in systems, culture, and equipment are needed to reduce exposure risk and severity level? How can the 4Is of transformational leadership be used in this regard?

10. Reflect upon how you will lead in a way that reconciles the need for profit with the imperative of developing people to their full potential, while protecting and saving the earth's natural resources. Why is such a balanced agenda necessary? How can you help advance such an agenda both locally and globally? How will you measure your progress in meeting your goals?

Notes

1. Packer-Muti, B., & Lockwood, R. C. (2008, June 12). Transformational change in higher education. *Gallup Management Journal.* Retrieved September 10, 2008, from http://gmj.gallup.com/content/107596/Transformational-Change-Higher-Education.aspx; and retrieved September 13, 2008, from http://chronicle.com/free/v54/i19/19a01501.htm.
2. Fleming, J. H., & Asplund, J. (2007). *Human sigma: Managing the employee-customer encounter.* New York: Gallup Press.
3. Deutschman, A. (2001). *The second coming of Steve Jobs.* New York: Broadway Books.
4. Sosik, J. J., Jung, D. I., Berson, Y., Dionne, S. D., & Jaussi, K. S. (2004). *The dream weavers: Strategy-focused leadership in technology-driven organizations.* Greenwich, CT: Information Age Publishing.
5. Kaplan, R. S., & Norton, D. P. (2004). *Strategy maps: Converting intangible assets into tangible outcomes.* Boston: Harvard Business School Press; and Voelper, S., Leibold, M., Eckhoff, R., & Davenport T. (2006). The tyranny of the balanced scorecard in the innovation economy. *Journal of Intellectual Capital, 7,* 43–60.
6. Kaplan & Norton (2004). As cited in Note 5.
7. Fleming & Asplund (2007). As cited in Note 2.
8. Fleming & Asplund (2007). As cited in Note 2.
9. O'Connell, V. (2008, September 10). Retailers reprogram workers in efficiency push. *Wall Street Journal,* pp. A1, A11.
10. For more information on EVA™, visit http://www.sternstewart.com/.
11. Welch, D. (2004, May 13). Mutual of Omaha's healthy preoccupation with talent. *Gallup Management Journal.* Retrieved September 15, 2008, from http://gmj.gallup.com/content/11608/Mutual-Omahas-Healthy-Preoccupation-Talent.aspx#1.
12. Sosik et al. (2004). As cited in Note 4.
13. Drucker, P. (1954). *The practice of management.* New York: Harper & Row; and Kaplan, R. S., & Norton, D. P. (1996). *Balanced scorecard: Translating strategy into action.* Boston: Harvard Business School Press.
14. Kaplan & Norton (1996). As cited in Note 13.
15. Elkington, J. (1994). Towards the sustainable corporation: Win-win-win business strategies for sustainable development. *California Management Review, 36,* 90–100; and Elkington, J. (1998). *Cannibals with forks: The triple bottom line of 21st century business.* New York: Capstone Publishing.
16. Savitz, A. W., & Weber, K. (2006). *The triple bottom line: How today's best-run companies are achieving economic, social and environmental success—and how you can too.* San Francisco: Jossey-Bass.
17. Burns, J. M. (2003). *Transforming leadership: A new pursuit of happiness* (p. 230). New York: Atlantic Monthly Press.
18. Litzky, B. E. (2008). *LEAD 582 entrepreneurship and community leadership syllabus.* Penn State School of Graduate and Professional Studies at Great Valley, Malvern,

PA; Mumford, M. D., & Moertl, P. (2003). Cases of social innovation: Lessons from two innovations in the 20th century. *Creativity Research Journal, 15,* 261–266; and Seelos, C., & Mair, J. (2005). Social entrepreneurship: Creating new business models to serve the poor. *Business Horizons, 48,* 241–246.

19. Eyal, O., & Kark, R. (2004). How do transformational leaders transform organizations? A study of the relationship between leadership and entrepreneurship. *Leadership and Policy in Schools, 3,* 209–233.

20. Barling, J., Loughlin, C., & Kelloway, E. K. (2002). Development and testing of a model linking safety-specific transformational leadership and occupational safety. *Journal of Applied Psychology, 87,* 488–496; and Kelloway, E. K. (2006, September 8). Managers should lead the way in workplace safety. *Halifax Herald Limited.* Retrieved September 16, 2008, from http://www.thechronicleherald.ca/external/sobeys/september06.html.

21. Harrison, G. (1981). Save the world. On *Somewhere in England* [CD]. Hollywood, CA: Dark Horse/Warner Brothers Records.

22. Waldman, D. A., Siegel, D. S., & Javidan, M. (2006). Components of CEO transformational leadership and corporate social responsibility. *Journal of Management Studies, 43,* 1703–1725.

23. Anonymous. (2008, August). Environmental winners to be honored at EFD. *American Agriculturist,* p. 7.

24. Bass, B. M. (1986). *The nurturing of transformational leadership.* Working Papers Series 86–99. Binghamton, NY: School of Management, State University of New York at Binghamton.

25. Lockwood, R. C. (2006). *The Gallup path* [DVD].Princeton, NJ: The Gallup Organization.

26. Wanberg, C. R., Welsh, E. T., & Hezlett, S. A. (2003). Mentoring research: A review and dynamic process model. *Research in Personnel and Human Resource Management, 22,* 39–124.

27. Sosik, J. J., & Godshalk, V. M. (2000). Leadership styles, mentoring functions received, and job-related stress: A conceptual model and preliminary study. *Journal of Organizational Behavior, 21,* 365–390.

28. Fleming & Asplund (2007). As cited in Note 2.

29. Bass (1986). As cited in Note 24.

30. Adapted from Anonymous (2008, August). *LexisNexis corporate innovation strategies.*

Appendix: Master of Leadership Development Program

Leadership and learning are indispensible to each other.

—John F. Kennedy

About the same time Henry Mintzberg was criticizing graduate business programs for being out of touch and unrealistic,[1] we were hearing similar complaints from several of our clients, students, and alumni. Their gripe was that some master's-level business programs were graduating myopic, short-sighted, or ethically challenged managers who could not see beyond the cubicles within their functional silos because their training lacked the right focus. This was not our opinion, but it did peak our interest. And it presented an amazing opportunity for new program development.

In our opinion, the MBA degree does provides a good overview of the accounting, finance, marketing, operations, IT, and strategy functions within organizations. But something very important is missing. Many graduate business programs lack a deep dive into leadership competencies, ethical reasoning, social responsibility and entrepreneurship, dynamic communication, innovation strategies, diversity training, conflict resolution, negotiation strategies, and coaching and mentoring. These are the core competencies required at middle and upper levels of management—the career goals that traditional graduate business programs claim to prepare students for. These programs simply do not have the room to include such critical topics without increasing the number of program credits to a number that is prohibitive to prospective students.

During the 2002–2003 academic year, a task force of faculty, staff, and administrators at Penn State's School of Graduate and Professional Studies at Great Valley examined this issue. They reviewed research on trends in business education conducted by the Gallup Organization, *U.S. News & World Report*, the Big 10 Universities, and the Conference Board, indicating the need for stronger graduate leadership education. For example, only 34% of U.S. companies report being effective at identifying future leaders, according to the Conference Board's *Developing Leaders for 2010 Report*.[2] They need the help of universities to create a pool of individuals suitable for leadership roles. Recognizing these trends, organizations such as General Electric, Lockheed Martin Corporation, and the Vanguard Group have made significant investments in leadership training through various organizations and institutions. However, they have recognized that there are significant gaps in their existing approach to company-wide leadership development, and they have requested university assistance in closing those gaps. The task force viewed this as an important opportunity to create a specialized graduate-degree program, the Master of Leadership Development (MLD) program, and to obtain accreditation from the Association to Advance Collegiate Schools of Business (AACSB).

This perceived gap between organizational need for leadership development and the opportunity to create a specialized graduate leadership degree energized the task force to continue exploring the possibility of creating such a degree. During the 2003–2004 academic year, the task force conducted a systematic marketing research study of over 2,000 alumni and prospective students to gauge potential interest in the proposed degree. Responses about the need for leadership development in corporations and program interest were strongly positive. These favorable results prompted the task force to then perform a competitor analysis. Results of this study indicated a competitive opportunity for the university, given the relatively small number of similar programs in the region. The task force then identified target markets for the program and evaluated needs for additional resources, including faculty, staff, and course development monies. Faculty collaborated to identify existing and potential courses. They then weaved these courses into the program's conceptual framework. The task force championed the program proposal as it was reviewed and approved by numerous university committees. In January 2005, Penn State's MLD program was finally launched. This appendix describes the MLD's philosophy, structure, and content.

MLD Versus MBA: A Difference in Focus and Philosophy

The MLD teaches students how to be exemplary leaders, while the MBA teaches students how to be exemplary managers. The MLD and MBA programs are quite different in their emphasis and content. For example, Penn State's MBA program prepares professionals to manage in an ever-changing, increasingly global economic environment. The curriculum includes both behavioral and more technical and functional courses on organizational operations. It provides students with the intellectual tools to integrate finance, accounting, marketing, information systems, operations management, human resource management, and organizational behavior, and articulate a vision, motivate colleagues and employees, and develop and execute business strategy. The MBA's primary focus is on constructing and maintaining organizational systems, emphasizing improvements in efficiency and bottom-line financial performance.

In contrast, the MLD program includes courses focusing on behavioral and ethical elements, such as adult human development, creativity, motivation, interpersonal and group influence tactics, role modeling, and moral development. This curriculum is primarily aimed at educating students regarding what constitutes authentic transformational leadership and enhancing the full positive potential of individuals, groups, organizations, and communities. It is directed toward challenging the status quo and creating change, formulating visions and meaning for others, bringing about organizational change congruent with long-term objectives, innovating the entire organization, transforming cultures, inducing change in values, attitudes, and behavior using personal examples and expertise, and empowering associates with shared values. While the MBA program provides an overview of leadership, the MLD program provides an *in-depth* analysis of the theory, research, and practice of authentic transformational leadership by providing an environment in which faculty and students can have a complete and open collaboration on what constitutes exemplary leadership. The MLD's primary focus is on promoting positive change in individuals, teams, organizations, and communities emphasizing improvements in effectiveness and triple-bottom-line performance.[3]

The MLD degree helps students develop leadership potential in themselves and in others. The program considers leadership across the life span, from early career through retirement, including parenting and community service, as well as leadership in the corporate realm. The program employs a multidisciplinary approach stressing social responsibility, ethics, and the value of the individual. Instruction develops real-world skills to foster positive change in individuals, groups, organizations, and community.

The MLD provides the competencies and actionable behaviors that can be readily applied in students' professional and personal lives. Cutting-edge information on leadership development is shared in an interactive, collaborative learning environment. The program's life span perspective on authentic transformational leadership development is reinforced through strong bonds formed with leadership practitioners, faculty and students, and the university's leadership events and alumni association.[4]

MLD Program Structure

The MLD is a 33-credit interdisciplinary professional program that blends the social and behavioral sciences with ethical studies to develop outstanding organizational and community leaders. It is accredited by the AACSB. At the time of this writing, the faculty were considering increasing the number of credits to 36. We will describe the updated 36-credit version of the program here.

When we designed the MLD's course structure, we decided to use Fulton Sheen's notion of "correlation of courses"[5] to tightly integrate aspects of FRLD, especially transformational leadership, throughout the courses. This approach serves to reinforce in the student's mind interrelationships between course concepts and the broad array of practical applications for transformational leadership. The conceptual overlap of several key topics illustrates the complex system of interdependencies often seen in leadership systems in organizations. This approach is quite different from the "cafeteria style" style of curricular design, where students select courses to check off a curricular requirement, without evaluating interdependencies of concepts within and between courses. This latter approach does little to develop strategic or systems thinking skills in students. Such thinking is required at the upper echelons of organizations for leaders to synthesize information from a variety of domains, identify similarities and differences between situations, and create entirely new solutions to novel problems. These requirements are similar to the tasks we challenged you to perform as you began reading this book (i.e., the meta-cognition and critical questioning discussion in Chapter 1).

This correlation of tightly integrated courses offers students a challenging and interesting overview of leadership development. To earn the MLD degree, students must complete four Leadership Cornerstone courses (12 credits), four Leadership Competency courses (12 credits), four Leadership Context courses (12 credits), and a Leadership Capstone course (3 credits). The Leadership Cornerstone courses provide basic foundation material that introduces the program's philosophy and FRLD concepts and assessments, including the Multifactor Leadership Questionnaire (MLQ). The Leadership Competency courses elaborate upon the components of transformational leadership and other leadership models and research methods as well. The Leadership Context courses teach students about the environment that surrounds their personal leadership situation and how to lead strategically and in a socially responsible manner. In the Leadership Capstone course, students apply FRLD to a local or global social entrepreneurial or community leadership service learning experience.

Leadership Cornerstone Courses

Students complete the cornerstone courses lockstep as a cohort. We have found that the sequential completion of these first four courses by students creates cohesiveness, common identity, and pride in the cohorts as they enter and progress through the program. The cohort also serves as a learning community where students share best leadership practices, network with their colleagues in professional and social settings, and form friendships. The content of these courses is a challenging and comprehensive introduction to the elements of the FRLD leadership system that are elaborated upon in more detail later in the program.

Leadership Across the Life Span

In the first course, we introduce students to the MLD program by framing leadership as a noble lifelong journey of personal development. We use a strengths-based approach to leadership development to transform students' innate talents into strengths, and build their hope, optimism, confidence, and resilience for success in the program itself, and in life in general. The course builds upon the concepts of positive psychology, positive organizational scholarship, and authentic transformational leadership to examine key developmental processes associated with leadership across the life span. Topics include an overview of leadership thought and theories, character strengths and virtues, individual differences, emotional intelligence, cross-cultural issues, self-construals, stages of moral and adult human development, personal meaning and vision, group dynamics, and self-leadership and its application in students' lives. Through both written and oral presentation assignments, students analyze results of executive coaching experiences, moral development tests, assessment centers, 360-degree feedback leadership development planning, and leadership and human development-related movies to enhance their self-leadership. This course also introduces students to the FRLD model.

Full Range Leadership Development

The second Leadership Cornerstone course is the keystone of the MLD program. This course presents all components of the FRLD as measurable, trainable, and actionable behaviors as they relate to the student. Learning modules include values clarification, leadership purpose, goal setting, contingent rewards, idealized influence, inspirational motivation, intellectual stimulation, individualized consideration, perspective taking, team leadership, shared leadership, cross-cultural dimensions of FRLD, and e-leadership (i.e., leadership in virtual or distanced settings). The MLQ is administered to students as a baseline measure of their FRLD potential. Students analyze results of Hartwick Classic Leadership Cases® using the FRLD model, MLQ reports, current events, personal values clarification, mission statements, and personal leadership development plans to enhance their transformational leadership potential. This course introduces students to issues of ethical decision making, role modeling, inspirational communication, innovation processes, team building, and diversity. These topics are elaborated upon later in the program.

Diversity Leadership

The third Leadership Cornerstone course is Diversity Leadership. This course expands students' understanding of the concept of individualized consideration through the analysis and application of models, theories, and strategies for managing an increasingly diverse workforce and customer base. Through guided exercises in self-reflection, students learn to appreciate the individual differences people bring to the workplace and how to leverage these differences to create potent and cohesive teams with a common identity. Learning modules include implicit bias, majority-minority identity development, intercultural communication, team diversity, and group identity and life experiences' impact on leadership. Students lead class discussions on diversity leadership issues, analyze Diversityinc.com articles to identify best practices, and participate in an activity where they are a minority. The capstone assignment is the Diversity Leadership Improvement Plan. The student assesses his or her skill set against an evidence-based set of diversity leadership competencies and develops an action plan for self-improvement. Students review a representative sample of the published research in the following areas: career experience of diverse individuals, the effect of diversity on team performance, the influence of leadership on setting and achieving diversity goals, best practices in diversity leadership at the organizational level, and the impact of best practices on organizational outcomes. The course moves the student systematically through the consideration of diversity leadership at the individual, team, and organizational levels.

Leadership Models and Methods

The fourth and final cornerstone course expands students' understanding of the array of leadership theories and models other than FRLD and the research methodology used to conceptualize and test them empirically. Students learn to explain these leadership models, identify their strengths and weaknesses, and discover potential applications for them. Because science backs the material taught in the MLD program, students are trained how to construct and evaluate leadership theories, test them, and draw conclusions from their analysis. This course develops students' critical thinking, logical reasoning, and technical writing skills required for contemporary leaders, and a growing number of our students are applying to doctoral leadership programs after completing the MLD. Learning modules include leadership theory overview, philosophy of science, conceptualizing theory, study design, measurement issues, data analytic procedures, and interpretation of results. Through both written and oral presentation assignments, students critique manuscripts and theories, conduct formal debates, and design and present an empirical study to become more informed consumers and producers of leadership research.

Leadership Competency Courses

Once students have completed the Leadership Cornerstone courses as a cohort, they branch out on their own to enroll in the Leadership Competency courses. They complete three courses in the areas of leadership communication, intellectual stimulation, and idealized influence.

Dynamic Communication for Leadership Contexts

The first required Leadership Competency course is the Dynamic Communication for Leadership Context course. This course expands students' understanding of the concept of inspirational motivation through theory and techniques of persuasion and rhetoric for articulating and promoting a vision, and facilitating interaction and communicating within and between groups. Students learn to craft and deliver visionary and charismatic speeches that inspire collective efficacy, trust, team synergy, intrinsic motivation, and engagement to create potent and cohesive teams and organizations with a common identity. Learning modules include meaning-centered communication and discursive leadership, intrapersonal and interpersonal communication, articulating a vision and promoting positive change, persuasion, social influence, and framing. Students present team talks on a leadership rhetoric topic, prepare a dynamic communication improvement plan, complete a series of essays, and make an emotive presentation to become more inspiring leaders.

Intellectual Stimulation Course Block

Students choose one of three courses that promote creativity and innovation. These courses expand students' understanding of the concept of intellectual stimulation through theory and practices from business, science, and the arts to foster creativity within people and teams, and innovation throughout organizations.

Students learn the antecedents, processes, and outcomes associated with creativity and innovation methodologies in individuals, teams, and organizations.

- *Developing High-Performance Organizations* uses a liberal arts and natural science approach to create high-performing organizations. Learning modules include philosophy of aesthetics, meaning making, behaviors and traits of creative individuals, and the elements of creative products. Students' assignments include assessment of original works of practicing artists, musicians, actors, scientists, and writers, and creating executive briefs on creativity topics. These activities help students become more intellectually stimulating contributors to the overall performance of their organization.
- *Corporate Innovative Strategies* surveys the issues involved in formulating and implementing innovation initiatives and large technology projects. Learning modules include the innovator's dilemma, stimulating new ideas through dialogue, identifying attributes of disruptive technologies and their threats and opportunities, discussing how existing business models constrain new ventures, and using storytelling and story listening to facilitate change and innovation. Through both written and oral presentation assignments, students learn through homework, presenting on issues of adaption, innovation, resilience, sustainability, globalization, and organizational learning. They examine these issues through storytelling and story listening to become more intellectually stimulating leaders.
- *Creativity and Problem Solving* explores the cognitive and behavioral approaches to fostering creativity in individuals, with an emphasis on pragmatic or problem-solving approaches to leadership and the paradox of structure. Learning modules include the brain's organization of problem solving, the catalytic nature of change, individual assessment of problem-solving style, and problem-solving leadership models. Through homework assignments, exams, and class participation that emphasize precision, students learn to use their own respective problem-solving abilities and cognitive styles to become more intellectually stimulating leaders.

Idealized Influence Course Block

Students also choose one of three courses that teach role modeling and ethical decision making. These courses expand students' understanding of the concept of idealized influence through an ethical lens focusing on virtues, values, moral development, ethical reasoning models, philosophy, and application to their personal leadership context. Students learn philosophies and frameworks for conducting themselves and their businesses in an ethical, morally developed, and socially responsible manner.

- *Ethical Dimensions of Leadership* takes a historical approach to the philosophical study of Western and non-Western ethical frameworks, with implications for contemporary ethical leadership. Learning modules include how the economy influences our ethics, the interrelationships between the ethical issues we face, ethical issues facing the earth and its life-sustaining systems, doing business in an ethical way, and ethical issues raised by the larger context of our life as part of a developing universe. Students prepare and present a research paper on the life, work, and significance of leaders such as Paul Robeson, Susan Adams, Desmond Tutu, and Eleanor Roosevelt; prepare news briefs that connect class readings with ethical issues in the news; and analyze case studies to enhance their idealized leadership.
- *Ethical Issues in Information Technology* presents an overview of ethical concerns related to computer-based information systems that pervade our lives in so many ways. Learning modules include ethical theories and history, conceptual frameworks, and analysis of issues, including e-leadership, spam, privacy, quality of work life, cybercrime and government snooping, online annoyances, intellectual property in the digital world, and free speech on the Web. Students use debates, current events analyses, and case analyses of the above listed topics to enhance their idealized leadership.
- *Ethical Dimensions of Management in Biotechnology and Health care* presents a comprehensive overview of ethical decision making in health care, pharmaceuticals, and biotechnology, including ethical implications of technological and scientific advances, medical interventions, and business decisions. Learning modules include ethical theories, history of research ethics, informed consent, scientific misconduct and the responsible conduct of research, industry management of ethical issues, and ethical issues in the health care sector. Through both in-class exams and student presentations and participation, students develop a greater understanding and awareness of the above-listed topics, which helps them to become idealized leaders.

Leadership Context Courses

Leadership does not occur in a vacuum. Transformational leaders are aware of the strategic opportunities and challenges that surround them. To gain such awareness, aspiring leaders must learn strategic thinking skills, how business and society interacts, and how to address special issues they face in their personal leadership situation.

Strategic Leadership

The first Leadership Context course is Strategic Leadership. This course focuses on executive-level leadership of larger systems and organizations. The course applies FRLD concepts to illustrate the impact of developing human, intellectual, social, structural, financial, and reputation capital that create wealth for shareholders. Students learn to think and lead strategically, guided by strategy tools such as the Gallup Path™ and Balanced Scorecard™. Learning modules include upper echelons theory, creating multiple forms of capital, environmental scanning and shaping, internal and external environmental analysis, the visioning process, shaping organizational culture and values, supporting innovation and learning, and measuring real profit and economic value-added. Students interview top executives responsible for their firm's strategy, assess their leadership style and culture, and create an executive coaching plan for them. They also analyze their own company's performance using strategy and performance management tools to become more effective strategic leaders.

Business Environment Course Block

Students choose either the Business Stakeholders Relations or Biotechnology and Health Industry Overview courses. These courses examine the industry practices, governmental regulations, financing, trends, problems, and issues facing organizations in general or in the life sciences industry in particular.

- *Business Stakeholders Relations* focuses on the exploration and analysis of the ethical, political, technological, social, legal, and regulatory environments of business. Learning modules include ethical problems in business and their importance, moral standards, famous cases in business stakeholders' relations, making moral decisions, corporate social responsibility, globalization, government regulation, consumer protectionism, "green" initiatives that protect the environment, economic regulation, and the political lobby. Through class discussion and debate, and report writing assignments, students learn to better understand the context surrounding today's transformational leaders.
- *Biotechnology and Health Industry Overview* focuses on the above-mentioned issues in the health, biotechnology, and pharmaceutical industries. Learning modules include current issues in the U.S. health care system, historical evolution of the U.S. health care system, global health care systems and markets, competition versus regulation, and health care costs and quality. Students write position papers on numerous issues explored in the course, present and analyze a current issue in the health care industry's business environment, and participate in debates and discussions to better understand the context and issues facing contemporary transformational leaders.

Table A.1   Sample MLD Context Elective Courses

- Collaborative Coaching and Mentoring
- Conflict Resolution
- Creativity and Problem Solving II
- International Business
- Negotiation Strategies
- New Ventures
- Organizational Culture and Development
- Organizational Change: Theory and Practice
- Organizational Power and Politics
- Problem-Solving Leadership

Context Electives

Leaders are often faced with special problems they need to tackle. The two Context Elective courses provide students with the opportunity to choose among a wide variety of special topic or boutique courses designed to provide insight into their personal leadership situation. Students use the knowledge, skills, and abilities they gain from these courses to address their specific leadership-related issue. Context electives come from multiple academic departments within the university and are too numerous to describe here in detail. The more popular elective courses are listed in Table A.1.

Leadership Capstone

When we designed the MLD program, we wanted students to finish the program by applying what they learned about FRLD in local and global businesses and communities. As a result, we felt that they would make life better for others. We also wanted to teach them the importance of measuring their organization's success in terms of the triple-bottom-line philosophy described in Chapter 10. With a focus on people, profit, and planet, students mentor high school and undergraduate students as they work on a social entrepreneurship or community leadership project. The Leadership Capstone course shows students how FRLD interacts with entrepreneurship principles to promote positive change in the social service sector. Learning modules include entrepreneurship versus social entrepreneurship, community leadership, social responsibility, sustainability, triple bottom line, how FRLD augments social entrepreneurship, MLQ assessment, moral development (i.e., perspective-taking capacity) assessment, and proper consulting engagement protocol with clients.[6] See Chapter 10 for a detailed overview of the Social Entrepreneurship and Community Leadership course and testimonials of students and alumni on the effectiveness of integrating the FRLD model into Penn State's MLD program.

Notes

1. Mintzberg, H. (2004). *Managers not MBAs: A hard look at the soft practice of managing and management development.* New York: Berrett-Koehler.
2. Retrieved January 22, 2004, from http://dayton.bizjournals.com/dayton/stories/2003/05/19/focus1.html.
3. Master of Leadership Development Task Force. (2004). *Master of Leadership Development program proposal.* Malvern, PA: Penn State University.
4. Retrieved September 23, 2008, from http://www.sgps.psu.edu/prospective/academicprograms/leadership/mld.ashx.
5. Sheen, F. J. (1980). *Treasures in clay: The autobiography of Fulton J. Sheen.* Garden City, NY: Doubleday.
6. Course description material in the appendix distilled from http://www.sgps.psu.edu/current/academicprograms/leadership/mld/schedule.ashx. Retrieved September 25, 2008.

Author Index

A

Abry, D. A., 237, 252
Ackoff, R. L., 47
Adams, J. S., 63
Adams, P., 161
Adamson, G., 148
Allen, C., 268, 270
Alsop, R., 5
Amabile, T. M., 166
Ante, S. E., 230
Arthur, M. B., 124, 144
Arvey, R. D., 35, 50
Asplund, J., 323, 325, 327, 346
Assayas, M., 60
Atkinson, A. A., 235
Attenborough, R., 83
Atwater, L. E., 108
Avey, J. B., 122
Avolio, B. J., 3, 6, 9, 10, 15, 18, 21, 31, 35, 36–39, 44, 47, 50, 98, 103, 112, 122, 151, 171, 172, 173, 174, 175, 176, 180, 183, 188, 201, 202, 208, 218, 224, 265, 267, 273, 301, 302, 305

B

Bai, M., 148
Bales, R. F., 298
Bandura, A., 130, 212
Barling, J., 140, 342
Barnes, B. K., 148
Barr, M. D., 240
Barrick, M. R., 212

Bartlett, C. A., 81
Bass, B. M., 3, 6, 8, 9, 10, 18, 19, 20, 27, 36–39, 98, 151, 172, 173, 174, 175, 176, 183, 188, 209, 212, 218, 224, 265, 267, 273, 288, 344, 348
Bassey, M. O., 136
Batson, C. D., 97
Baum, S. H., 81
Bebeau, M., 107
Belbin, R. M., 306
Bennis, W., 121
Bernstein, R., 309
Berson, Y., 51, 65, 90, 110, 146, 181, 255, 257, 265, 279, 325, 330
Best, G. F., 138
Blanchard, K., 21, 26
Bland, R. W., 84
Bloom, B. S., 33, 34
Bloomberg, M., 232
Blumenstyk, G., 185
Bogle, J. C., 228
Bono, J. E., 20, 22
Boyatzis, R., 2
Bradberry, T., 244
Braga, M., 63
Braithwaite, E. R., 45
Branson, R., 121
Bright, D., 98
Briley, J., 83
Brough, M. B., 137
Bullock, A., 138
Burns, J. M., 17, 156, 334
Burrows, P., 130, 239
Butcher, V., 140

C

Cacioppo, J. T., 148
Cameron, K. S., 98
Campbell, R., 130
Cartwright, D., 20, 25
Caza, A., 98
Chen, G., 216
Cheng, T. J., 127
Chun, J. U., 102
Clark, H., 209
Clavell, J., 45
Clifton, D. O., 253
Clinton, W. J., 50
Colvin, G., 3
Conger, J. A., 133
Conti, D., 81
Conti, R., 166
Conzemius, A., 248
Coon, H., 166
Covey, S. R., 203
Croce, P., 205
Csikszentmihalyi, M., 122

D

Dansereau, F., 199
Darrow, C. M., 71
Davenport T., 325
Dearwater, M., 253
Deci, E. L., 231, 251
De Cremer, D., 83
Denning, S., 148
Deutsch, C. H., 158
Deutschman, A., 324
Diener, E., 91
Dinger, S. L., 97, 98, 202
Dionne, S. D., 51, 65, 90, 102, 110, 146, 181,
        265, 279, 325, 330
Dirk, K. T., 294
Domjan, M., 250
Dreachslin, J. L., 166, 210, 211
Drexler, K. M., 81
Drucker, P., 238, 330
Dukerich, J. M., 81
Dungy, T., 86
Dworakivsky, A. C., 202
Dychtwald, K., 209

E

Eagleson, G., 299
Ebert, J. C., 265
Eckhoff, R., 325
Eden, D., 246
Edmondson, G., 177
Egolf, P., 156
Ehrlich, S. B., 81
Eidson, R., 205
Eilam, G., 15
Elkind, P., 127
Elkington, J., 333
Elliot, A. J., 119
Ellis, A. P. J., 211
Ellison, K. W., 274
Enterline, T., 156
Epitropaki, O., 140
Erickson, T. J., 209
Estevez, F. J., 96
Evans, J. M., 211
Eyal, O., 335

F

Felsenthal, C., 94
Feltz, D., 304
Fiedler, F. E., 21, 28
Finerman, W., 100
Firth, A., 64
Fitzpatrick, F., 90
Fleishman, E. A., 20, 24, 176
Fleming, J. H., 323, 325, 327, 346
Fleming, K. D., 254
Foden, G., 268
Foote, A., 156
Frankl, V., 71
Freud, S., 20, 22
Fuller, R. W., 214

G

Gandhi, M., 82
Gardenswartz, L., 212
Gardner, W. L., 15, 21, 31, 44, 103, 112
Generose, G., 229
George, B., 15, 82, 112
Gerhardt, M. W., 20, 22

Gerstner, L. V., 203
Gibney, A., 127
Godshalk, V. M., 62, 93, 216, 345
Goleman, D., 2, 20, 24
Gore, A., 172
Grabowski, J. F., 178
Graen, G. B., 21, 29, 62, 199
Greenleaf, R. K., 83
Gronski, J. L., 59
Gupta, N., 251
Guzzo, R., 130

H

Haga, W. J., 199
Hajim, C., 55
Hamel, G., 293, 294
Harding, F. D., 20, 24, 176
Harris, J., 148
Harrison, G., 298, 342
Hatfield, E., 148
Helfer, A., 136
Hemp, P., 230
Herron, M., 166
Hezlett, S. A., 214, 345
Hiller, A., 51
Hock, D., 157
House, R. J., 21, 28, 124, 144
Howell, J. M., 135, 246

I

Ilies, R., 20, 22

J

Jacobs, T. O., 20, 24, 176
Janis, I., 135
Jaussi, K. S., 51, 65, 90, 110, 146, 181, 255, 257, 265, 279, 325, 330
Javidan, M., 343
Jenkins, S., 194
Jensen, M. A. C., 310
Jermier, J. M., 280
Jeter, L. W., 134
Jolis, A., 14
Jones, D. R., 65
Jones, M. B., 65

Judge, T. A., 8, 20, 22
Julian, S. D., 212
Jung, D. I., 51, 65, 90, 97, 98, 103, 110, 146, 181, 202, 255, 257, 265, 279, 280, 303, 325, 326, 330

K

Kahai, S. S., 172, 180
Kanungo, R. N., 133
Kaplan, R. S., 235, 325, 330, 333
Karau, S. J., 279
Kark, R., 216, 335
Karlgaard, R., 105
Katzenbach, J. R., 294, 306
Kellerman, B., 193
Kelloway, E. K., 342
Kelly, M., 202
Kerr, S., 280
Kets de Vries, M. F. R., 20, 22
King, A., 32, 34
Kirkpatrick, S. A., 20, 22
Klein, E. G., 71
Kline, C., 156
Kohlberg, L., 140
Kohn, A., 251
Kopp, W., 196
Kouzes, J. M., 314
Kovatch, B., 205
Kram, K. E., 214, 215
Kroups, J., 148
Krueger, R. F., 35, 50
Kuhnert, K. W., 140, 217

L

Laine, A., 205
Lango, J. W., 137
Lash, K., 284
Latham, G. P., 234
Lazenby, J., 166
Leibold, M., 325
Lennon, J., 298
Letcher, G. E., 243, 257, 283
Levinson, D. J., 71
Lewis, P., 140
Linzmayer, O. W., 265
Lirgg, A., 304

Litzky, B. E., 335
Locke, E. A., 20, 22, 234
Lockwood, R. C., 322, 344
Lombardi Jr., V., 315
Long, R., 7
Lord, M., 284
Loughlin, C., 342
Lowe, J. C., 81
Lowe, K. B., 8
Luthans, F., 9, 15, 112, 122, 171

M

Maccoby, E. E., 181
MacDonald, R., 281
MacKenzie, S. B., 97, 98
Mair, J., 335
Manz, C. C., 50
Maslow, A. H., 246
Matsumura, E. M., 235
Matthews, C. J., 50
Maxwell, J. C., 287
May, D. R., 15, 112
McCartney, P., 298
McKay, B., 326
McKee, A., 2
McKee, B., 71
McLean, B., 127
Meindl, J. R., 81
Meyers, W., 53
Milner, C., 140
Minnier, S., 205
Mintzberg, H., 359
Mitchell, R. R., 21, 28
Moertl, P., 335
Montgomery, D., 238
Moon, H. K., 102
Morison, R., 209
Morris, B., 158
Most, R., 193
Mount, M. K., 212
Mumford, M. D., 20, 24, 176, 335
Mylander, M., 161

N

Nagel, T., 137
Narvaez, D., 107
Neck, C. P., 50
Newirth, S., 100

Newstrom, J. W., 280
Nijstad, B. A., 180
Norman, S. M., 122
Northouse, P. G., 27
Norton, D. P., 325, 330, 333

O

Obama, B., 120
O'Connell, V., 327
Ofori-Dankwa, J., 212
O'Neil, J., 248
Organ, D. W., 64

P

Packer-Muti, B., 322
Paulus, P. B., 180
Pearce, C., 299
Pearsall, M. J., 211
Peters, T. J., 239
Peterson, C., 200
Piccolo, R. F., 8
Pierce, J. L., 280
Pine, J., 148
Podsakoff, P. M., 97, 98
Posner, B. Z., 314
Priore, D., 167

R

Rapson, R. L., 148
Rath, T., 192, 253
Rest, J., 107
Riefenstahl, L., 138
Riggio, R. E., 27
Roberts, A., 138
Roth, E., 100
Rothwell, J. D., 279
Rotter, J. A., 213
Rowe, A., 212
Rubin, E., 184
Ryan, R. M., 231, 251

S

Sager, I., 230
Savitz, A. W., 2, 333
Schmitt, B. H., 294
Seelos, C., 335

Seligman, M. E. P., 200
Shamir, B., 15, 20, 22, 102, 124, 144, 216
Sharifi, J. M., 236
Shaw, J. D., 251
Shea, C. M., 246
Shea, G., 130
Sheen, F. J., 124, 362
Siegel, D. S., 343
Simons, R., 238
Sims, H., 299
Sims, P., 15, 82
Sivasubramaniam, N., 8
Slater, R., 286, 315
Smith, D. K., 306
Smith, D. L., 249
Smith, D. R., 237, 252
Smith, G., 194
Sosik, J. J., 15, 35, 44, 50, 51, 61, 62, 65,
        71, 90, 93, 97, 98, 102, 103, 110,
        146, 172, 180, 181, 202, 216,
        255, 257, 265, 279, 303, 325,
        326, 330, 345
Spink, K. S., 304
Starkey, S., 100
Starr, R., 298
Steidlmeier, P., 288
Stewart, T. A., 230
Stogdill, R. M., 20, 25
Strober, D. H., 62
Summitt, P. H., 194
Swartz, M., 134

T

Thoma, S., 107
Thomas, K. W., 282
Thompson, L., 211
Thompson, R., 243, 257, 283
Thorndike, E. F., 248
Thrash, T. M., 119
Tisch, S., 100
Treftz, D., 209
Tuck, R., 279
Tuckman, B. W., 237, 252, 310
Turner, N., 140
Turner, S., 298

U

Uhl-Bien, M., 21, 29, 62

V

van der Linden, H., 137
Van Doorn, J. R., 176
Van Steenhoven, T., 148
Velthouse, B. A., 282
Venter, J. C., 160
Voelper, S., 325
Vroom, V. H., 246

W

Waldersee, R., 299
Waldman, D. A., 343
Walumbwa, F., 15, 112
Walzer, M., 137
Wanberg, C. R., 214, 345
Waterman, R. H., 239
Waters, R., 46
Watkins, S., 134
Weber, K., 2, 333
Weber, T., 82
Weigel, G., 127
Welch, D., 330
Welch, J., 81, 277
Welch, S., 277
Welsh, E. T., 214, 345
Whitaker, N., 86
Williams, K. D., 279
Woglemuth, L., 52
Woods, R. B., 63
Wozny, M., 81

Y

Yammarino, F. J., 62, 102, 108
Yost, P., 130
Young, M. S., 235
Yukl, G., 27
Yunus, M., 14

Z

Zaccaro, S. J., 20, 24, 176
Zaleznik, A., 20, 22, 35
Zander, A., 20, 25
Zelleke, A., 121
Zemeckis, R., 100
Zhang, Z., 35, 50
Zigarmi, D., 26
Zimmerman, V., 281

Subject Index

A

AACSB, *see* Association to Advance
    Collegiate Schools of Business
Accountability, individual versus mutual,
    304
Active management-by-exception, 12
Activists, 193
Adams, Patch, 161
Agard, Michael, 79, 144
Agreeableness, 212
Ahrens, Lynn, 211
al-Bashir, Omar, 273
al-Gaddafi, Muammar, 273
Allstate, 179, 351, 353
Al-Qaeda, 58, 137, 138, 202
Altruism, 97, 129
Amazon.com, 130
Ann Taylor Stores Corporation, 327
Apple, 4, 119, 128, 265, 321
Aquinas, Thomas, 17, 137
ARC of Chester County, 338
Armstrong, Lance, 178
Association to Advance Collegiate Schools
    of Business (AACSB), 1, 360
Astra Zeneca, 350
Attribute, definition of, 9
Authenticity
    balance of self-monitoring and, 105
    damage to, 106
    Gandhi's call for, 15
Authentic leadership theory, 21, 30–32
Avolio, Bruce, 94, 111, 171, 208
Avon, 103

B

Baby Boomers, 4, 100
Bachelet, Michelle, 133
Baird, John, 218
Bales, Robert Freed, 298
Barclay Global Investors, 65
Barling, Julian, 339
Bass, Bernard, 111
Battle of Britain, 137
Beach Boys, 167
Beatles, 295
Behavior
    based theories, 26
    definition of, 9
Being in the zone (flow), 122
Berson, Yair, 111, 112
Best Buy, 321
Bezos, Jeff, 130
Bhutto, Benazir, 133
bin Laden, Osama, 19, 82, 133
Blagojevich, Rod, 273
Blair, Tony, 19, 23
Bloomberg, Michael, 231, 232
BMW (Bavarian Motor Works), 175–176,
    177
Bobko, Phil, 201
Body Shop, The, 59
Bogle, John C., 228
Bonaparte, Napoleon, 100, 349
Bonner, Patricia, 108, 179
Bono, 60
Bradley, Bill, 191
Brainstorming, 179

Brand image, 322, 346
Branson, Richard, 119, 120, 121, 128,
    160
Brooks, Herb, 309
Brown, Michael, 265
Buchan, John, 1
Buffet, Warren, 30
Burns, James MacGregor, 216, 334
Burns, Ursula, 158
Burrell, Pat, 302
Bush, George W., 19, 23, 105, 266
Butcher of Uganda, 268
Bystanders, 193

C

Camp Dreamcatcher, 155–156, 184, 337
Capital One Financial, 2
Career development, mentoring and, 215
Carey, Mariah, 132
Carlyle, Thomas, 263
Carroll, Pete, 304
Carter, Jimmy, 14
Cause-and-effect relationships in balanced
    scorecard, 328, 329
Center for Leadership Studies (CLS), 8,
    95, 344
Chairman Mao, 127
Chambers, John, 145
Chaordic Alliance think-tank, 157
Character, building, 90
Charisma
    dark side of, 132–141
        fatal attraction of Adolph Hitler,
            136–140
        leader profile, 134
        personalized versus socialized
            charismatic leaders, 133–136
        perspective-taking capacity and
            moral development, 140–141
    eye of the beholder, 132
    images of, 121
Chavez, Hugo, 134
Churchill, Winston, 19, 121, 133, 136
Cisco Systems, 131, 145
Clifton, Donald, 253
Clinton, Bill, 23, 50, 105
Clinton, Hillary, 47, 124
Clooney, George, 132
CLS, *see* Center for Leadership Studies

Coaching, 215
Cognition, description of, 32
Cold War, end of, 5
Collective efficacy, 130, 303
Communication
    distant leader, 101
    one-on-one, 201
    production control issues, 269
Communism, 127
Confidence, team-level, 303
Confident vulnerability, 208
Conscientiousness, 212
Conspicuous consumption, 6
Constructive transaction (CR), 302
Contingency theory, 21, 27–28
Contingent reward and management-by-
        exception active, 227–261, 335
    children's grades, 233
    conflicting evidence, 251
    contingent reward, definition and
            behavioral examples, 230–237
        actively monitor followers' progress
            and provide supportive feedback,
            235–236
        provide rewards when goals are
            attained, 236–237
        set goals for and with followers,
            233–234
        suggest pathways to meet performance
            expectations, 234–235
    corrective transaction, 238
    extinction, 249
    internal controls, 243
    leader profile, 232, 239, 240
    Malcolm Baldrige National Quality
        Award, 254
    management-by-exception active,
            definition and behavioral
            examples, 237–244
        arrange to know if and when things
            go wrong, 243–244
        closely monitor work performance for
            errors, 238–241
        focus attention on mistakes,
            complaints, failures, deviations,
            and infractions, 241–243
    negative reinforcement, 248
    parenting, 235
    Pathways to Education, 234
    positive reinforcement, 248

punishment, 248
putting transactional leadership into
         practice, 252–257
    applying contingent reward
         leadership, 252–255
    applying MBE-A leadership, 255–257
    assess risk and be alert, 256–257
    display behaviors described in chapter,
         252–253, 255
    give praise when it is deserved, 253
    preach accountability and
         responsibility, 256
    provide resources needed by followers
         to reach their goals, 253–254
    set standards, 256
    use rewards to support Six Sigma
         and Total Quality Management
         initiatives, 254–255
Pygmalion effect, 246
research-validated benchmarks, 258
risk assessment, 256
self-fulfilling prophecies, 246
summary questions and reflective
         exercises, 258–260
thinking about, 244–252
    advantages and disadvantages of
         extrinsic rewards, 250–252
    extrinsic rewards and punishments,
         248–252
    goal setting, 245–248
    set SMARTER goals, 247–248
    timing of rewards, 250
    when MBE-A is appropriate, 244–245
transactional leadership of Sam
         Palmisano at IBM, 229–230
waiting to strike, 242
Continuous Quality Improvement
         program, 64
Contrarian thinking, 169
Contrast, notion of, 184
Conventional moral reasoning, 140
Coolidge, Calvin, 265
Co-op America, 227
Cooperman, Gail, 73
Corrective transaction, 238
Costello, Elvis, 295
Covey, Stephen, 203
CR, *see* Constructive transaction
Critical questioning, 33
Croce, Pat, 204

Crocodile Catering, 67
Crowley Foods, 269
Cult of personality, 82
Cyrus, Miley, 80, 132

D

DAC, *see* Diversity Action Council
Dalai Lama, 133
Dance, leadership as, 192
Dangerous Minds, 45
Darwin, Charles, 139
Davis, Darrell, 202
DaVita, 64, 207
Definite Dozen, 194
de Gaulle, Charles, 19
DeGeneres, Ellen, 105
De-individuation, 91
Dependency, follower, 216
DePree, Max, 227
Diehards, 193
Dionne, Shelley D., 57
Disney, 327
Distant leader, 97, 101
Diversimilarity, 212
Diversity Action Council (DAC), 222
Diversity leadership, 210, 364
Dreachslin, Janice, 210
Dunkin Donuts, 11
Dushkewich, Lara, 220

E

Eagleson, Geoff, 298
Ebbers, Bernie, 134
EBS, *see* Electronic brainstorming
ECHO, *see* Educational Concern for Hunger
         Organization
Ecomagination, 333, 343
Economic turndowns, 49
Economic value-added (EVA) measures,
         327
Edison, Thomas, 180
Educational Concern for Hunger
         Organization (ECHO), 181
EHS issues, *see* Environmental, health,
         and safety issues
Einstein, Albert, 17
Electronic brainstorming (EBS), 180, 186
Ellison, Larry, 160

Emerson, Ralph Waldo, 43
Emotional contagion, 148
Emotional intelligence, 23–24, 109
Empathy, 203, 204
Empirically oriented thinking, 183
Empowerment
    follower, 216
    gift, leadership as, 192
    laissez-faire vs., 281
    women's, 349
Enright, Patricia, 349
Enron, 30, 127
Environmental, health, and safety (EHS)
        issues, 338, 340–341
Environmental initiatives, *see* Strategic,
        social, and environmental
        initiatives
Environmental leadership initiatives, 342
Environmental problems, 6
Equitable disengagement, 63
Estevez, Filipe J., 96
Evaluation, 34
EVA measures, *see* Economic value-added
        measures
Evocation, inspiration and, 119
Exception reporting, reactive leadership
        and, 282
Exercises
    contingent reward and management-by-
        exception active, 258–260
    idealized influence behaviors and
        attributes, 112–114
    individualized consideration, 221–224
    inspirational motivation, 149–152
    intellectual stimulation, 185–188
    introduction (FRLD), 34–40
    laissez-faire, 289–290
    management-by-exception passive,
        289–290
    strategic leadership, 355–356
    system (FRLD), 74–77
    teams, sharing full range leadership
        within, 316–319
Existentially oriented thinking, 183
External locus of control, 213
Extinction, 249
Extrinsic rewards, 231, 236, 251
Extroversion, 212
Eye catchers, 293

F

Facebook, 4, 119
Failure, fear of, 63
Family Support Line of Delaware County,
        Inc. (FSL), 69
Fantasy, 180, 181
Fear, motivation by, 63
Federal Emergency Management Agency
        (FEMA), 265
Feedback
    behavior adapted based on, 109
    MLQ, 208
    process improvement and, 269
    360-degree, 71, 108
FEMA, *see* Federal Emergency Management
        Agency
Ferguson, Vicki, 220
Fessenden, Tim, 343
Figure–ground reversal, 184
Fiorina, Carly, 105, 135, 238, 239
Firth, Aimee, 64, 66, 207
Fleming, Kirk, 254
Flip-flopper, 106
Flow, 122
Follower(s)
    confidence levels of, 131
    definition of, 51
    dependency, 216
    empowerment, 216
    extroverted, 212
    inappropriate behavior, 272
    locus of control, 213
    potential, tasks assigned appropriate for,
        198
    sharing of vision with, 149
    situation fit, 56
Ford, 327
Frankl, Viktor, 71
Franklin Institute, 352
Freakin' fitness, 205
Freedom of choice, employee engagement
        and, 166
Free riding, 278–279
Friday Night Lights, 45
Friends Association for the Care and
        Protection of Children, 338
FRLD, *see* Full Range Leadership
        Development

FSL, *see* Family Support Line of Delaware County, Inc.
Fuller, Robert, 223
Full Range Leadership Development (FRLD), 3, 43
  application of in organizational and social development, 69–70
  application of for people, profit, and planet, 347
  concepts, Web pages used to illustrate, 182
  expectations, 117
  ideas learned in, 192
  inaccurate perception, 231
  Mohandas Gandhi, 82
  process model for understanding, 61
  projects, can-do attitude, 130
  raising funds with, 351
  reaction to mistakes, 271
  relationship to other leadership theories, 20–21
  scholar profile
    idealized influence behaviors and attributes, 111
    individualized consideration, 217
    introduction (FRLD), 8
    leadership as system, 57
  sustainable changes, 350
  training by senior leaders, 102

G

Gallup Organization, 321, 360
  CE11 survey, 325
  Gallup path, appropriate fit, 344
  Q12 survey, 330
  StrengthsFinder 2.0, 107, 192, 222
Gandhi, Mohandas, 19, 82, 121
GE, *see* General Electric
General Electric (GE), 54, 81, 277, 315
General Mills, 2
General Motors, 54, 327
Generation X, 4
Generation Y, 4
Generose, Gary, 220
George, Bill, 30, 82
George Fox Friends School, 337
Gerstner, Lou, 203
Geshundheit! Institute, 161

Gestalt psychology, 184
Ghandi, Mohandas, 15
Giuliani, Rudolph, 62
Global war on terror, 5
Goals, SMARTER, 247–248
Goal setting, contingent reward and, 245
Godshalk, Ronnie, 92
Goebbels, Joseph, 138
Gore, Al, 171–172
Graham, Katharine, 93, 94
Great Man theories, 19
Greenacre, Grete, 352
Gronski, John, 56, 58–59, 125
Group potency, 130
Gulf War (Second), 202

H

Hamas, 138
Hamels, Cole, 302
Hannah Montana, 80
Harley-Davidson, 322
Harris, B. F., 321
Harrison, George, 295, 342
Harvest period, 333
Health care system
  assumptions, 161
  flawed, 159
Hewlett-Packard, 105, 135
Hillkirk, Patty, 155, 156
Hinson, Larry, 350
Hitler, Adolph, 19, 67, 134, 136
Hock, Dee, 157, 168
Howard, Ryan, 302
How Full Is Your Bucket?, 253
Hurricane Katrina, 339
Hussein, Saddam, 82, 134, 202

I

IBM (International Business Machines), 65, 182, 203, 229
Ibrahim, Anwar, 133
Idealistically oriented thinking, 183
Idealized influence behaviors and attributes, 15, 79–116, 342
  altruism, 97
  authenticity, 105, 106
  building character, 90

candidate of change, 103
clarity of direction, 96
de-individuation, 91
distant leader, 97, 101
dream, 88
flip-flopper, 106
Gallup StrengthsFinder 2.0 survey, 107
idealized influence attributes, definition and examples, 93–100
   act in ways that build others' respect, 98
   display sense of power and confidence, 98–100
   go beyond self-interests for good of others, 95–98
   instill pride in others for being associated with you, 93–95
   reassure others that obstacles will be overcome, 100
idealized influence behaviors, definition and examples, 83–93
   champion exciting new possibilities that can be achieved through teamwork, 92–93
   consider moral/ethical consequences of your decisions, 89–91
   emphasize importance of teamwork, 91
   specify importance of having strong sense of purpose, 88–89
   talk about importance of trusting each other, 86–88
   talk about your most important values and beliefs, 84–86
impression management, 102
in agreement/good leadership behavior, 108
in agreement/poor leadership behavior, 108
ingratiation, 104
inspiration, 89
modesty, 96
Mohandas Gandhi, idealized leadership of, 82–83
overestimators, 108
pride, 93, 95
purpose in life, 88
putting idealized influence into practice, 106–112

attribute of leaders who are aware or unaware of transformational behavior, 109–110
display behaviors described in chapter, 106
gauging your leadership self-awareness, 108–112
identify and leverage your strengths and those of others, 106–107
improve your perspective-taking capacity, 107
learn about becoming authentic transformational leader, 112
work on your self-awareness, 107–112
quiet confidence, 99
respect, 98
role model, 80, 83, 90
self-concept, 103
self-monitoring, 105
self-promotion, 104
servant leadership, 83
spirituality, 96
summary questions and reflective exercises, 112–114
Test of Defining Issues, 107
thinking about, 101–106
   close and distant leadership, 101–102
   desired identity images, 103
   hoped-for possible selves versus actual selves and impression management tactics, 103–105
   impression management, self-construals, and self-presentation, 102–106
   self-monitoring, 105–106
trust, 87, 109
underestimators, 108
values, 86
Identity images, desired, 103
Idi Amin Dada, 267, 268
IDP, *see* Individual development plan
Immelt, Jeff, 343
Impression management, 102
In agreement/good leadership behavior, 108
In agreement/poor leadership behavior, 108
Individual development plan (IDP), 208
Individualism, encouragement of, 195

Individualized consideration, 17–18,
191–226, 342
activists, 193
agreeableness, 212
bystanders, 193
collective skill set, 205
confident vulnerability, 208
conscientiousness, 212
cross-functional teams, 205
Definite Dozen, 194
definition and behavioral examples,
195–208
help others develop their strengths,
204–205
listen attentively to others' concerns,
202–203
needs, abilities, and aspirations
different from others, 196–199
promote self-development, 207–208
spend time teaching and coaching,
205–207
treat others as individuals, 199–202
developmental power of Pat Summitt,
193–195
diehards, 193
diversimilarity, 212
Diversity Action Council, 222
empathy, 203, 204
extroversion, 212
follower locus of control, 213
follower potential, 198
FRLD scholar profile, 217
Gallup StrengthsFinder 2.0, 192, 222
isolates, 193
leader profile, 196
listening, 204
neuroticism/emotional stability, 212
openness to experience, 212
participants, 193
putting individualized consideration into
practice, 218–221
become interested in well-being of
others, 219
celebrate diversity, 219–220
create strategies for continuous
personal improvement, 220–221
display behaviors described in chapter,
218–219
establish mentoring programs in your
organization, 220

rankism, 214, 223
self-efficacy, 212
sense of entitlement, 212
sources of irritation, 191
summary questions and reflective
exercises, 221–224
talking one-on-one, 201
thinking about, 208–218
benefits of mentoring, 214–215
developing followers through
delegation, 217–218
diversimilarity and transformational
leadership, 212–214
diversity leadership issues, 210–211
empowerment and dependency, 216
individuation, 209–214
mentoring, 214–216
mentoring and transformational
leadership, 215–216
training program principles, 200
Individuation, 209
Information
gathering, knowledge gained from, 176
shared, 301
Ingratiation, 104
Inspirational motivation, 15–16, 66,
117–154, 335, 342
altruism, 129
charting the right course, 118
collective efficacy, 130
definition and examples, 120–131
articulate compelling vision of the
future, 124–128
express confidence that goals will be
achieved, 130–131
provide exciting image of what is
essential to consider, 128–130
talk enthusiastically about what needs
to be accomplished, 122–124
talk optimistically about the future,
120–122
emotional contagion, 148
Enron philosophy, 127
enthusiasm, 123
evocation, 119
flow, 122
group potency, 130
inspiration concepts, 119
institutional memory, 124
intrinsic motivation, 122

leader profile, 121, 134
"little Hitler", 136, 140
metaphors, 128, 143
military command philosophy,
        125–126
moral development, 140
moral reasoning, 140
motivation, 119
narcissism, 135
nationalism, 124
positive psychological capital, 122
present-obsessed attitude, 127
putting inspirational motivation into
        practice, 144–149
    boost your self-confidence, 145
    build consensus around your vision,
        148–149
    display behaviors described in chapter,
        144–145
    use storytelling techniques to
        articulate your vision, 147–148
    work to improve your public speaking
        ability, 146–147
    write mission and vision statements
        for your organization, 145–146
rat race notion of time, 127
self-efficacy, 130
summary questions and reflective
        exercises, 149–152
thinking about, 132–144
    dark side of charisma, 132–141
    inspiring leadership of Winston
        Churchill and fatal attraction of
        Adolph Hitler, 136–140
    personalized versus socialized
        charismatic leaders, 133–136
    perspective-taking capacity and moral
        development, 140–141
    rhetoric of inspirational leadership,
        141–144
town meetings, 120
transcendence, 119
vision, 128
Institutional memory, 124
Instrumental compliance, 62
Intel, 65
Intellectual stimulation, 16–17, 155–189,
        335, 342
    behavior, 185–186
    Camp Dreamcatcher, 155–156, 184

collaboration, 162
contrarian thinking, 169
current state, 181, 188
definition and behavioral examples,
        159–171
    encourage nontraditional thinking
        to deal with traditional problems,
        168–170
    encourage rethinking those ideas that
        have never been questioned before,
        170–171
    get others to look at problems from
        many different angles, 163–165
    reexamine critical assumptions
        to question whether they are
        appropriate, 159–161
    seek different perspectives when
        solving problems, 161–163
    suggest new ways of looking at
        how to complete assignments,
        165–167
dynamic leadership duo of Anne Mulcahy
        and Ursula Burns at Xerox,
        158–159
fantasy, 180, 181
figure–ground reversal, 184
freedom of choice, 166
future state, 181, 188
independent thinking, 169
lateral thinking, 169
MBE-P and, 285
    mediocrity, incentive for, 168
mental frame, 168
notion of contrast, 184
photography, 163, 164
problem orientation skills, courses
        addressing, 175
putting intellectual stimulation into
        practice, 179–185
    alternative states, 181–182
    brainstorming, 179–180
    challenging questions, 183–184
    display behaviors described in chapter,
        179
    fantasy, 180–181
    learn to think differently, 182–183
    reverse figure and ground, 184–185
return on social investment, 157
scenario planning, 181
sharing of perspectives, 163

summary questions and reflective
exercises, 185–188
thinking about, 171–178
intellectual stimulation and
pragmatic/problem-solving
leadership, 175–178
roadblocks to intellectual stimulation,
171–175
your followers, 174
your leader, 173–174
your organization, 173
your problem orientation, 174–175
yourself, 175
think-tank, 157
Internal controls, auditing, 243
Internal locus of control, 213
Internet, 4
Internet start-ups, 204
Intimidation, motivation by, 63
Intrinsic motivation, 122
Intrinsic rewards, 231
Introduction (FRLD), 1–42
achievement-oriented leadership behavior,
28, 29
analysis, 33
application, 33
attribute, definition of, 9
behavior, definition of, 9
cognition, description of, 32
components of FRLD theory, 9–18
active management-by-exception, 12
contingent reward, 13
idealized influence, 15
individualized consideration, 17–18
inspirational motivation, 15–16
intellectual stimulation, 16–17
laissez-faire, 9–10
leader profile, 14
passive management-by-exception,
10–12
transformational leadership, 4Is of,
13–18
directive leadership behavior, 28
evaluation, 34
fight-or-flight behavioral reaction, 24
Gandhi's call for authenticity, 15
higher-level thinking skills, 33
history of leadership thought, 19–32
authentic leadership theory, 30–32
contingency theory, 27–28

emotional intelligence, 23–24
leader–member exchange theory, 29–30
path–goal theory, 28–29
pragmatic or problem-solving
leadership theory, 24–25
psychodynamic theory, 22–23
situational theory, 26–27
skills theory, 23–25
style theory, 25–26
trait theory, 19–22
knowledge-based learning skills, 33
leader–follower relations, 28
leader profile, 14
Least Preferred Coworker survey, 27
meta-cognition and critical questioning,
32–33
model, 10
need for FRLD, 3–9
demographic changes, 4
environmental issues, 6–7
FRLD scholar profile, 8
geopolitical alterations, 4–5
leadership for dynamic world and
lives, 4–7
new generations of workers bring new
ideas, 5
organizational modifications, 5–6
research, 7–9
technology trends, 4
participative leadership behavior, 28
positive psychological capital, 31
putting transformational leadership into
practice, 32–34
social entrepreneurship initiatives, 7
summary questions and reflective
exercises, 34–40
supportive leadership behavior, 28
teamwork, importance of, 15
transactional contingent reward, 13
Isolates, 193
Iverson, Allen, 197

J

Jackson, Jesse, 100, 143
James, William, 168
Japan Airlines, 30
Jesus Christ, 132
Jintao, Hu, 127
Jobs, Steve, 119, 120, 128, 148, 323

John Paul II, 127, 133
Johnson, Armando, 219
Jolie, Angelina, 105
Jordan, Bill, 79
Jung, Andrea, 103
Juniper Networks, 117
Juzbasich, John, 1, 68, 70

K

Kelleher, Herb, 59, 332
Kelly, Gary, 59
Kelly, Vesta, 293
Kennedy, John F., 23, 50, 121, 133, 136, 359
Kennedy, Robert, 121, 133
Kim Jong-il, 134, 267
Kindle, 130
King, Martin Luther, Jr., 16, 53, 71, 121,
    128, 133, 141
Knight, Bobby, 194
Knowledge
    based learning skills, 33
    problems and, 176
Kooks, 295
Kopp, Wendy, 195, 196
Kouzes, James, 314

L

La Comunidad Hispania, Inc., 338
Lag indicators, 325
Laissez-faire, *see* Management-by-exception
    passive and laissez-faire
Lake Placid Olympics, 307
Lateral thinking, 169
Lay, Ken, 134
Leader
    definition of, 50
    distant, 97, 101
    follower fit, 56
    irresponsible, 277
    lazy, 265
    member exchange (LMX) theory, 21,
        29–30
    personal confidence, 131
    personalized versus socialized
        charismatic, 133–136
    profile
        contingent reward, 232
        idealized influence attributes, 94

idealized influence behaviors, 84
individualized consideration, 196
inspirational motivation, 121, 134
intellectual stimulation, 160, 178
introduction (FRLD), 14
laissez-faire, 274
leadership as system, 52, 58–59, 60
management-by-exception active,
    239, 240
management-by-exception passive,
    268
strategic leadership, 326
teams, 309
transformational leadership, 13
transformational behavior, 109–110
Leadership
    authentic, 21, 30–32
    behavior
        in agreement/good leadership
            behavior, 108
        in agreement/poor leadership
            behavior, 108
        overestimators, 108, 186
        underestimators, 108, 186
    development, professor–student
        collaboration, 162
    diversity, 210, 364
    global perspective, 43
    inactive forms of, *see* Management-by-
        exception passive and laissez-faire
    initiatives, environment, 342
    passive, 280
    people-oriented, 25
    principles, idealized influence
        attribute, 96
    process as drama production, 44
    production-oriented, 25
    profile, intellectual stimulation, 177
    reactive, 282
    relationship-oriented, 25
    self-awareness, 108–112
    shared, 303
    significance of present, 124
    strategic, 324, *see also* Strategic, social,
        and environmental initiatives
    substitutes for, 280
    system, components of, 48
    task-oriented, 25
    team, 299, *see also* Teams, sharing full
        range leadership within

trust, 87
values, 86
Lead indicators, 325
Learning
    love of, 220
    partner, 71
    perspective, organizational goals, 325,
        332
Least Preferred Coworker survey, 27
Lee, Spike, 180
Lennon, John, 133, 180, 295
Levinson, Daniel, 71
Lexus, 321
Lieberman, Lori, 211
Lincoln, Abraham, 124
Linneman, Kurt, 67
Listening skills, 203, 204
Litzky, Barrie, 183
LMX theory, *see* Leader–member exchange
    theory
Lockheed Martin, 65, 72
Lockwood, Robert, 321, 333
Locus of control, follower, 213
Lomax, Michael, 179, 353
Los Angeles Lakers, 294
Louis XVI, 265
Love of life, 123
Lowe, Gregory, 218
Luthans, Fred, 171

M

Major League Baseball World Series, 302
Malcolm Baldrige National Quality Award,
    254
Malcolm X, 133, 136
Management-by-exception active (MBE-A),
    237–244, *see also* Contingent
    reward and management-by-
    exception active
    arrange to know if and when things go
        wrong, 243–244
    closely monitor work performance for
        errors, 238–241
    corrective transaction, 238
    focus attention on mistakes, complaints,
        failures, deviations, and
        infractions, 241–243
Management-by-exception passive (MBE-P),
    267

Management-by-exception passive and
    laissez-faire, 263–292
business entrepreneurship program, 287
control system, 272
fruitless outcomes, 271
lack of responsibility, 277
laissez-faire, definition and behavioral
    examples, 272–278
    avoid emphasizing results, 277–278
    avoid getting involved, making
        decisions, or solving problems,
        273–275
    be absent when needed, 275–276
    delay and fail to follow up, 276–277
    leader profile, 274
legacy of lazy leaders, 265–266
management-by-exception passive,
    definition and behavioral
    examples, 266–272
    believe that "if it ain't broke, don't fix
        it", 270–271
    intervene only if standards are not
        met, 267–269
    leader profile, 268
    react to mistakes reluctantly,
        271–272
    wait for things to go wrong before
        taking action, 269–270
passive leadership, 280
Pedals for Progress, 284
punishment, 290
putting passive forms of leadership into
    practice, 283–289
    avoid behaviors described in chapter,
        286–287
    display behaviors described in chapter,
        283–284
    enforce corrective action when
        followers make mistakes, 284–285
    fix problem and get back to coasting
        along, 285–286
    laissez-faire leadership, 286–289
    let things settle naturally, 289
    MBEP leadership, 283–286
    place energy on maintaining status
        quo, 284
    show lack of interest when things go
        wrong, 288–289
    talk about getting things done, but let
        others take the lead, 287–288

research-validated benchmarks, 289
sense of entitlement, 287
substitutes for leadership, 280
summary questions and reflective
        exercises, 289–290
thinking about, 278–283
    empowerment versus just
        laissez-faire, 281–282
    exception reporting and reactive
        leadership, 282–283
    letting things settle naturally,
        279–281
    social loafing and free riding,
        278–279
Management-by-objectives (MBO),
        330
Mandela, Nelson, 14
Marcos, Imelda, 83, 274
Marshall, Thurgood, 84
Marxism, 139
Master of Leadership Development
        (MLD) program, 106, 148,
        359–370
    Camp Dreamcatcher, 156
    diversity leadership, 210
    ethical reasoning, 359
    evidence derived from, 336
    in-depth analysis, 361
    learning modules, 365
    MBA versus, 360–361
    problem orientation skills, 175
    professors, 167
    program structure, 362–370
        business environment course
            block, 368
        context electives, 369
        diversity leadership, 364
        dynamic communication for
            leadership contexts, 365
        FRLD, 363–364
        idealized influence course block,
            366–367
        intellectual stimulation course block,
            365–366
        leadership across life span, 363
        leadership capstone, 369–370
        leadership competency courses,
            365–367
        leadership context courses, 367–369

leadership cornerstone courses,
        363–365
    leadership models and methods,
        364–365
    strategic leadership, 368
recruiting event, 179
self-concept, 202
Materialism, rampant, 6
Maxwell, John C., 287
MBE-A, *see* Management-by-exception
        active
MBE-P, *see* Management-by-exception
        passive
MBO, *see* Management-by-objectives
MBTI, *see* Myers–Briggs Type Indicator®
McCain, John, 103
McCartney, Paul, 295
McGroary, John, 72
McKeon, Dan, 73
McKinnon, Kate, 353
Mediocrity, incentive for, 168
Medtronic, 30, 82
Mental frame, 168
Mentoring, 110, 214–216
    benefits of mentoring, 214–215
    career development and, 215
    establish mentoring programs in your
        organization, 220
    mentoring functions, 215
    mentoring and transformational
        leadership, 215–216
    psychological support, 215
    psychosocial support through, 345
Merit Systems LLC, 1, 68, 69
Meta-cognition, 32–33
Metaphors, 143
Military command philosophy, 125–126
Mind Garden, Inc., 181
Miracle, 307, 308
MLD program, *see* Master of Leadership
        Development program
MLQ, *see* Multifactor Leadership
        Questionnaire
Montapert, Alfred A., 117
Moral development, 140
Moral reasoning, 140
Moran, Marty, 72
Moses, Andy, 43, 44
Most, Robb, 181

Mother Theresa, 208
Motivation, *see also* Inspirational motivation
  by fear, 63
  inspiration and, 119
  by intimidation, 63
  intrinsic, 122
  personality and, 80
  values and, 85
Motorola, 254
Mr. Rogers' Neighborhood, 241
Mugabe, Robert, 267
Mulcahy, Anne, 158
Multifactor Leadership Questionnaire
      (MLQ), 8, 35, 68–71
  exercises, 149, 185, 221, 258, 289
  feedback, 36–39, 108, 208
  FRLD scholar profile, 111
  MLD program, 362
  ordering, 68
  personal leadership mission statement
      and, 71
  promotion and transfer, 344
  results, 74, 117
Mutual of Omaha, 328
Myers–Briggs Type Indicator® (MBTI), 22, 222

N

Nagel, Thomas, 137
Namath, Joe, 304
Nano-manager, 88
Narcissism, 135
NASA, 128
Nationalism, 124
Natural environment, company interaction
      with, 43
Navy SEALs, 294, 312
Nazi Germany, 137
Nazi propaganda, 138
Negative reinforcement, 248
Neuroticism/emotional stability, 212
Newell, David, 241
NeXT Computer, 323
Nguyen, David, 130
Nishimatsu, Haruka, 30
Nixon, Richard, 50
  Nixon vs. Frost, 50
Nobel Peace Prize, 171
Nokia, 2

Nontraditional thinking, 169
Nooyi, Indra, 103, 326

O

Oasis, 295
Obama, Barack, 16, 22, 100, 103, 120, 121,
      124, 141, 315
OCB, *see* Organizational citizenship behavior
Openness to experience, 22
Optimism, inspirational motivation and, 120
O'Reilly, Phillip, 117
Organic organizations, 54, 348
Organization
  collective skill set, 205
  commitment to, 109
  diversity leadership processes, 211
  knowledge gained from, 176
  mission statement, 145
  organic, 54, 348
  reputation, 322
Organizational citizenship behavior
      (OCB), 97
Organizational development, application of
      FRLD in, 69–70
Organizational goals, perspectives, 325
Organizational-level effects, teamwork
      creating, 65
Organizational vision, 129
Orlando, Nancy Dart, 283
Overconsumption, 6–7
Overestimators, 108, 186

P

Paar, Jack, 175
PainBeGone Central, 337
Palmisano, Sam, 203, 229
Parenting
  FRLD and, 235
  overbearing parents, 286
Participants, 193
Passive leadership, 280
Passive management-by-exception, 10–12
Pasteur, Louis, 180
Paterno, Joe, 89, 91, 304, 313, 314
Path–goal theory, 21, 28–29
Pathways to Education, 234
Pausch, Randy, 16

PBS, *see* Public Broadcasting Service
Pearl River School District, 254
Pedals for Progress, 284
Pennsylvania Home of the Sparrow, 338
Penske Trucking, 43
People-oriented leadership, 25
PepsiCo, 103
Personality
   cult of, 82
   motivation and, 80
Personalized charismatic leaders, 134
Personal leadership mission statement
   (PLMS), 71, 72, 74
Perspective-taking capacity, 44
Philadelphia Phillies, 302
Philadelphia 76ers, 204
PhillyCarShare, 263, 264
Photography, intellectual stimulation
   and, 163, 164
Pink Floyd, 46
PLMS, *see* Personal leadership mission
   statement
Poitier, Sidney, 45
Pomager, Richard, 354
Positive psychological capital, 31, 122
Positive reinforcement, 248
Posner, Barry, 314
Postconventional moral reasoning, 140
Pragmatic or problem-solving leadership
   theory, 24–25
Preconventional moral reasoning, 140
Present-obsessed attitude, 127
Pride, team, 93, 95
Princetongreen.org, 347
Private self-awareness, 107
Problem orientation skills, courses
   addressing, 175
Problems, knowledge gained from, 176
Proctor and Gamble, 2
Production-oriented leadership, 25
Psychodynamic theory, 20, 22–23
Psychological support, mentoring
   and, 215
Public Broadcasting Service (PBS), 150
Public self-awareness, 107
Public speaking ability, 146–147
Punishment, 248
Purpose in life, 71, 74, 88
Putin, Vladimir, 19, 124
Pygmalion effect, 246

Q

Q12 survey, Gallup, 330
Qualcomm, 65, 220, 280
QVC, 199

R

Rabin, Yitzhak, 133
Radiohead, 168
Ramil, Mike, 270
Rankism, 214, 223
Rationally oriented thinking, 183
Ray of Hope Children's Hospital of India,
   337
Reactive leadership, 282
Reagan, Ronald, 105
Reframed reward contingencies, 62
Relationship-oriented leadership, 25
Remember the Titans, 305
Respect, building, 98
Rest, James, 107
Return on social investment, 157
Rice, Condoleeza, 105
Risk assessment, 256
Ritz Carlton Hotel Company, 254
Roddick, Anita, 59, 133
Rolins, Jimmy, 302
Rook, Terry, 266
Roosevelt, Franklin Delano, 19
Russell, Kurt, 307

S

Sanofi-Aventis, 79, 144
Santostefano, Eric, 130
Saraceno, Anthony, 197
Scenario planning, 181
Schneider, Ashley, 205
Schoolhouse Rock!, 211
Schultz, Howard, 53
S. C. Johnson, 2
Scott, Michael of *The Office*, 52
Scott, Robert, 164, 166
Scully, John, 265, 323
Selene Whole Foods Cooperative, Inc., 337
Self-awareness
   leadership, 108–112
   types, 107
Self-centered leaders, 51

Self-concept, 103, 109, 202
Self-confidence, tips to boost, 145
Self-construals, 102
Self-development, promotion of, 207
Self-efficacy, 130, 143, 212, 242
Self-fulfilling prophecies, 246
Self-interest, teams and, 301, 313
Self-monitoring, 105
Self-promotion, 104
Self-rewards, 73
Self-sacrifice, 129
Servant leadership, 83
Shakespeare, William, 30
Shamir, Boas, 216, 217
Sharifi, Jackie, 235
Shaw, George Barnard, 246
Sheen, Fulton J., 124, 127
Shiu, Melissa, 130
Shwe, Than, 267
Situational leadership theory (SLT),
        26–27
Situational theory, 26–27
Six Sigma, 254
Skill sets, overlapping versus
        complementary, 305
Skills theory, 20, 23–25
Skłodowska-Curie, Maria, 17
SLT, see Situational leadership theory
SMARTER goals, 247–248
Social contagion, 65
Social entrepreneurship, 334, 337
Social Entrepreneurship and Community
        Leadership course, 183
Social initiatives, see Strategic,
        social, and environmental
        initiatives
Social investment, return on, 157
Socialized charismatic leaders, 133
Social loafing, 278–279
Social networking sites, 4
Society for Industrial and Organizational
        Psychology, 181–182
Socrates, 30
Southwest Airlines, 59, 332, 345
Spielberg, Steven, 180
Springsteen, Bruce, 132, 295
Stalin, Joseph, 139
Stand and Deliver, 45
Starbuck's Coffee, 53
Starr, Ringo, 295

Storytelling techniques, use of to articulate
        vision, 147
St. Paul, 132
Strategic, social, and environmental
        initiatives, 321–358
    balanced scorecard, 325, 355
    brand image, 322, 346
    cause-and-effect relationships, 328, 329
    corporate social responsibility, 333
    customer perspective, 325, 331
    financial perspective, 327, 332
    Gallup Organization CE11 survey, 325
    Gallup path, appropriate fit, 344
    harvest period, 333
    idealized influence, 342
    individualized consideration, 342
    innovation, 325
    inspirational motivation, 342
    intellectual stimulation, 342
    internal business process, 327, 331
    lag indicators, 325
    lead indicators, 325
    management-by-objectives, 330
    more evidence that FRLD promotes
            prosperity and well-being,
            348–354
        creating sustainable changes with
                FRLD, 350–351
        developing righteous minds through
                FRLD, 352–353
        empowering women with FRLD, 349
        life-changing experience, 349–350
        most noble form of transformational
                leadership, 354
        negating the naysayers with FRLD,
                353
        raising funds and lifting spirits with
                FRLD, 351–352
    opportunities for happiness, 335
    organic organizational structure, 348
    putting full range leadership development
            into practice, 344–348
        build strong brand and corporate
                image, 346
        periodically examine and redesign
                organizational structure,
                348–349
        recruit and select the best, 345
        reengineer jobs and processes,
                345–346

use transformational leadership as career development tool, 345
use transformational leadership measures for promotion and transfer, 344
shared vision, 327
Steve Jobs and resurrection of Apple, 323–324
strategic leadership defined, 324–334
balanced scorecard, 325–330
how FRLD enhances this process, 330–333
triple bottom line, 333–334
summary questions and reflective exercises, 355–356
sustenance period, 333
thinking about, 334–343
environmental, health, and safety issues in workplace, 339–342
environmental leadership initiatives, 342–343
social entrepreneurship, 334–339
Strength, weaknesses, opportunities, and threats (SWOT) analysis, 336
Stycharz, Stan, 219
Style theory, 20, 25–26
Summitt, Pat, 193–195
Sun Micro Systems, 160
Sustenance period, 333
SWOT analysis, *see* Strength, weaknesses, opportunities and threats analysis
Synergy, definition of, 302
Synthesis, 33
System (FRLD), 43–78
antecedents, 61
competition, 53
components of leadership system, 48
Continuous Quality Improvement program, 64
economic turndowns, 49
equitable disengagement, 63
fear, motivation by, 63
follower–situation fit, 56
geographic context, 54
instrumental compliance, 62
intimidation, motivation by, 63
leader–follower fit, 56
leadership as system, 47–60
confluence of leader, follower, and situation, 56–60

follower, 51–53
FRLD scholar profile, 57
GE and its passion for leadership development, 54–55
leader, 50–51
leader profile, 52, 58–59, 60
situation, 53–54
online leadership intervention, 66
organic organizations, 54
organizational contexts, 54
outcomes of leadership at individual, team, and organizational/macro levels, 64–65
perspective-taking capacity, 44
process model for understanding FRLD, 61–63
purpose in life, 71, 74
putting systems thinking into practice, 67–74
applying FRLD in organizational and social development, 69–70
first step, 67–68
FRLD process model lens, 68
learning partner, 71–73
make FRLD reflection part of your schedule, 73
Multifactor Leadership Questionnaire, 68–71
personal leadership mission statement, 71, 72
self-rewards and positive affirmations, 73
set goals with personal leadership development plan, 74
reframed reward contingencies, 62
self-centered leaders, 51
Sidney Poitier and *To Sir, With Love*, 45–47
social contagion, 65
summary questions and reflective exercises, 74–77
systems thinking, 60–66
360-degree feedback, 71
total quality management, 76

T

Task-oriented leadership, 25
Teams, sharing full range leadership within, 293–320

blame, 301
collective efficacy, 303
common expectations, 300
differences between groups and teams, 306
lessons from the Beatles, 295–298
    carry that weight, 295–296
    come together, 296–297
    don't let me down, 296
    tell me what you see, 297
    within you without you, 298
levels of team development, 310
norms, 300
putting FRLD into practice, 312–316
    emphasize importance of having collective sense of mission, 314–315
    go beyond self-interest for the good of the team, 313–314
    help team members develop their strengths, 315–316
    instill pride in team members for being associated with team, 312–313
slacking off, 314
summary questions and reflective exercises, 316–319
team leadership defined, 298–300
thinking about FRLD in groups and teams, 300–312
    differences between groups and teams, 301–306
    individual versus mutual accountability, 304–305
    information and workflow, 301–302
    levels of team development, 310–312
    overlapping versus complementary skill sets, 305–306
    shared leadership and miracle on ice, 307–310
    synergy, 302–304
Teamwork
    idealized leaders and, 92
    importance of, 15, 91
    pride, 93, 95
    risk assessment, 256
Tennessee Lady Volunteers, 194
Test of Defining Issues, 107

Thatcher, Margaret, 19
Theory
    authentic leadership, 21, 30–32
    contingency, 21, 27–28
    leader–member exchange, 21, 29–30
    path–goal, 21, 28–29
    pragmatic or problem-solving, 24–25
    psychodynamic, 20, 22–23
    situational leadership, 21, 26–27
    skills, 20, 23–25
    style, 20, 25–26
    trait, 19–22
Thinking
    contrarian, 169
    empirically oriented thinking, 183
    existentially oriented thinking, 183
    idealistically oriented thinking, 183
    lateral, 169
    nontraditional, 169
    rationally oriented thinking, 183
    rethinking, 170
    unconventional, 158
Thirteen, 46
Thiry, Kent J., 64
Thoreau, Henry David, 155
Time, rat race notion of, 127
Tolson, Melvin, 353
To Sir, With Love, 45
Total quality management (TQM), 76, 254
Toyota, 333
TQM, *see* Total quality management
Trait theory, 19–22
Transactional contingent reward, 13
Transactional leadership, two faces of, *see* Contingent reward and management-by-exception active
Transcendence, inspiration and, 119
Transformational behaviors, leader attributes, 109–110
Transformational culture, examples experiencing, 65
Transformational leadership
    emotional side of, *see* Inspirational motivation
    humane side of, *see* Idealized influence behaviors and attributes
    idealized influence, 15
    individualized consideration, 17–18
    inspirational messages of, 142
    inspirational motivation, 15–16

inspiration triggered by, 119
intellectual stimulation, 16–17
nurturing side of, *see* Individualized
    consideration
rational side of, *see* Intellectual
    stimulation
significance of past, 124
Treaty of Versailles, 138
Triple bottom line, 333
Trust, 109
Tutu, Desmond, 14
Twitter, 4

U

Underestimators, 108, 186
Unilever, 333
United Way, Executive Fellows Program, 3
Urban decay, 288

V

Vanguard Group, 65, 220, 228
Venter, Craig, 159, 160
Verbal persuasion, 212
Verizon, 252
Verizon Wireless, 353
Vertex Corporation, 283
Vietnam War, 103, 160
Vigorous love of life, 123
Virgin, 119, 128, 160
VISA International, 157
Vision
    alignment of people around, 133
    compelling, 128
    shared, 327
    statement, organizational, 145
    use of storytelling techniques to
        articulate, 147

W

WAATCO, *see* West Africa American
    Trading Company
Waldersee, Robert, 298
Waldrop, Mary, 79
Walzer, Michael, 137
Washington, Denzel, 305
Waters, Roger, 46
Weber, Max, 132
Weekly, Jack, 328
Welch, Jack, 55, 81, 277, 285, 315
West Africa American Trading Company
    (WAATCO), 2, 338
Whole Foods Market, 293–294, 300
Williams, Robin, 161, 187
Wilson, Brian, 167
Winfrey, Oprah, 16
Wischum, John (Jay) G., 106, 351
Wooden, John, 236
WorldComm, 30
Wyeth Pharmaceuticals, 205
Wynn, Jim, 1

X

Xerox, 158

Y

Yammarino, Francis J., 8
Yew, Lee Kuan, 240
Yunus, Muhammad, 14

Z

Zuckerberg, Mark, 119, 120
Zuma, Jacob, 134
Zutons, 295